CRISIS COUNSELING
FOR A QUALITY
SCHOOL COMMUNITY

CRISIS COUNSELING FOR A QUALITY SCHOOL COMMUNITY:

Applying Wm. Glasser's Choice Theory

Larry L. Palmatier, Ph.D.
Author and Editor

ACCELERATED DEVELOPMENT
A member of the Taylor & Francis Group

USA	Publishing Office:	ACCELERATED DEVELOPMENT
		A member of the Taylor & Francis Group
		1101 Vermont Avenue, N.W., Suite 200
		Washington, DC 20005-3521
		Tel: (202) 289-2174
		Fax: (202) 289-3665
	Distribution Center:	ACCELERATED DEVELOPMENT
		A member of the Taylor & Francis Group
		1900 Frost Road, Suite 101
		Bristol, PA 19007-1598
		Tel: (215) 785-5800
		Fax: (215) 785-5515
UK		Taylor & Francis Ltd.
		4 John Street
		London WC1N 2ET
		Tel: 071 405 2237
		Fax: 071 831 2035

CRISIS COUNSELING FOR A QUALITY SCHOOL COMMUNITY: Applying Wm. Glasser's Choice Theory

1 2 3 4 5 6 7 8 9 0   E B E B   9 0 9 8 7

This book was set in Times Roman. The editors were Heather Worley, Cindy Long, and Judith L. Aymond. Photograph of author/editor by Indira Palmatier. Cover design by Michelle Fleitz. Cover photograph: K-8 grade students at Lawton Alternative School in San Francisco—Jolie Weinroth, Principal.

A CIP catalog record for this book is available from the British Library.
ⓧ The paper in this publication meets the requirements of the ANSI Standard Z39.48-1984 (Permanence of Paper)

Library of Congress Cataloging-in-Publication Data

Crisis counseling for a quality school community: applying Wm.
    Glasser's choice theory/[edited by] Larry L. Palmatier.
        p.   cm.
    Includes bibliographical references and index.

    1. Glasser, William, 1925– . 2. Educational counseling—United
States.   3. Teacher participation in educational counseling—United
States.   4. Reality therapy—United States.   5. School crisis
management—United States.   6. School improvement programs—United
States.   I. Palmatier, Larry L.
LB1027.5.C685   1998
371.4'0973—dc21   97-25094
                                                                          CIP

ISBN 1-56032-398-1 (paper)

DEDICATION

To all the children of the world: those who have felt the pain of ridicule, loneliness, illness, misunderstanding, abuse, and war; and to those who are mostly free of threat, trauma, and tragedy.

May those who enjoy more security share some of their good fortune, happiness, and strength with their needy brothers and sisters so that *all children* can become part of the same safe circle.

CONTENTS

CHAPTER 2
REALITY THERAPY AND CHOICE THEORY:
MAKING PERSONAL CHOICES FOR A CHANGE   27
Larry L. Palmatier

CHAPTER 3
CRISIS THEORY: COUNSELING OUT-OF-CONTROL PEOPLE   55
Mary B. Ballou and Larry Litwack

CHAPTER 4
ETHICAL SCHOOL COUNSELING: MANAGING
A BALANCING ACT   77
Terence E. Patterson

CHAPTER 5
THERAPIST AS TEACHER; TEACHER AS THERAPIST: EVOLUTION OF THE RESPONSIBLE ROLE MODEL   91
Barbara I. Bratter, Carole Jaffe Bratter, and Thomas Edward Bratter

PART II
CRISES AND SOLUTIONS—PERSONAL TRAUMAS

CHAPTER 6
HANDLING PERSONAL PROBLEMS: SHOWING FEAR, TEARS, INACTIVITY, APATHY, IMPULSIVITY, AND TRUANCY   117
Larry L. Palmatier

PART III
CRISES AND SOLUTIONS—
INTERACTIONAL TRAUMAS

FOREWORD

William Glasser, M.D.

For the last few years, my number one professional interest has been improving the quality of schools in this country and around the world. I propose doing this through a consortium of participating school districts that have voluntarily joined me in a mission to revitalize schools. I believe that making this transformation a reality depends on mastering three distinct models and practices. These three keys are choice theory, quality management, and reality therapy.

THREE ESSENTIAL INGREDIENTS FOR QUALITY

Control Theory: Powers

William Powers (1973) introduced me to control theory through his fine book, *Behavior: The Control of Perception.* I translated his powerful ideas for counselors and the average person on the street because his explanation of human motivation and behavior is one of the most significant clarifications of human psychology available. I also refined Powers' theoretical model so that educators would have a means for getting students to take effective control of their learning.

Quality Management: Deming

The second key in the formula for quality schools is adoption of the powerful quality management practices that the late W. Edwards Deming developed in his rich and productive 92 plus years. Dr. Deming was truly a remarkable human being whose ideas will continue to affect the world in profound ways. My publications revolving around his thinking are *The Quality School* (Glasser, 1992), *The Quality School Teacher* (Glasser, 1993), *The Control Theory Manager* (Glasser, 1994), and my newest—*Choice Theory* (Glasser, 1998).

Reality Therapy: Glasser

The third key is my counseling model that I call reality therapy. This counseling method dovetails with choice theory and provides an organized framework for counseling that can help individuals face personal challenges more efficiently and take charge of their lives.

QUALITY SCHOOLING: MEETING NEEDS RESPONSIBLY

Taken together, the above three pragmatic sets of ideas have proven useful in effecting root changes in the cultural values of schooling in America. The model presented in this book for improving the quality of education at the core is not a top-down prescription or yet another set of mandates and restrictions that passive educators must endure reluctantly. "This too shall pass" does not apply. After working in schools for more than three decades, I have concluded that three simple notions are at the heart of the shift to quality: *eliminate fear, focus on quality,* and *involve learners in goal-setting and self-evaluation.* Eliminating fear and coercion will insure that students and teachers find more enjoyment and cooperation. Focusing on genuine quality learning experiences and products will lead to more meaningful results for all. Involving everyone in goal-setting and self-evaluation will encourage responsibility and a clearer purpose.

Quality School Consortium: A Partnership for Improvement

I wake up every morning buoyed by the thought that many thousands of devoted professionals have committed themselves to seeking a common purpose. They all aim to transform schools into safe and creative places that feature supportive relationships and high quality learning. Many associates within my organization—*The William Glasser Institute*—have taken the ball and run with it in creative and meaningful ways. Many of those certified in the practices that I teach and strongly endorse have taught workshops in the U.S.

and abroad, and many too have written books and journal articles on counseling and quality schooling. Larry Palmatier is one of those associates. He has been with me since 1969. Once, he told me that he immediately applied my initial book, *Reality Therapy* (Glasser, 1965) to his first year of teaching—1964-65. The junior high school had a significant number of culturally diverse students from lower middle income families. While completing his doctorate at the University of California, Berkeley in 1969, Larry came to hear me speak in northern California about insuring success for all students. From that first contact in the Bay Area, he became certified in reality therapy, joined my international staff of instructors, and regularly organized speaking engagements and workshops for me at the University of Utah and the University of San Francisco. This book represents a comprehensive effort by Larry and many professionals in mental health and education.

This Book Can Help You Transform Education

Transforming schools from coercive institutions to vibrant, enjoyable, and safe settings where everyone is working hard to learn is no small task. Dr. Palmatier's wide-ranging book, *Crisis Counseling for a Quality School Community: Applying Wm. Glasser's Choice Theory,* addresses some of the most intractable, individual, and relational problems that teachers, administrators, and counselors could face in today's difficult classrooms. Those schools that have signed on with the *Consortium for Quality Schools* represent a full spectrum of social, economic, cultural, and intellectual backgrounds. Thus far, however, few inner-city schools have come aboard. Dr. Palmatier's book addresses the need to have remedies for the entire range of students who attend public school— from the most neglected and bereft to advantaged children who crave more security and affection at home and academic success and social impact at school. His work is a comprehensive and methodical prescription for applying choice (control) theory principles and reality therapy strategies for handling most of the serious problems seen in schools at any location. By taking the risk of trying some of these noncoercive ideas and putting energy into these new directions, a very high quality learning place can be created. I encourage you to work with others who are similarly committed to changing the norms of schooling at the heart. The process of transformation will not occur if professionals remain socially isolated. Teamwork is crucial.

Solving Problems at School, at Home, and between Home and School

To keep matters clear, I always suggest that educators solve school problems at school and that parents solve home problems at home. Unfortunately, we cannot neatly keep parents from hearing about all the troubles we confront at school. Working together with students' families on joint problems often will help them find a new level of responsibility. Asking the parents of your students about their goals and wishes for their children will give you a fuller picture of the family's view of the world. This collaboration between teachers and parents can offer you added leverage and improve your relationships and your students' learning. The children also will be more likely to put you into their quality worlds as a need-satisf ing person if they know that you respect their parents.

Teachers as Communicators. I never have tried to turn teachers into counselors—only to show them some very forthright methods for helping students cooperate better by selecting better behaviors to get what they want. Good counseling is artful communication. People who choose to learn about my ideas and to apply my methods usually do not reject my attempts to show them problem-solving strategies. They also do not plead with me to lecture them on delving into the past or analyzing their psyches. What I teach is that life is too short to stand around and paw the earth. Our job is to help each and every young person learn better ways to meet personal human needs without violating the rights of others to do the same. Larry Palmatier has gotten the message, and he brings it to you in a comprehensive book that deals with the whole human drama in clear and down-to-earth language. Besides the four chapters and the epilogue that he personally has written, he has tapped the minds and creative experience of 21 other counselors, teachers, and school administrators. Collectively, these authors have a few hundred years of valuable lessons to pass along to others in the field.

Getting Started. I am sure that you will learn many new ways to think about problems that are staring you in the face. More important, perhaps, I have no doubt that you also will find countless practical ideas in this book and that you will enjoy the whole process. I recommend that you first read the introductory material in the first five chapters because these create the context for the rest of the book. Next, feel free to pick chapters by topics of special interest to you. After reading a particular selection, try out the educational tips or counseling strategies and see for yourself how helpful these suggestions are.

Larry has taught in public schools, directed his own private model school, trained teachers, counseled individuals and families, and trained and supervised counselors. As a licensed psychologist in California and also as a marriage, family, and child counselor, he has worked out many solutions to the very dilemmas you must handle almost daily. I think his experiences and insights will be very useful to you. I wish you well and extend my personal admiration and encouragement to you for your serious dedication to education and to those students whom you teach.

William Glasser, M.D.
June 15, 1997
Los Angeles, California

REFERENCES

Glasser, W. (1965). *Reality therapy: A new approach to psychiatry.* New York: Harper & Row.

Glasser, W. (1992). *The quality school* (2nd ed.). New York: HarperCollins.

Glasser, W. (1993). *The quality school teacher.* New York: HarperCollins.

Glasser, W. (1994). *The control theory manager.* New York: HarperCollins.

Glasser, W. (1998). *Choice theory: Redefining our personal freedom.* New York: HarperCollins.

Powers, W. (1973). *Behavior: The control of perception.* Chicago: Aldine Press.

PREFACE

Larry L. Palmatier

THE WAY IT USED TO BE

Things are not always as clear and simple as they used to be, when they weren't as clear and simple as they seemed to be. Historically speaking, when it comes to schooling, everything seems to have happened either in boxes or in chapters. The little boxes were represented by the isolation of all those individuals who plugged away in the lonely confines of their own separate four walls and, of course, studying anything in school all came down to following a textbook. History happened in chapters. Too often what we ended up with by following the coercive model of the past was a tight little domain in which uptight little characters interacted for huge blocks of time. Educators shared the undaunted hope that, sooner or later, all children somehow would land on their feet and survive the experience.

I wish I could say that these narrow routines have changed, but many top-down practices still go on in many places. Even today, for example, one otherwise enlightened school district notifies all parents that not getting the car started in the morning is no excuse for tardiness; furthermore, "three tardies and a child will be considered truant." Being proactive is fine but not when schools are throwing stones at parents.

Some administrators still do not have the message: Treat parents the way you want them to treat you and their children. Rigidity and coercion still thrive in too many schools. Creating a positive mental expectation that school is a good place is essential to having a quality school. A memorandum stating that the school would like to work with the parents to insure that everyone starts the school day on time would not be inappropriate. An example of such a little note might be: "Dear Parents: We realize that, from time to time, something may delay you or your child in getting to school on time. These unexpected interferences happen to everyone periodically—teachers included. Please let us know if we can be of help in any particularly pressing situation." Self-discipline is good, but alienating parents before the fact through relentless policies and procedures is counterproductive and damaging.

HOW FAR HAVE WE COME?

The counseling intern took a closer look. Was that a rope burn on the boy's neck? Her heart pounded. This nine-year-old was her first case, and no supervisor was available; even the principal had left for the day. She did what seemed to her the most prudent thing in the circumstance and rushed to a telephone. The police arrived within minutes.

Ronnie's story unfolded as one of continuous chaos and threats. The boy was living with his eight siblings (ages 2 to 14) in one room of a motel in a marginal section of town. The night before, two of his younger brothers also had tried to kill themselves by slashing at their wrists with a broken beer bottle. Ronnie's uncle lay on the double bed, gulping down one beer after another and slurringly encouraging the boy to hang himself. Ronnie's mother was not home, and his father would not be out of prison for another three months.

The counselor's call to the police gave the boy an immediate respite from the unbearable family violence. While an emergency psychiatric unit evaluated him, the intern notified the child protective service. Sadly, within two days, Ronnie was back at school. The hospital claimed that what he did was not all that irrational under the circumstances, and since no one would guarantee payment for his medical and psychiatric treatment, the hospital had no choice but to release him. The day the hospital released him, the school staff sent him back to join his classmates. At the end of the day, in desperation, he hid at school in order to avoid getting on the school bus for home.

This story of a young man's traumatic predicament is only one of probably thousands that occur each day throughout the country when children find themselves trapped in seemingly hopeless situations. All schools could benefit from pragmatic, kind, and common sense problem-solving services. For some schools, a responsible counseling service is an absolute must.

LIMIT SCHOOLS AND SCHOOLS–WITHIN–SCHOOLS TO 300 STUDENTS

Most of the schools that have joined William Glasser's Quality Schools Consortium are good places, relatively safe, and mostly suburban (Dryden, 1994). For some reason, the large educational fortresses in America's inner cities have not yet signed on to join the journey to quality. Does this absence mean that the city schools are disinterested in organizational transformation? Perhaps contemporary urban schools are spending most of their intellectual and emotional energy staying afloat and dealing with matters of survival.

One brief visit to a randomly selected urban school will convince anyone that teachers there often act in even more isolation than their peers in more pleasant surroundings. Many big city educators seem to convey a sense of caution as if trying warily to survive. In some cases, they appear in the school hallways as walking wounded. This book addresses these teachers' needs, as much as all students' challenges, and the conditions of all schools. The contributors assume the worst case as a starting condition but hold out the possibility of dramatic improvement.

As a counselor educator, I hear what every year's new crop of university hopefuls hears as they enter schools and begin gathering their counseling internship training hours. "Don't expect to change anything. You won't be able to make any difference in anyone's life. The problems are too big. Just make sure that you watch out for yourself and drill your 500 to 1,000 students on the graduation requirements. Learn how to make schedule changes so that you can move the unhappy students from one disgruntled teacher to another."

I have heard this pessimism for years and have rejected these negative attitudes. Working together, administrative leaders and serious faculties can discard a casualty status and reclaim their positions of influence with young minds and hearts. They can set their schools on a new course of hope and positive improvement. To many sincere teachers, principals, and counselors, the alternatives of fraying nerves, increasing cynicism, worsening violence, and running in place have lost all appeal.

This book offers a cohesive set of ideas and practical alternatives to help front line educators. They can use the book to face their daily conflicts with new leverage and gradually shift schooling to an optimistic, and even fun, adventure. Schools with less dangerous conditions can take heart, resolve the crises, and apply preventive steps to avoid the experiences of the most desperate schools out there.

Stories that show schools as mirrors of society can range from pathetic to inspiring. Educators urgently need effective solutions to the critical problems in their schools. Following the theme first reported in *A Nation at Risk* (U.S.A. Research, 1984), tons of "at-risk" literature has flooded out, and teachers find themselves increasingly playing social workers and counselors as well as dispensers of information.

When the brutality of society comes to school, responsible men and women in government propose a social worker in every school. A governor in a major state established a cabinet position for Education and issued just such a call. Ideally, a team of professionals working together would operate in any school with social hardships that interfere with a safe environment and a fundamental focus on learning. The team would include a counselor, social worker, and, at some sites, a police officer and a corrections specialist. Where possible, a higher education teacher educator and counselor educator would work closely with large school districts or consortia of smaller districts to ensure realistic training for young professionals and a continuous supply of fresh thinking to the schools. When all is said and done, however, teachers still must take a large share of the burden of setting everything right. These extra demands go with the territory as teachers still stand *in loco parentis.*

An essential first step may be to limit all schools, at every level, to 300 students—a proposal that many educational observers and critics have offered over the years. Smaller units could share the same roof when necessary but would operate as physically separate and mostly autonomous divisions. Capping the numbers would help faculty teams work together in personalizing education and moving toward quality schools. When school enrollments reach 1,200, 1,800, or 2,800—as happens in many secondary urban schools—the subschools could follow their own separate schedule for two-thirds of the day with students from all the subschools enrolling in specialty courses and advanced electives for the remaining one-third. Thus, school districts would not have to replicate computer facilities, auto shop, drama, and music for six different minischools.

THE TIDE IS TURNING

Fortunately, the dismal picture that has been true for many sincere teachers and vast battalions of students for far too long is now changing to a more vibrant, more collegial, and more enjoyable schooling experience. What is making the improvement possible is a shift in definition of schooling and a corresponding transformation of roles of professionals and the clientele with whom they work. One part of the transformation is related to content. In the midst of an overwhelming knowledge explosion, many are abandoning the view of schooling as stuffing curriculum into narrow little minds. The second part of the metamorphosis is a qualitative shift in the way educators are defining relationships. Finally, many are seeing school as a series of significant interpersonal relationships in which teachers masterfully involve themselves with their young learners. These enlightened teachers are spending their energy encouraging kids to want to ask questions and to pursue knowledge out of genuine desire and not out of fear. Schools appear to have changed their public relations agency.

Paradigm Shifts Take Time

The radical transformation in academia has to do with a paradigm shift in the role teachers will play in America's schools. More and more, teachers are becoming a *resource* for students who are starting to think for themselves and to share in determining what they deem most useful. Teachers know that they must act as guides more than guards, and friendly persuaders more than domineering bosses. Once the change of view occurs in relation to "discipline," schools cannot remain the same. This book is about this fundamental shift from fear and threat to responsible choices and accountability. The old methods were harsh; these practices also kept students out of the loop of making responsible choices. Schools joining William Glasser's Quality School Consortium are discovering that discipline and good order greatly improve when students feel free to take some risks in learning. Trusting their teachers leads to more enjoyment of school, higher grades, and more cooperative behavior.

What can we add to this mix? The first task is to see the heart of teaching as allowing students to work hard to meet their own important needs and wants. Next, the major resource all educators can tap to make their jobs more than tolerable is to create the conditions for ready involvement by parents. The secret weapon of successful teaching—after providing a choice theory context in the classroom and introducing creative and relevant curricula—is keeping a family perspective in mind. Teachers who enlist the genuine support and active participation of their students' parents will succeed far beyond their initial expectations.

Most, but not all, of the chapters in this book show applications of William Glasser's (1998) choice theory. Those chapters that do not explicitly contain choice theory samples do not contradict the theory's emphasis on taking personal responsibility for one's own learning and relationships. I invite everyone—teachers, administrators, and counselors—to enjoy reading this book. I have enjoyed putting together this comprehensive work, which I expect will assist many in finding solutions to what has become one of the most challenging careers anywhere.

BIBLIOGRAPHY

Deming, W. E. (1982). *Out of crisis.* Cambridge, MA: Massachusetts Institute of Technology (MIT), Center for Advanced Engineering Study.

Deming, W. E. (1993). *The new economics for business, government, and education.* Cambridge, MA: Institute of Technology, Center for Advanced Engineering Study.

Glasser, W. (1990). *The quality school.* New York: HarperCollins.

Glasser, W. (1993). *The quality school teacher.* New York: HarperCollins.

Glasser, W. (1998). *Choice theory: Redefining our personal freedom.* New York: HarperCollins.

REFERENCES

Dryden, J. (1994). *The quality schools initiative: Analysis of an educational reform as perceived by principals in K-12 consortium schools.* Unpublished doctoral dissertation, University of the Pacific, Stockton, CA.

U.S.A. Research. (1984). *Nation at risk: The full account.* Portland, OR.

ACKNOWLEDGMENTS

My gratitude to all the teachers, students, contributing writers, parents, school administrators, and counselors who have added to this book.

First, I want to single out my own teachers outside the formal schoolhouse—William Glasser, Cloé Madanes, Jay Haley, Milton Erickson, John Weakland, and Virginia Satir. Second, my in-school teachers from kindergarten (Sr. Eugene Marie) to 7th and 8th grades (Sr. Margaret Therese) at Sacred Heart Elementary School in Aurora, Illinois; to St. Louis Prep High School (Frs. Brennan, Matthews, and Gaydos); on through college at Glen Ellyn, Illinois (Larry Murphy, Paul D'Arcy, and Greg Keegan); to graduate school at USF (Ed Griffin, John Devine, and Henry C. Hall III) and UC Berkeley (Jim Stone, Paul Heist, and John Hurst); and post-graduate studies and internship in clinical and counseling psychology at the University of Utah (Ernst Beier).

I appreciate what I have learned from all the other teachers who have taken classes from me and all the ones I have met, in and out of their own classrooms, who spontaneously and energetically put themselves on the line each and every day and almost always give their best to their students.

I acknowledge all of the K-12 students whom I have taught and who have taught me. I got a lot out of all of those real-life lessons, even though many were tough ones to learn. Thank you to my university students who have discussed, debated, grappled with, and applied most of the ideas included here.

I thank my fellow authors who have passed along their special gems, insights, over 200 cumulative years of practical experience, and brilliant hopes for a brighter future for all children and adolescents.

I extend my appreciation to all the parents I have met, sometimes advised, and always respected. To those who need an extra bit of encouragement right now, I recommend this book.

To all those sincere administrators in the schools who sometimes endure bad press, but who always want what is most meaningful and useful for their faculties and student bodies, I extend my special support and thanks. Countless of these school managers have trusted me and offered me opportunities to be of service to children. I thank them all even though I mention only a representative few: Art Wiscombe, M. Donald Thomas, Carol Ellis, Harley North, Kim Bricker, Steve Moreno, Armando Flores, Mark Klinestecker, Reneé French, and Mike.

A sincere and cordial word of special resonance to my colleagues in the broad fields of psychology, mental health, and counseling—educational, marriage and family, and clinical social work. To all of you who have worked in schools or who plan to do school-based work, I thank you and applaud your contributions. Thank you to my University of San Francisco colleagues in our counseling psychology department—Joan Avis, Steve Zlutnick, Elena Flores, Brian Gerrard, Terence Patterson, Terry Soo-Hoo, and Dan McPherson—and to the others throughout the School of Education—Allen, Susan, Alma, Rosita, Sr. Mary Peter, Paul, Robi, Bob, Patricia, Dody, and the rest.

To my own immediate family, beginning with my beautiful wife, Indira, and on to my terrific daughter, Laurel, and my three great sons—Brent, Tristan, and Laurent. Also, a tender hug to my three granddaughters—Brittney, Amanda, and Faith—and to my family of origin and my extended family in both directions. Thanks to all my friends and associates—Len, Bruce, Yolanda, and Mike—and especially to Gary Brown for his moral support and technical assistance in this project.

Finally, to the two people at the heart of Accelerated Development—Dr. Joe Hollis, publisher, for his unswerving strength and solid help, and Ms. Cindy Long, office manager, for her unflappable style and impressive competence in helping me rein in this tiger of a book.

Larry Palmatier
June 15, 1997

been going into schools for 30 years, spending time in classes, talking to both students and staff, what strikes me most is the lack of actual change. With the benefit of visiting the front lines and not having to work day and night in the trenches, I do gain an outsider's perspective. Sometimes I view schools as quarantine zones that protect those within the walls from becoming aware of the many ideas for improvement on the outside. Here and there among these socially isolated buildings, I do come across glimmers of innovation as I learn of those rare schools where something new and much better is actually in place. How can education improve itself, especially if schools continue policies and methods that have never worked and are still ineffective? I think the problem is political as much as anything: schools do not change because the way almost all teachers are managed from above has led them to be fearful of doing anything different from the cautious, conservative, and safe things they always have done.

Excuses for Lethargy Are Common

Naturally, other forces are at work that keep things the same in schools, but my goal here is not to write about all of the complex sociology involved. We all know that pressure from the community and from parents has a powerful impact on schools. Look at what happened from the start with the awkward attempts to introduce sex education years ago. The more recent attempts to provide students reliable information on safe sex regularly raise a huge furor. Frank talk about AIDS or VD or making condoms available in schools elicits one outcry after another. The logic for both educators and obstructers is the same: students automatically will want to apply what they learn in school.

What about the pressure on schools from state and local government, as well as parents, to raise standardized test scores, move kids along from one grade to another smoothly, and graduate most students on schedule with few dropouts? And while focusing on their primary academic task, school officials are supposed to keep youngsters off the streets, out of everyone's hair, and somehow remove all the ideas of drug use and violence from their heads!

If we are looking for excuses to explain the ineffectiveness of contemporary schooling, we could identify countless causes. Those who spend too much time and energy wringing their hands or citing problems, however, create a stalemate and end up doing nothing. No one seeking drastic changes in education should overlook, for example, the pressure of sports, especially for minorities. This may sound trivial compared to other problems, but the problem is very real for some students and in some parts of the country. In many states,

Chapter 1

MANAGING FOR QUALITY
IN THE SCHOOLS

William Glasser

Editor's Note

   Dr. William Glasser needs no introduction and is not interested in hearing anyone sing his praises. A major shift in labeling is Glasser's use of the word "choice" theory in place of "control theory," conveying, as clearly as possible, the responsible decisions that every individual human being naturally and continually makes from the inside out. Control, although technically accurate in describing people's search for a sensory match to a particular perceptual picture in their heads, has implied their control over other people. Control theory—now choice theory—always has been about controlling for one's own wants and controlling one's own life. The best complement that I can offer Dr. Glasser is to suggest that readers try these ideas in their own schools and be the judges of the merit of his expertise and strategies.

SCHOOLS KNOW HOW TO REPEAT
PAST PRACTICES

   Whenever I read books such as this, as well as article after article in educational journals, I am struck by the soundness of almost all of the ideas. No shortage exists of proven suggestions for improving our schools. Yet as I have

3

PART I
SEEING CRISES
IN A CONTEXT

coaches and parents (especially) often have "red-shirted" boys as early as junior high—that is, pulled strings or whatever to keep Junior back a year or two so that when he finally gets to high school he'll be bigger and stronger, hence likelier to make the football team. In some states such as Texas, Ohio, and Hawaii, high school football is *the* sport, more so than at the college or professional levels. Needless to say, for some students, their sole reason for doing *anything* in school, or even staying, is to make a college and then a professional team.

Changing the Teacher's Role to Manager

All of these very real pressures and realities aside, I think I have learned some fundamental principles about learning and teaching within an institutional setting that truly could transform the nation's schools at the grass roots, and I intend to stay focused on one main idea in this chapter. We can *do* something about the problem that I consider to be the main obstacle we need to change. If we redefine a teacher's role from *controller* of others to *manager,* we can effect a revolutionary change in schools and even get a handle on the morass of political considerations I just mentioned.

Students Do Not Find School Worthwhile

Down under all of these symptoms, the problem of schools is simple: regardless of the school they attend, far too few students are working hard to learn. To check this out with a small sample, I asked about 40 high school student leaders attending a conference in Pittsburgh (sponsored by the Fox Chapel School District) to define a *good student.* My student volunteers had no problem in responding to that question. I then asked how many of these good students were in their school. The consensus was between 20% and 45%. When I asked them if this number was so low because many students were handicapped or retarded, they said, "No, they don't work enough because they don't like the schoolwork teachers ask them to do." Those students with whom I met in Pittsburgh came from schools that were preselected for excellence—no "troubled" inner-city schools were represented. All schools were well-funded, and the students who attended were mostly from homes where parents strongly supported education.

Focusing on a single sample of 40 students has its obvious limitations when it comes to generalizing, but remember that these kids were the elite from more or less elite schools. Moreover, I felt these responses were more than just anecdotal or flippant because I have heard this story so consistently in every school in every part of this country over many years. No one needs a research technician to help draw the conclusion that I reached then and still hold today: in our *best* schools, fewer than one-half of the students are "good students." In the underfunded, overcrowded schools of our big cities, this number probably drops to less than 10%. To put the problem bluntly, capable students are not working in school. This disinterest in other people's agendas is *the* problem and really the only problem. Apathy has been the problem for over 100 years.

To talk about ragged discipline, dropouts, drugs, teenage pregnancies, learning disabilities, dysfunctional homes, poor financial support, breakdown in societal values, pressure to get into professional sports, or any other related problems is to avoid facing the real issue—huge numbers of capable students do not like their present schoolwork and refuse to make the effort to become good students. If we could run schools where these students were willing to make the effort, we would eliminate many if not all the other problems about which we complain. Quality schools are my answer. Many districts, starting with the Johnson City School system in New York, have joined the Quality School Consortium that I initiated. Today, Evergreen in Victoria, Washington, Evergreen in north central California, Huntington Woods in Michigan, and 150 others nationwide are working hard at transforming schooling for children and adolescents. Managers in these schools follow the ideas suggested in *The Quality School* (Glasser, 1992). The result is that almost all students are working hard, producing high-quality results, and not antagonizing teachers, the administration, or their parents (Dryden, 1994).

TEACHING IS PRIMARILY MANAGING

We will not have quality schools until we face the fact that almost all efforts to improve any school do not even address the main issue. Why do we call those who direct what occurs in classrooms throughout the western world "teachers?" They may teach some of the time, but teaching is not what most of them do most of the time. What most people who teach in public schools really do most of the time is *manage*. In my view, anyone who is unwilling to face the fact that management, and not teaching, is the challenge will not implement one good suggestion from this book or from any other source. Problems and complaints will continue while students lose interest, make trouble in old and new ways, and, finally, drop out of school altogether.

We can accurately define a *manager* as a person with an agenda and the duty of persuading workers (i.e., in school, the students) to accept that agenda, work hard, and do a good job (Glasser, 1994). Whether the manager works in a shop or factory, oversees children at home, or teaches in a school, the essence of the task is the same. Effective managing is very tough work, perhaps the most difficult of all jobs. Furthermore, what we call teaching is without a doubt the most difficult kind of managing. The reason teaching presents such a challenge in managing is that society has no real goals beyond test scores and grades for evaluating teaching effectiveness.

Pure Teaching Is Rare

I am not saying that professionals who do nothing but teach do not exist. They do, lots of them, but few exist in the academic classes anywhere in grades 1 through 12 of our public schools. A pure teacher, one who does not manage at all, is someone whose students not only want to learn but also are willing to work hard to learn what the teacher teaches. Examples are nonacademic teachers such as driver education instructors as well as those who coach or teach in purely voluntary academic classes (e.g., advanced science, math, or foreign language teachers in private institutes). Schools would have no problems if all the students wanted to learn, because almost any knowledgeable person could teach a student who is willing to work hard.

What workaday teachers seem unable to do is teach the vast majority of students who, liking neither *what* teachers ask them to learn nor *how* they ask them to learn it, refuse to put in much effort. Because even our best schools have well over 50% of all students in this minimal-learning group, we must face the fact that managing students successfully—helping them enjoy learning—is a very difficult job but is still the job that we all must learn to do much better.

When I refer to quality in teaching or a quality school, I am not proposing a new elitism, a return to so-called permissive education, or the "do your own thing" days of the late 1960s. Perhaps distinguishing between *teaching* and *training* would be useful. No one talks about "basic teaching" in the armed forces or "job teaching" rather than "job training." *Training* is narrowly goal-oriented and aims at a specific body of skills that can be certified and measured quantitatively. Information can be poured out within a framework of rigid assignments.

I define pure teaching as a process of imparting specific skills and knowledge through a variety of techniques, such as explaining and modeling, to people who want to learn these skills and knowledge because they believe that, sooner or later, these skills and knowledge will add quality to their lives. Therefore, no one can *teach* unwilling learners, which characterizes most students today. With such passive seat-warmers, a competent person first must *manage* the reluctant learners in the sense that I just have described. Managing in new ways is guiding, suggesting, and respecting the free choices of self-motivated learners who feel safe in a climate of noncoercion. Students will work toward goals if they have a major voice in laying out their own objectives. The goals they can control or, at least, have a strong voice in setting typically defy quantification. Gone are the punitive restrictions of indoctrination and some schools' ideas of training—the extra assignments, special papers, detention study halls, in-school suspension, and the dreaded "five points off" list.

Managing in Business Versus Managing in School

To put the difficulty of managing students into perspective, take a look at how much easier managing in industry is where goals are much clearer. Managing employees is easier than managing a class, for at least six reasons:

1. However much workers may not like a job, usually they *have a clear goal*—for example, money—and a clear way to get where they are going. Most students did not seek out a school and have little or no goal in mind.

2. Workers almost always *can see the sense of what a boss asks them to do* and easily can judge whether or not they are doing a good job. Further, if workers see the basic inefficiency or nonsense of a task, very often they *earn a reward for dropping a proposal for improvement* into a suggestion box. A poor manager would, of course, discourage workers from suggesting any changes. Students typically have no clue about the value of the work their teachers ask them to perform.

3. Employees in industry almost *never have to take work home.* Homework is common in school.

4. Bosses *can discharge workers who do not do a good job,* and new workers are usually both eager and able to take their place immediately. For the most part, schools are stuck with the students who happen to attend.

5. If workers decide they really do not like a work environment, they *can quit* and go find another employer with a work environment more to

their liking. Students in some locales have some degree of choice about the school they attend but not the same freedom to come and go that a worker has in a company.

6. Unlike a school, a business *will recognize that when shortcomings become obvious, poor management is often to blame*; companies are willing to spend millions of dollars to try to improve the effectiveness of their managers. Schools seldom label a problem with students as a systemic problem.

Even with all these advantages, most industries still are not able to persuade their employees to do what they are fully capable of doing, further proof that managing effectively is very difficult.

What's More Difficult: Parenting or Teaching?

Although not exactly easy, parenting can appear to be easier than teaching because, in most cases, children love their parents and want to please them. Except for very young children, students usually do not *love* their teachers, at least not at the outset. Students, of course, do not receive money for studying, yet they must continue to carry out a lot of boring work that neither they nor anyone else sees much sense in doing. Teachers ask them to do a lot of homework, often mindless drills, which is even less sensible than their in-class assignments. Finally, students have little or no choice about the school that they attend.

Coercive Tactics That Currently Beat Out Persuasive Ploys in Schools

Given these dismal disincentives, most classroom teachers fall flat on their face when it comes to their skills in managing. They simply cannot persuade a class of reluctant learners to choose to do the schoolwork the students are capable of accomplishing. In frustration, the motivation that almost all teachers use, perforce, is coercion, usually punishment. If punishment worked, we would have no problem, but pushing, shoving, taunting, and finger-pointing do not stir up any enthusiasm for study. Our schools are overflowing with threats and punishments, but the more people try to manage through coercion, the less students choose to do. Not only does force not help, but also coercion of both teachers and students actually intensifies the complaints we have.

LOOKING FOR GOOD MANAGEMENT MODELS

If you agree that management is the skill that teachers and principals have to learn (and most people do not think of teachers as managers), the sensible thing is to look for good management models. In schools, few models do exist outside a handful of schools in the Consortium for Quality Schools. Even in the vast arena of industry, few examples of effective management stand out. We have to look halfway across the globe to Japan, where many managers in the world also currently are looking. The Japanese evidently have figured out how to manage industrial employees so that they work hard and build quality products. In fact, their ability to manage for quality has been a major contributor to their quick ascent from devastation to being the wealthiest country in the world. Japan has been very fortunate in other ways too, enjoying the luxury of spending little or no tax monies on national defense and diverting enormous sums into their free markets.

Who can say what would have happened to the world had Hiranuma, Japan's civilian Minister of Economics, prevailed at a special government meeting in early 1941? As a member of the government's conference on going to war, Hiranuma (Ike, 1967, pp. 100-101) suggested an alternative to initiating an international conflict. He proposed that Japan should rely on the natural loyalty and enthusiasm of its people and gain virtual economic dominance in the world through the development of its industry. One member of the conference commented that the economic minister "made us all feel a little funny," suggesting that many agreed with this idea, but few felt in a position to show public support. That historical opportunity was then, and we all know too well that the Japanese government did not opt then for the path of a commercial battle. We are living in the 1990s, not the 1940s, and what we need to do is learn how the Japanese have managed for quality and apply this knowledge to managing students in our schools.

MANAGING FOR QUALITY

Discovering that what the Japanese are doing today in factories is not inherent in their traditional culture may be intriguing to some. Their cultural norms and traditional values encourage an open willingness to follow the advice of authorities, to leave the decisions to the higher-ups, and to accept a superior's evaluation of their efforts. Instead Japan learned how to manage effectively from an American, W. Edwards Deming (1982), who had taught the same ideas in America for many years before he went to Japan. Deming passed away in the late autumn of 1993 and is still revered as the leader among teachers of quality management. During World War II, he was active in training American factory managers in how to handle unskilled workers so that they could do quality work in America's war industries. After the war, when he suggested to the same companies that they continue to emphasize managing for quality as they converted to peacetime production, boards and bosses scoffed at him. The leaders of the American automobile industry were especially incredulous when he told them what the Japanese since have proven: building a quality car is less expensive than producing a shoddy car with style changes.

The Japanese heard Dr. Deming's message and implemented his proposals. Someone in the MacArthur administration took Deming to Japan in 1950 and, in contrast to the American industrialists, the Japanese listened to him. He told them that, if they would learn what he taught, they could become the world's leader in any product they wanted to build. To a nation of shamed, crushed, and vulnerable people, Deming's promise of regaining some power and influence on the world stage sounded like a very good idea indeed. With Deming's help, the Japanese have gone from a prewar reputation for tinny, shoddy products to a reputation for quality that is unprecedented in history. Deming himself said that everything he taught could be applied in any country and that these ideas would work just as well in schools as in factories.

Deming's Fundamental Beliefs

Deming presented his ideas in four parts—the psychology of managing workers well, the statistical standards that workers must meet to achieve quality, systems theory, and profound knowledge or a sound theoretical base (Crawford, Bodine, & Hoglund, 1993). *The Quality School* (Glasser, 1992) has been my own effort to bring Deming's management psychology to the schools. Deming's statistical work for production and quality is an important element in quality management; however, I will not cover this topic because school leaders may want to examine statistical variance as a natural phenomenon that affects their programs every day. Taking action on events that happen by chance, as if one could control naturally occurring variations, is a foolish waste of time (e.g., schools making a huge fuss when a student is tardy). Everyone in life is late from time to time, teachers included. We easily could apply Deming's notion about natural variation and allow for some reasonable number of tardies—say, 10 a year—as a fact of life.

Choice Theory Makes Deming's Ideas More Effective in Schools

The quality school project is more than an application of Deming's ideas to schools. My main contribution, as I see it, has been to provide what Deming does not offer—a rationale for adopting his ideas and a practical system for implementing his methods in education. The explanation I offer provides a context for managing people in any setting and is embedded in *Control Theory* (Glasser, 1984; Powers, 1973; Robertson & Powers, 1990). Another book I can suggest on this topic that connects choice theory to quality management is *New Paradigms for Creating Quality Schools* (Greene, 1994).

CHOICE THEORY HELPS STUDENTS ACHIEVE QUALITY ON THEIR OWN

What is puzzling is that Deming's management psychology, which has led the Japanese to riches and success, has not been adopted widely yet in American industry, much less in the noncorporate world. This oversight probably should be no more surprising than the fact that Japan's schools are managed much the same as they were in the 1930s, still apparently characterized by rote learning and memorization. Great pressure remains on students for grades, substantial competition, and threats leading to a wave of suicides after the completion of the annual university placement exams. Hazing and a competitive spirit abound in many schools, sometimes leading students to choose reckless behavior, including suicide. Within the past two or three years, the Education Ministry in Japan has proposed eliminating the conventional grading system throughout the country, so someone, at least, has been listening.

Some Japanese worry that their schools produce workers and managers who are great at efficiency and synthesizing ideas from elsewhere, but poor at real innovation and entrepreneurial skills. Sadly, their schools remain encrusted in an elitist, feudal system, but this sorry condition does not mean that we should settle for inadequate schools ourselves or that we cannot learn management methods from Japanese businesses and apply those proven strategies and tactics to schools.

Changing a School's Social Norms Is Difficult

Many American manufacturers have tried to adopt Deming's principles by hiring Deming or Deming-trained consultants and spending millions on training managers and workers. With very few exceptions, as described in detail in a book about quality in the workplace (Gabor, 1990), they have been unable to put into practice in their factories what the Japanese have learned and implemented so successfully. Even though some schools have tried to follow the Wyoming, Michigan model (which is similar to the Deming model), almost all schools, both in the U.S. and in Japan, have been unable to adopt the model thoroughly to create a quality school. How can anyone account for this?

I believe that what stops both schools and factories from changing to Deming's way is his fundamental challenge that they change their basic belief about the way people function; accepting this charge is too much for most managers. Additionally, most managers possibly carry a shortsighted view of their own power and wrongly believe that, if they sponsor a collaborative role for workers or students, they somehow might lose control over the entire situation. What foreman wants a line worker promoted over his head? What teacher really wants to see students running the class? For cultural reasons, American managers (far more so than Japanese managers) are unwilling to accept the words of an authority—even one with good evidence that the recommendation will work—unless that authority also is willing to explain clearly why these changes need to be made. Deming did not provide a rationale for changing organizational norms, and this void, in my view, explains why his recommendation has been so difficult for Americans to put into practice. I can suggest one other recent book for guiding school principals through the transition between conventional and quality schooling. The book is *Creating the Conditions: Leadership for Quality Schools* (Gossens & Anderson, 1995).

Choice Theory Makes Quality Schools Possible

Setting aside cultural considerations, anyone's best chance of persuading others to change their beliefs is to offer them a "better" set of beliefs as a substitute for those they are rejecting. What I offer in *The Quality School* is an organized theory about the way human beings function. This new structure is *choice theory,* which explains clearly why we should change to the management psychology that Deming has recommended in industry, in schools, and elsewhere. I am asking those who manage (i.e., teach) to substitute choice theory for their traditional belief in action-reaction or stimulus-response psychology (sometimes called punish and reward psychology), a belief about human functioning that many people have held for years.

The request to transform one's current belief system and to adopt choice theory is a major shift in one's viewpoint and attitude toward the world. The invitation to convert one's frame of reference is even more difficult in light of choice theory's relative newness. The *practical application of choice theory* to the lives of human beings is probably less than 25 years old. This relative newness, though, is not a problem because almost everyone who discovers the new perspective shows much interest in choice theory. Starting with the original work of William Powers (1973), the first to apply this theory to people in pragmatic ways, I have expanded and clarified the theoretical ideas to make learning how to use control (choice) theory in everyday life and work an easy task. I also have trained a cadre of 100 or more people who teach this theory all over the world to make these ideas readily available to any school or business that wants to learn this powerful model.

I believe that choice theory is the key to implementing Deming's management concepts in schools or anywhere else. I began introducing the Johnson City, New York schools to choice theory in the early 1980s and, without any direct input or training from Deming, the staff now views this theory as basic to their success in managing both students and parents. They also acknowledge that knowing *about* Deming has helped them even more. Therefore, a fair statement would be that *creating a quality school requires learning and applying a combination of Deming's management psychology and choice theory, which explains why the management principles work.*

DEMING'S CONTRIBUTION

Deming summarized his management psychology in his famous 14 points and laid out 7 deadly diseases and 5 obstacles that successful managers need to avoid (Deming, 1982). By coupling my version of Powers' (1973) control theory with my long-term understanding of schools, I have reduced Deming's 26 principles to three key premises. If we could persuade a school administrator and, at least, three-quarters of the teachers in any school to use these three core concepts for managing education, we could, with a small amount of staff training, transform any school into a quality school in five years or less. What exactly is a *quality school?* A quality school is one where 90% or more of the students are making serious efforts to do competent work in all of their academic classes; even the few students who are not doing competent work in all their classes are doing some work in at least one class that both they and their teachers could consider quality work. Although defining "quality" in any exact sense is slippery, I can say that, regardless of how small the quantity of work, the effort will be *the very best* that the student is capable of doing. The work will be meaningful to the students, useful, satisfying, and never destructive.

I have derived three principles from Deming's extensive teachings and from choice theory as the minimal essential starting points in building a quality school:

1. manage without coercion or scare tactics;
2. emphasize quality, not quantity, in assigned schoolwork; and
3. remove obstacles to students evaluating all their work honestly.

Manage without Coercion

To persuade workers or students to do quality work, Deming said that a manager must eliminate all fear in a managerial relationship. The manager must refrain from doing anything that could be construed as coercive (e.g., "Do this right, or you're out, Charlie"). In light of Deming's commitment to a secure workplace, a school principal must never coerce teachers and teachers must never coerce students. In practice, noncoercive managing and teaching mean eliminating all threats, punishments, ridicule, lowering of grades, and anything else that students could construe as negative coercion to force them or teachers to do what they do not want to do. Most educators have become so familiar with coercion in the educational system that they may be unable to envision what will motivate students with no sanctions at all. We know, of course, that the strongest motive in a quality school is the student's own self-respect and the responsible pursuit of inherent goals and important wants. For those who insist on some coercion, make it positive. A carrot may be present, but no stick is in sight. Even a carrot is not an external stimulus that an outsider artificially creates. Any reward is a carrot only insofar as students so define the reward from within their own value system. This way of operating is clearly not stimulus-response psychology because students, like everyone else, are internally motivated.

Since the purpose of a quality school is to persuade almost all students to work hard and do some quality work, managers and workers *cannot* be adversaries. The more adversarial the relationship, the lower the quality of work. The more collaborative, trusting, and encouraging the relationship, the higher the quality of the work. Deming taught that managers and workers (i.e., teachers and students) must be friends. They must care for each other, and in school both students and teachers really must believe that a major goal of those who manage them is to treat them well. This emphasis on friendship will be particularly difficult for some teachers to swallow because they believe that school is a place where students engage their heads and not their hearts.

In the quality school, I see a noncoercive manager as a *lead-manager* or simply a leader. Unfortunately, even this term may conjure up thoughts of a military leader, carrying images of much negative coercion, general abasement, and even chewing out. My connotation for the word *leader* is someone people want to follow because they believe that this person primarily has *their* benefit in mind. I also mean to convey that a leader focuses on success in the task at hand. This definition of leader contrasts sharply with the usual coercive manager. A boss tries to get people to work hard by threats and bluster. In a boss's mind, his/her personal benefit and satisfaction are paramount, not the workers or the task.

Emphasize Quality, Not Quantity, in Assigned Schoolwork

In a quality school, the emphasis is on quality work, meaning work that both teacher and student see as a cause for pride. Teachers will talk with their classes about quality and explain that whenever we choose to do something, quality is what we all want. One "perfect" sonnet is worth a thousand lines of doggerel. The teacher-manager's goal would be to persuade each class member in every academic subject to do what that student would consider quality work. What makes all of this discussion much more tangible is that one of the requisites of quality is *usefulness.* Therefore, in a quality school, not only is punishment nonexistent, but also students are never held responsible for schoolwork that seems of little or no use in their lives.

Usefulness is not limited necessarily to the practical or utilitarian in a physical sense, but could refer to any use, including enjoyable or aesthetic. A teacher must explain to all students, in an acceptable way, why what the teacher is teaching is so useful for students that it would be worthwhile to learn even at the cost of strenuous effort. Learning relevant material will be fun for some students; those who do not like it do not have to continue, and meanwhile they can enjoy helping their friends and feeling vicarious satisfaction.

In almost all schools, too much is taught and demanded back on tests that has no use for anyone and that students will soon forget, no matter how well or poorly they do on the tests. Memorizing the presidents of the United States in the correct chronological order, as my older son once had to do for a test, is a good example of useless schoolwork, unless he wanted to make a career out of trivia games or TV game shows. (For a while, I was worried that such a career was a top priority with him.) This guideline of usefulness, however, should not prevent a teacher from teaching anything of value; however, teachers should not ask students to remember for a test what teachers themselves do not deem useful.

What should be emphasized and tested in a quality school should be skills, not facts, information, or formulas available both in books and in computer software or other references. The librarian becomes an even more significant person because the thrust is learning how to learn and discovering resources. Computer hotlines and databases are usually excellent, but these are not always complete and a good librarian is a key person in the quality school. Memorizing facts that people do not use in their daily lives does not correspond to any legitimate need. No possibility exists for quality in students memorizing anything that has no use because it has no real, continuing interest. This would not prevent a teacher from asking a student to memorize a short poem, for example, for an aesthetic purpose in the hopes that the student would find this valuable. Many students would be so motivated, but those who do not should not be punished for their unwillingness to agree. Again, the skill to persuade and not the willingness to coerce is the hallmark of a good teacher-manager.

Skills are always useful, especially general skills such as writing or public speaking. Learning in school how the *Constitution* protects our civil rights, for example, eventually can add quality to most students' lives, even though some kids may find the subject tiresome. No quality comes from mechanically repeating the words of the "Bill of Rights"; however, the quality is in learning how to use the protection guaranteed by the "Bill of Rights." A quality school would test for the skill of using the *Constitution* and not merely the rote memorization of its words.

In the schools that I am proposing, no busy or tedious work, such as doing problem after problem in long division, would be present. As soon as students could demonstrate competence in an arithmetical process such as long division by correctly doing one or two problems by hand and showing their understanding, they would be encouraged to use calculators to do further computations. This would free them from drudgery and allow them to concentrate on learning that *what* to calculate, not *how* to calculate, is the real reason to study mathematics.

Except for the possibility of taking practice tests to prepare for the senseless mass-testing obsession of the everyday world, students would have no objective tests in a quality school because very little if anything can be measured on an objective test that will have any inherent quality. All tests would have written or oral answers calling for the student's opinion, evaluation, or ability to use what he/she has learned. Teachers would give students take-home tests and encourage them to consult with parents or others, as one often would when learning in the real world or solving actual problems. Teachers should foster group work even on tests; after all, this reflects real life in a society where people more and more must learn to work together. In today's schools, no one can say with certainty that students are honest because they cannot display genuine honesty if they have no opportunity to cheat. In a quality school, a teacher has better things to do than watch students like a hawk. No cheating would occur, because the need for it would be zero. A student's ability to use what is learned (and not just stow away facts) would be tested, and no one can cheat on usage. You either can or cannot do something.

Usage is like throwing a basketball through a hoop; cheating is not possible. The significant questions become, for example, can students show the teacher how they would use a road map to find a city, or have they received an answer to a letter they wrote to someone? What students cheat on currently is nonsense knowledge like the height of a mountain, a date in history, or the name of a person. Students will continue to enjoy the possibility of enlisting others to write a paper or buying a ready-made term paper, but they would be less inclined to do so in light of the qualitative shifts in schools and in their relationships with teachers. When you discard definite letter grades or rankings for a class, you remove most incentives to come to a class armed with crib notes. Eliminating busywork and all academic nonsense, emphasizing skills and using these skills on tests, would bring the chance for quality and absolutely no reason would be present even to think about cheating.

Remove Obstacles to Students Evaluating All Their Work Honestly

Deming claimed that quality work costs *less* than shoddy work and that one way to save this money is to ask workers to evaluate their own work instead of paying an inspector to do so. Deming claimed that workers know more about their work than anyone else and that, in a noncoercive working environment, workers *want* to do quality work and do not need an outsider to inspect what they do. Naturally, as time goes by and students stop associating feedback with criticism and pain, they may request an outside review of certain tasks. Writers always will benefit from the services of a proofreader and editor for their own work because a second, objective opinion is extremely important. Sometimes a writer is just too close to the subject and forgets that readers may not be as familiar with ideas left unstated or stated ambiguously. Students must know from the start that they are in the driver's seat when it comes to evaluating and directing their learning. Asking for an inspection is different from unsolicited correction and outside control.

Where quality is concerned, the problem with external inspections—whether an inspector checking a machine part or a teacher grading a paper—is that the worker tends to do only enough to get by, and the inspector sets the level far below what the worker is capable of doing. Inspectors have their own constraints;

they are afraid for their jobs if they reject too much work. Teachers experience similar pressures to promote students onward, to improve test scores in a class, and, most of all, to keep 'em in school lest the budget allocation called average daily attendance (ADA) go down.

Inspections, whether in schools or in factories, cost more, work against quality, and emphasize "passing" as the standard. "It's good enough" is what most students answer when they first are questioned about the quality of their work. They do not believe that quality is their responsibility; *that* judgment belongs to the teacher or inspector. But when students are given the task of inspecting their own work in a noncoercive atmosphere strongly emphasizing quality, they do not want to judge themselves inferior. Basic to Deming's ideas and the quality school, therefore, is the idea that all students can and should be taught to inspect all of their work.

Deming was correct in assuming that factory workers know more than anyone else about their work because they do it over and over and become very familiar with the procedures. In school, however, much of what a student does is new, so the student needs help from a teacher in evaluating the work accurately. In a quality school, the evaluation of the work is done by both the student and the teacher (who concentrates on teaching the student how to do a good job of self-evaluation). Once the teacher is confident that a student knows how to self-evaluate, the student's decision will count for more and eventually may be given as much weight as any teacher's evaluation, if not more.

Asking students to evaluate their work in the absence of a chance to improve the project or paper makes no sense. Ideally, no final grades show up in a quality school. Grades simply would indicate where students were when they decided to stop trying to improve. Both teachers and students have expressed concern that if students knew at the outset that they had a chance to improve and would not be graded, they might not try very hard the first time. This is possible, especially in the beginning, but most students will find that doing something over is more difficult than doing it once; thus, in time, this problem diminishes. Besides, most students have pride and gradually will become uncomfortable having little to show for the extended time they spent for their personal efforts.

If students want to improve a grade after evaluating their work, they will know that they always have a chance to do this. This procedure can encourage students to look over anything they do with the idea of improving it, a process that is necessary for quality and almost nonexistent presently in schools that follow the maxim "it's good enough." What follows is that students have very little, if any, assigned homework in a smoothly running quality school. Instead, the students themselves will assign their own homework and simply take work home that they want to improve. Their rationale for doing self-assigned homework would be to improve the quality of their work or to get a better grade (i.e., if the school assigns grades during the transitional period between conventional school and quality school). Students use class time to study new work but select home as the place where they can improve what they started in class. In any case, students always will receive some form of credit for increasing the quality of what they do by engaging in their own form of homework.

THE CURRENT SITUATION

Up until recently, I could not name a specific school in the entire U.S. where all three Deming principles were in active use. The first district I found, Johnson City in New York, and countless other school districts in the Quality School Consortium are working hard to make self-evaluation a key component and to eliminate testing for nonsense. Both of these changes are necessary changes if quality is to prevail. I now can state with a wonderful sense of delight that the Huntington Woods Elementary School in Wyoming, Michigan has fully accomplished the major shift to quality, and on May 13, 1995, we officially declared this fine school and staff a quality school. My congratulations to Kaye Mentley, principal, for her excellent leadership in collaborating with the Huntington Woods teachers, staff, children, parents, and community to move to quality schooling.

As I continue to work closely with schools and districts, I try to keep a little ahead of those whom I advise, but schools that practice lead-management are capable of great flexibility and always show continuous improvement. Sometimes I feel that we are running neck and neck. I learn something daily, and I always admire the sincerity of all the professionals committed to quality. I do not claim a lock on quality schooling. Many perceptive teachers have used one or more of these principles successfully for years. Outside observers universally acclaim these standouts as good teachers. Unfortunately, no one operating alone can change the cultural norms of an entire system. By definition, making this dramatic shift requires a team effort.

Any school that incorporates the three basics into its program will become a quality school within a few years. Administrators who have been implementing Deming's managerial methods have confirmed my own conviction that all who wish to create the conditions for an authentic transformation *must know and practice choice theory.* This was confirmed in Dryden's (1994) fine doctoral study of quality schools in the Consortium. In fact, schools in the Consortium say that part of the process of becoming a quality school is teaching choice theory to all the students beginning in kindergarten. In general, the earlier staff and students apply choice theory, the easier the journey to quality and the more comfortable the students and schools will be with Powers' model of thinking actively and behaving responsibly. Many materials are available already, especially through New View Publishing Company, and, of course, this book contains more specific ideas for reaching the goal of quality. Interested readers can write the William Glasser Institute to obtain more information on quality school programs all over the country. The addresses for New View Publications and for the Institute are at the end of this chapter.

CHOICE THEORY

Choice theory (Glasser, 1984) is a biological theory of our functioning as living creatures. The main way this view of human behavior differs from the generally accepted cause and effect or stimulus-response (S-R) notion is that choice theory has as its basic premise the contention that all behavior is an attempt by individuals to satisfy needs that are built into the genetic structure of the brain. By taking action, we seek to satisfy these needs. Simply stated, all of our motivation is *internal*—a sharp contrast to stimulus-response (S-R) theory, which claims that we are externally motivated. External motivation is an oxymoron.

In a stimulus-response world, environmental events cause us to behave. In such a linear cause-and-effect model, we answer a telephone, for example, because it rings. Choice theory contends that this predetermined cause and effect chain is never the case. The ring of the phone does not *make* us do anything. Events outside of us, commonly called environmental stimuli, are, in fact, only pieces of information. Information in itself never makes us do anything. Always we are the ones who decide how to act on the information that we take in, and how we act is always in the direction of what we think will fulfill one or more of our five basic needs at that time. In other words, we *choose* the behavior that looks like a response. In actuality, our response is really a *sponse.* This means, with the obvious exception of a stronger person using greater physical force to make an unwilling person move or fall down, no one can make another person do anything that that person does not want to do.

We do not answer a phone because it rings but because answering satisfies one or more of our needs, such as love and belonging, better than anything else at that time. If we have something better to do, we are free to let the phone ring and some people often do just that. What this means is that our behavior is always our best attempt at a given time to choose an action that will satisfy one or more of the five basic needs: *love and belonging, power, freedom, fun, and survival.* We do not do anything *because of* what happens outside ourselves.

The world, in general, seems to accept that one can force, bribe, or coerce others into doing what they stubbornly do not want to do. Many who hold this viewpoint present examples of people doing what they do not want to do when pressure is applied—for example, people often do what is distasteful to them because they either are threatened with a great deal of pain or are promised a great reward. But the final decision to acquiesce came after they carefully appraised their needs and wants. They reached the decision inside their own heads and decided it was better to do what was distasteful rather than suffer the consequences or fail to reap the reward. Some people have given up their lives rather than doing something against their principles; but even those principles come from their personal needs and not from the world around them.

QUALITY REVISITED

To understand quality better, choice theory is most helpful. Generally stated, according to choice theory, no one can compel or bribe a person into doing quality work. In school, you can make students do some work to avoid pain or other sanctions, but you cannot make them do quality work. If you examine your own life, you will see that whenever you did quality work, you did it not because someone else forced you but because doing it satisfied you. You may have done it because you loved or respected another person but, in doing it for that person, you were able to satisfy your own internal need for love.

As we live our lives, we keep careful track of what is satisfying to our needs, and choice theory is an explanation that we store this information in a special place in our memory that I refer to simply as the "Quality World" (Glasser, 1986). In the past, I also have used the more generic term "Internal World." As we live and learn what is satisfying, this hypothetical place becomes an internal representation of an ideal world in which we would like to live permanently if we could. In this special world are all our loved ones, our prized possessions, our ideals and values, and everything we consider most important, for we have found these things most satisfying to our needs. Remember, the basic needs are genetically encoded and are the same for everyone, but people's wants vary and they meet their needs differently.

In order to manage people successfully, you must persuade them to put what you want (i.e., the managerial agenda) into their own quality worlds. When they do, then and only then will they work hard and do a quality job on what a teacher asks them to do. In schools then, the whole thrust of Deming's three basics is to persuade students to put into their quality worlds their schools, their teachers, and, of course, the schoolwork they encounter. When students agree and customize their quality worlds in this way, they will do quality work. When all students and teachers do this, they will transform the school into a quality school.

Learning choice theory is fundamental to the whole process. When we employ this framework, students will not be in a place where they experience coercion in their quality worlds, nor will they be taught by a coercive teacher. If we ask students who have placed schoolwork in their quality worlds to evaluate their work, they cannot help trying to improve it if they believe that this is possible.

A quality school has much more to all aspects than I possibly can explain here. For further information, I suggest that you start by reading *The Quality School* (Glasser, 1992) and *The Quality Teacher* (Glasser, 1993). The book that you presently are reading, on teaching and counseling in a quality school, has many suggestions about getting started. Here you will find the practical steps that you will need to create the quality school in spite of the serious challenges many students bring to school. If you decide that you want to learn more after reading these books, contact the Institute and ask how your school can become part of the Quality School Consortium. For information on making the transformation to a quality school, contact me at the following address:

The Quality School Consortium
The William Glasser Institute
22024 Lassen Street, #118
Chatsworth, CA 91311

You also may wish to telephone us at 818-700-8000 or 800-899-0688, or reach us via FAX at 818-700-0555. New View Publications can be contacted at P.O. Box 3021, Chapel Hill, NC 27515-3021. The telephone number is 800-441-3604.

BIBLIOGRAPHY

Glasser, N. (1989). *Control theory in the practice of reality therapy.* New York: HarperCollins.

Powers, W. T. (1989). *Living control systems.* Gravel Switch, KY: The Control Systems Group.

Skinner, B. F. (1969). *Contingencies of reinforcement: A theoretical analysis.* New York: Appleton-Century-Crofts.

REFERENCES

Crawford, D., Bodine, R., & Hoglund, R. (1993). *The school for quality learning.* Champaign, IL: Research Press.

Deming, W. E. (1982). *Out of the crisis.* Cambridge, MA: MIT Center for Advanced Engineering Study.

Dryden, J. (1994). *The quality schools initiative: Analysis of an educational reform as perceived by principals in K-12 consortium schools.* Unpublished doctoral dissertation, University of the Pacific, Stockton, CA.

Gabor, A. (1990). *The man who discovered quality.* New York: Random House.

Glasser, W. (1984). *Control theory.* New York: HarperCollins.

Glasser, W. (1986). *Control theory in the classroom.* New York: Harper & Row.

Glasser, W. (1992). *The quality school* (2nd ed.). New York: HarperCollins.

Glasser, W. (1993). *The quality teacher.* New York: HarperCollins.

Glasser, W. (1994). *The control theory manager.* New York: HarperCollins.

Gossens, D., & Anderson, J. (1995). *Creating the conditions: Leadership for quality schools.* Chapel Hill, NC: New View Publications.

Greene, B. (1994). *New paradigms for creating quality schools.* Chapel Hill, NC: New View Publications.

Ike, N. (1967). *Japan's decision for war: Records of the 1941 policy conferences.* Stanford, CA: Stanford University Press.

Powers, W. (1973). *Behavior: The control of perception.* New York: De Gruyter Press.

Robertson, R. J., & Powers, W. T. (Eds.). (1990). *Introduction to modern psychology: The control-theory view.* Gravel Switch, KY: The Control Systems Group.

Chapter 2

REALITY THERAPY
AND CHOICE THEORY:
MAKING PERSONAL CHOICES
FOR A CHANGE

Larry L. Palmatier

Many readers are probably familiar with reality therapy because Glasser's (1965, 1969, 1984) problem-solving method is a classic framework for handling some of the most troublesome complaints people can devise. His ideas mainly help others become responsible, and his strategies work well anywhere—in correctional facilities, hospitals, schools, social service agencies, mental health centers, and private practice. Some educators and counselors who claim familiarity with Glasser's counseling model do not apply his methods accurately and consistently. Others miss one small piece and end up with poor results; worse still, they become frustrated with someone whom they are trying to help and resort to tongue-lashing, making a mockery of the method. If the helper is trying these methods in a school setting, perhaps he/she asks students *why* they did such and such. Glasser recommends avoiding asking why directly because the word *why* automatically evokes excuses and blaming from the average person. In addition, people naturally feel that someone asking *why* must be talking down to them. Also, when we hunt for an answer to *why*, we intellectualize and stay removed from action. When we feature the word *how*, we look for practical solutions that we can act upon at once. Principals report that almost all

27

parents whom they telephone about a disturbance at school will say, "Did you ask him 'why'?" This comment may help someone save face temporarily, but my advice to administrators is to ask the parents, "Could you tell me more? Have you found the *why* question *useful?*"

In concert with reality therapy, Glasser has adapted Powers' (1973, 1989) control theory to his own work with schools. The next few pages will address reality therapy first and then control (choice) theory—the same order Glasser presented these ideas. For some, control theory conjured up images of straight jackets and nylon ropes. My task will be to explain both models—one, choice theory, showing why and exactly how humans behave; and two, reality therapy, providing a straightforward method of counseling. To accomplish this dual task of clarifying Glasser's version of choice theory and his own problem-solving methods, I present specific examples so that readers can try out these tools immediately with actual renegades or those youngsters struggling with some extra pressures. Professionals who want to learn more about these two topics or to become certified through Glasser's Institute will find information at the end of chapter 1.

REALITY THERAPY: FICTION OR FACT

First of all, reality therapy works best when teachers or counselors understand choice theory (CT) and can point to positive applications of choice theory principles in their lives. Choice theory explains the system that operates for all conscious creatures. Our focus will be to explain why and how humans do the things they do. Reality therapy (RT) is a method of counseling that emphasizes solving problems in our lifetime and not dwelling on the past too much or bemoaning one's history. Both formulations, RT and CT, are friendly and effective; not harsh and blunt as some may have misinterpreted the techniques. As in anything else, a *little* knowledge may be dangerous.

One teacher told me that Glasser should change the names of his strategies so teachers would not cringe at their labels. "Reality therapy!" she said, "What's that? Get real, man?" With control theory, she was equally emotional: "Control theory! I am going to control the devil out of you." I explained that control theory is an established system model in cybernetics and other hard data sciences. No one has a unilateral right to drop the label for a well-established theory. I did suggest to the teacher, though, that she think of control theory as *personal choice theory* because the main person one is trying to control is oneself, not others. She said she felt relieved to hear the new phrase. Regarding reality therapy, I told her that I thought she would come to respect the title once she heard some of Glasser's classic statements in his counseling demonstrations. His comments are sometimes so incisive and true that their simplicity bowls a person over. One example: Glasser is speaking with a juvenile offender who has landed in a detention facility and is not accepting the reality of being there. He does what most *fish* do—fights being caught and shoved into a bucket. The original reality therapist says to him, "I think what's happening is that you are having trouble being 14. Is that right? But being 14 is a fact. You can't be anything but 14 when you're 14." This statement and 1,000 other ones much like it show educators that answers to problems are often much closer than we might imagine. Solutions most often depend on new ways to think about a situation as well as new actions to take; not trying too hard is a talent worth honing.

Doing It Wrong

A few years back, I met a teacher named Frank who was very likable. He had already taught for six years and he took his work seriously. One problem: decent Frank spent too much energy trying to control other people, namely, his eighth-grade students in a nice suburban junior high school in Utah. To show me his sincerity, Frank listened intently as I described reality therapy to a small group of professionals who had voluntarily attended an inservice workshop at his building. Over the next week, he practiced the counseling method by seeking out students as targets of opportunity. When I returned to the school and asked how the week went, Frank's hand shot up. He said, "I tried reality therapy and it didn't work." I asked Frank to tell me exactly what he had done and said. "I saw this student who had been getting on my nerves, and so I called him aside in the hall and practically shouted, 'All right, Jim, up against the wall. What are you doing?'" I reminded Frank that students deserve a fair warning and maybe an ounce of courtesy. Frank correctly had heard me say that he should target the "here and now" and not the past. What he did not register was "first, make friends."

Reality therapy starts with the assumption that no one can force anyone else to do anything. To elicit a willing agreement to act in ways *we* would prefer requires, first and foremost, a warm and friendly environment. Persuasion requires some trust between people. Set the stage by being supportive and nonpunitive. By the way, to Frank's credit, he later interviewed his students about his manner with them and he invited me to sit in and listen. They gave him an earful about his tendency to overcontrol. Micro-managing is out; encouraging initiative is in. Creating a courteous context for a counseling dialogue is just as important in solving problems as kindness is in winning students' cooperation in a classroom. First, make friends and ask, "What do you want?" This sounds simple enough and, as a positive idea, is a beginning. Unlike some heavy duty therapies, reality therapy *looks for what is right* and builds on positives—quite a contrast to clinical methods that hunt for deviance and pathology. One of Glasser's favorite statements is, "You never build anybody up by tearing 'em down." This observation is so simple and so true that people may sometimes forget it.

REALITY THERAPY'S EVOLUTION

Glasser credits another psychiatrist, G. L. Harrington, with teaching and modeling the concrete practices that Glasser took as the basis for what he later labeled reality therapy. He published his classic book, *Reality Therapy* (Glasser, 1965), in the mid-1960s. From the beginning, he decided to keep his ideas down to earth, so he structured his principles in seven or eight straight-forward steps.

1. Positive relationship. Make friends. Establish rapport by being friendly and supportive.

2. Current behavior. Ask what are you doing? Focus on current behavior and avoid the past.

3. Self-evaluation. Ask students to evaluate how well the present behavior is working to get them what they want.

4. New plan. If the behavior is not working well, ask about an optional plan of action.

5. Commitment. When a student has agreed on a new plan, seal the bargain with an agreement or commitment.

6. Do not accept excuses.

7. Do not punish (hurt) people in any form—ridicule, threats, intimidating.

8. Do not give up easily. (Glasser added step 8 several years later after extensive time working with teachers.)

Any theory or methodology worth its salt is not static; people change the ideas to serve their purposes better. Glasser noticed that he was asking people to evaluate their behavior and to draft a plan for new action if they saw their present behavior as not working out, but he had not asked them first about their own particular goal. He fixed this oversight by changing the first point. While making friends, ask a simple question: "What do you want?" By asking people early about their goals, he joined Milton Erickson and many others who asked this question at the beginning of a session (Adler, 1963; Haley, 1991; Lankton & Lankton, 1986). In this way, clients could evaluate their behavior in relation to a specific goal. This simple addendum changed the first point to "Make friends and ask, 'What do you want?'"

Drop the Recipe Book Approach

Over time, professionals practiced reality therapy as if by rote, taking one logical step after another. They stymied their own spontaneity and, if students did not give predictable answers to classic questions, teachers and principals felt stuck. The mechanical style called for another paradigm. Wubbolding (1988, 1991) developed a briefer synthesis of the original seven and then eight steps, but he still retained a step-by-step system, labeling his framework radio station WDEP. Can you figure out the acronym? W is for *wants*, D is for *doing*, E is for *evaluation*, and P is for *plan*. This abbreviated outline served many practitioners well by giving them a simple and clear structure to guide their questioning.

Fishing for Love in All the Right Places

Other devices are available today, but all fall into two categories: (a) creating a counseling context or environment, and (b) using particular counseling techniques. Kathy Curtiss, a senior faculty member with Glasser's Institute, has created a "fishing" model that works well in two ways. *Fishing* is a better description of the spontaneity any psychological process contains. Steps imply more order and logic than may be present, and Curtiss's questions parallel the choice theory model piece by piece. Psychology, like fishing, is more spatial, random, and nonrational. Curtiss's method will appear later in the choice theory portion so readers not only may understand the connection between CT and RT but also will have lists of exact questions to use with students.

I Was Angered and Hurt: Everybody's Theory

Before showing how clear choice theory can be, I will discuss an opposite theory, one the whole world seems to follow. Most people on the planet believe that what happens in their environment not only affects them but also influences them directly and even controls them. They believe that events "out there" *make them respond* in prescribed ways and even determine their future. A majority believes that outside events (i.e., stimuli) shape people's behavioral reactions (i.e., responses). To challenge this stimulus-response theory of *external motivation,* just imagine pouring yourself a cup of your favorite hot drink. Let's say you like rich, aromatic Colombian coffee. You also like something in your coffee. How do you know whether to put cream or milk in your java? Should you use whole, low-fat, or non-fat milk? How much sugar and milk is correct for a cup of your fresh brew? Some people say they just know. When pressed, they say they have learned through trial and error what tastes good to them. The question remains: "How do you determine that the coffee is *just right* for you? If a little sugar is good, why not keep spooning in more? How do you know when to stop? The answer is obvious: people know what they want from the inside out. The coffee does not tell us how we like it; our taste-buds do. Our job is to get the coffee to cooperate with us.

Everything that we think, feel, and do is in response to a picture inside our head and not in reaction to an environmental cue outside ourselves (Glasser, 1984). If a car drives up over the curb and heads toward us, we all would take evasive action. We would try to protect ourselves, not because a car shape is looming ever larger in our direction, but because a picture in our head tells us our need for survival is in jeopardy and we need to vacate the area fast. We *never* are externally motivated. Carrots dangling outside our window will entice us only if, inside our head, we have placed a picture of a carrot as need satisfying. The environment does not control or shape us outside of our control. We control ourselves from a mental file or a picture album that shows us, moment to moment, what we need and what we are attempting to match through our senses.

Choice Theory Made Simple

Glasser has referred to two kinds of people. One type says, "I don't like what I see out in my environment, so I am going to try to change the world around me." The other type says, "The world is not totally to my liking. What can *I do* to get what I want from the reality out there?" The underlying assumptions for all the case samples in this chapter and throughout most of the book come from choice theory. Plainly stated, all any of us does from birth to death is *behave,* and our *behavior controls our perception.* Our behavior is always our best attempt to meet our needs, get what we want, and match the sensory picture (i.e., the view we have of the world through our senses) with an internal mental picture that serves as a reference or goal for us. Contrary to popular opinion, what we choose *to do* directly affects the way we see the world and our place in it. Many people believe that, if they first change their attitude or their feelings, they then will be ready to act. In choice theory, people are urged to act first and then review their feelings and attitudes. Feelings *follow* actions, a premise that many other schools of psychology employ (Erickson & Rossi, 1981; Fisch, Weakland, & Segal, 1982; Glasser, 1965, 1984; O'Hanlon & Weiner-Davis, 1989).

We all are born with five genetically encoded fundamental needs: (a) survival at the lower physical level, (b) love and belonging, (c) power and competence, (d) fun and diversion, and (e) freedom and options at the higher psychological level. We are internally motivated and have a flexible behavioral system that allows us to manage an endless array of competing demands and variation. We become aware of major unmet needs in the form of very specific personal wants at a given moment. As we focus on wanting something, we feel an urge to satisfy that want and to find a peace of mind that comes from meeting our needs. We seek closure to the pain signal that goes off in the comparing place in our brain when we want something we do not have. Inside the deepest chamber of our mind and heart lies our prizing place—our quality world.

If we mentally cringe because the pictures in our quality world are out of focus, we simply choose to *do* something different in our best attempt to find a match with those intrinsic pictures. One who takes new action soon begins to see the world differently because *behavior controls pictures.* Choosing to act first and to delay emoting has the same effect on our emotional lives: change what you do and you will change how you feel. The average person may think he/she is constantly on the lookout for new behavioral choices, but our behavioral system does not drive us. We control for (i.e., seek to satisfy) the inner wants we see as pictures in our heads. Wanting what we value and do not have is what drives us to action. Those detailed desires form our minigoals from moment to moment, and our behaviors help us obtain those goals and satisfy those needs. "Controlling for" translates to looking for an alignment between our inner reference pictures of very specific wants and the pictures from the external world that we develop in the photo lab of our sensory camera. For every mental reference picture, we naturally seek a matching sensory picture. When viewing a discrepant mental picture, meaning we want something and do not have it, we see an out of focus picture. We feel this discrepancy as an urge that prompts us to search for a focused pictorial match in reality. Behavior is the only way we can satisfy our awareness of an endless stream of demanding needs and wants because we use our thinking, acting, feeling, and physiological behaviors to align the world with our private picture album.

Our Behavior Focuses Our Camera. When our sensory camera shows us a blurred picture of outside reality in relation to our inside pictures, we feel urges to select behaviors to bring the sensory and mental reference pictures into focus. Behavior is to a human being what the focusing mechanism is to a camera. Pain is an out of focus sensory camera, and the focusing mechanism in the lens is our behavioral system—thinking, acting, feeling, and physical functioning. Do something more effective and bring a whole new focus to your life.

Throughout time, religious thinkers have presented this choice theory notion in more lofty and existential terms than labeling a "want and have not" as a perceptual error or a frustration signal. When one is carrying a major unmet need, that person is not "at one with the universe." The Buddhist concept of nirvana is living beyond an awareness of unmet needs. This state of universal oneness is mostly theoretical, perhaps true of only isolated individuals throughout history. Many teachers of one spiritual path or another have emphasized the value in denying oneself physical pleasures. They commonly have recommended sacrificing oneself for a life of asceticism and transcendence over pestering and mundane human wants.

Shaffer (1993) interviewed 12, 30- to 45-year-old women who had become widows abruptly through the sudden and accidental death of their recently healthy husbands. The women in this qualitative investigation reported immense shock and grief immediately following their loss. In follow-up interviews, two to four years after their husbands' deaths; however, all 12 women reported remarkable changes in their sense of personal identity and self-definition. Once they overcame their internal struggles and sense of instability, they universally felt that external accomplishments became far less important to them than a new commitment to generativity and a strong sense of the preciousness of life. They became more assertive and felt they had developed an enlarged capacity for caring. No matter what the outside event—and the death of a spouse imposes a great demand for adjustment—we always can do *something* to take better control and meet our needs in more satisfying ways.

Two Kinds of Problems: Developmental and Accidental

I will give some practical suggestions to help you keep your head clear and your feet on the ground as you work with students and periodically consult with their families about their children's classroom work. Two components affect everyone's life—generic *developmental challenges* and *special events*. The spectrum of human drama includes one or the other of these two elements, known as common cause events and special cause events.

Common Cause. Examples of normal developmental or typical life transitions may be growing up, establishing intimate relationships, marrying, having a baby, letting a first-born child go off to kindergarten, moving, divorcing, managing old age, and dying. These normal patterns of growth and development often reflect a theory that life is comprised of *stages* (Haley, 1973; Levinson, 1976).

Special Cause. Unique family twists and idiosyncratic crises may be abandonment by parents, child abuse, alcohol and drug abuse, shoplifting, violence, illness, and natural disasters such as tornadoes, earthquakes, flooding, fires, financial loss, and other random misfortunes.

When a school interested in quality cannot handle a problem *at school* because the problem may span home *and* school, the staff member most directly involved must make a decision about what to do. Consulting with a counselor, administrator, or other trusted peer is often a prudent first step. A counselor who stays in the present and evaluates the facts of the case may be useful to the student and the family. By taking into account the interpersonal connections in any human conflict, a counselor will be more helpful than one who automatically runs from trouble or whose knee-jerk inclination is to pin down a culprit who created the mess in the first place.

Grab Bag Therapy: Reality Therapy with a Twist

A guaranteed procedure for creating change in the midst of conflict and trauma is a little known counseling modality I call "Grab Bag Therapy" (Palmatier, 1990). With a solid grasp of choice theory, people eventually can eliminate any problem in their life merely by picking a new "to do" and acting on the new behavior at once. The two aspects of one's total behavior most under voluntary control are *thinking* and *doing*. Because behavior controls (i.e., aligns) pictures that we judge important, anyone willing to do something new and different can create a new picture. If you change your attitude and decide to look at an event, friend, or situation differently, you will hold a different belief about the reality of a given circumstance and, in following the theory to its logical conclusion, you will feel differently as well.

Of the four components of our total behavior—acting, thinking, feeling, and bodily functions—the single aspect most amenable to voluntary change is the doing or acting part. To some extent, we can change our thinking about a disturbing situation, as we do, for example, when we hear a powerful reframe that allows us to shift our focus away from the dilemma. Whenever an objective and supportive person helps us reframe our current views, we may say, "Ah hah! I never looked at this predicament in that way." Unfortunately, this process does not work as easily in the emotional realm, probably because our feelings are rooted in a primitive part of the brain—in the limbic system. Because our emotions are not neurologically housed within the cerebral cortex—

the locus of rational thinking—we find making quick changes in our feelings and physiology easier to imagine than to do directly.

If you are game for Grab Bag Therapy, you can use yourself as a guinea pig and immediately implement the following five-step plan.

Grab Bag Therapy

1. *First, pick a particular topic or dilemma that you consider currently unsatisfying in your own life.*
2. *Secondly, decide what is not perfect about the situation you selected and specify what you would like to see happen. What would you like to change? How would your ideal look?*
3. *Third, holding in your mind's eye a clear sense of what you want, specify carefully all of the things you currently are doing to meet your goal. What are your solutions to the dilemma now?*
4. *Fourth, write out for yourself or get your friends to list on paper 5, 10, or even 50 new actions you could take. (These may or may not be logically related to your complaint.)*
5. *Draw one of the suggestions and implement it.*

Picking up on step 4 in the five-step plan, put the suggestions on separate pieces of paper and drop them into a box. One clue that can make developing a list easier is to think of the tasks or general activities that you believe you should be doing but are putting off. You may end up with a long list such as this one: eating out at a new restaurant that specializes in foods you have not eaten yet; taking a new vehicle for a test drive; walking around a lake with friends at 5 a.m.; reading a novel and talking it over with an interested person; joining a class on a topic you like; seeing three films this week; starting a savings account; drinking only tomato, orange, mango, pineapple, banana, or guava juice for breakfast for two weeks; bowling in a carefree style; loafing at a plant nursery and checking out their specials of the month; and writing a letter in real ink to a special relative.

COMMUNICATION PRINCIPLES
TO GUIDE YOUR COUNSELING

The communication principles that I apply in the average short-term contact with acting out children in schools are functionally compatible with the specific procedures of reality therapy as long as you bear in mind the fluidity of the approach. Reality therapy is not a counseling-by-the-numbers game or following a recipe from a psychological cookbook (Wubbolding, 1988). These principles bear amplifying and are repeated here.

Counseling Framework for Children

- *Listen to a child's story with no judgment or criticism.*
- *Identify the person's behavioral pattern that ends up as a problem. This step will tell you where the pain resides.*
- *Connect the symptomatic pattern of behavior to an unmet need or want.*
- *Convey your view that the problem behavior is understandable and makes sense, considering the situation. Minuchin (Minuchin & Fishman, 1981, p. 43) called this procedure normalizing, and the "Milan group" wraps the presenting problem in a reframe called "positive connotation" (Boscolo, Cecchin, Hoffman, & Penn, 1987, p. 5).*
- *Ask a child to evaluate the actual usefulness of the problem behavior.*
- *Permit the child to feel the discomfort from a symptom he/she plays out, and even suggest safe ways to express the symptom except, of course, for harmful acts such as cutting into one's body.*
- *Find out whether a student would like to find a better long-range way to handle things. Create some optional activities the student can do in order to meet the thwarted need and, thereby, arm the child with a practical plan to do something different and to take control.*
- *If a child's family is intact and willing to come regularly for counseling, hold out hope that a longer-term family solution may be possible and may be worked out in another meeting.*

Holding out a hopeful picture is especially useful for children. Using the example of a sobbing child, reflect the child's own goals by drawing a verbal picture of the way everything will look after you and the youngster spend a little time together and the child replaces her present weeping style with new ways to act. If the new mental image you paint matches an inner picture of someone who has met a particular need, you will have succeeded indeed. The solution will work when it matches a child's mental picture of an important want that the child is able to satisfy.

Students sometimes want something they cannot have. What if they want to do something that the school does not allow, such as enjoying the freedom to roam the halls at will or sleeping all day at their desks? Naturally, teachers cannot accommodate all the pictures of inner wants that every child can imagine. Choice theory holds that some of these inappropriate or inconvenient choices are really masks that cover the hurt that children call up when they are not meeting a more basic need, such as belonging to a warmly accepting group of peers. Roaming halls is a protective act for some students who view staying in a room and cooperating with others as too risky, and, therefore, as unsatisfying for some reason. Your task includes helping children set unrealistic wants aside and putting their goals into realistic and attainable plans.

Problems Themselves Are Not the Enemy

Most of us expend endless energy trying to eliminate problems as soon as we become aware of them. Our own problems are bad enough, but children's difficulties can strike us as genuine irritants. Schools, in fact, would be good places to work if it were not for children. During a clinical psychology internship in a medical hospital, I learned early the value of not treating anyone's problem as the enemy.

A Case Sample. I met Dan in the waiting room just outside the medical records office in a veterans hospital. I said, "Dan?" A rather pale, bulky fellow, about 25 to 30 years old stood up and said cautiously, "That's me." I *didn't* say, "I am glad to see you because you are my first 'patient'." (I was just beginning the long quest for 3,000 postdoctoral clinical internship hours for licensing as a psychologist.) We started down the hall toward one of the look-alike consultation rooms and, with a hand gesture toward the office, Dan said, "My file's in there." I knew that he, like every patient, had a thick file clamped between two shiny metal covers; but I already had decided that if I were to read his medical record then and there, as he was suggesting, I would be reviewing solid documentation that this man was "sick." I could not see how that psychiatric documentation could be helpful to either of us at that time, partially because I was not heavily trained in medical explanations about people's psychology and did not value intrapsychic theory because of its inefficiency and negative connotations; my view was due partially to the fact that I recently had passed the therapy certification program sponsored by the psychiatrist William Glasser and partially due to the fact that I did not want this patient to wield the full power of the entire medical system that he was caught up in. I automatically responded, "We don't need it."

We walked to a small office, and I started our meeting with a fresh greeting and a question.

Larry: *Welcome, Dan. Tell me your story.*
Dan: *I have high blood pressure, tension, nervousness, anxiety, and depression.*
Larry: *Are you taking medication?*
Dan: *Yes I am.*

I asked Dan to sign a release so I could consult his psychiatrist about his emotional and physical condition and his medication. Then I asked Dan about his personal life. In the course of the next 15 to 20 minutes, I learned that he was 26, had just been discharged from military service, and was living at home with his mother. He had an 18-year-old brother who had friends, money, and a car.

Larry: *How about you, Dan? Do you have a job?*
Dan: *No.*
Larry: *Friends?*
Dan: *No.*
Larry: *Do you have any short or long range plans that you are looking forward to doing?*
Dan: *Not at this time. Maybe moving some day.*
Larry: *You know, Dan, I would be more worried about you, considering what you are doing and what you have going on in your life right now, if you weren't depressed, nervous, and anxious.*

Dan immediately displayed a visible sigh of relief and otherwise indicated that he had just shed a heavy weight. I saw just how powerful a tactic "normalizing" can be (Minuchin & Fishman, 1981, p. 68) as the man relaxed right before my eyes. I stated that last sentence with a great deal of conviction because I believed it. Who wouldn't have stress amid a drab routine and a total absence of any sense of control and power? Anyone out of options is out of luck.

The end of the story was positive for Dan. He showed up at his fifth counseling appointment about six weeks later wearing a jacket that was part of the uniform for his job with a national car rental franchise. In the meantime, he had gotten a haircut, lost about 15 pounds, and reported to me that he was no longer taking a prescribed drug to relieve his anxiety. I attributed his productive new choices to the encouragement I had offered him *and* to his own agreement that the complaints he described to me at the first session made sense in the context of his post-army life. After our meeting, he came to see some tangible options for changing many important conditions of his life and realized he had the power to make his life better. He began slowly with walks around the block in place of popping a pill to relieve his anxiety. Anxiety, as most pains, can signal a person to do something else or perhaps to take even more drastic action in the face of an obvious demand to change course.

Problems Are Not All Bad. After I understood that problem behaviors are people's best attempts at the time to get what they need, I took an open attitude about anything any client or student might say. As I counseled others, I began doing all I could to minimize the loss of face or feelings of foolishness people experience when they describe their problems to an outsider they have just met. They tell themselves they shouldn't feel this way or that they ought to know better. They were off schedule in their lives, compared to their peers who were long into the career they themselves were still scrambling to enter. Once I stopped trying to keep the problem at bay or to eliminate it all together through swift therapy, I was able to invite the clients (and later on students) to befriend their own symptoms. As people stopped trying so actively to stamp out their woes permanently, I watched the "guide wires" holding their troubles in place fall away. Whenever troubled kids or harried adults would give themselves a breather from their struggle to free themselves completely from their complaints, I could see them focusing more on *solutions* than on apologizing for having a problem in the first place (O'Hanlon & Wilks, 1987). Giving up the battle to obliterate a problem leads to a willingness to see the problem differently and to the principle that Paul Watzlawick (1990) suggested of deliberately retaining an *unresolved remnant.* You can overcome a problem much faster if you try to get over some, but not all, of it.

No One Makes Mistakes. Ask anyone; no one sets out to fail intentionally or to make a mistake, at least by one's own definition. Whatever anyone does always seems the best choice of behavior at the time. Only in retrospect does anyone ever look at a particular behavior and label it a mistake (and people often blame others for their own misfortune). How many adults look back and wish they had all the money they wasted on cars. "Oh, I should have bought that house at that time." If only we had known then what we know now.

Children do many things at school—some curricular activities and some interpersonal behaviors—and teachers and administrators often stand poised to cast quick judgment on all their school activities as good or bad. Making schoolwork relevant, enjoyable, and not "for keeps" can turn students around and make their job of learning more meaningful.

Four Foolproof Formulas for Frustration

Students believe they have solid reasons for feeling ticked off. They also may lack the communicative tools for expressing their frustrations and presenting their needs clearly and directly to somebody who can do something about their predicament. Teaching students to say forthrightly what they want and helping them succeed at no one's expense is the essence of good counseling.

Four conditions that always lead to the familiar frustration signal that we all experience as an urge to behave (Glasser, 1991) are carrying around *unmet expectations*, *not expressing a communication* we feel strongly about, maintaining a batch of *unfinished tasks*, and *thwarted intentions.* The common element in all these conditions is a discrepancy or dissonance between what we want and what we perceive as having at any moment—choice theory at work.

Unmet Expectations. When we have a picture in our head of what we expect and other people have a different picture, we have set the stage for discomfort and frustration. Conflicting prior assumptions almost always cause difficulties in communication, and we will save ourselves much grief if we learn to clear the air early and convey what we expect from a person or situation, so that the interaction does not end up with unmet expectations and frustrations for both sides. Students' telling their own teachers what they need and expect is fair to themselves and to teachers, as is first negotiating an agreement when starting a formal association with a professional therapist, lawyer, or accountant. On a personal level, we lower the chances of conflict when we talk over with our family what each member expects in regard to a planned vacation, organizing a party, selling a house, or moving to a new area.

An example of unmet expectations is not knowing something we think we should know. Intellectually, everybody knows the axiom that knowledge is power. Conducting a computer-assisted survey of the literature and tracking relevant research in a matter of minutes usually produces a special thrill of discovery and control. Students who work harder than their friends and present technical information to classmates preparing for an important test, report a special feeling of command and control (Glasser, 1986). The opposite of this sense of power coming from a contributive style is also true. When we do not know something that we think we should know, we experience a pain signal. If we lack knowledge in an area we consider out of our area of specialty or interest, we feel no frustration because we had no prior expectation.

Unfinished Tasks. How about unfinished tasks? We all know that toting around a mental list of "to do's" and reaching the end of the day with an intact list can be a foolproof formula for frustration. Shortening the list and aiming at completing fewer tasks or putting more realistic completion times next to the tasks will minimize or eliminate our need to frustrate when we do not get all the jobs done within an allotted time. Those who like to confuse motion with progress often find themselves driven by an insurmountable workload that never seems to diminish.

Unexpressed Communication. Probably more ulcers develop from withholding communication than from any other discrepancy because we choose to remain silent when we are burning to say something. Many of us choose to sit on a message we believe we should deliver and prefer to fume silently than say something directly to someone. We put off expressing communications and make a hundred excuses because we rationalize that the message might hurt someone's feelings, be too difficult to say, or not be helpful anyway. Most troublesome human problems result from unclear and inadequate communication that requires someone to say something to someone who does not want to hear the message. We could handle 50% of the confrontational challenges and conflicts through appropriate training and the practice of assertive "I" statements (Gordon, 1989). Many people carry around for years communication that they refuse to express. Expressing these tough messages will lead to a lighter step, a happier heart, a clearer sense of self, and more satisfying interpersonal relationships. I can see the lines of teachers now heading for their principals' offices in schools all over the place. I can also see a few principals making notes.

Thwarted Intentions. Unlike unmet expectations, which reside somewhat passively in our heads, we also can develop noble plans, set out to accomplish those ends, and encounter opposition. If we weigh all the data and still decide to open a business, run for public office, or campaign for a greener earth or animal rights, we still may be frustrated. Even if we limit our expectations and allow for a certain amount of organized resistance, we still do not want our intentions to go completely unfulfilled. When we see our goals as especially noble or altruistic, we can frustrate ourselves even more when we see forces working to sidetrack or sink those goals. Some of the hottest issues today are abortion, immigration, race relations, and gun control. Some individuals in the civil rights movement and in abortion rights debates have gone over the edge and have resorted to shooting their opponents. This escalation in tensions might represent the seeds of the next civil war in America. Many believe that gun control is closely connected to racism. Whites, some say, want to be well-armed in the event the lid blows off and citizens choose battle sides on the basis of color.

Solutions are difficult to find in this arena, but people who become too socially isolated and one-issue thinkers create destructive conditions for themselves. Some make their cause (a) a paintbrush to make others wrong or (b) a death plunge. We certainly will do better if we remind ourselves that we are not the center of the universe and if we maintain regular contact with a group of friends who do not share our convictions at the same high level. Politicians receive wide credit for taking themselves too seriously and surrounding themselves with yes-sayers. They most often end up as the butt of pundits' columns and just as often the objects of scorn in the monologues on national talk shows. Hosting a talk show, of course, is easy: the critic does not have to perform—only blast those who are out in front doing something.

CHOICE THEORY AS PART OF EVERYDAY LIFE

Who wants to understand choice theory thoroughly? You see a lopsided picture hanging on a wall. What is your first inclination? "Well," you say, "to get up, go over, and straighten up the picture so it hangs straight." I ask you, "What motivates you to take such an action?"

> **You:** *Because it looked funny hanging crooked.*
> **Me:** *How did you know it was crooked?*
> **You:** *I know how pictures should look on a wall.*
> **Me:** *How do you know how pictures should look?*
> **You:** *I learned this information.*
> **Me:** *Explain how learning something helps you organize your thinking on a particular topic.*
> **You:** *I just knew that I wanted to see that picture straight.*
> **Me:** *How'd you know?*
> **You:** *I moved it because it was crooked.*
> **Me:** *So the picture made you get up and change it.*
> **You:** *Now you got me confused. Please tell me what I should think.*
> **Me:** *You would not know that the picture was hanging crookedly unless you had a clear idea in your head that pictures are supposed to be straight. You first mentally envision how it should be and then compare your image of the norm with the way you see the actual picture.*
> **Me:** *Two more questions for you, though. Why do you stop when you have straightened out the picture? Why not go on experimenting and putting more effort into straightening an off-centered picture in front of you right now?*

This brief dialogue represents a practical scenario that teaches choice theory in a nutshell. Environmental cues or stimuli do not make us behave. We act from the inside out and not from the outside in. We always behave in an attempt to match a mental picture with what we want to see out there. The pictures in our head do not in and of themselves make us behave. *What makes us act is picturing a want in our head for which we can see no matching picture in the real world.*

Is this a game of semantics? Tedious as this description of choice theory may appear, the implications for turning around the conventional wisdom on motivation are dramatic. For teachers and counselors, discarding a passive and robotic view of human beings (i.e., that other people and external events make people think, feel, and act in certain ways) in favor of choice theory literally transforms the job of working with students. Applying stimulus-response theory from the *outside in* is ineffective over time because students see through it. They know that the responsible decision is crucial for any extrinsic manipulation to work. Shaping children's behavior through reward and punishment allows students to hide behind excuses and say, "The devil made me do it." Choice theory puts the responsibility squarely on students for all their actions. Teachers and counselors who are immersed in choice theory readily admit to students that they cannot control any person or make any human being do anything.

All Behavior Is Purposeful

Alfred Adler (1959) was the first psychological theorist to suggest that all behavior is purposeful. Adler arrived at his conclusion because he viewed people in much more benign ways than his former mentor, Sigmund Freud, who took a very pessimistic view of human beings. Reality therapy (Glasser, 1965) and control theory (Powers, 1973) also take an optimistic view and demonstrate that all behavior is purposeful and that most behavior is chosen. Can anyone say what all the possible purposes of behavior are? The purpose of all behavior—effective behavior that works to get what we want or symptomatic behavior that does not help us get what we need—is the same: people are attempting to meet one or more unmet need(s) in the form of a specific want.

Most Behavior Is Chosen

Behaviors that are not chosen are few in kind, especially in light of the general notion that purposeful behavior is voluntary (N. Glasser, 1989). One class of nonchosen behaviors is the knee-jerk reactions to perceived threat to one's life—the automatic fight or flight mechanism that resides within the autonomic nervous system. A second class of nonchosen behaviors is responses to physical force or domination. One is not choosing to fall when a greater force compels that response. A third type of nonchosen behaviors is comprised of those actions someone takes while in a psychotic state. Injecting someone with a truth serum, of course, would put a person in an altered state of consciousness and elicit nonchosen behaviors. People who "go crazy," however, may have control over many of the behaviors they engaged in prior to "losing it," such as taking harmful drugs, remaining in an argumentative and conflicting social setting, and depriving oneself of sufficient sleep for endless days and nights. Fourth, the brain mechanisms in the choice theory cycle related to awareness of wants or unmet needs and evaluation before and after taking action are spontaneous and automatic. In this way, we can protect ourselves even when we are tired.

Behavioral Output. The decision to behave does not represent a free choice in choice theory. One's behavioral system *automatically activates* whenever the brain scan identifies an unmet need (e.g., thirsty for apple juice, hungry for a vegetarian taco, wanting a fun time, aching for an intimate relationship); however, the particular behavior one chooses to do is *voluntary*.

Choice Theory Has Five Elements

1. *Inherent basic needs: love, power (competency and influence), fun, freedom, and survival*
2. *Outside reality: our physical and social context*
3. *Perceptual system containing knowledge and values*
4. *Comparing place through which we judge what we want and whether we have succeeded*
5. *Behavioral system through which we act on the world to get what we want*

FIVE ELEMENTS OF CHOICE THEORY

Basic Needs

Inside our brains are genetically encoded needs. In the brain stem or old brain is the most primitive and fundamental need for survival. In the cerebral cortex, the new large brain, are the higher order, psychological needs for (a) love and belonging, (b) power and competence, (c) fun and diversion, and (d) freedom and options.

Reality

The world outside of us contains information only. None of these pieces of information cause us to do anything. We constantly face a large number of disturbances in our environment that we must interpret, accommodate, and manage. We make sense of external data through our perceptual abilities in our brains. Our perceptual system has two components.

Perceptual System

Part One of our perceptual system is the *All We Know* world, which relates to sensing the external world and making meaning of what we observe. Part

Two of the perceptual system is the *All We Want* world. Here we assign value to what we know. We filter all data through a values screen, labeling our intake as good, bad, or neutral. The *All We Want* world is our *quality world*.

Comparing Place

We have a special place in our brains where we weigh and measure the outside data and reference these pieces of information with the mental pictures of our current wants to see if we have a sensory match. The wants are specific instances of more generic needs.

Behavioral System

Whereas perception is the *input* part of our two-part, closed-loop control system, behavior is the *output* part through which we act on the world to get what we want. We take the world into our heads perceptually and we act on the world through our capacity to behave.

CHOICE THEORY IN THE PRACTICE
OF REALITY THERAPY

How about blending choice theory and reality therapy (N. Glasser, 1989)? This combination is a natural marriage, and, to demonstrate the suave resonance among Glasser's *what*, *why*, and *how*, a case will follow to clarify what a teacher or counselor might do with the blueprints that choice theory and reality therapy provide.

Applying Choice Theory to Reality Therapy

The most direct way to use reality therapy is to do two things: (a) adopt a friendly and supportive attitude toward a student and (b) be sure to cover the four key elements in the framework—wants, doing, evaluation, and plan. As teachers gain confidence in talking with students the way that William Glasser suggested, they then will want to add to their arsenal of responsibility developing language. One model for doing this is to develop specific questions for the various components of the choice theory model. One example of this alignment of self-evaluative reality therapy questions and choice theory is available in the teaching modules that Kathy Curtiss has developed and for her work with Glasser's Institute. (To contact this instructor or any other certified reality therapist, see the information at the end of William Glasser's introductory chapter to this book.)

The Context of a Problem: School, Home, or School and Home

Children come to school with a headful of ideas already. Regardless of their age, they bring their entire world to school daily. Children and adults live in their heads. The perceived world is the only one we have. Teachers constantly must be on the alert to perform academic and psychological triage—observing, intervening, sorting, and referring—according to students' needs. The first decision after identifying trouble is categorizing at two levels. First, how serious is the behavioral display—mild, moderate, or serious? Second, whose problem is this? The school's, the family's, or the home and school working in concert?

One day, while visiting a school in transit to quality, a group of teachers invited me to talk with three particular students whom the teachers said were out of bounds with emotional struggles. We obtained parental permissions to meet with the students and to videotape the chats. One of these meetings was with a 6-and-a-half-year-old lad who recently had moved from another part of the state in order to escape a pattern of traumatic abuse from the mother's boyfriend of six years. To little Reginald, the pain of moving away from his primary relationships was as dreadful as surgery without anesthesia. His two problems were crying at the drop of a hat and not talking.

He must have been dying to talk because when I sat down with him, he freely unloaded his personal misery and endured my questions and suggestions for almost an hour. When his teacher viewed the taped conversation, she said, "This is not the Reginald I know." I first determined that his story was a home and school matter and I felt that a classroom teacher should not be expected to handle this situation. A school counselor or community-based social worker would be in a better position to intervene in this case.

Reggie was hurting from the sudden removal from his mother's male companion and from his young friends whom he had known for most of his first six plus years. The abrupt shift of geography with no warning was impossible for him to handle smoothly. As a result of his feeling out of control, he naturally attempted to regain some sense of control. He did this in the best way he knew—telling his new comrades how badly he felt. When he did this, however, they made fun of him and his sense of rejection and hopeless feelings only swelled. At home with his mother's parents, he found himself sobbing almost all of the time. When he resorted to tears, however, all three adults descended on him with both fists and both feet, so to speak, and consoled him with the admonition that "Big, tough boys don't cry." He felt trapped in the double binds he felt in both social contexts—the family and the school.

My job was to identify what was most painful about his story. What was important to him that was not under his control? He wanted his family ties restored. He wanted his old friends back. Most of all, he wanted the security of his mother's attention and her settling for a partner who could serve as the boy's father. Being teased at school for his tears and his silence was another distressor, but this part was only the tip of the iceberg.

I intervened at three key points: (a) I reminded Reggie that his mother's choice of a romantic partner was her business. I asked him, in light of her prerogative, to stop trying to find his mother a mate, suggesting that he was trying to do something that only *she* could do. (b) After I learned that he could not cry, even at home, I requested his permission to consult with his mother and grandparents to see if they would let him show his hurt at home. We set this up by having him pretend to be a baby because he had said the happiest time for him thus far was the days of babyhood when he laughed all the time (according to his mother's reports). (c) I suggested that he pretend not to be sad around two or three of his peers who used the information about his hurtful feelings to tease him. He could, of course, disclose his sad moments to his family, his teacher, and his counselor.

Choice Theory and Reality Therapy in the Classroom

Eventually, all teachers who (a) master the fundamentals of choice theory, (b) apply these principles to their lives, and (c) learn to apply reality therapy methods can begin to teach all of their students practical ways to apply choice theory in the classroom (Glasser, 1986). Shifting to a choice theory view is a major transformation but, by then, teachers definitely will know what to do and will not be plodding around in the dark. Keep in mind the main thrust of choice theory: encouraging students to empower themselves and to take full responsibility for their behavior at school. First, of course, the teacher must remove the barriers to teaching choice theory. The rest of this book is about managing crises and discovering specific suggestions for creating a context for quality teaching and learning. Some examples of materials that teachers have found useful in teaching choice theory are listed below the citations.

BIBLIOGRAPHY

Adler, A. (1969). *The science of living.* New York: Doubleday Anchor Books.

Aguayo, R. (1990). *Dr. Deming.* New York: Simon & Schuster.

Amatea, E. (1989). *Brief strategic intervention for school behavior problems.* San Francisco: Jossey-Bass.

Archambault, R. (1974). *John Dewey on education.* Chicago, IL: University of Chicago Press.

Bandler, R., & Grinder, J. (1982). *Reframing.* Moab, UT: Real People Press.

Beier, E., & Young, D. (1984). *The silent language of psychotherapy* (2nd ed.). Hawthorne, NY: Aldine Publishing.

Beier, E., & Valens, E. (1975). *People-reading.* Briarcliff Manor, New York: Stein and Day Publishers.

Carkhuff, R. (1987). *The art of helping six: Trainer's guide.* Amherst, MA: Human Research Development Press.

Chance, E. (1985). An overview of major discipline programs in public school since 1960. *Dissertation Abstracts International, 46*(08-A).

Corey, G. (1986). *Theory and practice of counseling and psychotherapy* (3rd ed.). Pacific Grove, CA: Brooks/Cole.

Covey, S. (1989). *The seven habits of highly effective people.* New York: Fireside Publishing.

Deming, W. E. (1982). *Out of crisis.* Cambridge, MA: Massachusetts Institute of Technology, Center for Advanced Engineering Study.

de Shazer, S. (1985). *Keys to solution in brief therapy.* New York: W. W. Norton.

de Shazer, S. (1988). *Clues: Investigating solutions in brief therapy.* New York: W. W. Norton.

Dinkmeyer, D. , & McKay, G. (1973). *Raising a responsible child.* New York: Simon & Schuster.

Dinkmeyer, D., McKay, G. D., & Dinkmeyer, D., Jr. (1980). *Systematic training for effective teaching.* Circle Pines, MN: American Guidance Service.

Dinkmeyer, D., & McKay, G. D. (1989). *The parent's handbook* (rev. ed.). Circle Pines, MN: American Guidance Service.

Dinkmeyer, D., & McKay, G. D. (1982). *STEP/teen parent's guide.* Circle Pines, MN: American Guidance Service.

Dobyns, L., & Crawford-Mason, C. (1991). *Quality or else.* Boston: Houghton-Mifflin.

Eagan, G. (1990). *The skilled helper* (4th ed.). Pacific Grove, CA: Brooks/Cole.

Ellis, A. (1988). *How to stubbornly refuse to make yourself miserable about anything—yes, anything!* Secaucus, NJ: Lyle Stuart.

Ellis, A., & Harper, R. (1975). *A new guide to rational living.* North Hollywood, CA: Wilshire Books.

Erickson, M., & Rossi, E. (1976). *Hypnotic realities.* New York: Irvington.

Faber, A., & Mazlish, E. (1980). *How to talk so kids will listen & listen so kids will talk.* New York: Avon Books.

Faber, A., & Mazlish, E. (1987). *Siblings without rivalry.* New York: Avon Books.

Faber, A., & Mazlish, E. (1990). *Your guide to a happier family.* New York: Avon Books.

Featherstone, J. (1971). *Schools where children learn.* New York: Liveright Publishers.

Felt, M. C. (1985). *Improving our schools.* Newton, MA: Educational Development Center.

Gabor, A. (1990). *The man who discovered quality.* New York: Times Books.

Ginott, H. (1976a). *Between teacher and child.* New York: Avon Books.

Ginott, H. (1976b). *Between parent and child.* New York: Avon Books.

Glasser, N. (Ed.). (1980). *What are you doing?* New York: Harper & Row.

Glasser, W. (1990). *The quality school.* New York: HarperCollins.

Gordon, D. (1978). *Therapeutic metaphors: Helping others through the looking glass.* Fenton, MI, Meta Publications.

Juran, J. (1992). *Juran on quality by design.* New York: The Free Press.

Lankton, S., & Lankton, C. (1983). *The answer within: A clinical framework of Ericksonian hypnotherapy.* New York: Brunner/Mazel.

Lazarus, A. (1989). *The practice of multimodal therapy.* Baltimore, MD: Johns Hopkins University Press.

Madanes, C. (1981). *Strategic family therapy.* San Francisco: Jossey-Bass.

Madanes, C. (1984). *Behind the one-way mirror.* San Francisco: Jossey-Bass.

Minuchin, S. (1974). *Families & family therapy.* Cambridge, MA: Harvard University Press.

Okun, B. (Ed.). (1984). *Family therapy with school related problems.* Rockville, MD: Aspen Systems.

Okun, B. (1991). *Effective helping: Interviewing and counseling techniques* (4th ed.). Monterey, CA: Brooks-Cole.

Parish, T. (1988). Helping teachers take more effective control. *Journal of Reality Therapy, 8*(1), 41-43.

Piaget, J. (1975). *The child's conception of the world.* Lanham, MD: Littlefield Adams Quality Paperbacks.

Rogers, C. (1951). *Client-centered therapy.* Boston: Houghton-Mifflin.

Rosen, S. (Ed.). (1982). *My voice will go with you: The teaching tales of Milton H. Erickson.* New York: W. W. Norton.

Satir, V. (1988). *The new people making.* Palo Alto, CA: Science and Behavior Books.

Steinem, G. (1992). *Revolution from within.* New York: Little, Brown and Company.

Whitaker, C. (1989). *Midnight musings of a family therapist.* New York: W. W. Norton.

Zeig, J. (1985). *Experiencing Erickson.* New York: Brunner/Mazel.

REFERENCES

Adler, A. (1959). *Understanding human nature.* New York: Premier Books.

Adler, A. (1963). *The practice and theory of individual psychology.* Patterson, NJ: Littlefield, Adams.

Boscolo, L., Cecchin, G., Hoffin, L., & Penn, P. (1987). *Milan systemic family therapy.* New York: Basic Books.

Erickson, M., & Rossi, E. (1981). *Experiencing hypnosis.* New York: Irvington.

Fisch, R., Weakland, J., & Segal, L. (1982). *Tactics of change.* San Francisco, CA: Jossey-Bass.

Glaser, E. (1991). *In the absense of angels.* New York: Berkley Publishing.

Glasser, N. (Ed.). (1989). *Control theory in the practice of reality therapy.* New York: Harper & Row.

Glasser, W. (1965). *Reality therapy.* New York: Harper & Row.

Glasser, W. (1969). *Schools without failure.* New York: Harper & Row.

Glasser, W. (1984). *Control theory.* New York: Harper & Row.

Glasser, W. (1986). *Control theory in the classroom.* New York: Harper & Row.

Glasser, W. (1991). *Control theory chart.* Chatsworth, CA: The William Glasser Institute.

Gordon, T. (1989). *Teaching children self-discipline . . . at home and at school.* New York: Random House.

Haley, J. (1973). *Uncommon therapy: The psychiatric techniques of Milton Erickson.* New York: W. W. Norton.

Haley, J. (1991). *Problem-solving therapy* (2nd ed.). San Francisco: Jossey-Bass.

Lankton, S., & Lankton, C. (1986). *Enchantment & intervention in family therapy: Training in Ericksonian approaches.* New York: Brunner/Mazel.

Levinson, D. J. (1976). *The seasons of life.* New York: Knopf.

Minuchin, S., & Fishman, H. C. (1981). *Family therapy techniques.* Cambridge, MA: Harvard University Press.

O'Hanlon, W., & Weiner-Davis, M. (1989). *In search of solutions.* New York: W. W. Norton.

O'Hanlon, W., & Wilks, J. (1987). *Shifting contexts.* New York: Guilford.

Palmatier, L. (1990). Reality therapy and brief strategic interactional therapy. *Journal of Reality Therapy, 10*(1), 3-25.

Powers, W. (1989). *Living control systems.* Gravel Switch, KY: The Control Systems Group.

Powers, W. T. (1973). *Behavior: The control of perception.* Chicago: Aldine.

Shaffer, S. (1993). Young widows: Rebuilding identity and personal growth following spousal loss. Ann Arbor, MI: *Dissertation Abstracts International, 54*(1).

Watzlawick, P. (1990). *Midnight musings of a family therapist.* New York: Brunner/Mazel.

Wubbolding, R. (1988). *Using reality therapy.* New York: Harper & Row.

Wubbolding, R. (1991). *Understanding reality therapy: Metaphors.* New York: HarperCollins.

RESOURCES FOR TEACHING CHOICE THEORY

Floyd, C. (1990). *My quality world workbook.* Cherry Hill, NC: New View.

Good, P. (1987). *In pursuit of happiness.* Cherry Hill, NC: New View.

Good, P. (1989). *The happy hour guide.* Cherry Hill, NC: New View.

Good, P. (1992). *Helping kids help themselves.* Cherry Hill, NC: New View.

Gossen, D. (1989). *Control theory in action.* Cherry hill, NC: New View.

Gossen, D., & Anderson, J. (1994). *Creating the conditions.* Cherry Hill, NC: New View.

Green, B. (1994). *New paradigms for creating quality schools.* Cherry Hill, NC: New View.

Greene, B., & Uroff, S. (1991). *Self-esteem and the quality school.* Cherry Hill, NC: New View.

Kiefer, S. (1994). *Give them wings.* Cherry Hill, NC: New View.

Smith, G., & Tomberlin, K. (1992). *Quality time for quality kids.* Cherry Hill, NC: New View.

Sullo, R. (1993). *Teach them to be happy* (2nd ed.). Cherry Hill, NC: New View.

Sullo, L., & Sullo, R. (1990). *I'm learning to be happy.* Cherry hill, NC: New View.

Switzer, D. (1992). *Teacher's guide to "In Pursuit of happiness."* Cherry Hill, NC: New View.

Tinsley, M., & Perdue, M. (1992). *The journey to quality.* Cherry Hill, NC: New View.

Chapter 3

CRISIS THEORY: COUNSELING OUT-OF-CONTROL PEOPLE

Mary B. Ballou
Larry Litwack

Editor's Note

Today's post-industrial society is filled with technical complexities, shifting economic patterns, serious diversity among people, and tensions within most social structures (Toffler, 1990). Limited resources on the globe and less than effective human coping mechanisms threaten to overwhelm many traditional organizations in our communities, particularly, the schools. Often we see few answers for such intense problems. Singling out crisis counseling as an intervention, we face the same paucity of answers since we have up to now developed little agreement on theory and few solutions to actual crises occurring in schools. This chapter provides a useful framework for conceptualizing the issues and effective tools to deal with such crises.

Finding an alternative description of the crisis process can change the meaning an individual assigns to a crisis and, thereby, put the individual more in control. This explanation reverses the original definition of crisis and invites a victim to assign a variety of possible attributions and, of course, to choose from a pool of behavioral options after the crisis has subsided. This line of thinking is consistent with choice theory, which posits that people mainly act and do not react except insofar as they might attempt automatically to escape a perceived direct threat to their survival. In the face of an *intense danger, even choice theory states that a person may act on impulse or* pure feeling *and not* choose *the behavior of self-protection. Where choice theory leaves off in cases of shock and trauma, Drs. Ballou and Litwack present a comprehensive framework for understanding crises and handling the challenges these special circumstances pose.*

The subjectivity of one's view of reality is the starting point of choice theory. In this theory, any event—critical or calm—is information only, and people are free to interpret outside phenomena in any direction they choose. Choice theory does not entertain the notion that people spend their lives dodging triggers *and precipitating events. Environmental phenomena or stimuli are merely pieces of information that either catch our attention or pass right on by us. We can attend to the information or overlook these environmental cues. If our sensory observations match our brain's pictures, we automatically enjoy a* controlled perception. *If the information we sense is out of kilter with our internal reference pictures, we attempt to* gain *a controlled perception. The only way we can* control *the discrepant pictures is through a decision to behave. In any case, what happens outside of us—even observations of particularly nasty events—cannot* make *us suffer for the rest of our lives. To the contrary, choice theory contains the view that a person is never condemned to suffer life endlessly but is free to redefine all experiences. By taking control, we, thereby, can live more comfortably and freely.*

A useful theoretical model in the field of psychological and social relationships must be versatile enough to explain human behavior clearly, and possibly to suggest specific techniques for resolving problems. Otherwise, we reverse the natural order, and actual reality serves a theoretical construct of reality. We become tourists who view the Grand Canyon on videotape in a motel room near the awesome spectacle. The crisis theory the authors present here serves reality and contains the versatility necessary to account for a range of human behaviors that often occur but can never really be completely codified. The model is not choice theory but a viable framework for viewing severe problems. This model is a contribution because readers learn how to view circumstances for which choice theory has no detailed explanation. Choice theory says that people in crisis are out of control.

Behavior, by definition, is what we do when we want something we do not have. This definition applies equally when we already know what to do and when we do not know what to do. Behavior, therefore, is intrinsically creative and flexible, representing our way out of binds and new situations. We do not control *for behavior (output); we* control *for pictures (input). Our primary focus is not on our behavior but on the pictures in our head. We are always trying to match our perceptual view of the world with our internal pictures of what we would like to see.*

Ideally, teachers would respond to all of the crises and potential calamities they observe in their classrooms, but handling every trauma directly is not always practical.

Therefore, a school counselor, wishing to meet more students' needs and address the reality that teachers can do only so much, would do well to learn the crisis theory to follow and to work with teachers in helping them learn appropriate community resources and referrals.

HISTORY AND DEVELOPMENT OF CRISIS THEORY

Crisis theory and crisis intervention have had a long and multidisciplined history. Early on, these approaches concentrated primarily on individuals, later expanding to families, groups, and organizations; currently, crisis theory is being applied to different social systems. Thus, schools are not the only systems for the application of crisis models, but they are certainly among the most important. As crisis theory has evolved, simple views of individual variables such as personal strengths and vulnerable states have expanded and become more complex. The leading edge of current theory includes such influencing factors as ethnic, class, and gender diversity, cultural norms, and social barriers or supports. In addition, developing ideas within education and mental health—prevention, health promotion, and systems analysis and intervention—have shaped the meaning and study of crisis. An understanding of the history, development, and theoretical rationale of crisis theory clearly will be helpful to school personnel faced with increasing needs in the schools. Crisis theory underlies most of the topics ahead and leads naturally to crisis intervention.

The precipitating factors that lead up to a crisis, the crisis itself, and the intervention strategies to resolve a crisis have appeared with regularity in the psychological literature since Lindemann (1944) wrote a report of his interviews with the survivors and bereaved families of the Coconut Grove fire in Boston in 1942 in which 500 people lost their lives. He recounted the crisis reactions of those who survived that disaster. Caplan (1964), using Lindemann's initial work, presented the first formal theory of crisis, applying the notions of homeostatic balance and vulnerable states to the crisis process.

In addition to this early professional literature dealing with crisis, a second area soon developed. In the 1960s and 1970s, direct crisis intervention emerged as a grassroots approach that was responsive to community needs. *Crisis centers* and *hotlines* evolved in response to such specific problems as drug overdoses, suicides, rapes, and runaways. In the main, these centers were paraprofessional responses to crises by individuals drawing from their practical experience and their intuitive understanding of the needs of individuals with whom they worked. Individuals, such as Kubler-Ross (1970) with her work in clinical settings on death and dying and Fink (1967) with his work on generic crises in individual and organizational contexts, actively sought to pull together the random budding strands of crisis theory and crisis intervention and weave these into a meaningful tapestry.

Interest in the professional literature increased during the 1970s when Auerbach and Kilmann (1977) wrote an article reviewing research on crisis intervention and concluding, as many researchers do, that the subject of crisis theory and treatment needed serious attention and more solid empirical research. Smith (1977) wrote another review of crisis theory and intervention and identified major overlaps in the various models appearing in the literature. Baldwin (1979) published a review of various crisis intervention strategies, integrating many of the existing models into a general language descriptive of the stages within a crisis response, and suggesting specific actions to deal with crises.

The 1980s have seen the application of crisis interventions in a variety of settings, accompanied by crisis training for such diverse caregivers as police, teachers, medical personnel, and volunteers in a wide range of crisis centers. Additionally, the increasing demands for crisis intervention from individuals, systems, organizations, and communities has heightened the general awareness of crisis theory. The 1980s have also seen well-designed research studies assessing the effectiveness of crisis intervention and the further development of crisis theory and application (Parad & Parad, 1990; Roberts, 1990; Slaikeu, 1990).

The application of crisis theory and intervention to contexts beyond individual problems is especially characteristic of the latest work in crisis. *Cataclysms, Crises, and Catastrophes: Psychology in Action* (VandenBos & Bryant, 1987), part of the Master Lecture series of the American Psychological Association, included the application of crisis intervention to victims of natural disasters; and the above two 1990 texts by Roberts and the two Parads each contain substantial sections presenting crisis interventions in diverse settings, including schools, jobs, medical and legal practice, and communities at large. The literature of the current era is also more concerned with ethnic, class, race, and gender diversities as these affect the causes, perceptions, and resolution of crises.

Basic Theoretical Concepts and Definition

In the early days, crisis was understood to be something that *happened to* people when they experienced traumatic events such as rape, natural disasters, unexpected deaths of loved ones, and the like. Indeed, the early literature reflects this *precipitant event* definition of crisis. As crisis theory evolved, however, a different understanding of crisis came to the forefront. Rather than judging the strength of the precipitant event to determine whether or not a person was in crisis, the continuing effect of the event on an individual became the focus. This development is important because it acknowledges the differences in individual perceptions and allows for the conceptualization of a crisis process across different kinds of crisis precipitants. This emphasis on the subjectivity of one's view of reality is the starting point of choice theory.

Current definitions of crisis vary somewhat from author to author, but Fink's (1967) definition of crisis as *a perceived threat that overwhelms the individual's coping abilities* still stands. Fink's definition is important not only because it subsumes many other definitions, but also because it points toward possible interventions for the resolution of a crisis as well as preventive actions for dealing with future crises.

This broad definition of crisis is more useful than Caplan's (1964) crisis theory for a variety of reasons. First, the earlier concept implies that growth and improvement can result from a crisis. Caplan's theory posited that normal human functioning requires a homeostatic balance, such that the stresses on a person and the reactions of that same individual are held in opposition at a balanced point. When events or *precipitating factors* upset that balance, a crisis occurs compelling a person to seek to reestablish the balance. Caplan assumed that this process occurred within two to four weeks. Fink's definition offered an alternative to such intrapsychic thinking and emphasized *perceived* threat and one's coping skills. His model sets the defining features squarely with the person in crisis, both in the perceived meaning of the event and in the coping skills the person uses over an indefinite time.

Thus, rather than people living in constant danger of an upset to the homeostatic tension, with crises being almost inevitable, Fink's model presents both individual perceptions and coping skills as variables essential to crisis. Perceptions and skills are neither fixed features nor static conditions. At any one time, a person can change, develop, learn, and practice both perceptions or assignment of meaning and skills or coping strategies. In fact, crises can be opportunities for such development, and some crises actually can be prevented by working with and developing new perceptions and coping skills to create a significant increase in a person's strength and resistance to stress. This parallels choice theory in that people are capable of putting new pictures into their quality worlds and of changing their perceptions. Reality therapy offers people the clear option of choosing new coping behaviors when they move beyond a crisis state.

Fink's crisis model is not limited to individuals because neither does he presume that the phenomena of developing new perceptions and coping skills come from a person's primary or secondary processing, id-ego-superego, nor does he posit an ego that is more vulnerable to trauma at particular developmental stages. His model can be used just as easily to explain crises in families, groups, organizations, and systems (Table 3.1).

A second advantage of Fink's concept of crisis is that factors external to, yet influencing an individual, are integrated readily into both the theory and the interventions. Slaikeu (1990), for example, in summarizing work in the area of crisis theory, has begun to consider the context of crisis, in particular, the various levels (i.e., microsystem, ecosystem, and macrosystem) of social organizations and structures relevant to an individual in crisis. As he describes the context of a crisis, each of four systems, in increasing levels of complexity, is made up of subsystems.

Five modalities define the personal in the person system. The family or social group (i.e., microsystem) describes the immediate social milieu within which a person lives. The immediate social group can be a source of support or stress. In some crises, the precipitating event—known as information in choice theory—comes from the family or social context (e.g., a marital fight). Also, family and social groups are capable of offering psychological first aid or first-order crisis intervention. From the viewpoint of crisis theory, the family's social group is the chief provider of support. In identifying the role of community systems, particular attention is given to governmental, political, and social service structures that can exacerbate crises as well as assist in their resolution.

TABLE 3.1
Crisis in Context: Systems Variables

System	Variables
Person	Behavioral, affective, somatic, interpersonal and cognitive aspects of a person's functioning
Family or social group	Family, friends, and neighbors, and the nature of their relationships with the person in crisis (cohesion, communication patterns, roles, responsibilities, flexibility, and openness, values)
Community	The characteristics of an individual's community, including: geography; material and economic resources; the policies of political and governmental structures; the individual's place of employment plus other businesses and industries; schools, churches, and neighborhood organizations
Culture	Predominant values, traditions, norms, customs

Cultural variables include both national policy issues (e.g., funding for community mental health programs and disaster preparedness plans) and the traditions, customs, and values that determine how particular individuals will work through crises (Slaikeu, 1990, pp. 27-28).

A person's perceptions and abilities can no longer be viewed in isolation, nor can anyone resolve crises without attending to the contexts and structures surrounding a distressed individual. Obviously, the schools are one of the major systems affecting children and children, as we all know, frequently experience crises.

CRISIS TYPES:
SITUATIONAL AND DEVELOPMENTAL

Crises most often are either situational or developmental. Situational crises are precipitated by a specific event or series of events; mugging, gang violence, death, major surgery and illness, divorce, moving, sexual abuse, natural or man-made disasters, loss of a job, or sudden wars are all examples from the literature; however, events not so consensually traumatic also can precipitate crises. Exclusion from a desired group at school, parent-child conflict, or peer pressure for drug use or sexual activity (i.e., particularly when conflicting with strong family, religious, or cultural rules) might cause a crisis for some. The individual's perceived threat and own coping abilities shape the crisis.

Developmental crises are related to transitions from one developmental stage to another and the demands of the new stage. Leaving home for kindergarten might precipitate a crisis for a child who has not yet developed many coping abilities and who perceives strangers as fearsome. Similarly, transitions to middle or high school cause many students to worry about their personal identity or values; and this bind comes at a time when any personal decision may lead to sharp conflicts between one's family and culture versus one's peers and social group. At such times, crises may be precipitated by any particular event, but some situations are more predictable and thus can be averted more easily.

We want to stress that crises are normal and not uncommon events, especially for children. Social myths that only weak or abnormal people experience crises are clearly wrong. Such myths may protect subscribers from a real awareness of crisis for themselves or others; but these tenuous beliefs interfere with improved human functioning and preventive efforts. Well-developed or fragile, healthy or unhealthy, rich or poor, white or people of color, man or woman, young or old, all may experience crises, as may families, groups, organizations and systems.

Just as people experiencing greater stress with fewer resources and supports may be more likely to experience crisis, so, too, may people with no prior experience with a given stressor. Some *marginal* people have learned through prior experience to cope with many events that would be perceived as overwhelming to others more in the mainstream. For instance, many black children learn early from their families and communities how to cope with urban violence, whereas many white, middle-class counterparts are not streetwise and have not developed the skills necessary to cope in a neighborhood of a typical American inner city.

Another key point deals with the concept of secondary symptoms or reactions experienced by one or more individuals in contact with the person in crisis. This is particularly true of siblings and classmates who may find themselves with a range of problems following their interaction with a child in crisis. In such situations, the helper also may need to focus on the needs of the sibling or classmate to help in an understanding of what is happening.

Timing

The literature indicates that the period of intense distress in a crisis is typically two to six weeks, but the final resolution often takes much longer. Crises resulting from the loss of a parent or friend may not be resolved for years, although the intensity of the crisis certainly diminishes. In addition, crises may invite people to recall other past conflicts and unresolved difficulties. Thus, the full resolution of a crisis is often an extended process in which the intensity diminishes only gradually. When crises are genuinely resolved and not just managed or temporarily reduced, the person in crisis addresses not only the precipitating events, but also finds the necessary coping skills. The one with the crisis then ends up with changed perceptions and a stronger identity and also may resolve past conflicts successfully. For all their disruption and threat, crises bring with them the opportunity for growth. Golan (1978) stated the following:

> The phase known as crisis resolution is the period when the person seems to be especially amenable to help. Traditional defense mechanisms have broken down, traditional coping patterns have been found to be ineffective, and the ego has become more open to outside influence and change. . . . A small amount of help, appropriately focused, can prove more effective than more extensive help at a period of less emotional accessibility. (p. 9)

Crisis intervention, then, is important not only because of the intensity of need of the person in crisis and the potential for growth toward effective resolution, but also because a crisis is often the best time for major changes in attitudes, defensive structures, coping patterns, cognitive abilities, interpersonal relationships, and even value orientations. One finds substantial motivation for changing one's lenses, for using a choice theory image, and for putting new pictures into the quality world at a time of stress, turmoil, and crisis.

Crisis Stages and Intervention

Baldwin (1979), Roberts (1990), and the Parads (1990) all have proposed useful integrative models for crisis intervention, but each is loosely based on Caplan's (1964) crisis theory. The model we are presenting in this chapter is the earlier Fink-Ballou model that is based on Fink's crisis model. As we discussed earlier, this framework applies not just to individuals, but also more widely to organizations and systems. Through its thorough assessment of a person's subjective experiences, psychological structures and coping actions in the crisis process, a physical dimension emerges and the theory is not narrowly centered on intrapsychic assumptions.

Fink (1967) developed the scheme in Table 3.2 as a thorough and sequential account of an individual's reactions to a crisis. This model shows that a person's reactions will vary according to the stage of the crisis one faces and also that an individual's reactions within each stage may vary. Ballou (1986, 1987) has developed specific interventions for helping people in crisis within each stage and these follow the psychological phases of crises described in the Table 3.2.

Interventions

The strategies proposed here as appropriate interventions for each stage of a crisis process are not intended for mental health professionals only. With appropriate training, teachers, classroom aides, principals, student peer coaches or counselors, and other members of a school staff often can provide children effective crisis intervention; but training (even if it comes only through long experience) is *vital* for both professionals and others. Training helps one to understand a crisis, identify the stages, and provide stage specific interventions. A counselor or other concerned person can use this training in crisis counseling to intervene effectively in an emergency. Crisis theory, particularly in the latter stages of intervention, clearly overlaps with reality therapy and choice theory, as cited in chapter 2 (Wubbolding 1988, 1991). For convenience, we

TABLE 3.2
Fink's Psychological Phases of Crisis

Aspect	Shock (Stress)	Defensive Retreat	Crisis Stage Acknowledgment (Renewed Stress)	Adaptation and Change
Self-experience	Threat to existing structures	Attempt to maintain old structures	Giving up existing structure; self-depreciation	Establishing new structures; sense of worth
Reality perceptions	Perceived as overwhelming	Avoidance of reality; "wishful thinking"; denial and repression	Facing reality; facts *impose* themselves	New reality testing
Emotional experience	Panic, anxiety, and helplessness	Indifference or euphoria (except when challenged, in which case, anger (low anxiety)	Depression with apathy or agitation, bitterness, mourning, high anxiety; if overwhelming—suicide	Gradual increase in satisfying experiences; gradual lowering of anxiety status
Cognitive structure	Disorganization; inability to plan, reason, or grasp	Defensive reorganization; resistance to change	Defensive breakdown: (1) disorganization; (2) reorganization abilities in terms of altered perception	Reorganization in terms of present resources and the situation
Physical disability	Acute somatic damage requiring all medical care	Physical recovery from acute phase; functional return to maximum possible level	Physical plateau; gradual slowing of improvement until no change happens	No change in physical disability status

shall refer consistently to anyone intervening in a crisis—teacher, administrator, or counselor—as a *helper*. Similarly, our discussion here will concentrate on crises that manifest themselves in a school setting even though the real causes or problems of these traumas may lie outside the school.

SHOCK STAGE

Unless the helper is present at the moment of the precipitating event, a child in crisis seldom is seen during the *shock stage*. At that time, the child temporarily has broken down and may be operating on what Glasser (1984) terms *pure feelings*, which may evolve into emotional numbness. The child frequently chooses to withdraw rather than seek help. If the child does seek help, he/she usually makes the request hesitatingly, articulates poorly, and is quite confused owing to the anxiety and disorganized thinking common in this stage. Often a child simply will look for the friendly, generalized support of others (especially peers) in an attempt to dissipate some of the emotional pain. Particularly with young children, this stage may involve significant changes in behavior, such as enuresis, somatic complaints, absences, or an escalation of sibling rivalry. What such individual children need at this time is an opportunity to vent emotional intensity in an atmosphere of total acceptance and caring, supportive, human contact. Such contact may be little more than physical hand-holding or a calm attentive presence.

The helper may intervene by simple acceptance if he/she can tolerate the altered behavior or other signs of crisis in a child at this stage. Obviously, if a child engages in behaviors that are destructive to self or others, the helper must provide for an emergency intervention in order to prevent injury or even death. Whether communicated verbally, nonverbally, or both, the helper must express acceptance clearly and consistently. To state, "It's O.K. for you to cry," and then walk out of the room (i.e., rationalizing that the child needs privacy) is not a congruent message and children are notorious experts on detecting discrepant messages. They hear the impact of the message and not simply the words, and the bottom line for them in the above comment is, "Go ahead and cry, but don't expect me to stay; crying makes me uncomfortable."

During the shock stage, a reticent child may need help in dealing with feelings. One excellent way is to listen fully to the child and respond to any feelings he/she may express. The ability to respond to perceived feelings rather than to what is actually being said can be important, but be careful. The child may be functioning poorly, and the feelings experienced during the shock stage may be so overwhelming that youngsters, especially young children, frequently cannot deal with these intense emotions without assistance. The helper's ability to recognize this shock stage and to help children talk about a crisis situation and express their feelings openly, whether verbally, nonverbally, or through techniques such as play therapy or classroom meetings has several benefits. Fink (1967) remarked that the helper's openness to listen provides acceptance and permission for those feelings to exist in the first place. Also, the helper's accepting posture communicates that the helper can sense accurately both the real world and the ideal world the child may be feeling and perceiving. This ideal world is what Glasser refers to as the quality world. Finally, nonjudgmental listening allows the child to express emotions. At this stage, the helper must provide stability for the person in crisis by making necessary decisions regarding physical safety, medical care, and resources for support.

Responses During the Shock Stage

Some desirable interventions during the shock stage are the following:

1. Stabilize the system. Assess the need for medical or other treatment and obtain any needed treatment.
2. Provide a safe, quiet, private atmosphere, perhaps moving the child to a warm, nondistracting room where privacy is possible.
3. Help the child talk about a problem by listening understandingly and offering support in an effort to capture the real feelings. Establish a warm and caring connection by making eye contact without staring, listening alertly, and using touch appropriately. Within this framework of support, make an assessment of the nature and dimensions of the crisis.
4. Seek information about the precipitating event and the child, both from the child and significant others.
5. Identify and contact other appropriate support systems (e.g., school counselor, parents, and involved community groups and resources).

The helper should be careful not to make value judgments about the significance of any visible behaviors or the precipitating event until learning more about the child's own feelings and perceptions.

Responses During the Defensive Retreat Stage

The interventions are more difficult for the helper who is faced not with a confused, anxious child, but with someone who may be angry, denying, fantasizing, ultradependent, or unrealistically optimistic. Use whatever coping strategy may suggest itself. The child in crisis has reverted either to defensive behavior or to the denial stage as described by Kubler-Ross (1970) in relation to the terrible loss one feels over the death of a loved one. A helper's task is to intervene with strong support for the child but not the child's inappropriate behavior or unrealistic thinking. This can be very tricky. A helper cannot, for example, confront a child with any mention of the problem behavior. To do so may both strengthen the child's defenses and force the child to begin viewing the helper as an additional threat that the child must ward off. A helper's role is to support such troubled children by emphasizing their needs for self-worth and recognition while concurrently acknowledging their right to volatile private feelings.

Additional Strategies

The following techniques sometimes work.

1. Reflect the child's feelings; that is, empathize.
2. Summarize the content of the child's messages as you understand these, letting the child correct any false impressions.
3. Help the child clarify feelings.
4. Gently ask the child to explain the probable consequences of his/her intended behavior—both those the child may be hoping for and those you think might possibly follow.
5. Avoid personalizing any angry or hopeless feelings that the child may be expressing, but acknowledge his/her right to feel this way.

The goals are to form a solid and trusting relationship with the child and to indicate the helper's availability whenever the child is ready to communicate further. The stronger the involvement a helper fosters during this stage, the greater will be the helper's effectiveness in the next stage.

Acknowledgment Stage

Interventions appropriate in the third stage, acknowledgment, will start the real helping process. At this point, the child is beginning to accept the reality of the shocking event and starting to see the differences between the real word and an inner picture of an ideal, personal, quality world. At this crucial stage, the child may entertain thoughts of suicide or feelings of severe depression and guilt. The child again is viewing the precipitating, traumatic event(s) in a highly emotional way, but this ability to feel—painful as it may be—is a tangible sign that a child is moving through a serious trauma. A helper even may normalize the anguish a child experiences in stage three by labeling the feeling of despair as a clear indication that the shock is receding and the child will be able to move through this phase as well.

Any event may become a crisis because of its importance to children, given their limited repertoire of problem-solving abilities and their dearth of behaviors to cope with a crisis. With a clearer view of reality, the child now must confront the same problem, still lacking the ability to cope. Clearly, a helper's role now must be to help the child develop practical ways to deal with the challenge while encouraging the continued development of trust within their own relationship.

Responses in the Acknowledgment Stage

Some specific interventions that might work during the acknowledgment stage follow.

1. Fully communicate an understanding of the situation and a special caring for the child.
2. Explore the child's developing awareness and feelings.
3. Clarify and define the precipitating event, its implications, and its dimensions whenever the child communicates a willingness to hear about these aspects. This point is similar to a reality therapy method of focusing on current behavior.
4. Remain supportive and realistic as you help the child evaluate unsound alternatives in light of his/her value system. This step aligns with a key move in reality therapy—evaluation.
5. Supply necessary data and resources to assist the child in making a good decision.
6. Explore tentative plans for the problem's solution. This follows the planning stage of the reality therapy problem-solving model.
7. Offer an understanding ear as you listen to a child's expressed feelings as long as necessary.
8. Make sure the child knows that options exist for changing feelings by solving the problems with new actions.
9. Mobilize support systems and help create new ones as needed.
10. Get some commitment from the child to follow through on any plans developed in this dialogue.

Adaption and Change Stage

In the fourth stage of adaption and change, individuals in crisis have acknowledged reality, understood it, and are ready to begin reorganizing their lives. The goals here are for the helper and the individual to decide together upon the most workable solutions to the problem(s) and to begin to work toward them. The helper and child work together to communicate clearly with each other and with parents, teachers, social workers, and courts about the effectiveness of the plan as the child perceives it. The helper and child also work together to integrate the new skills and meanings the child has gained through the crisis and to gain the lessons from the "baptism of fire" into one's life and understanding. Finally, the helper terminates the problem-solving phase of the crisis intervention and maintains involvement and personal contact as needed.

Helper's Responses to the Adaption and Change Stage

Some specific strategies for intervening at this stage are as follows:

1. Maintain positive communication with the child, but freely support, highlight, and confront as appropriate.
2. Work to increase a child's problem-solving abilities.
3. Identify any unconsidered options that may be available.
4. Facilitate the child's own decision about resolving the problem.
5. Support the child's movement and progress toward any new goals.
6. When solutions are underway, see if the child is willing to talk about the crisis, its progress, and the skills and understandings gained through it.
7. Aim to move the child toward greater self-reliance.
8. End your relationship as a crisis counselor and refer a child to another counselor when you agree the child is ready or needs follow-up or friendly assistance. Remain a friend if possible.
9. Keep some interest in the child and remain available until the child has reached his/her goals and regained a solid sense of autonomy. Afterwards, maintain involvement on a mutually agreed basis.

Related Issues

The interventions that we have presented above are the options open to a helper during each stage of a crisis, but an actual crisis is never cut and dried. The amount of time anyone spends in each of the four stages will vary greatly, ranging from as little as five minutes to as much as six or more days, or even weeks, depending on the child and the event. The stages always play in real life as variations of the theoretical model, but disparities between a mental construct and actuality is true of every theory. Some children may slide gradually from one stage to another and sometimes even show signs of two stages at the same moment. A crisis is a process but not necessarily an orderly or logical one. These stages represent an interactive process more than a lockstep progression. Seldom do children move sequentially and neatly forward from shock to defensive retreat, to acknowledgment, and, finally, to adaption and change. Some might go, for example, from shock to acknowledgment to defensive retreat and then move back to new acknowledgment. Finally, they might come out of the loop by moving on to adaption and change.

Although the four stages of a crisis presented here portray a successful encounter, every case may not end in a satisfying resolution. The process may remain incomplete for a variety of reasons. Insufficient psychological strength may keep a person from moving beyond defensive retreat. Some may return to defensive retreat if they label the reality they perceive in the acknowledgment stage as overwhelming to them. Death, suicide, or another shock may intervene in the process. Someone in the total system interacting with the individual in crisis may disagree with the decisions, block the actions, or disallow desired changes of other parts of the system. Such squabbles are not unusual in the interaction of a family, a child, a school, and other sociopolitical bureaucracies.

The interventions in each stage of Fink's (1967) model are congruent with the goals and the dynamics that occur within that stage. These strategies give the helper some concrete ways to guide a troubled child through a time of great stress. Crisis intervention is important because of the critical nature of a live situation, the real and immediate need for assistance, and the intensified potential an individual child has for growth or regression at that moment.

One important development that first must take place in schools is a new emphasis on the critical role of a teacher as helper. As this counseling role evolves, as it inevitably will, teachers will gain increased finesse in managing children's critical needs.

Up to now, we have focused our discussion on an individual in the midst of a crisis and have specified appropriate interventions a counselor or other helper can employ once a crisis occurs. Although this individual focus is a necessary and appropriate starting point, important and broader issues surface for any helper working at the elementary and middle school levels.

The first issue relates to the stage of adaption and change. To resolve a crisis successfully, a helper must be able to contact and influence various systems surrounding a person in crisis. A teacher or other helper in a school must be alert to signs that other children in a class may experience shock and defensive retreat by association. When a crisis flares up at school, a counselor or other helper must operate within the system as part of a team that includes many school personnel. The team also may call on other external systems, such as police, medical services, mental health agencies, youth services, and crisis centers. The decision to involve others depends on the nature of the crisis. See the prologue for step-by-step suggestions about coordinating one's effort in helping a child, contacting various institutions, and dealing with the pervasive red tape of those agencies.

A helper not only must tend directly to the child in crisis, but also must oversee the needs of those in related systems as well. These wider contacts can be anything from disseminating information to insisting on any additional aid. When the need is urgent, the helper must ensure immediate therapeutic treatment and not tolerate a delayed appointment with a community-based child therapist.

Ideally, teachers would have the perspective and emotional energy to observe potential or actual crises in their classrooms and take initial steps to respond to the crises but, in the real world, such ideal actions do not always become part of teachers' routines in spite of their best intentions and talents. Therefore, school counselors who wish to meet more students' needs will become proactive. Starting with acceptance of the reality that teachers' tolerance of ambiguity and stress is limited, the counselors can enjoy more progress by informing teachers of appropriate community resources and referrals. Teachers find some comfort in knowing and utilizing the school's own internal resources and in validating with a counselor and principal that their job does have some serious limitations. They are teachers, not paramedics.

Besides grappling with a plethora of community agencies and working with teachers to learn to spot brewing crises and make appropriate referrals, a counselor also involves the developmental aspect of all crises. Professionals educated in helping skills and principles of human growth and development know that individuals have particular concerns at certain developmental stages and also know about the corresponding vulnerabilities at those stages. Because these growth pains are common, a helper often can predict problems, employ preventive and psychoeducational techniques, and offer training in intervention skills. Thus the counselor is one of the key people in the school and the community who serves the role of a supportive advocate for children who daily present challenging developmental nuances or other vulnerabilities. Educating teachers about the signs of child abuse and working with school administrators to increase parents' access to school services are examples of programs and activities that can be important to children. (See Loar's work in chapter 7 on spotting child abuse and taking responsible and effective steps to solve the problem.) With support, children may be less vulnerable to developmental and situational crises.

SOCIAL CONTEXT OF A CRISIS

Another perspective involves aiming efforts at the larger social system that contributes to vulnerability and predisposes individuals and families to face a crisis. These shockers can happen to anyone. Often a counselor or other professional at the scene can do little about the larger contextual realities, yet accounting for these influences would be most useful to both helper and child. Medicine, psychology, and education traditionally have focused primarily on individuals in isolation and not the unique environment in which those persons live. Crisis prevention requires a broader focus on the social systems that impact people's lives and that, therefore, have the potential of effecting primary prevention.

Among examples of primary prevention, children may face such deplorable conditions at home that they need a foster home placement, an unavailable option in some communities with a very limited number of foster home placements. Another social stigma may be living with a parent or parents whose best intentions may exceed their emotional and/or economic resources to provide for their children. Minority children often experience problems of crisis proportions as they try to join in with the majority culture despite their language difficulties, or the problems they have from forced bussing. Finally, many children who need one-to-one assistance might benefit from family counseling but live in communities with inadequate resources. For many communities, this under-funding of social and counseling services can happen even in *good times.*

If a counselor wants to intervene fully in crises that tend to overwhelm an individual's ability to cope, he/she must include preventive programs sponsored by community agencies and other social systems. Perspectives that look beyond individuals to the social contexts of their lives are a necessity if counselors are to gain a full understanding of crises. A helper cannot afford to give in to a fatalistic attitude—"one cannot fight city hall." Rather, determined advocacy to modify or change community and societal forces affecting individuals is an integral part of a helper's role.

We must not overlook the social context of children in crises—their families, neighborhoods, communities, or even country. One has to look only at the effects on children of life in impoverished rural communities or inner-city neighborhoods in the United States or abroad. Whether anticipated or unexpected, death, divorce, family abuse, hunger, and abandonment by a parent are stressors that most see as crises in a family. This book is about all of these troubles—handling children's crises and doing so in the full context in which the misfortunes occur. School personnel have to deal with the effects of these crises upon the children who give them a reason for being there. In such situations, a school counselor must know every community resource for families in crisis and must collaborate with others in the community in applying the power of these services.

INTEGRATING CHOICE THEORY
AND CRISIS THEORY AND INTERVENTIONS

We have designed this chapter to provide you with a theoretical framework for understanding crisis theory and for formulating useful interventions for your students when they present themselves under highly stressful conditions. Together with the previous chapter by Palmatier on choice theory and reality therapy (chapter 2), our model provides a foundation for the contributions in the remainder of the book that overall applies reality therapy and choice theory to crisis intervention in schools. We have presented two issues and have made an effort to distinguish between these—first, learning and applying the principles of crisis theory and, second, seeing the connection between crisis theory and interventions and the main thrust of the book captured in choice theory and reality therapy. As you read the many case examples in the ensuing chapters, you will see our crisis counseling model come to life, and your fuller understanding of this basic framework will contribute to your facility in applying the crisis model with real students who bring their distress to elementary, middle, and junior high schools all over the country.

Beyond our foundational theory, the second factor we have described relates to clinical practice and counseling strategies. We have shown the interrelationship of our model of crisis theory and choice theory. The interaction between these two theories and approaches to crisis management and rational problem solving will become increasingly clear as you examine the practical cases woven throughout this book.

Just as in crisis theory, choice theory places a major emphasis on the subjectivity of one's view of reality and on the notion of personal power, decision-making, or control over one's behavior through personal choice. Any external event, according to choice theory, is only *information* and people are free to interpret such input and to redefine the external experience or event so that reality becomes more congruent with the pictures in their quality worlds. We take the position that a person in crisis is operating on choice theory's notion of *pure feelings* and cannot make choices entirely rationally in that state because the person is mainly *controlling for survival*. In the early stages of a crisis, people's thinking may be unfocused and their behaviors may be more automatic than chosen. They are attempting to control for inner pictures through their gut feelings and natural bodily responses rather than through rational behavior and prudent action steps. Choice theory and crisis theory have much in common, but timing is crucial in effective intervention. Only when children and adolescents reach the stage of adaption and change in our model can they revert fully to reason that typifies the driver's seat position of one who is fully in control.

Finally, crisis theory allows counselors or helpers to focus single-mindedly on the emotional aspect of people's total behavior during crises and does not rush them to come to an intelligent decision while engaged in a survival mode. Under these emergency circumstances, of course, a reality therapist would follow the principles contained in crisis theory and show the same respect for a client's agitation or disorientation. Reality therapy is a rational problem-solving method designed for use at subsequent stages of a crisis—certainly after the shock and defensive retreat stage. A helper can shift gears as people show that they are capable of rationally examining their current behavior, evaluating the usefulness of their present actions in achieving their goals, and carving out new plans of action that are more likely to help them meet their needs well.

REFERENCES

Auerbach, S., & Kilmann, P. (1977). Crisis intervention: A review of outcome research. *Psychological Bulletin, 84*, 1189-1217.

Baldwin, B. (1979). Crisis intervention: An overview of theory and practice. *The Counseling Psychologist, 8*, 43-52.

Ballou, M. (1986). Crisis intervention. In G. Miller (Ed.), *The middle school counselor*. Cranston, RI: Carroll Press.

Ballou, M. (1987). Physical violence against children and crisis topics. *Acute Care and Trauma Rehabilitation, 2*(1), 45-53.

Ballou, M., Fetter, P., Litwack, K., & Litwack, L. (1992). *Health counseling.* Kent, OH: American School Health Association.

Caplan, G. (1964). *Principles of preventive psychiatry.* New York: Basic Books.

Fink, S. (1967). Crisis and motivation: A theoretical model. *Archives of Physical Medicine and Rehabilitation, 48*, 592-597.

Glasser, W. (1984). *Control theory.* New York: Harper & Row.

Golan, N. (1978). *Treatment in crisis situations.* New York: Free Press.

Kubler-Ross, E. (1970). *On death and dying.* New York: Macmillan.

Lindemann, E. (1944). Symptomatology and management of acute grief. *American Journal of Psychiatry, 101*, 141-148.

Parad, H., & Parad, L. (1990). *Crisis intervention, Book 2.* Milwaukee, WI: Family Services of America.

Roberts, A. R. (Ed.). (1990). *Crisis intervention handbook: Assessment, treatment and research.* Belmont, CA: Wadsworth.

Slaikeu, K. (1990). *Crisis intervention: A handbook for practice and research* (2nd ed.). Boston: Allyn & Bacon.

Smith, L. (1977). Crisis intervention theory and practice. *Community Mental Health Review, 2*(1), 5-13.

Toffler, A. (1990). *Powershift: Knowledge, wealth & violence at the edge of the 21st century.* New York: Bantam Books.

VandenBos, G. R., & Bryant, B. K. (Eds.). (1987). *Cataclysms, crises, & catastrophes: Psychology in action. APA Master Lectures.* Washington, DC: APA Press.

Chapter 4

ETHICAL SCHOOL COUNSELING: MANAGING A BALANCING ACT

Terence E. Patterson

Editor's Note

Many educators confuse morality in a narrow denominational sense with ethics. Ethical standards, especially as contained in professional associations of teachers and counselors, typically move beyond the parochial interpretations of one religious group or another. No one, however, can argue that, when ethical issues require interpretation in relation to community values, politics enters the discussion. Standards that may vary across communities show that the field of ethics does not represent some kind of eternal "truth," except perhaps as such standards or positions become universal across cultures and historical periods. An example of such a generic stricture is the practically universal prohibition against murder.

Sound ethical practices are wholly compatible with choice theory and noncoercive schooling. A humanistic philosophy underlies ethical norms in most societies and the guidelines for quality schools. This convergence between a spirit of humanism on the one hand and both social ethos and academic quality on the other becomes especially apparent in relation to eliminating coercive tactics, respecting all children, creating helpful opportunities for handicapped children to enjoy school and to succeed, and fostering a friendly sense of community among teachers and learners.

Both the chapter author and the author–editor encourage all counselors and teachers to join a professional association for accessing information and eliciting professional support. Finally, I endorse an idea many counselors have found useful—forming a support or consultation group in a school, district, region, or state in order to overcome isolation. Connecting to an Internet chat room with other counselors is also a prudent and efficient way to remain aware of current community practices and standards.

ETHICAL COUNSELING IN SCHOOLS

The legendary Dionysius searched in vain for one honest person; contemporary school counselors might search for a practitioner who is thoroughly versed and skilled in the applications of contemporary law, ethics, and standards of community practice. The complex, severe problems of today's students and their families, the proliferation of laws and regulations affecting practice, and the increasing awareness and shifting values of society combine to create an ethical mine field in which counselors must operate (Lakin, 1988).

Ethics in the broadest sense addresses issues that are universal to the human condition: life and death, basic human rights, and dominance and control in society. In the professions, the aim of ethical codes is primarily to protect the consumer of services. Secondarily, codes of ethics serve as criteria for professions to regulate themselves and as benchmarks by which individuals maintain professional integrity. Contemporary ethical codes seek to define both minimal and aspirational (ideal) standards for practitioners (Nagy, 1990). Legal codes, of course, derive from legislation and case law regulating consumer affairs and licensing laws, usually at the state level. Notable instances can arise in professional practice in which the proscriptions of ethical codes and those of the law come into grave conflict (Thompson, 1990). Finally, community standards enter into the definition of acceptable standards of practice. Thus, the counselor often faces complex dilemmas in the application of these guidelines to school environments.

In the sections that follow we will examine specific aspects of role clarification for school counselors, confidentiality, assessment, abuse of children in the school setting, cultural sensitivity, and a variety of methodological and miscellaneous issues. This paper is an attempt to negotiate the boundary between clear legal, ethical, and community guidelines and ambiguous areas that depend upon the counselor's informed judgment for resolution.

ROLE CONFLICTS:
SERVING MANY MASTERS

Professionals employed in public settings meet with unique dilemmas in defining their roles. To delineate school counselors' areas of competence according to their training and experience and to specify the ethical principles of their professional associations may be a simple matter. State laws may present clear guidelines regulating practice in the consumer's interests.

Counselors who interact regularly with colleagues on an informal basis and in continuing education seminars develop a pragmatic sense of community standards that affect their work. Counselors also must pay attention to standards and practices that an individual school and school board may have established. Similarly, unions and the community at large promote expectations and standards affecting counselor practice. Some counselors may view themselves as community educators on relevant issues, while the community may attempt to limit the counselor to activities within the school itself. Just when a counselor feels that he/she has a clear professional identity and function, a constituency or governing body may dictate a shift in emphasis, values, or practices.

Realistically school counselors must ask whether they are primarily school employees, union members, educators, or mental health professionals. Are all of these roles compatible? Do school boards or administrators who significantly dilute counselors' roles prevent them from practicing ethically and legally? Do community pressures prevent legal, ethical, or school policies from being implemented? If counselors define their roles primarily as mental health professionals, how can they integrate this identity with public, parental, and administrative pressures?

Perhaps the potential for conflict is most acute in public school systems, especially on controversial issues. Employer demands can stress counselors' abilities to define their roles clearly. Counselors may function well advising students on personal and family matters, leading groups, and consulting. Budget cuts then may dictate that their roles be limited to course scheduling and student discipline. The school board may be pressured by a segment of the community that is uncomfortable over counselors dealing with family or birth control issues. What should counselors do when the union calls for a protracted strike in the midst of counseling a student on a critical issue? The proper course of action may be clear-cut from an ethical viewpoint, but there may be a significant cost in job security and peer relationships. These are but a few of the ethically-based role conflicts that can arise for school counselors.

Aside from the complexity of role definition, shifting trends in ethical codes and community standards create ambiguous contexts in which counselors must practice. Challenges to ethical codes involving testimonials by clients and public statements about areas of competency recently have resulted in substantial modification of the principles of the American Psychological Association (Nagy, 1990). Ethical principles promulgated by various professional associations (e.g., The American School Counselor's Association, The American Psychological Association, The American Association for Counseling and Development, The National Association of Social Workers) are seldom in conflict, although differences in interpretations of general principles may occur by the various organizations to which counselors belong. With regard to community standards, counselors who have been involved in malpractice litigation have discovered that the most salient factors in settling a case often are based on what a reasonable counselor practicing in a specific community according to current community standards might do in a similar case. School counselors need to apprise themselves of ethical and legal codes and community standards and need to create a framework to use in practice. The most common ethical pitfalls encountered by school counselors, as indicated by Fischer and Sorenson (1985, p. 42), are listed in Table 4.1.

Confidentiality: To Tell or Not To Tell

Counselors in training learn the meaning of confidentiality, which is a term referring to "the ethical responsibility of mental health professionals to safeguard clients from unauthorized disclosures of information given in the professional relationship . . . *Privilege* . . . refers to the right of clients not to have their privileged communications used in court without their consent" (Corey, Corey, & Callanan, 1988, p. !77). In some situations the privilege can be claimed by the counselor, most notably when clients are dangerous to themselves, when

---

TABLE 4.1
Common Ethical Pitfalls for School Counselors

- Prescribing or administering drugs
- Giving birth control advice
- Giving abortion-related advice
- Making statements that might be defamatory
- Assisting in searches of students' lockers
- Violating the privacy of records

Source: Reprinted from L. Fischer & G. Sorenson, *School Law for Counselors, Psychologists, and Social Workers*, p. 42. Copyright © 1985 by Longman.

a third party is in danger, and when documents are subpoenaed. Claiming the privilege means that the counselor overrides the client's prerogative to withhold confidential information and, therefore, may disclose in court any information discussed in counseling. A notable example would be cases of child abuse or sexual molestation in which a student would not want the incident to be divulged, but where the counselor legally is obligated to file a report in order to protect the child. In claiming the privilege, the counselor incurs the ethical obligation to protect the child from retribution insofar as possible.

Confidentiality in regard to school counseling in particular is an extremely complex issue. As with all laws pertaining to counseling, each state regulates the professions as it sees fit. The California law known as the Hart Bill (AB 763) and its amendments (AB 428) enacted as Education Code 35301 establishes specific regulations pertaining to confidentiality in school counseling and will be used in this section in reference to school counselors. As of this writing, a majority of states have passed bills with similar provisions. A Pupil Personnel Services credential covers only school counselors under this law, not teachers, school psychologists, educational psychologists, social workers, nurses, administrators, or other mental health professionals.

Ignorance of the law is no excuse for counselors who may prefer ignoring their obligations to protect a client's privilege at selected times and to claim it when indicated (Bernstein, 1982). The prevailing standard in all mental health professions is to obtain a written release for each disclosure of information (Conidaris, Ely, & Erikson, 1991). The counselor in some situations may be in a precarious position in relation to ethics and the law. A court may subpoena client records and the client may refuse to sign a release of information, or a client may release information but the counselor independently may determine that disclosure to a third party would be detrimental to the client. In such cases the counselor may follow an ethical mandate but violate the law. Counselors, therefore, need to be aware of ethical and legal guidelines, to specify clearly their values and priorities, and to establish reasonable safeguards and practices regarding record-keeping, support from professional associations, and malpractice insurance.

Many counselors hold a common misperception about group counseling, generally thinking that professional privilege protects information clients disclosed in such settings, but this is not the case. While counselors should uphold ethical principles pertaining to confidentiality so that students or clients can feel that members will not disclose their statements wantonly, courts historically have held that where more than two people discuss personal matters, the privilege does not apply (Fischer & Sorenson, 1985). With this in mind, the counselor must attend sensitively to the impact of disclosures made by group members upon the group process and the ability of participants to feel safe in discussing sensitive issues with one another (Terres & Larrabee, 1985).

California Education Code 35301 states that students who are 12 years of age and older (and their parents) have a right to confidentiality when engaging in counseling with a credentialed school counselor. No one has a right to include information from group counseling in a student's cumulative academic record, and cannot disclose such content to anyone (except under the following seven conditions):

1. discussing a case with another health care provider for purposes of making a referral;
2. having the student sign a written waiver;
3. reporting child abuse or neglect;
4. providing information to law enforcement officials under court order;
5. disclosing information to the principal or parent in order to avert a clear or present danger to self, others, or property;
6. conferring with school staff regarding modification of the academic program; or
7. reporting crimes, intended or committed.

Thus, clearly, no school official may compel a school counselor to break confidentiality under threat of disciplinary action, charges of insubordination, or dismissal. Similarly, school counselors may not routinely discuss with colleagues or parents information their clients reveal to them during counseling unless the situation is covered by the exceptions specified in the law. Interestingly, although school counselors are not defined as mental health professionals by California Evidence Code 49424, the State Department of Education refers to the ". . . 'clinically trained' school counselor. [Counseling] is a therapeutic growth process through which individual students or groups of students are helped" (California State Department of Education, 1982). A sharp contrast exists between the more liberal law that applies to school counseling in which 12-year-olds can give informed consent independently and the stricter law pertaining to outpatient psychotherapy that requires therapists to document their attempts to notify parents and requires a child to be in psychological or physical danger. School counselors benefit from a relative lack of restriction and enjoy a welcome degree of flexibility.

CASE COMMENTS

When disclosing confidential material concerning the counseling of minors, the general policy is this: At the beginning, emphasize a student's right to confidentiality along with the potential benefits of their including appropriate adults on certain matters. Following these guidelines may prevent misunderstandings from the start and prevent ethical and legal problems later. Also, a frequent possibility is to "take the middle ground" concerning confidentiality with minors by making an agreement with students that counselors will inform their parents only that their child is in counseling and of the general nature of treatment (except for mandated reporting and certain crisis situations). Most counselors prefer this procedure because such a practice maintains the integrity of the counseling relationship, involves parents, and satisfies legal and ethical guidelines.

The following two vignettes illustrate actual situations in which legal, ethical, and professional issues intersect to create various choice points for school counselors. Read the examples and sketch a few notes on how you might handle each situation before you read the case comments.

Case of Sara

Sara, age 15, comes to you in crisis over fears of possible pregnancy. Sara is afraid to inform her parents about her situation and requests counseling regarding her options. As a school counselor you have concerns about her health, her future, and her family's lack of involvement. What is the best course of action?

Case Comments. The best course of action is to form a trusting alliance with Sara and to attempt to bridge the communication gap with her parents. She is old enough to receive confidentiality in school counseling and to give consent to medical treatment regarding pregnancy without her parents' permission, if that becomes necessary.

Case of John

Counselors disagree about their obligation to breach confidentiality on such controversial issues as the presence of HIV infection. One work on the subject (Gunderson, Mayo, & Rhame, 1989) indicated that professionals have a clear obligation under the Tarasoff ruling (Tarasoff, 1974) to warn the sexual partners of patients who test HIV seropositive. Generally, however, current standards of practice in psychology do not view HIV-positive status as a clear and imminent danger to others as required by Tarasoff (William Schachter, Ph.D., J.D., personal communication, 1991). Davis (1987) asked a series of questions on the matter of divulging the condition of a person with an HIV-positive diagnosis. Who should be notified? What about an afflicted person's right to privacy? Common sense may dictate avoiding any action that would burden an afflicted individual with being stigmatized or ostracized because of his/her condition (Davis, 1987). What about an HIV-positive man, however, who knowingly continues to engage in unprotected sex with his wife and who states unequivocally that he has no intention of revealing his status to her?

Consider the following case example: John, age 18 and about to graduate from high school, discusses with you in counseling that he has tested HIV-positive as a result of his intravenous drug use. He is concerned about the possibility of his girlfriend (who is not a student at your school) contracting HIV from their sexual activity but says he will not tell her because he is not sure of the degree of risk involved and because he sincerely does not want to lose her. Do you have a duty to warn her?

Case Comments. Current legal guidelines do not establish a clear duty to warn; ethically, however, you may decide to save the girlfriend from any possible risk by telling her yourself if you cannot persuade John to do so. Telling her places you at risk for violating confidentiality, however, and John may file a civil suit for damages.

Another special situation in which counselors and teachers must be knowledgeable, especially in regard to confidentiality, is crisis management. Good skills in establishing rapport, reducing anxiety, and guiding the student through a prudent course of action are essential in crisis counseling, but do the same rules of confidentiality apply as in routine situations? In fact, the guidelines mentioned earlier in this section do apply to crises, particularly when the student is a danger to self or others or when abuse has occurred; however, numerous circumstances exist in which the informed judgment of the counselor rather than a legal statute or ethical code might indicate the proper course of action. In a situation where there is suicide potential and a student does not want his/her parents notified, the counselor would be remiss not to do so as part of a reasonable plan to protect the student. Similarly, whenever contact is made with an agency such as a probation department or a medical or mental health clinic and complete confidentiality cannot be guaranteed to the student, the counselor is advised to notify the parents whenever possible, preferably with the student's involvement. These are examples of situations where the individual judgment and community standards (i.e., what a "reasonable" professional might do) are the salient guidelines.

ABUSE IN THE SCHOOL SETTING

As mandated reporters, counselors are usually well-informed about issues regarding child abuse and neglect. But what happens when school or district policy permits or does not monitor adequately such practices as physical punishment or restraint, extensive isolation, or ridicule? Numerous situations exist in which counselors can be reasonably certain that institutional abuse or neglect is occurring. In malpractice or other court action, the burden of proof is on counselors to demonstrate that abuse does not exist or that they had no awareness of it. A policy that allows for any form of corporal punishment, extensive isolation, restraint, or large amounts of unstructured time or perfunctory activity at the expense of learning can involve unethical practice for counselors who participate in it.

Behaviorally-disordered and learning-disabled children frequently may be restrained mechanically or manually "in their own best interests," and the line between abuse and appropriate management can become blurred (Schloss & Smith, 1987). Due to the institutionalized nature of the abuse or neglect, reporting may not be required by statute, but counselors nonetheless incur an ethical obligation to take action; otherwise they may become liable for damages if litigation occurs.

A more insidious instance of abuse involves the improper use of commonly accepted methods of behavioral management. With the use of the time-honored techniques of time-out and extinction (punishment), children may be isolated for undue periods of time or may experience harsh treatment due to misapplication of a technique by a teacher, administrator, or counselor. School personnel may think they are using behavior modification techniques correctly when actually they are applying an undue amount of control and noticing serious negative consequences (Chwee-Lye & Giles, 1985).

Another example of insidious abuse involves the all too common practice of recommending that hyperactive children be placed routinely on medication. Such recommendations may place pressure on parents (and subsequently on physicians) for an immediate cure for a multidetermined problem (Simms, 1985). Prescribing and managing prescription drugs are clearly not within the scope of school counselors' jobs, even though during informal discussions or in the course of an Individual Education Plan (IEP), teachers and counselors often may suggest that parents check out medications for a particular behavior problem their children exhibit. These casual recommendations can carry a great deal of weight with parents who feel pressure to solve their children's difficulties quickly. Frequently, no one provides adequate monitoring of children taking medication for hyperactivity and these youngsters then may remain on medication far longer than necessary. Similarly, in an IEP conference, teachers and counselors unwittingly may cause children with other types of special needs to be placed inappropriately or without timely reviews of their progress. Lack of objective, specific behavioral descriptions and of competent psychometric testing can result in misplacement and inappropriate treatment of children with all types of special needs (Jenkins, 1985).

ASSESSMENT: A UNIQUE CHALLENGE

Assessment has become much more prominent over the past two decades. Parents, educators, psychologists, and counselors have questioned the validity of tests for educational placement. In the noted Larry P. case (Larry P. v. Riles, 1979), the use of standardized intelligence tests such as the *Wechsler* scales was prohibited in some school districts for determining placements in special education. Educators carried the burden of proof to demonstrate that placement tests were free from cultural bias. A number of substitute instruments for placement in special education classes were developed. Test users increasingly are required to scrutinize the normative sample used in the development of a test as well as the test's usefulness in making educational and administrative decisions. Some schools or states may require standardized achievement tests such as the *California Test Battery* and aptitude tests such as the *Scholastic Aptitude Test.* School counselors can be instrumental in selecting and interpreting tests of scholastic achievement and vocational interest. As guidelines for the ethical use of tests and the interpretation of test results, counselors must use test manuals and the standards for testing that the American School Counselor's Association and other professional associations publish.

Whenever testing, counselors need to offer an explanation of test results to students, parents, and others. Counselors have an obligation to present information in a language and context that clients can understand. One procedure that is often helpful and that facilitates understanding, for example, is presenting a range within which test scores fall and anchoring scores to a percentile ranking. Identifying competencies, deficits, and patterns on a continuum rather than presenting a static condition or a formal diagnosis avoids labeling and allows readers to view scores in their proper perspective (Shea, 1985). Clarifying misunderstandings that could result from nonanchored and ambiguous test results and identifying assessment goals and resources as specifically as possible give important background to drawing conclusions and making recommendations.

CULTURAL CONTEXT: A MAJOR CONSIDERATION

The implications of testing without cultural sensitivity have been explored in the previous section. Subtle yet powerful distortions may interfere in other aspects of working with ethnic clients. Students, particularly those who have recently arrived from non-Western societies, may fail to comprehend the very nature of Western "talking" as a means of problem solving (Westermeyer, 1989). Clients may question the motives of a counselor who suspects that their family's immigration status or public benefits may be in jeopardy if they reveal certain types of information. Counselors may misinterpret results on the basis of inadequate understanding of cultural factors.

Lack of eye contact, passivity, and dialect may be culturally specific and professionals sometimes see these elements as psychological, characterological, or linguistic disorders in need of treatment (Russell, 1988). Conversely, various behaviors and characteristics of clients may be viewed as cultural manifestations when a disorder is actually present. Incorrect evaluation may have the effect of establishing either excessively low or high academic, career, and behavioral expectations and either misplacing students or ignoring appropriate interventions altogether.

Although counselors in an increasingly multicultural society have the obligation to understand as much as possible about diverse cultural values and practices, they can never understand fully everything that pertains to a client's cultural situation. Immersion in a specific culture is an optimal method for gaining information and empathy, but individualizing one's approach to working with students is inevitably the best course of action, regardless of ethnicity. Whether knowledge about specific cultural issues is abundant or minimal, a deliberate interviewing pace, including frequent questions about cultural meaning, promotes both counselor understanding and client rapport. Systemic, contextual assessment and intervention based on an individual's situation is particularly appropriate for multicultural clients. Individuals from the client's culture may aid in explaining cultural meanings, though caution must be used against using any ethnic individual's interpretation as the definitive explanation of cultural phenomena. Ethical, multicultural counselors are advised to participate in peer consultation groups, in-service training, travel, and extensive reading on a regular basis in order to deepen cultural sensitivity and enhance their effectiveness.

INTERSECTING JUNGLES:
WHERE DO WE GO FROM HERE?

Law, ethical principles, and standards of practice all provide salient guidelines that directly affect the practice of school counseling, but acting in accord with the imperatives in one of these three realms does not dispense counselors from violations in any other area. Instead of a defensive, moralistic, or legalistic approach to practice, this article suggests that practitioners follow the prudent course of remaining aware and assertively integrating the law, ethics, and community standards in their day-to-day application of counseling services in schools. Counselors best serve clients' interests and their own by means of a synthesis in which they maintain an acute awareness of their own personal competencies, limitations, and current standards governing practice. Counselors must balance sensitivity to the needs of client groups with effective management of the pressures of overseeing organizations. Counselors, teachers, and administrators must stay abreast of ethical and legal practices and foster a safe environment in which they routinely may discuss ambiguous issues. The practice of "see no evil, hear no evil" is most dangerous as it pertains to law and ethics. A pretense of certainty about the legal and ethical implications in every situation is not conducive to raising questions or consulting regularly with colleagues.

School staffs can take a variety of positive steps to increase their legal and ethical acumen. Raising questions at staff meetings and discussing the lessons they have learned in specific cases can help them integrate legal and ethical topics into the fabric of the school environment. Staff members with particular interests in law and ethics can organize study groups to explore matters of current relevance to the school. A regular consultant knowledgeable in all facets of ethics and the law can be a valuable asset. Finally, teachers, administrators, and counselors can take advantage of workshops and seminars by local universities and training centers in order to stay informed about rapidly changing developments.

Contemporary ethical practice is truly a balancing act which can be served less and less by default—that is, by side-stepping controversial issues. In the current climate, school counselors who plan to survive well will practice assertively in order to meet the needs of a diverse population of students. The profession of school counseling can establish a hallmark for itself by clearly defining its objectives and competencies and by sensitively negotiating the ethical complexities that are part of contemporary professional practice.

REFERENCES

Bernstein, B. (1982). *Values, ethics, legalities and the family therapist.* Rockville, MD: Aspen Systems.

California State Department of Education. (1982). (brochure).

Chwee-Lye, C., & Giles, G. (1985). Behavior modification in the classroom: Some ethical reservations. *Education, 105*(4), 360-365.

Conidaris, M. G., Ely, D. F., & Erikson, J. T. (1991). *California laws for psychotherapists.* Gardena, CA: Harcourt Brace Jovanovich.

Corey, G., Corey, G., & Callanan, P. (1988). *Issues and ethics in the helping professions* (3rd ed.). Pacific Grove, CA: Brooks/Cole.

Corey, G., Corey, M., Callanan, P., & Russell, J. (1992). *Group therapy techniques* (2nd ed.). Pacific Grove, CA: Brooks/Cole.

Davis, D. (1987). Children with AIDS in the public schools: The ethical issues. *Journal of Medical Humanities and Bioethics, 8*(2),101-109.

Fischer, L., & Sorenson, G. (1985). *School law for counselors, psychologists, and social workers.* New York: Longman.

Gunderson, M., Mayo, J., & Rhame, F. (1989). *Aids: Testing and privacy.* Salt Lake City, UT: University of Utah Press.

Jenkins, D. (1985). Ethical and legal dilemmas of working with students with special needs. *Elementary School Guidance and Counseling, 19*(3), 202-209.

Lakin, M. (1988). *Ethical issues in the psychotherapies.* New York: Oxford University Press.

Larry P. v. Riles, 495 F. Supp. 926 (N.D. Cal 1979.)

Nagy, T. (1990). *Revision of the ethical principles of psychologists.* Unpublished manuscript.

Russell, D. (1988). Language and psychotherapy: The influence of nonstandard English on clinical practice. In L. Comas-Diaz & E. Griffith (Eds.), *Clinical guidelines in cross-cultural mental health* (pp. 33-68). New York: John Wiley & Sons.

Schloss, P., & Smith, M. (1987). Guidelines for ethical use of manual restraint in public school settings for behaviorally-disordered students. *Behavioral Disorders, 12*(3), 207-213.

Shea, V. (1985). Overview of the assessment process. In C. Newmark (Ed.), *Major psychological assessment instruments* (pp. 1-10). Boston: Allyn & Bacon.

Simms, R. (1985). Hyperactivity and drug therapy: What the educator should know. *Journal of Research and Development in Education, 18*(3), 1-7.

Tarasoff v. Regents of California, 118 Cal Rptr. 129, 529 P. 2d 553, 559 (1974).

Terres, C., & Larrabee, M. (1985). Ethical issues and group work with children. *Elementary School Guidance and Counseling, 19*(3), 190-197.

Thompson, A. (1990). *Guide to ethical practice in psychotherapy.* New York: John Wiley & Sons.

Westermeyer, J. (1989). *Mental health for refugees and other migrants: Social and preventive approaches.* Springfield, IL: Charles C. Thomas.

Chapter 5

THERAPIST AS TEACHER; TEACHER AS THERAPIST: EVOLUTION OF THE RESPONSIBLE ROLE MODEL

Barbara I. Bratter
Carole Jaffe Bratter
Thomas Edward Bratter

Editor's Note

The Bratter team presents a compelling case for transforming two roles. First, therapists transform their role from neutral mirror to healing teacher through a strong and separate identity. Second, teachers transform their role from dispassionate information dispenser or talking head to caring and strong counselors. The authors go one step further: teachers become therapists. The authors feature adolescents here but, in the end, teachers and therapists become responsible role models to all children.

As Adler (1959, 1963, 1969) so eloquently portrayed and Glasser (1965, 1984, 1993) concretized: Therapists are teachers (inspirers and role models of responsible living); teachers are therapists (healers and role models of responsible living). The key to understanding the intensity of the new therapeutic relationship magically appears after erasing Freud's original untenable role of the therapist—*too distant, too flat, too robotic, too fearful, too inhuman, too unreal. The Bratters Three suggest a much more interesting, multilayered role for the teacher-therapist: from cool and emotionless mirroring to charismatic, caring, and fully human role modeling of responsible living. Therapists are not the only professionals who must transform themselves. Teachers too must undergo a metamorphosis: from controller to guide, from boss to friend, from neutral observer or vigilant watchdog to passionate advocate, and from keeper of narrow factoids to fully human role model of responsible living.*

In my work as professor, psychologist, family counselor, consultant, and writer, I generally replace the word therapy *with* counseling. *Therapy sounds too intense and psychiatric. Counseling conveys a more user-friendly relationship with a focus on helpful advice. The original meaning of therapy from the Latin* therapia *and the Greek* therapeia *and was to heal by treating medically. A later, more naturalistic meaning was also more benign than the early scientific slant: to heal by getting out into the fresh air and sunshine. The thrust in this chapter is in the direction of using more common sense and fresh air, creating human bonds, and sponsoring responsible choices.*

I will leave further therapy talk alone because the authors are not defining the term within the science of mental disorders. In their day-to-day work with troubled young people at the John Dewey Academy, they have blended the most noble, illuminating, and responsible aspects of the teacher's and the therapist's roles. This compatible union results in an awesome transformation producing a responsible role model who relates to students in curative ways. I invite you to ready yourself for a dynamic and restorative journey.

EMERGENCE OF THE RESPONSIBLE ROLE MODEL

The concept of responsible role model took hold initially in a residential treatment milieu where teachers interacted for prolonged periods of time with children and adolescents. Unable to remain invisible in a live-in setting, therapists and teachers first permitted, then encouraged, students to identify with them. Program administrators encouraged the educators who shared the residence to play out a parental role to children and adolescents whose parents were unavailable to nurture and guide them. Later on, these care givers were able to move easily and naturally from parenting to responsible role modeling.

Creating Community versus One-Upping Patients

Alcoholics Anonymous (AA), a derivative of the Oxford Movement of the 1850s, used the inspiring example from alcoholics in recovery as the quintessential component of the helping process. Still struggling alcoholics could identify with the stronger role models among them and take inspiration from their determination to live sober lives. "We are all in this human condition together" was the message. People agonized in isolation to do the best they could do. When they united their humanity with their brothers and sisters, they experienced a bond of moral support that buoyed them for the battle at sea.

One-Upping Becomes an Art Form. In contrast to this deeply human connection in AA, however, academically trained psychotherapists encountered resistance and even censure for tampering with the treatment role that Freud had defined. Sigmund had decreed that psychoanalysts remain benign observers whose chief task was to help patients become fully aware of their unconscious processes.

Teachers Were There First. Ironically, while teachers developed the concept of responsible role models and were the first professionals to practice this role over much of this century, psychotherapists, who have written about the subject, generally have taken credit for this emphasis. The aims of this chapter are (a) to help teachers learn some new behaviors from psychotherapists and, in so doing, (b) to persuade them to become more effective by becoming more directly and personally involved with their students. Hechinger (1992) urged teachers to recognize the value of relating more humanly.

> Adrift in a desolate and often hostile environment, [youngsters] need adults to whom they can turn with trust and support. . . . The young person must feel that the recommendation is coming from someone who understands his or her emotions and fears, and who truly cares . . . on a personal, not simply a professional level. . . . Adolescents need adults who can be positive role models and mentors. (pp. 27, 53)

Leaders in the field of mental health increasingly and openly have pleaded with therapists, family counselors, clinical social workers, and other psychological specialists to join teachers in becoming responsible role models to clients. This relatively recent development applies especially to therapists working with children and adolescents and is revolutionary in light of Freud's taboo on such a friendly human touch.

Competency Is a Key to Respect. As proposed by Redl and Wattenberg (1959), teaching personnel in residential programs have assumed the awesome parental role, which has been the *sine qua non* for this special breed of educator for many years:

> If one wants to aid a child, it is not always necessary to give him a complete psychoanalysis. A teacher may give a child the affection he needs by helping him to learn. . . . When any youngster needs affection, the simplest way for teachers to administer it is not the honeyed words or sympathetic smiles, but by friendly assistance in learning. . . . For this reason, the skills of a good teacher who can help children find success in learning are as specialized as those of a psychiatrist. . . . Good teaching gives [adolescents] a type of support which they can see as meaning they are liked and which can be accepted. (pp. 206-207)

This chapter, admittedly, is ambitious because the primary message urges therapists and teachers to become responsible role models rather than remaining anonymous, one-up, and distant. Because teachers and therapists can be responsible role models, we will use the terms *role-model* and *helper* interchangeably.

The Adverse Impact of Freud: Therapeutic Neutrality

Until the 1950s, psychoanalytic thought was the predominant method influencing therapists and teachers. Psychological prudes watching those who dared to challenge Freud's sacrosanct "benign observer" edict, often labeled the offenders unprofessional or worse, they insisted that the deviates seek psychoanalytic treatment for their inappropriate countertransference. They were simply showing too much *self,* not to mention blatant kindness, encouragement, and friendship. Knowing the history of psychoanalytic thought will provide better historical perspective of the profound influence Freud has had on psychiatry and psychological practice.

To Be or Not To Be . . . Human. Goldman (1988) wrote, "The personal relationship between patient and therapist in psychoanalytical therapy has . . . been a source of confusion and conflict." Greenson (1967), a practicing psychoanalyst, addressed the conflict between analytic practice and being human.

> All analysts recognize the need for deprivations in the procedure of psychoanalysis; they would agree in principle about the analyst's need to be human. The problem arises, however, in determining what is meant by the term humanness in the analytic situation and how one reconciles this with the principle of deprivation. (p. 213)

Freud's restrictions created great tension for practitioners and, ultimately, his caveats became untenable to those employing alternative therapeutic methods. Conservatively, 90% of therapies are variations or opposites of Freud's psychodynamic posturing. The main difference is the analyst's obsession with pathology and the unconscious, on the one hand, and the alternative focus on hope and human potential to tap inner resources, gain personal strength, and live more effectively.

An Emotionally Disengaged Mirror. Freud (1912) urged the psychoanalyst to "put aside all his feelings" and "The doctor should be opaque to his patients and, like a mirror, should show them nothing but what is shown to him" (p. 115). Remarkably, Carl Rogers (1951, 1980) picked up on this mirroring role in mid-century but emphasized positive regard and empathy more than pathology. Freud (1915) continued this theme when he wrote, "In my opinion . . . we ought not to give up the neutrality towards the patient, which we have acquired through keeping the countertransference in check" (p. 225). In fairness to Freud, therapists who cross the boundary between themselves and those who seek their help lose their perspective and cannot be as helpful. Therapists offer two special services: caring and objectivity. This emotional distance does provide a context for seeing pathways out of the trouble.

Adler Influences Freud . . . for a Change. For all his universalism, Freud warned that the psychoanalytic process could not be effective for all. Significantly, Freud excluded from treatment those persons, especially adolescents, who created crises.

> We cannot avoid taking some patients for treatment who are so helpless and incapable of ordinary life that for them one has to combine analytic with educative influence; and even with the majority, occasions now and then arise in which the physician is bound to take up the position of teacher and mentor. But it must always be done with great caution. (1912, p. 117)

Remaining Neutral about Intimate Matters. Not surprisingly, neutrality in psychoanalytic circles became the therapeutic ideal. Before undergoing his own radical shift in theory, Szasz (1965) counseled the psychoanalyst, "Not to show that you are human, that you care for [the patient]. . . . Your sole responsibility to the patient is to analyze him" (pp. 114-115). Understandably, this treatment ideal of objectivity created dilemmas for those who practiced this mode of psychotherapy. A young psychoanalyst described his ambivalence regarding the code of anonymity when a homosexual patient fantasized his analyst wanting to seduce him. Rather than deny this concern or to offer reassurance to the patient with whom he had become engaged, Glazer analyzed the patient's fears. Not receiving any reassurance agitated the patient who, during a session, opened a box on the analyst's desk. Glazer (1981) reported the incident as follows:

> I clearly remember him smiling and visibly relaxing. Examining the box after the session revealed a love note to me from my fiancee, from whom it had been a gift. I had never looked inside. . . . My unintentional self-disclosure had facilitated the process. (pp. 147-148)

The temptation to react personally and emotionally remains too great to resist. Wouldn't any analyst reasonably try to open a closed box, symbolizing the unconscious, preconscious, and subconscious? (Why Glazer did not open the box remains for the reader to conjecture, or analyze if you will.)

Distancing Can Be Dangerous. Therapeutic neutrality, in fact, may be an epistemological impossibility and, in many critics' minds, is counter-therapeutic. Guntrip (1969) contended that the psychotherapist may need to become "a good object—i.e., a real person (and) a good mother—a role that was absent in childhood to help the individual grow which becomes more important than technique" (p. 132). Guntrip (1969) defined psychoanalytic psychotherapy in these words:

> The provision of a reliable and understanding human relationship of a kind that makes contact with the deeply repressed traumatized child in a way that enables one to become steadily more able to live, in the security of a new real relationship. . . . [It] is a process of interaction, a function of two variables, the personalities of two people working together towards free spontaneous growth. . . . To find a good parent at the start is the basis of psychic health. In its lack, to find a genuine "good object" in one's analyst is both a transference experience and a real life experience. (p. 155)

A Rescuing Urge. This crucial dynamic appears to be either misunderstood or ignored by psychoanalysts. The rescue fantasy of psychotherapists often has been viewed to be pathogenic. Palmer, Harper, and Rivinus (1983) viewed the "adoptive process" in the residential treatment of adolescents as acting out the rescue fantasy by professionals who have not resolved their conflicts or who seek to become parental surrogates due to their unfulfilled needs (p. 183).

The Adolescent in Every Therapist. Shay (1987) attributed the need to rescue to be an unresolved countertransferential need:

> Adolescents in particular may evoke the therapist's need to be idealized because they sound an echo of our teenage years. When we were teens, many of us were concerned with where we stood with our peers, with who would include us or exclude us, and with who,

if anyone, loved us. With our newfound sexual yearnings, many of us had the developmentally appropriate wish to be the object of someone's "crush," to be adored by someone. . . . As we aged, we made peace with these needs as we shaped our identities, found groups to include us, found significant others to love us. . . . The wish to belong, the yearning to be admired, the need to feel loved are frequently revived by our adolescent patients who live these issues passionately every day. And our borderline adolescents may be our most passionate adolescents. To borrow a phrase, "we have met the adolescent and he is us."

If one accepts this notion of an inherent over-identification with adolescent patients, then the countertransference wish to rescue them is readily comprehensible. This process leads to something like the Golden Rule of Countertransference: rescue others as you yourself would have liked to have been rescued. (Shay, 1987, p. 715)

Glenn, Sabot, and Bernstein (1978) warned, "The child analyst who sees parents as neglectful, abusive, or abandoning . . . reacts by wishing to replace . . . 'bad' parents . . . rescue fantasies in which an analyst identifies with an ideal parent and replaces a realistic stance" (p. 401).

Therapist as Parent. Frequently, the psychotherapist assumes the role of positive parent, not to replace the biological family, but instead to provide what Alexander (1948, pp. 286-287) has described to be a "corrective emotional experience." Writing about his experiences in group psychotherapy, Grotjahn (1972) described the personal qualities of the leader:

The therapist is the central figure, symbolizing the parent in all the shades of various transference. His peripheral looseness toward the different members of the group must allow him to perform his duties by being father to one, mother to all, affectionate friend to someone who needs one, disciplinarian to someone who may at that time be working on problems of authority. (pp. 196, 197)

Making Parents Wrong. The potential for abuse exists when the helper competes with the family for control and/or affection of the adolescent, minimizes psychopathology, fantasizes becoming the good parent, or deems parents incapable of changing and hence excludes them from treatment by refusing to work with them. Strupp (1968, p. 198) suggested that one goal of psychotherapy is to offer the adolescent a healthy replacement for a pathogenic family; that is, a "new, if temporary, 'home' from which the patient can venture forth." Grotjahn (1972) suggested that the group psychotherapist

must accept in himself a considerable amount of maternal identification. . . . The therapist's maternal attitude facilitates the experience
of weaning and individuation. The breaking of the mother-infant
symbiosis may amount to an experience of rebirth in the group.
(p. 179)

A few families, however, remain so dysfunctional that severing youngsters'
connections is in their best interest. Still, even such a seriously high level
of conflict and interpersonal dysfunction in a family does not justify the role
model attacking the parents or the family or attempting to compensate for the
gross deprivation by completely replacing one or both parents. The dual urges
to rescue children from their parents by making parents wrong is a very insidious problem that new therapists and teachers must resolve early in their
careers. Over and over again, well-meaning people try to save offspring from
their heritage but, to paraphrase the late Virginia Satir (1988), people who criticize the stock they come from cannot feel good about themselves.

NEGATIVE ROLE MODEL:
PROFOUND IMPLICATIONS FOR PSYCHOTHERAPY

During the 1960s, society witnessed the demise of the nuclear family. The
family has been devastated by desertion, divorce, and death. More children and
adolescents live in single or reconstituted families during the last decade of the
twentieth century than ever before. Stability erodes further when grandparents
leave home to live in adult communities or migrate to warmer climates.

Criminals and Other Negative Heroes

During the 1980s, as Bratter, Bratter and Bratter (1995) asserted, the primary preoccupation was the acquisition of material goods. Predictably, the new
heroes to adolescents now have become those whose earning power is excessive. The most visible males in many communities are drug dealers and criminals. Today's idols personify alienation and anger. The public has elevated
musicians, athletes, and entertainers to a state of nonstop adulation. (One could
argue about athletic heroes being miscategorized—perhaps they could join the
drug dealers and criminal class since so many of them act as highly paid pros-
titutes.)

Quick to recognize the disillusionment and mistrust of adolescents, movies
glorify the anti-hero, the anti-Christ, the misfit, and the mutant. Dalton (1974)

has described James Dean (1931-1955) who, more than any other actor, personified the role of mutant king. Sadly, the enduring heroes and heroines of the adolescent subculture have died from drug overdoses or violent deaths. The music of Sam Cooke (1937-1964), Otis Redding (1941-1967), Brian Jones (1942-1970), Janis Joplin (1943-1970), Jimi Hendrix (1942-1970), Jim Morrison (1943-1971), "Mama" Cass Eliot (1943-1974), and Elvis Presley (1935-1977) are all more popular today, decades after their deaths, than when they lived. The athletes who have been convicted of drug offenses and are dead from drug-related incidents are too numerous to list.

Hungry for Charism: Judicious Self-disclosure

Void of spiritualism and morality, nihilism must be confronted by society before adolescents will be amenable to psychotherapy. Like it or not, as Samorajczyk (1971) contended:

> as uncomfortable as a therapist may feel in the role of therapist-parent, he cannot ignore one of the basic cries for help by the alienated losers. They want to know where the limits are and that someone "gives a damn enough to guide me in my search of what's expected of me. . . ." Uncomfortable or not, a therapist must provide information where it is lacking in order to help someone who is being misled by peer pressures. There are times when he must be persuasive as well as an understanding parent who is the source of sexual identification to . . . adolescents searching for self-definition. (p. 115)

Often a helper must assume a charismatic role. Some adolescents seek parental approbation, encouragement, understanding, acceptance, and/or forgiveness. Others project their hostility, hurt, anger, mistrust, and/or rejection. If a role model is not prepared to be charismatic and to use judicious self-disclosure, a positive treatment alliance probably cannot be forged.

RESPONSIBLE ROLE MODEL:
THE CRUCIAL AND CATALYTIC
INGREDIENT TO FORMAL HELPING

The justification for therapist transparency and vulnerability has been offered by Glasser who urges adult helpers to become more involved with clients by becoming more personal and friendly. Glasser (1965, p. 22) described the personal attributes of a helping person. Therapists must be very responsible people—tough, interested, human, and sensitive. They must be able to fulfill their own needs and willing to discuss some of their own struggles so that clients can see that acting responsibly is possible though sometimes difficult. Neither aloof, superior, nor sacrosanct, they must realize that clients will test what they do, stand for, and value, and they must be prepared to withstand even intense criticism by those they are trying to help. Clients may pick apart every fault and defect. Willing to admit that, like the patient, they are far from perfect, therapists must nevertheless show that people can act responsibly even if it takes great effort.

Therapists as Catalysts

Alcoholics Anonymous (AA) (1939, 1952) was the first to utilize recovered persons in the treatment process to be catalytic, responsible role models who present themselves to alcohol addicted persons as living proof that constructive change is possible. To the organization's credit, AA has extended the responsible role model concept to include sponsorship, which is the most potent form of mentoring. The person who has become responsible—that is, abstinent—encourages the active alcoholic not only to identify but also, more importantly, to begin to believe that sobriety is an attainable goal.

Therapeutic Community (TC)

The residential self-help therapeutic community (TC) that Bratter and Greenfield (1985) described traces its psychotherapeutic origins to Alcoholics Anonymous (AA). This treatment form has been the most effective modality for character disordered addicted adolescents. The difference between AA and the self-help concept developed by a therapeutic community is minor. After establishing a treatment relationship based on identification, the TC uses a confrontational approach that helps the addicted person learn how to become more responsible and productive and, in the process, to unlearn dysfunctional behavior.

More specifically, Bratter (1977a) asserted that the clinical staff of the TC should do the following:

> function as responsible role models who are living proof that creative and constructive personal change is possible. In addition, the staff is prepared to share significant experiences in an effort to identify with and relate to the resident. The staff becomes involved with the resident. Credentialed professionals, in contrast, have been trained to treat symptoms, not to identify with the patient. (p. 166)

Engaging Therapy

In view of the countertransference prohibition that Freud articulated, this type of therapeutic bonding has not been well-received by academically trained mental health workers until recently. No one doubts that children and adolescents gain their unique identities when they interact with adults and their peers. The teacher needs to understand this effect because this dynamic has implications for teaching, especially now when a sense of desperation, disillusionment, insecurity, and frustration causes adolescents to mistrust most adult authority figures. A most inspirational responsible role model who became a mentor and subsequently a trusted friend was Anne Sullivan of the Keller-Sullivan (i.e., Helen Keller and Anne Sullivan) relationship that Lash (1980), Gibson (1956), and Keller (1955) have described. Initially, Sullivan defined and carefully enforced behavioral limits but, by maintaining high expectations for improved behavior, used this remarkable relationship to produce dramatic results in the client. Bratter (1977b), Meichenbaum, Bowers, and Ross (1969), Rosenthal (1973), Rosenthal and Jacobson (1968), and Shaw (1914) have discussed the potency of positive high expectations, perhaps the most neglected aspect of the treatment relationship.

Looking for Ultimate Security: Father

Adolescents continue to search for the Supreme Being and a corresponding sense of security and mission. Thomas Wolfe (1935), the novelist, recognized this adolescent need by cogently summarizing the pervasive quest as the following:

> to find a father, not merely the father of his flesh, not merely the
> lost father of his youth, but the image of a strength and wisdom
> external to his need and superior to his hunger, to which the belief
> and power of his life could be united. (p. 39)

Looking for Mama

Walkenstein (1972) urged her psychiatric colleagues to become *mamas*. Therapists' training and commitment to helping others to help themselves rests on the presupposition that therapists are saner than those whom they seek to help. This assumption recognizes and justifies parental surrogate roles for therapists. No matter how scrupulously a helper attempts to maintain neutrality and anonymity in the therapeutic relationship, students incorporate some of the role model's implicit beliefs and values. By insidious default if nothing else, the social context of a school, a student's own needs, or other relational factor thrusts a teacher into the position of parental surrogate. Jourard (1968) stated that a psychotherapist's judicious self-disclosure can stimulate adolescent growth, exploratory spirit, and positive change. In contrast, the psychoanalyst has been trained to avoid answering personal questions, no matter how legitimate these may be. Tangentially, Breggin (1991) lamented the "Brave New World," which endorses norms that reduce psychiatrists' professional role to prescribing medicine and drastically deemphasizes talking with patients.

> **Dehumanizing Psychiatry.** As the medical and biological wing of the profession (i.e., psychiatry) has taken over, compassionate psychologically oriented psychiatrists have been replaced by biochemists and lab researchers as department heads. Major journals devote nearly all their space to studies on the brains, blood and urine of psychiatric patients—without so much as a passing mention of patients as people with thoughts and feelings relevant to their condition and their recovery. People suffering from what used to be thought of as "neuroses" and "personal problems" are being treated with drugs and shock. Children with problems that once were handled by remedial education or improved parenting are instead being subjected to medical diagnoses, drugs, and hospitals.
>
> Yet the only biochemical imbalances that we can identify with certainty in the brains of psychiatric patients are the ones produced by psychiatric treatment itself. (p. 12)
>
> Depressed people don't tend to hurt themselves when they have a good relationship with a therapist and some hope of improvement. I try to help individuals experience their feelings, to understand the sources of their despair, and to overcome hopelessness, while providing a caring, morale building relationship and guidance toward more effective ways of living. Often this involves the client learning new, more positive values and a more daring, caring approach. (p. 171)

Distinguishing between Honesty and Disrespect

In contrast, therapists working with alienated and angry adolescents often find themselves in an uncomfortable and potentially compromising position when they decline to answer legitimate personal questions. This refusal to relate can provide adolescents with whatever justification they may need to stay apart and to rationalize dishonesty. If counselors are to serve children and adolescents as role models, surely they can answer reasonable questions about their beliefs and personal life. They should answer these legitimate inquiries forthrightly. When adolescents clearly intend to use their personal queries to discredit adult authority by becoming intrusive or manipulative, therapists should respond to the confrontation in kind. To overlook the dishonesty is to default on the demands of role modeling. The counselor must use common sense in distinguishing between adolescents' sincere desire for information and their attempt to hurt or humiliate the role model. Naturally, role models need to refrain from answering questions involving immoral or illicit acts not only to avoid self-incrimination, but also to avoid encouraging adolescents to engage in similar self-destructive behaviors.

Personal Disclosures

After counselors have formed reasonably strong relationships with their clients, they can respond to sincere questions about their own personal experience with drugs by helping their adolescent clients to identify and internalize important data. Discussing current illicit activity with clients is unethical because such disclosures by adult authorities place adolescents in untenable positions. Since the authors have never used dangerous drugs, this question is moot for them. What if adolescents challenge the role model's credibility and ability to understand the impact of drugs? Helpers may mention appropriately that they too have personal feelings and face the same pressures as adolescents confront. If role models have abused drugs in the past and/or have been dependent on illegal substances, they can relate honestly by stressing the mistakes they committed earlier in their lives when they were impulsive and immature. They can say, "I hope you do not need to be as stupid and self-destructive as I have been when I was your age." They also may say, "I may be able to help you save yourself much grief by telling you about these errors of my youth."

Being transparent at appropriate times conveys a most potent therapeutic message: existence frequently can be stressful and unpleasant, but individuals can control their personal responses. Painful and difficult as restraint may be, young people can remain responsive and responsible. Rachman (1975) has discussed judicious self-disclosure as it pertains to conducting adolescent group psychotherapy. Expecting adolescents to assume the role of the helper's treatment agent or to offer support is inappropriate, unfair, and unethical. Such a move would be unethical as the client then would experience a dual relationship with a therapist turned patient. The therapeutic alliance can be reciprocal but cannot be predicated on equality. In the absence of therapeutic issues, the helper should terminate the relationship. Easson (1976) suggested, in a few cases, that renegotiating a relationship of friendship may be acceptable when manipulation and exploitation are not present. We prefer a more purist view of this, however, and suggest maintaining a professional relationship. In any case, the role model remains the responsible leader until the age factor can be neutralized through the passage of many years.

At times, helpers cannot conceal current realities, so remaining anonymous is impossible. A pregnant female, for example, inevitably will need to face up to this experience and manage the consequences of her condition. Similarly, one author of this chapter confronted a medical emergency involving involuntary hospitalization that absolutely prevented him from conducting "business as usual."

One Author's Personal Aside

I knew I needed triple bypass surgery requiring an absence of at least two months. I decided eliciting the reactions from the group before going to the hospital would be more beneficial to me and the community rather than waiting until after the ordeal to relate the terrifying experience of facing the trauma of major surgery alone. When we notified the adolescents, they were frightened because they needed to view me as invincible. Some identified with me as being unjustly victimized by conditions beyond my control. I explained with my best logic that my poor eating habits and continual avoidance of daily exercise had caused occlusions in my arteries. Rather than complaining that I had been unfairly treated, I publicly accepted full responsibility for creating the conditions that required surgery. In so doing, I helped group members recognize they could control their self-destructive behavior by conscious choice. This type of unavoidable self-disclosure is not controversial in any way. Maneuvering the group to offer me special sympathy or support, however, would have been countertherapeutic because I would have burdened them inappropriately.

To establish a therapeutic rapport with gifted, angry, and alienated adolescents, helpers need to accept their burden to relate honestly in order to promote trust and respect. The role model must have the courage of personal convictions to communicate these beliefs rationally. Perhaps, in the final analysis, to choose to be a responsible role model requires courage and personal integrity, which Bratter, Bratter, Fiske, and Steiner (1991) described as five dimensions:

1. Courage to be human, to risk, and to invest in students when the continually hurt and disappoint those who care for them
2. Courage to be innovative and creative to devise persuasive strategies that practically compel students to want to change
3. Courage to insist that adolescents perform to the best of their personal ability
4. Courage to continue to believe passionately that anyone can improve personal performance rather than to accept excuses for continued mediocrity or failure
5. Courage never to give up, knowing that each individual is capable of achieving success and can become a worthwhile person by becoming more responsible, honest, and decent. (p. 15)

RESPONSIBLE ROLE MODEL'S CONTRIBUTIONS TO COUNSELING

The role model explicitly communicates a concern with the "bottom line"—that is, accountability and productivity, which are reasonable intermediate goals of any relationship. Demanding the best from students is a primary ingredient of a caring relationship. Mayeroff (1971) has written, "To care for another person, in the most significant sense, is to help him grow and actualize himself" (p. 1).

As usual, Glasser (1972) was even more concrete:

> Because [students] are lonely, they need involvement with educators who are warm and personal and who will work with their behavior in the present. They need teachers who will encourage them to make a value judgment of their behavior rather than preach (at them) or dictate; teachers who will help them plan better behavior and who will expect a commitment from students that they will do as they have planned. They need teachers who will not excuse them when they fail their commitments, but who will work with them again and again as they commit and recommit until they finally learn to fulfill a commitment. When they *learn* to do so, they no longer are lonely; they gain maturity, respect, love and a successful identity. (p. 24)

Fromm (1956) added the crucial dimension of caring when he answered a rhetorical question that he had posed for readers to ponder:

> What does one person give to another? He gives of . . . that which is alive in him; he gives him of his joy, of his interest, of his understanding, of his knowledge, of his humor, of his sadness—of all expressions and manifestations of that which is alive in him. In thus giving of his life, he enriches the other person, he enhances the other's sense of aliveness by enhancing his own sense of aliveness. He does not give in order to receive; giving is in itself exquisite joy. But in giving, he cannot help receiving that which is given back to him. Giving implies making the other person a giver also and they both share in the joy of what they have brought to life (together). (p. 25)

Counselor as a Person

Responsible role models have a personal imperative to establish a clear and congruent personal identity. Students can assess the authenticity of their helpers' character through interacting with them and communicating their moral and social integrity. Erik Erikson (1968) described the correlation between adolescents' development of their ego identity and expressions of social integrity. Fromm (1968) added an important dimension with his suggestion that "Integrity means a willingness not to violate one's identity" (p. 87). In describing the function of the John Dewey Academy, Bratter, Bratter, and Radda (1989) stated that the staff "Attempts to instill principles of moral conduct by educating the student to become responsible, trustworthy, and accountable for their personal acts" (p. 53). Glasser (1972) asserted:

> Students are responsible for fulfilling their needs, they are responsible for their behavior, they are not mentally ill, but are making bad choices when their behavior is [self-destructive]; nevertheless they can't make better choices, more responsible choices, unless they are strongly involved with those who can. In education, involvement may start with one person, be he teacher, counselor, or administrator. . . . Both in psychiatry and in school, teachers and therapists too often stand aloof from children; they do not get emotionally involved; they are not warm, personal and interested; they do not reveal themselves as human beings so that children can identify with them. Thus they fail to alleviate the loneliness of the many children who need human warmth so desperately. Only in a school where the teacher and student are involved with each other and equally involved with the curriculum through thinking and problem solving does education flourish—an education that prepares students to live successfully in the world. (p. 19)

Moral Strength Comes from Living Well. The John Dewey Academy offers a pragmatic education where students learn how to love and be loved, how to respect others and to gain their respect, how to give and to receive help, how to trust and be trustworthy, and, most importantly, how to live a good, decent, moral, and responsible life. Bratter, Bratter, and Bratter (1995) suggested the goal of psychotherapy with adolescents is to help them gain or regain their self-respect by doing the right thing for the right reasons. Erikson (1963) wrote that children need to feel trust that caregivers can nurture with "the assured reliance on another's integrity" (pp. 268-269). Students learn when (a) a meaningful relatedness and respect exists between themselves and their responsible role models, (b) their parental surrogate takes on a charismatic role, and (c) the role model places legitimate and humane demands on the students to do the very best that they can do.

Helper's Traits. The helper needs to be (a) honest and transparent so students can respect, trust, and admire this person; (b) caring, optimistic, and passionate while concurrently being assertive, demanding, and direct; (c) definite by expressing personal values and opinions; and (d) willing to develop a relationship predicated upon reciprocity, sharing, and caring so that students can have a meaningful dialogue. All of these traits forge a substantive relationship within which students can begin to develop their unique identities. Glasser (1993) defined this relationship between teacher and students in a school of quality.

CONCLUSION: A PLEA AND A WARNING

Fromm-Reichman (1948) affirmed the judicious sharing of personal values in psychotherapy. By implication, teachers may put themselves on the line in the same personal way. She wrote

> It is not correct to say there is no inherent set of values concerned with the goals of psychotherapy. . . . The psychiatrist should not be afraid of being aware of these standards which guide him in this therapeutic dealings with patients, no matter how eager he may be to establish his personal evaluational neutrality. (p. 269)

Helping Involves Risk

By extending themselves to depressed and demoralized adolescents, adult authority figures give students a chance to relate to strong individuals with whom they can identify. Responsible role models can relate to personal painful past mistakes, which include failure and rejection, to convince adolescents that no one realistically wins and succeeds all the time. Helpers must use self-disclosure exclusively to benefit adolescents and not as a means of gratifying themselves. Counselors are not self-centered. Exhibitionists seek personal attention and benefits. They need to examine and eliminate their grandiose tendencies. Role models must keep in mind that acknowledging any personal experiences that they now regret may involve risk because adolescents are adept at confronting personal inconsistencies of their significant others. Helpers should read any lingering discomfort following personal disclosure as an indication that such expressions were probably counter-therapeutic. Disclosures by a counselor are certainly harmful if this information gives students leverage with their helpers to behave irresponsibly.

Modeling, Not Molding

Responsible role models need to have the strength and patience to permit students to challenge and criticize their personal values. They also must relate so rationally and realistically to students that young people not only will clarify their issues but also can begin to determine solutions in the process of internalizing their developing beliefs. Finally, responsible role models need to recognize that, under some circumstances, adolescents will not heed advice or adopt personal values, no matter how compelling the message or messenger. Adolescents can gain invaluable insights when adults show that they can relate to painful and depressing events that substantiate their resilience and determination to remain responsible through adversity and failure.

Baring One's Heart

The male author (i.e., T. Bratter) elected to disclose a painful and tragic experience when requested to deliver a eulogy for a young adult who had a fatal driving accident while intoxicated. This story served to dramatize the consequences of substance abuse and to personalize the despair of those who survive. Eliciting sympathy, admiration, and support was not the goal. Neither did he seek to glorify his position of being invited to officiate at a funeral. Instead, he emphasized the issue of personal obligation. Rejecting this request to speak would have been easier than subjecting himself to pain. The speaker rebuffed those adolescents who misunderstood the speaker's message and tried to become sympathetic and supportive. His harsh response was the following:

> Do not pity me. I have no guilt. I did my best to prevent Michael from killing himself. Imagine how his family and friends feel. Imagine how your parents would feel if this happened to you. . . . Their sense of loss. Their sense of impotence. . . . Their grief. . . . Their rage at the waste and injustice.

The speaker made no attempt to turn a difficult eulogy into a *cause celebre* by glorifying mental toughness. He only shared a painful experience, which he could more easily have withheld. The adolescents in attendance learned about obligation and took away an explicit antidrug message because, in many ways, the deceased young man, Michael, was similar to them.

PRIVILEGE OF COUNSELING AND TEACHING

Undeniably, the mistrust and disrespect for the therapist and teacher, both as a technician and person, is at its zenith during the 1990s. This flagrant disregard has profound implications for the future of both fields. Kafka (1915) wrote a short story, *Metamorphosis,* in which the protagonist who failed to actualize his humanity was turned into a cockroach. All teachers and psychotherapists should take these ominous warnings seriously. Perhaps helpers who fail to become responsible role models who inspire their clients to engage in active learning and thinking positively about change deserve to become symbolic cockroaches.

Those who dismissed Skinner (1984) as too radical or cynical when he proposed that teaching machines could educate learners of all ages obviously did not comprehend the legitimacy of his proposition. If therapists fail to provide therapy and teachers fail to teach, why *not* replace their disservice with suitable machines? Industry has learned the lesson of human obsolescence. Welding and screwing robots have replaced inefficient assembly line workers. The elevator operator is extinct (except in one nostalgic manager's operation in a downtown Hong Kong YMCA) because technology has automated elevators. Librarians face extinction because of the Internet and the computer terminal. Telephones are less personal by the day. Unless teachers recognize their mandate to assert their humanness and to relate to students fighting relentlessly for their own identify, classrooms and offices of psychotherapy in the twenty-first century may contain neither teachers nor therapists, only machines. The choice is ours: Risk obsolescence or become human!

BIBLIOGRAPHY

Bratter, T. E. (1976). The Three 'R's' of educational reform. In A. Bassin, T. E. Bratter, & R. L. Ration (Eds.), *The reality therapy reader: A survey of the works of William Glasser*. New York: Harper & Row.

Bratter, T. E. (1980). Educating the uneducable: The little 'ole' red schoolhouse with bars in the concrete jungle. *Journal of Offender Counseling, 4,* 95-108.

Bratter, T. E., Bratter, E. P., Radda, H. T., & Greenfield, L. J. (1986). The evolution of the responsible role model. In A. Acampora & E. Nebeikof (Eds.), *Proceedings of the Ninth World Conference of Therapeutic Communities.* San Francisco: Abacus Printing.

Glasser, W. (1969). *Schools without failure.* New York: Harper & Row.

Glasser, W. (1990). The John Dewey Academy: A residential college preparatory high school—A dialogue with Tom Bratter. *Journal of Counseling and Development, 68,* 582-585.

Glasser, W. (1992). *The quality school: Managing students without coercion.* New York: Harper & Row.

REFERENCES

Adler, A. (1959). *Understanding human nature.* New York: Premier Books.

Adler, A. (1963). *The practice and theory of individual psychology.* Patterson, NJ: Littlefield, Adams.

Adler, A. (1969). *The science of living.* New York: Doubleday Anchor Books.

Alcoholics Anonymous. (1932). *Alcoholics anonymous.* New York: Alcoholics Anonymous World Services.

Alcoholics Anonymous. (1952). *Twelve steps and twelve traditions.* New York: Alcoholics Anonymous World Services.

Alexander, F. (1948). *Fundamentals of psychoanalysis.* New York: W. W. Norton.

Bratter, B. I., Bratter, T. E., Fiske, R., & Steiner, K. M. (1991). The effective education professional: Politician, psychologist, philosopher, professor, and parent. *Journal of Humanistic Education and Development, 30,* 4-18.

Bratter, C. J., Bratter, B. I., & Bratter, T. E. (1995). Beyond reality: The need to (re)gain self-respect. *Psychotherapy: Theory, Research & Practice, 32,* 53-59.

Bratter, T. E. (1977a). Confrontation groups: The therapeutic community's gift to psychotherapy. In P. Vamos & J. J. Devlin (Eds.), *Proceedings of the First World Conference on Therapeutic Communities* (pp. 164-174). Montreal, Canada: Portage Press.

Bratter, T. E. (1977b). The positive self-fulfilling prophesy of reality therapy. *Together: Journal of the Association for Specialists in Group Work, 2,* 60-75.

Bratter, T. E., Bratter, B. I., & Radda, H. T. (1989). The John Dewey Academy: A pragmatic, moral, thinking curriculum in a drug-free environment. *The Journal of Reality Therapy, VIII,* 52-60.

Bratter, T. E., & Greenfield, L. J. (1985). Toward a theory of realistic, relevant, pragmatic education: Challenges and concerns for the 1980's and 1990's. In J. Corelli (Ed.), *Proceedings of the Eighth World Conference on Therapeutic Communities.* Rome, Italy: Il Centro Press.

Breggin, P. R. (1991). *Toxic psychiatry: Why therapy, empathy, and love must replace the drugs, electroshock, and biochemical theories of the "new psychiatry."* New York: St. Martin's Press.

Dalton, D. (1974). *James Dean: The mutant king.* San Francisco: Straight Arrow Books.

Easson, W. M. (1976). Patient and therapist after termination of psychotherapy. In A. Bassin, T. E. Bratter, & R. L. Rachin (Eds.), *The reality therapy reader* (pp. 144-153). New York: Harper & Row.

Erikson, E. H. (1963). *Childhood and society.* New York: W. W. Norton.

Erikson, E. H. (1968). *Identify, youth and crises.* New York: W. W. Norton.

Freud, S. (1912). *Recommendations to physicians practicing psychoanalysis* (standard ed., vol. 12). London: Hogarth Press.

Freud, S. (1915). *Observations on transference-love* (standard ed., vol. 12). London: Hogarth Press.

Fromm, E. (1956). *The art of loving.* New York: Harper & Brothers.

Fromm, E. (1968). *The revolution of hope.* New York: Bantam Books.

Fromm-Reichman, F. (1948). Notes on the development of treatment of schizophrenics by psychoanalytic psychotherapy. *Journal of Psychiatry, 11,* 263-273.

Gibson, W. (1956). *The miracle worker.* New York: Bantam Books.

Glasser, W. (1965). *Reality therapy: A new approach to psychiatry.* New York: Harper & Row.

Glasser, W. (1972). *The identity society.* New York: Harper & Row.

Glasser, W. (1984). *Control theory.* New York: Harper & Row.

Glasser, W. (1993). *The quality school teacher.* New York: HarperCollins.

Glazer, M. (1981). Anonymity reconsidered. *Journal of Contemporary Psychotherapy, 12,* 143-149.

Glenn, J., Sabot, L. M., & Bernstein, I. (1978). The role of parents in child analysis. In J. Glenn (Ed.), *Child analysis and therapy.* New York: Jason Aronson.

Goldman, S. B. (1988). To be or not to be a real object: Monitoring the therapeutic relationship. *Journal of Contemporary Psychotherapy, 18,* 160-166.

Greenson, R. (1967). *The technique and practice of psychoanalysis.* New York: International Universities Press.

Grotjahn, M. (1972). The qualities of the group therapist. In H. I. Kaplan & B. J. Sadock (Eds.), *New models for group psychotherapy.* New York: E. P. Dutton.

Guntrip, H. (1969). *Schizoid phenomena, object relations and the self.* New York: International Universities Press.

Hechinger, F. (1992). *Fate choices: Healthy youth for the 21st century.* New York: Hill & Wang.

Jourard, S. M. (1968). *Disclosing man to himself.* New York: Van Nostrand Reinhold.

Kafka, F. (1961). Metamorphosis, judgment day, 1915. In F. Kafka, *The penal colony: Stories and short pieces.* New York: Schocken Books.

Keller, H. (1955). *Teacher: Anne Sullivan Macy.* New York: Doubleday.

Lash, J. P. (1980). *Helen and teacher: The story of Helen Keller and Anne Sullivan Macy.* New York: Delacorte Press.

Mayeroff, M. (1971). *On caring.* New York: Harper & Row.

Meichenbaum, D. K., Bowers, K., & Ross, R. (1969). A behavioral analysis of teacher expectancy effect. *Journal of Personalized and Social Psychology, 13,* 306-316.

Palmer, G., Harper, G., & Rivinus, T. (1983). The "adoptive process" in the inpatient treatment of children and adolescents. *Journal of the American Academy of Child Psychiatry, 22,*178-189.

Rachman, A. W. (1975). *Identity group psychotherapy with adolescents.* Springfield, IL: Charles C. Thomas.

Redl, F., & Wattenberg, W. W. (1959). *Mental hygiene in teaching.* New York: Harcourt & Brace.

Rogers, C. (1951). *Client-centered therapy.* Boston: Houghton-Mifflin.

Rogers, C. (1980). *A way of being.* Boston: Houghton-Mifflin.

Rosenthal, R. (1973). *The Pygmalion effect lives. Psychology Today, 7,* 56-62.

Rosenthal, R., & Jacobson, L. (1968). *Pygmalion in the classroom: Teacher expectation and pupils' intellectual development.* New York: Holt.

Samorajczyk, J. (1971). The psychotherapist as a meaningful parental figure with alienated adolescents. *American Journal of Psychotherapy, XXV,* 110-116.

Satir, V. (1988). *The new people making.* Palo Alto, CA: Science & Behavior Books.

Shaw, G. B. (1914). *Pygmalion.* New York: Brentano's.

Shay, J. J. (1987). The wish to do psychotherapy with borderline adolescents— and other common errors. *Psychotherapy: Theory, Research & Practice, 24,* 712-719.

Skinner, B. F. (1984). The shame of American education. *The American Psychologist, 39,* 946-949.

Strupp, H. H. (1968). Psychoanalytic therapy of the individual. In J. Marmor (Ed.), *Modern psychoanalysis: New dimensions and perspectives.* New York: Basic Books.

Szasz, T. S. (1965). *The ethics of psychoanalysis: The theory and method of autonomous psychotherapy.* New York: Basic Books.

Walkenstein, E. (1972). *Beyond the couch: A psychiatrist's new therapy of contact, risk, and involvement.* New York: Crown Publishers.

Wolfe, T. (1935). *The story of a novel.* New York: Charles Scribner's Sons.

PART II
CRISES AND SOLUTIONS—
PERSONAL TRAUMAS

HANDLING PERSONAL PROBLEMS: SHOWING FEAR, TEARS, INACTIVITY, APATHY, IMPULSIVITY, AND TRUANCY

Larry L. Palmatier

Editor's Note

In this chapter, I describe a series of common misbehaviors and give a framework for helping students resolve their own troubles. The principles within the framework follow, of course, the main choice theory and reality therapy ideas that run throughout this book. After a while, readers will know how to approach almost any problem: be supportive and understanding of a hurting child; remind yourself that you cannot make others do anything regardless of their age; pinpoint the goals the students have in mind; ask self-evaluative questions; and, finally, have the students examine their overarching degree of happiness as they decide whether to plan more responsible behavior to get what they want.

CRISES ARE OFTEN PREDICTABLE

As with most human behavior, a problem usually starts small and grows with time. Except for sudden tragic accidents or a catastrophic event as a brain aneurysm, people usually notice their pressures becoming critical only gradually. Overworked teachers report that they necessarily give the most attention to the students whose troublesome behavior bursts out as a crisis that they cannot ignore. Sometimes a crisis *does* erupt spontaneously, but far more commonly, little warning signs do appear earlier in the form of personal problems that an alert teacher or counselor can detect and resolve at a more primitive stage. This chapter concerns "nipping these personal problems in the bud" before they get out of control and create chaos.

I will discuss ways of detecting and coping with a number of the most common danger signs of personal trouble: choosing tears and sadness, angering and acting aggressively, entertaining apathy and passivity, displaying an impulsive style, depressing emotions and choosing loneliness, fearing, and advertising physical problems such as body odor. Any of these problems can show up in schoolchildren of any age, although some problems and their outward symptoms are more common at certain ages and grades. A second-grader, for example, is a lot less likely to suffer social problems from severe acne than someone in grade six or seven. With the right kind of practical help, though, most troubled sixth-graders might have resolved their problems much more easily back in the third grade.

Most of this discussion applies equally to teachers and counselors. True, almost all the strategies I suggest are counseling strategies and were developed as such but, based on my own classroom teaching experience and my consulting with teachers about these strategies, I believe teacher can profit from most of these examples. Classroom teachers literally can bypass avoidable traumas. Indeed, the teacher on the scene is very often in the best position to spot the earliest signs of problems and head them off, perhaps calling in a counselor or administrator when needed. After all, everybody is in the trenches together. Those not burdened by the direct emotional impact of children's various stressors may have a better vantage point and more emotional flexibility to assist youngsters with their personal pangs.

Unfortunately, every possible problem cannot appear in this one chapter, but you will see how choice theory principles apply to most personal problems. Keep in mind that *only one psychological problem exists* anyway: people, of any age, do not have what they want. The premise is that teachers not only must teach students various school subjects but also must guide young people in learning to behave responsibly. When it comes to coaching about living skills, as the Bratters eloquently stated in chapter 5, teachers join counselors in the task of showing students how they can get what they want responsibly.

BEHAVIORAL METHODS VERSUS CHOICE THEORY

The thrust in this chapter for defining and resolving trouble in the classroom is choice theory and reality therapy, an *inside out* approach. The emphasis in this chapter is on *personal* difficulties. *Interpersonal problems* and solutions begin in chapter 12. The choice theory ideas here represent a sharp contrast to one of the most common methods found in schools, behavioral techniques (Lazarus, 1976; Catania & Harnad, 1988). Operant conditioning and behavior modification may work as interim tactics, but, for the most part, these tools represent *outside in* applications. Somebody is doing something to someone else—a sharp contrast to inviting students to identify their goals, pull some of their own strings, and shift their gears themselves. Even the behavioral technique of praising can backfire and lead to less of what teachers would like students to do at school (Kohn, 1993).

Critique of Behavioral Therapy

Strictly speaking, operant conditioning and behavior modification are *proactive* models (Catania & Harnad, 1988)—contrary to popular interpretation. Passive creatures do not lie around waiting for selected environmental stimuli to bombard them. Many professionals misunderstand the stimulus-response viewpoint and behavioral practitioners do little to clarify and sell their notions. Many critics believe that, by adamantly rejecting the mental aspects of human behavior and retaining most of Skinner's original mechanistic language, behavioral "shapers" merrily maintain the long established ritual of shooting themselves in the foot with their robotic jargon, cognition-devoid explanations, and packaging that many neophytes find alien.

Teachers often report four problems with behavioral methods:

1. The decision about what is wrong and what ought to be done comes from the behavior modifier and not the student. Teachers holding these reservations agree with Glasser that, with some guidance, students ought to modify their own behavior without coercion.
2. In gathering baseline data and intermittently reinforcing students'

behavior, teachers automatically carry too much logistical responsibility for monitoring and following up with trouble makers.
3. Some of the tools in a behaviorist's arsenal are aversive and punitive.
4. Teachers object to Skinner's mechanistic jargon: "the organism responds to environmental stimuli," "shaping through successive approximations," "intermittent reinforcement," and "manipulating the social contingencies."

On the other hand, every approach uses a specialized jargon; behavioral contingency managers are more often than not kind and friendly human beings, and few therapeutic methods are as rigidly empirical in their methodologies. The counter charge to the latter claim that Skinnerians rely exclusively on data is that the outcomes they tout are most often narrow explanations about relatively insignificant topics. Time on task is a good example of one such finding. Students who sit at their desks staring at their sheets of teacher-assigned material usually show fewer disruptive classroom behaviors. Philosophically, this way of thinking about teaching and learning runs counter to choice theory, which envisions students as having their own cognitive maps, their own sense of what is good for them, and their own inherent need to self-evaluate on a continuing basis. Needless to say, this book is about a choice theory philosophy and the interactive practices that accompany such a value system. For a powerful critique of Skinner's experiments with animals and people, see the writings of Kohn (1993), Glasser (1984), and Powers (1973, 1992).

Choice Theory: Students Taking Responsible Control

Choice theory has its own jargon as all counseling models do; however, teachers who learn Glasser's version of choice theory almost automatically reject operant conditioning. Choice theory or *responsible choice theory* places personal accountability directly on the students' shoulders. Teachers in a quality school do not even try to manipulate environmental reinforcers to control their students; instead, they remove the barriers that inhibit students from controlling their own behavior. Such teachers work hard at conveying friendliness and using normal English terms: "If you could have whatever you want—without interfering with anyone else's rights—what would that be?" "What are you doing?" "How is this action (e.g., wandering around or calling another student a derogatory name) helping you get what you want?" "Is what you are doing taking you in the direction that you want to go?" "How happy are you?"

Before discussing any specific problems and solutions, let's look at some general information and communication concepts as these apply to students' personal problems. In essence: how does a student communicate the first signs of a problem? Equally important, how can *you* let that student know that help is at hand?

COMMUNICATION THEORY:
SENDER, RECEIVER, MESSAGE, CONTEXT

Every human informational exchange, verbal or nonverbal, contains at least four components: a sender, a receiver, a message, and a context. *Someone* says *something* to *someone* in a particular *context* (Haley, 1963, p. 89). Human communication carries just as much potential for misunderstanding as for understanding because messages of any value usually contain multiple referents that can throw us off the track and mask a speaker's intentions. A discrete message that refers to only one concrete object or fact is a literal or "digital" communication. Messages that deal with multiple interpersonal possibilities, interlocking relationships, and the factors that maintain problems are "analogical" or figurative (Liddle, Breunlin, & Schwartz, 1988).

We Relate to Others Only Through Communication

We use words to name specific objects and we call this arbitrary verbal labeling *digital communication.* All of nonverbal communication that alludes to relationships and always includes multiple possible referents, we call *analogical communication* (Watzlawick, Beavin Bavelas, & Jackson, 1967, pp. 60-65). We are always simultaneously communicating both content and emotional impact on others. Although everyone wants to know the facts, the part of our interpersonal links that makes life most interesting (and often confusing) is the relationship component. Lovers and mathematicians (two distinct groups) especially enjoy analogical or multi-referent communication.

Simple and Complex Messages. Beier and Young (1984, pp. 11-16) has suggested two types of messages in interpersonal communication: simple and complex. *Simple messages* are literal and obvious and speakers are fully aware of their intent. They are not trying intentionally to code messages to include hidden contextual and nonverbal cues that they design to create an emotional climate within a listener. Advertisers work on the hidden part. An example of a simple message is "Please pass the pepper."

Persuading and Agitating. *Complex messages,* on the other hand, may be persuasive or evocative—the former being a conscious attempt by the sender to include subtle contextual and nonverbal cues in order to invite the receiver to answer in a certain way. Everyday examples of persuasion include sending flowers, offering to do someone a favor, or serving chicken soup. A *persuasive message* is designed to constrict the emotional climate of the other person and invite the receiver to agree with the sender or do what the sender has in mind. In common parlance, this method is manipulative, as the sender tries to get others to comply. We all send these persuasive messages much of the time. Ministers use these, as do parents, counselors, teachers, and politicians. In the *evoking message,* senders refuse to admit their manipulative methods, but, nevertheless, they still are pushing a receiver to respond in a specified manner.

An example of an evoking message is an overt signal that depressed people convey that they do not want to be lonely, coupled with subtle cues that everyone should stay away from them. The good news is that communication about relationships makes our lives richer and far more interesting than static finger pointing at chairs and tables. The bad news is that the multiple possibilities within any relationship guarantee that we may distort everyday messages in a thousand ways. We process meanings through our subjective perceptual system, which includes our valuing filters that add emotional tints. Our ultimate interpretation depends on the intentions and awareness of a sender, the perception of a receiver, the diverse interpretations in any message that inherently contains multiple possible meanings, and our special decoding according to the context.

Context Is Everything

When sports fans shout, "Kill 'em" at a professional football game, they mean something quite different from a crowd of furious citizens, shouting the same words while armed with ropes and clubs as they await a mass murderer's plane to land. How about a mother yelling, "Kill 'em," as she freaks out in front of her children, who, armed with a can of bug spray, are frantically running around the kitchen, trying to gun down a cockroach. In therapy, we often can help someone merely by changing the context in which they relate or communicate (O'Hanlon & Wilks, 1987).

Practical Example of Recontextualizing. Every day a mother drives to school to pick up her fourth-grade son, Homer. As he climbs into the family car, he begins reciting horror stories about the number of warnings and detentions he was assigned during the day. His mother automatically tenses up and shows him anxious looks. For months the daily interaction unfolds with little or no variation. If Mother decides to make her contacts with Son more pleasant, she simply could modify the context of the problem pattern by interrupting the routine and breaking up the "fixed action pattern" between them (Beier & Young, 1984, p. 44). One way to break the cycle, for example, is for mom to decree that she is not interested in hearing the boy's bad news as the two of them drive off from school at day's end. She could suggest instead that he save his tales of trouble until later and try very hard to frighten both Mother and Dad at the evening meal. In this new context, the boy cannot easily hold his mother emotional hostage, and soon he will behave differently in relation to the problem.

RELATING DESTRUCTIVELY: "REFUSING" TO CONNECT AND AFFIRM

Fortunately, in spite of its apparent complexity, we can simplify the broad field of communication theory and still capture its essence in four elements: sender, receiver, message, and context. We also can typify communication *breakdowns* and even categorize four simple ways that interpersonal communication goes astray, following the human validation model of Satir (1988). As sender, people can invalidate or deprecate themselves and play the *placater*. Invalidating another while sending a message converts a sender into a *blamer*. Ignoring or discounting any emotional content in the message makes the sender an *intellectual computer* who overrationalizes and fails to relate humanly. Finally, the worst communicative dysfunction—*distracting* and refusing to acknowledge any interpersonal relationship—invalidates the context of any human connection and conveys to children a fundamental statement: "In my mind, you do not exist."

A Family Example

Suppose you have a student in your classroom who keeps to himself to a disturbing degree. Hearing an extreme but actual story about such a boy may offer some fresh perspective for understanding some withdrawn youngsters. One family came to a training clinic for counseling because of problems with their two troubled teenage sons. The woman was unhappy and felt that she was bearing too much of the burden of the marital relationship. Because she lacked a full perspective to see just how dreadful her status had become, she did not realize that she was "dying on the vine." Even though both boys showed signs of confusion and stress, her immediate driving concern was the welfare of her 15-year-old boy, who already had made a serious attempt at suicide. In a session with only the husband and wife, the highly trained counselor struggled with the man's sullen hostility that heated up as the meeting progressed. He not only was openly aggressive in his distancing style but also refused contact with anyone. He intended to exude relationally neutral messages. His sons and wife could have worked with a hostility dance much more easily than with his indifferent refusal to contact anyone. More than either his older brother or his mother, the 15-year-old son tuned into the father's main cue: "In my mind, you do not exist." The boy took that statement to heart and expressed his loyalty to his father by responding in suicidal gestures, "Okay, Dad, I won't—exist, that is."

In a briefing after the session, the therapist explained to the training group that the husband clearly was trying to refuse all relationships—marital, paternal, and even therapeutic. His communication was an attempt to evoke frustration and fury in the therapist. The lethal game was alive and *unwell,* and the therapist-trainer led the brainstorming to plan a more aggressive intervention to rebuild a communicative pattern that was destroying all the family's relationships. Could the family rediscover wholeness? For therapy to be effective, any intervention had to touch the father, who communicatively had "committed suicide" already and was signaling to family members that he was dead to all three of them. The 15-year-old had tuned in and concluded that he could relate to his father only by sacrificing himself. In this example, one can see that suicide is at least a three-person act. The reality therapy question at that point would be to the mother: "Do you think staying in this frozen wasteland of a relationship will work to your general happiness or your sons' welfare?"

This commentary on the counseling session may or may not be an accurate account. The analysis differs from a psychodynamic interpretation by keeping the focus on behavioral outcomes. What are the effects of the man's style of communicating and the family's attempt to relate in these hog-tying double binds? Wouldn't anyone want to climb out of a cesspool, once they realized that is what they had? What is valid here is that the above description of the family's interactive pattern is completely plausible, links to the choice theory notion that all behavior is purposeful, and will cause no damage if the scenario turns out to be inaccurate.

Aloofing. Refusing human contact at either end—sender or receiver—can have the direst effects on others, for denying a relationship turns people into socially isolated nobodies. Parents who do this can make their children want to fight, run away, hide, or erase themselves in compliance with the parents' desperate messages, sometimes overtly stated as "I wish you kids had never been born." In her lectures, Satir used to call these communication games "lethal." Studying the tragic effects of this harsh process was the preliminary double bind work on schizophrenia in the 1950s by the Gregory Bateson group at MRI, the Mental Research Institute, in Palo Alto, California (Bateson, Jackson,

Haley, & Weakland, 1956). Parents who pretend to be attentively present for children and then refuse any level of connection literally can drive children crazy. The effect on strong adults who already have developed their psychological inner ears can be unbalancing but is probably not as destructive. A classic example of a man who could not connect was Jack Nicholson's character in *Five Easy Pieces*, stunning his female companion with his sudden disappearance from a truck stop and leaving his "immediate other" thinking the breakup was all her fault.

THREE PROBLEM SETTINGS: SCHOOL, HOME AND SCHOOL, HOME

The first task of a counselor working in a school, or a teacher for that matter, is to determine the *context* of the problem at hand. No personal or interpersonal problem ever exists in a human vacuum; and because relationships form the backdrop for any dilemma or disturbance, the first question is, "Whose problem is it?" Ask yourself if this is a problem we can resolve at school? If so, the school should handle the matter. Naturally, most school problems have some home connections, but the school should make an effort to give students a chance to resolve school problems at school. If the problem is a more obviously a family matter, possibly the school and home can work together to provide joint help for a confused child. If the problem is exclusively a home matter—say, terminal illness—the school should not try to intervene directly but only offer encouragement and possibly make appropriate referrals to a community counseling service.

The key question is, "What can I control?" *Control* here does not mean forcing a student to do anything—only persuading a student to do something smart about a school-related matter. In keeping with good management practices, counselors in a school or other responsible staff members first identify the trouble spots and then sort the problems into three categories: matters they can control completely, those they can control partially, and those they cannot influence at all. For another view of this common sense framework, see the direct, indirect, and no control model presented by Covey (1989). Being realistic about one's chances of success in handling these conflicts is the best starting position. The following chart shows some samples of each type. Reality therapy does not look for hidden causes of current discomfort. The assumption is that people are generally capable of being in charge of their lives and that everyone periodically lets go of the steering wheel for a time. "What the counselor sees is what everyone gets."

Assessing a Problem's Locus		
Teacher: Influence (School Troubles)	Teacher: Partial Influence (Home & School Matters)	Teacher: No Influence (Home Troubles)
Disrupting classes	Depressing after a divorce	Spousal abuse
Fighting on playground	Mourning a death in family	Alcoholism at home
Low quality schoolwork	Adjusting to a remarriage	Runaway child

The problems throughout this chapter are mostly the kind that students can work out at school with a few examples of counseling children and parents together. Counselors can gain a larger vantage point and substantial leverage by inviting a parent or parents to participate directly. Giving students the first opportunity to resolve the messes they make at school is always wise. If an early resolution seems unlikely or impossible, counselors can involve parents, foster parents, grandparents, or any others who influence the students. Starting by asking each and every individual's unique personal goals and moving to their goals for the *index person* (IP) usually works well.

Guidelines Paralleling Reality Therapy

The following guidelines may shed some light on the intricacies of this method.

Special Guidelines for Reality Therapy
1. Listen as students talk about what hurts.
2. Translate their bad feelings into specific wants they are not satisfying.
3. Connect the symptoms (ineffective behavioral attempts at a solution) to their unmet wants.
4. Normalize students' feelings of frustration with themselves for having a problem; and, when reasonable, permit them to acknowledge and maintain their problems—even to display these misguided attempts at solution in safer ways or in altered circumstances.
5. Ask students to evaluate the usefulness of symptomatic behaviors—their acting out, exhibiting emotional upset, or withdrawing. "How does being grouchy full-time help you feel happier?"
6. In consultation with students, create optional actions they can imple-

ment in place of the symptomatic behaviors they are using to try to get what they want.

7. Link new behaviors of the present to the future by tying the payoffs to their stated goals.

8. Move to the next disturbance on their list until they have resolved each complaint in turn and have learned a method they eventually can apply without your coaching.

All of these guidelines fit reality therapy methods and show that, even though Glasser's procedures are forthright, the counselor offers 100% respect in the process. Harsh students who have not learned to relate to anyone in relaxed trust may answer your befriending with stony silence. These crusty kids find trusting anyone a chore because to enjoy another person requires a willingness to risk being vulnerable. Some students who join gangs often appear shell-shocked when a counselor or other adult at school reaches out to them. They may be casualties of early childhood violence and abuse, and heavier therapeutic guns may be needed to counter the blasts of danger they continue to feel.

The first obligation of any school is to insure physical and psychological safety for everyone, so that all can meet their primary need for survival. A school can hold meetings with a mix of successful students and some less successful ones and invite their ideas about their own futures. What educational goals can they list that may make sense to them and how can they make their lives better while they are there? Instead of calling out only low achievers to discuss new threats, intersperse an equal number of honors students. This practice confuses many observers.

FRAMEWORK FOR RESOLVING PROBLEMS

In general, a counselor will choose to follow the procedures of choice theory and reality therapy as I have described these in chapter 2. Also, Wubbolding (1988, 1991) has summarized the four key elements in counseling with reality therapy in the radio station call letters "WDEP." This acronym refers to W—wants, D—doing, E—evaluation, and P—plan. Another way to think about the basic reality therapy framework as a guide to teachers' and counselors' work is the above eight-step sequence. The first three steps help children replace hurt with hope, self-doubt and shame with encouragement, and confusion with perspective.

As a human bond forms, students experience friendship with a caring adult and soon learn to define pain as behaviors, see more clearly the wants they are ignoring, discover what is useful about their complaint, list one or more optional paths out of the dilemma, and look to the future with confidence. The two devices that make these classic reality therapy methods even more powerful are *making sense of the trouble by normalizing it* and *befriending the symptom*. Normalizing usually reduces anxiety rather swiftly, and viewing a complaint as something other than the enemy allows students to go into the storm and make some new decisions. The harder people fight against their troubles, the more attached to their problems they become because they spend all their energy on selected problem behavior. Compulsive eaters or smokers who constantly tell themselves they "shouldn't do such nasty habits" actually give themselves permission to carry on the undesirable activities by feeling they have paid some dues by merely decrying the symptoms. Befriending a complaint and looking to see how the problem may be helpful is usually much more productive. They could start a cessation of smoking program with "I would rather not smoke. While I continue to smoke, however, I will not condemn or criticize myself. Instead, I will choose to do something about it."

The more people resist their problems, the more the problems persist. This principle of emotional resistance originates in the physical universe. Physical resistance from a physical object will hold another physical object in place if the two objects are of similar force. The more the resistance, the more the persistence in the standoff. Psychologically, the same principle applies as many people are able to hold a problem in place by resisting it. The self-criticisms and even self-condemnations serve as a counterbalancing force that may keep in place the very problem behavior that the individual presents as a complaint.

KEY PRINCIPLES:
RESOLVING ONE PROBLEM AT A TIME

Crying and Entertaining Sadness

The example here is about a girl. A boy just as easily could have had the same problem. Rachel was a little six-year-old with tears in her eyes as she sat in a big wooden chair alongside the principal's desk. Nancy, a remarkable woman approaching her 60s, had been in charge at Kawana School for as long as anyone could remember. If the teachers there had been consulted, they may have voted for a lifetime contract for Nancy. Her credentials? She loved children, consistently backed the teachers and their classroom aides, and kept one hand extended to the parents of the 650 families that the school served.

Glancing up briefly, Nancy motioned for me to come in and join her in talking to little Trisha. She said, "You do this for a living. Show me what you would say." (I was only a professor. What did I know about child development, especially when it happened outside a textbook?) Nancy knew I had four children of my own and, therefore, must have learned *something* over the years. In "principal's code," she signaled me that Trisha had shown similar emotional outbursts around Nancy on many occasions before this one. In fact, nearly every day she used her spontaneous and uncontrollable crying to find her way out of her kindergarten classroom and down the sidewalk to the principal's office. I took up a part of the chat and noticed Nancy's relief as she sat back a bit and just listened. I felt the same thrill I had as a young kid: "Here's the bat, Larry. Your turn at the plate."

Children Can Teach *Us* Too

> **Larry:** *Hi. What's your name?*
> **Trisha:** (Mumbling and containing her emotions slightly), *Trisha.*
> **Larry:** *This morning you are feeling sad.*
> **Trisha:** *Mm-hmm.*
> **Larry:** *I feel sad sometimes. When you feel sad, do you come and see Mrs. Padden?*
> **Trisha:** (Nods yes).
> **Larry:** *Lots of times when people feel the way you do, Trisha, I think they have a reason to be sad. Do you have something to be sad about?*

With that question, Trisha produced a new flood of tears and sad tales, surprising me with her willingness to pour out her soul. She obviously felt safe and judged me to be all right, especially if her beloved principal invited me to participate. This counseling approach does not define emotional venting as intrinsically therapeutic. Rather than hear someone out about their feelings, the counselor hears them out about their unmet goals.

We Ignore Problems at a Cost

Looking back on my individual or group contacts with children at different grade levels, I have noticed that, almost universally, children hesitate to show their true feelings, especially negative ones, such as sadness, anger, or fear. Vengeance may be an exception, as they are often too willing to show anger and revenge. They obviously must feel trust and safety first, but perhaps, too, we typically do not give much of a hearing to these feelings in school. Schools do not feature negative feelings. One second-grade boy once told me,

"It's okay to be sad in school." Unfortunately, he added another sentence: "You just can't cry." The good side of all this repression, I suppose, is saving some money on big towels. Many educators seem to have little time for tears . . . or fury . . . or depressing . . . or monkey business.

Are Schools Heartless?

Can we really say that schools are innately numb? As institutions, schools are neither friendly nor mean-spirited. The social norms that a staff follows will show at once how human the place is. Perhaps teachers have discovered that if they, too, show their feelings openly, as suggested in the writings of Haim Ginott (1976a, 1976b) and the communication model of Thomas Gordon (1989), they will become embroiled in an emotional swirl, lose their concentration on the subject matter, and focus less on teaching than on the tragic stories their students silently embody. Understandably, everyone fears the stream of emotions that would appear in any classroom if they spoke with students as persons and not just as objects. With a little encouragement, students might express their feelings and opinions spontaneously and uncap all the energy they now use in fighting what they feel.

Students who stringently hold back their emotions pay a price for putting on the emotional brakes. Suppose a girl feels sadness welling up inside. Sensing that no one is supposed to be openly tearful at school, she automatically squelches those stirrings because she knows she cannot cry at school. The same little girl then experiences desperation when she realizes no ear will tune into her sad tale, and no warm adult is at hand to understand. Feeling confused, she coats her sadness with a secondary symptom (Ellis, 1975, 1988; Maultsby, 1975) of floundering alone and feeling constant urges to leave the room.

Feelings Are Behaviors Too

Realistically, no teacher has the time to allow children to speak endlessly about their state of mind and heart; but a teacher *can* manage conflicts one at a time. By acting as conflict manager and letting students know they are not alone, the teacher actually can insure that students obtain a sense of control and power in the long run. When teachers add regular class meetings to their routines, they say to students even more clearly that what *they* label important is also significant to teachers. When students are more relaxed about themselves, the teacher faces a more comfortable classroom. Some teachers will struggle with conflict among the students for an entire school year and never move in with some open and blunt talk about these painful inconsistencies. Communication in an open atmosphere wards off most crises and resolves those that have gotten out of hand.

CHOICE THEORY IS IN THE MIND

What I first did with Trisha was convey my willingness to hear her story. Anyone who resists a child's secondary emotional message will watch the problem persist and even balloon out of proportion. Attending to these affective expressions of pain, however, does not mean we should dwell on the bad feelings; in actuality, we have little leverage for change when we emphasize these fleeting buggers. Glasser (1991) showed that highlighting emotions is like trying to steer an auto with the rear wheels. You should, however, spend some time *acknowledging* students' pain and talk about their conflicts, fears, or traumas. Noticing the negative is a practical way for them to get a handle on their hurts and do something constructive about the matter so that they do not have to let these nagging troubles—in their words, "push their lives around." Talking about these painful topics from a choice theory viewpoint shows children that *they* can take charge and not live at the mercy of any feeling or problem.

Being consciously aware of an unmet want produces a slight pain signal that we notice as an "urge to behave." This urge only gets the ball rolling. The focus quickly shifts from what one *has* or *does not have* to what one can *do* to make that wish come true or satisfy the inner urge. The best time to talk about feelings in some detail is after the student has done something about the problem and starts feeling better. *Acknowledge* negative feelings associated with useless behavior; *feature* positive emotions that accompany useful behavior.

We know from chapter 2 that choice theory explains pain as an awareness of an unmet want or as a frustrated goal and that we all automatically feel discomfort when we see a gap between what we want in our minds and what we have in reality. In the face of such a deficit, we will continue to feel some degree of anguish until we do something to get what we want. Trisha had not yet figured out just how many different emotional disguises she could use to cover over her frustration. By contrast, most adults have learned to shield themselves with many protective devices and mental processes. Freud had a name for all 11 of these defenses, but it is widely held that Freud often stooped too far and became far too analytical for his own good. He reportedly even resorted to using cocaine to enhance his preoccupation with his own mind and his psychological insights. Sadly, he became paranoid in the process and, for a long stretch, was so terrified that he could not even leave home.

OUR "DEFENSES" MAKE SENSE

Some options available to people when they want something they do not have are listed below. Put more simply and in much fewer psychiatric terms than Freud's list of intrapsychic defenses, people either can give up or hide behind one of five symptoms (i.e., behaviors they use to regain control):

- going to extremes of displaying certain emotional upsets, such as depressing, anxietizing, guilting, or fearing;
- acting out, angering, and causing havoc in society;
- withdrawing into a psychosis (i.e., devising a *make believe* world);
- withdrawing into a psychosomatic illness; or
- taking on a narrow and destructive addiction such as eating, drinking, drugging, gambling, working, or making life about sex.

Shorthand for these categories of disturbing and ineffective behaviors might be the following:

- giving in to discouragement;
- taking on a symptom such as blaming others, sulking in a corner, emoting oneself silly, or threatening someone;
- becoming numb or giddy, living in a make believe world, or paining one's body; and
- hiding one's misery in an addictive lifestyle or distracting oneself with a busy schedule.

Back to the Tearful Girl

Trisha just showed us her obvious need by crying, leaving Nancy and me the task of decoding her message. I started by telling her that she *could* cry at school and stated that, when children cry, they usually have something to cry about. When Trisha heard the comforting comment that her emotional expressions were *normal,* she was free to change her messages and communicate with regular talk unclouded by tears. She started steering a front wheel of her car instead of pecking away at a rear wheel only.

As suspected, we soon found that Trisha's actual problems had little to do with her classmates or her kindergarten teacher whom she liked very much. She felt worried and unsafe at home and, because she was unable to access those feelings and describe her plight clearly, she did what made sense at the time—crying and troubling herself and a few others until someone listened. I ended our 17-minute conversation on the topics of herself, her school, her family, and her friends on a note of multiple permissions: to cry when she was really sad, to notice ahead of time when she sensed the first signals of her sadness at school, and to ask the teacher if she could go to Nancy's office *ahead of the flood,* and talk with her for a minute or two. Finally, I asked her what she thought about my telephoning her parents and asking them to drop by for a little meeting to share with me their ideas about their daughter's worries. She approved that plan. Nancy and I watched her leave dry-eyed and skip all the way back to her classroom. She was armed with a plan and knew that no one was making fun of her or telling her to shape up. In the bargain, she started feeling more in control of her life. She locked on when someone she assumed important in the school told her he would arrange a meeting with someone important in her family.

I planned also to talk with the teacher privately about Trisha and her problem of involuntary crying. Maybe early in the morning the teacher could ask her to come to the side of the classroom and cry in order to get her tears out of the way early and move right into her schoolwork. Strange, how taking action *before* the problem becomes full blown can have an impact on the whole problem (O'Hanlon & Weiner-Davis, 1989; Palmatier, 1990, 1994). Stoop right down next to the child's desk and quietly say, "This is an okay time if you feel like crying now." The child often will admit, "I can wait." If not, let that student have the floor; the crying will not go on forever.

Holding Out a Hopeful Picture

This perennial hope is especially useful for kids. To use my earlier example of the sobbing child, reflect the child's own goals by drawing a verbal picture of the way everything will look after you and Trisha work together and after she replaces her current weeping style with new ways to act. If the new mental image you paint matches the child's inner picture of a person who has met a particular want, you will have succeeded indeed. The solution will work when it matches the child's mental picture of a satisfied want or goal. But what if students want to do something that the school cannot allow, such as enjoying the freedom to roam the halls at will or sleeping all day at their desks? Naturally, teachers cannot accommodate all the pictures of inner wants that every child can imagine. Choice theory explains some of these inappropriate or inconvenient choices as masks that cover the hurt that children call up when they are not meeting a more basic want, such as belonging to a friendly group of peers. Roaming halls is a protective act for some students who view staying in the room and cooperating with others as too risky and, therefore, as unsatisfying for some reason. Your task includes helping kids sort "wants" into realistic and attainable goals and plans.

Problems Themselves Are Not the Enemy

Most of us expend endless energy trying to eliminate problems as soon as we become aware of them. Our own problems are bad enough, but children's difficulties can strike us as genuine irritants. Many say that schools would be good places to work if it were not for the children. As the reader may recall, a story in chapter 2 describes an incident during my post-doctoral clinical psychology internship in a medical hospital. Here I learned early the value of not treating anyone's problem as the enemy. Please refer back to this story of Dan and I as an illustration of a minor way of thinking about mental disorders. The focus here is on solutions.

The end of the story was positive for Dan. He showed up at his fifth counseling appointment about six weeks later wearing a jacket that was part of the uniform for his job with a national auto-rental franchise. In the meantime, he had gotten a haircut, lost about 15 pounds, and reported to me that he was no longer taking a prescribed drug to relieve his anxiety. I attributed his productive new choices to (a) encouragement from our meetings and (b) to his own agreement that the complaints he described to me at the first session made sense in the context of his post-army life. By the end of our session, he came to see some tangible options for changing many important conditions of his life and realized he had the power to make his life better. We began slowly by my asking him to take walks around the block in place of his popping a pill to relieve anxiety. Anxiety, as most pains, can signal a person to do something else or perhaps to take even more drastic action in the face of an obvious demand to change course.

Problems Are Not All Bad

After I understood Glasser's point that problem behaviors are people's best attempts at a particular time to get what they need, I took an open attitude about anything any client or student might say. What goal are they aiming at and constantly missing? As I counseled others, I began doing all I could to minimize the loss of face or feelings of foolishness people experience when they describe their problems to an outsider they have just met. They tell themselves they should not feel this way or that they ought to know better. They were off schedule in their lives, compared to their peers who were long into the career they themselves were still scrambling to enter. Once I stopped trying to keep the problem at bay or to annihilate it instantly, I was able to invite clients (and, later on, students) to befriend their own symptoms. As people stopped trying so actively to stamp out their woes permanently, I watched the guide wires holding their troubles in place fall away. Whenever troubled kids or harried adults would give themselves a breather from their struggle to free themselves completely from their complaints, I could see them focusing more on *solutions* than on apologizing for having a problem in the first place (O'Hanlon & Wilks, 1987). Giving up the battle to obliterate a problem leads to a willingness *to have the problem resolved differently* and to the principle Paul Watzlawick (1988) suggested of deliberately retaining the unresolved remnant. You can get over a problem much faster if you try to get over some but not all of it.

No One Makes Mistakes. Ask anyone; no one ever sets out intentionally to fail or to make a mistake, at least in one's own terms. Whatever anyone does always seems the best choice of behavior at the time. Only in retrospect does anyone ever look at a particular behavior and label it a mistake (and people often blame others for their own misfortune). Children do many things at school —some interpersonal behaviors and some curricular tasks—and teachers and administrators usually stand poised to cast quick judgment on all school activities as good or bad. Making schoolwork relevant, enjoyable, and not for keeps can turn students around and make their job of learning more meaningful.

Solving Problems One by One: Alternatives to Angering

Fury or anger is a perennial reaction to problems and an old-time favorite emotion even for teachers at times. When examined through choice theory lenses, fury is a choice of emoting that students select when they are unaware of better alternative. Perhaps they simply are disinterested in choosing a more rational behavior in the face of the natural frustration anyone would feel when a want goes unattended. Think about a time when you were really angry. Is your memory unpleasant? Often people report a certain amount of pleasure in openly expressing fury, especially if the angry outburst worked to draw a new recruit to their cause. If you felt your anger was justifiable, you probably enjoyed the feeling of being right and powerful—at least for a moment. Students display the same strong sense of entitlement or concern about rights that people in the general society display. Teachers must take these attitudes into account. Coupled with their sense of competing with the colorful and highly technical media, many teachers report feeling more pressure than ever to perform, entertain, and even to cater to students.

Pandering is clearly too strong a word for teachers' attempts to meet the current demands of students, but some teachers have reported widely that more students are expressing their wants with a new sense of urgency. Some of this increasing clamor may spring from a new level of political candor in the media, ranging from tabloids to talk shows and virtual reality. Some of the literature—as good as the material may be—connotes a new focus on self and conveys the new priorities. *Pulling Your Own Strings* (Dyer, 1991) and *The Sky's the Limit* (Dyer, 1993), for example, are but two examples of books that emphasize getting yours before someone else gets you and yours.

We probably cannot return to yesteryear when the streets were a bit safer, but we can and must redefine propriety. Puritanism and the euphemisms that went with it finally may be on the decline, but politeness and civility still reign in some parts of the world. On a recent family visit to the small village of Pebworth, nine miles from Stratford-upon-Avon, I recall the landlady's comment when we told her the rental fee that we had paid on her English country cottage. By going through a U.S. based broker, we ended up paying three times the amount of money the company passed along to her. We only could imagine her real thoughts because she appeared quite shocked and upset. What we heard, however, was, "How naughty!"

The danger of America's social problems and the intensity of national politics demand more directness. People should be able to shop at their favorite supermarket without fearing the loss of their automobile to a carjacker or their physical security to a drive-by shooter. Talk about AIDS and other sexually transmitted diseases is more open in America than in many other countries because business as usual proves fatal. The private lives of public figures and the particular ills of education are well-known. Watching the world headlines every 30 minutes cannot possibly be helpful to the average citizen who has no control over the minute-by-minute tubal stream of tragedies. Focusing on topics and challenges that one can manage makes more sense. Watzlawick is one philosophical therapist who has managed to keep his sense of perspective on consuming an endless deluge of irrelevant information called *news*. Besides cautioning against subjecting oneself to a constant barrage of traumatic events that are all out of one's personal control, Watzlawick has kept his book titles in perspective (e.g., *The Situation Is Hopeless, But Not Serious* [Watzlawick, 1983]). Tee vee or not tee vee; that is the question.

We have little choice about facing up to some harsh realities. Many programs are available to help schools with practical ideas for handling insidious problems such as drugs, sexual harassment and abuse, and threats of violent physical harm. The fundamental ingredient that students, their families, and their teachers learn in order to ward off these dangers is a new set of confrontational skills. Training in *Tribes* (Gibbs, 1995), *Here's Looking at You 2,000 Curriculum*

(1991), and a host of other public and private efforts designed to empower students and the entire body politic rely on the same key component: assertive communication. If students learn these lessons well, some school staff members become nervous. If the adults in schools elicit students' opinions, they probably should not act too surprised when children and adolescents express their views.

Choosing Apathy and Withdrawal. Inactivity is another common way to show excessive caution or discouragement. Not grappling also is a way to avoid personal connections or to engage in a power struggle. Most of us want to speed up students' changing by pushing them to try something new. First, take the time to acknowledge to the apparently resistant students that remaining passive and inactive could make sense if those who opt out were to look at the entire context of their lives and their current choices for action. Ask these students what the disadvantages might be in becoming actively involved in your classroom. Soon you will isolate a need that these students are ignoring, and you then can decide with them whether their boycott makes sense and whether they should continue it. Usually, students either will blame their mother or tell you that they do not like what they are doing and, for some reason, cannot figure out a reasonable alternative. If you help such students stop fighting their problems, they actually may learn to befriend their symptom—that is, stop fighting their hesitation). You can ask them to "do their passivity" differently, and they often come out of their self-imposed exile rather swiftly.

Refusing to Participate in a Class Activity

One nine-year-old student refused to participate in the rope jumping that his P.E. teacher had organized, probably because he saw the exercise as a girl's game and felt too embarrassed to try something new. Luis was Hispanic and saw jumping rope as singularly "unmacho," and, at first, his teacher tried to pressure him to join her and the class. Using logic to convince him that this sporty exercise was not any more feminine than other games, she argued that everyone else was willing to jump. After these tactics failed, she sheepishly confessed thinking she should compel him to join in or face detentions, rote writing exercises, and other penalties. Notice that her first instinct was not to drop the requirement and invite the boy to select an alternate exercise. Such flexibility might solve the problem but also could scare a teacher with images of mass revolt. Being fluid is not backing down.

How could the teacher handle Luis' refusal? Real or not, the teacher feared that she had to win the power struggle with this boy because all her other students were witnessing her attempts to persuade Luis to join the jumping. Otherwise, she reasoned, the rest of the class might feel inclined to boycott the P.E. program themselves if one student succeeded in remaining inactive. "After all, why should we exercise if Luis doesn't have to?" Frankly, my own private thoughts were that the physical conditioning of the teachers in that school was already too good. Everyone looked like a champion volleyball player, especially the women, and not one person smoked that I could see. The students might have felt a bit in awe of such excellent body tone, shape, and stamina.

In any case, the teacher ran over some optional tactics she might use with this boy who feared the "sissy" label. She quickly decided to discontinue forcing him to do anything because she realized no one could compel him to action. She agreed with Luis that anyone was entitled to feel any reaction without pressure or fear of ridicule. The teacher was not convinced that his cultural rules kept him stuck. Maybe he opted out because he was afraid of appearing foolish by being physically awkward and incompetent to jump well.

Avoid Challenging a Student Directly in Front of a Class. The P.E. teacher reminded herself of the predictable dangers of challenging a student in front of a class. She decided to talk with him alone—a very smart move on her part. She would take five minutes with him during the class after the others had begun a game and tell him she would make a deal with him. For her part, she would stop nagging him if he would agree either to get involved directly on his terms—for example, jumping rope at home for two minutes each evening, verified by an adult's signature or phone call—or to suggest an alternative exercise that would be equally beneficial to his physical conditioning in a similar way to jumping rope.

The teacher also planned to have Luis examine the film catalogues and order a training film of a professional boxer such as José Camacho or Jorge Rodriguez displaying his artistic talent for creative rope jumping. After viewing the training tapes, he still would not need to join the group if he felt shy about jumping in public. To prompt his own brainstorming about alternatives, she also considered having him come up with a more "macho" exercise related to ropes that would be safe, valuable, and impressive, such as swinging across a sand pit on a rope or climbing a few feet up a rope and dropping into a soft landing area that he could help prepare. In any case, the boy could present an alternative activity that would produce the same or greater health benefits as jumping in place.

Objections to this scenario include taking far too much time with only one student, pushing a kid who clearly sees jumping rope as an activity for sissies, and catering to a disrespectful child. The point of the story is that a teacher learned what many teachers already know: if a student refuses to participate, yell, demand, and sentence them to detention. A quality school, employing lead management in the main office and in the classroom, handles such problems differently. Spending so much time on this matter pays off in many ways. The other students see a teacher who is trying to reach a student, not to steam roll one. The boy who must face a persistent teacher who doggedly pursues alternatives to standoffs ultimately will feel some human connection. The teacher will never have to work this hard again with this young fellow. The story shows a qualitative shift in classroom values that leads to a new basis for a positive and satisfying relationship.

Class Meetings. Another way to approach this particular problem would be through a *class meeting* but not one that would put Luis on trial. Sometimes, the more you push, the more a student pushes back, and so backing off is the way to go. Discussing with the class the matter of opting out of a class activity would be a legitimate exercise. Asking for Luis' agreement to discuss this topic at a class meeting and at least to try one of the many solutions that would surely bubble up in that forum would be a good plan. Humor goes a long way, and a warm teacher sometimes can talk a child into trying an activity that he otherwise might not dare to do. The quality of the relationship between teachers and students is really the critical factor in all personal problems and solutions presented here. One of my all-time favorite definitions of school that applies here is a "series of significant interpersonal relationships" (Featherstone, 1971).

USING CHOICE THEORY AND REALITY THERAPY WITH SPECIFIC PROBLEMS

Most of this chapter shows examples of problem solving with reality therapy. The next six examples again include methodical procedures from this counseling model. Any behavioral anomaly usually can be resolved through the persistent and courteous application of reality therapy and choice theory, the earlier the better. After talking with the child and identifying the bugaboo, make sense out of the symptom and explain it to the child's satisfaction. Show how this choice of action might interfere with successfully meeting an important want and search for alternatives that do not necessarily disavow the option of troubling. Be patient and do not give up on the child.

Acting Impulsively and Demonstrating Hyperactivity

First, rule out any real medical or organic causes of this bothersome behavior by interviewing children and consulting their parents. Ascertain the children's general diet and ask whether they get sufficient sleep. Also, be sure to find out if the boy (usually this is a problem boys exhibit) or girl is able to concentrate at any time—watching TV, for example. Is the student hyperactive mainly at school? Next, try to find some way to label the action in a neutral or positive light. "Where did you get all of that energy?" "You can't keep a good woman (or man) down." "You would make a good night watchman (or watch-woman) or a great sailor at sea." Then move to a consideration of the wants that the student is not taking care of as he absorbs so much energy fidgeting or acting impulsively. Perhaps the student is lonely and keeps a healthy distance from others by popping up here, there, and everywhere. A child who has been abused often will go into a morose state or fly around a room looking for targets of opportunity. In these cases, a teacher should refer the student to the school counselor or to the school principal. In turn, a school leader needs a referral procedure for advising a family about finding low cost help. Making attending school contingent on actually going for that assistance may serve as an effective way to make progress with the complaint.

Keep Energetic Children Busy. Some teachers have tried assigning a "bouncer" the task of carrying things back and forth throughout the day. A teacher can ask this student to be a runner, so to speak, and to remain standing (near the teacher's desk). After checking to make sure the student's health is good, explain that sitting down and getting comfortable would be a problem. Make sure that these healthy runners get the maximum time during breaks to do all the exercise they have coming. Finally, put runners onto the jump rope (or similar exercise) periodically throughout the day.

Case of Hyperactive Boy

Jacob was a real charmer—one to one. In a classroom, he was as vibrant as a vivid nightmare. His mother and father had split up some time before his fourth-grade teacher referred him to a counselor, and he had lost almost all contact with his mother. When a child is in Jacob's shoes, he usually goes into a numbing state or shows constant motion. Jacob was a real gadfly among his peers. He had trouble with the idea of videotaping the meeting with the counselor even though his dad had authorized the taping and all the other students that day did not question the filming.

What came out was that this young fellow lacked a clear-cut picture in his mind about his role within his family. He felt that neither his father nor his dad's new wife gave him much time and, mostly, he felt very desperate to have current information on his mother's whereabouts and condition. She had had problems with drugs for many years and he was understandably worried about her safety and health. Children and mothers in similar circumstances often feel as if they are going to go crazy with worry for the absent family member. They crave contact and reconnection. These family ties help them define who they are. As typically happens, step-mother and father openly criticized the boy's mother as an irresponsible derelict and refused to allow him to write her or telephone her. In addition, they would not fill the emotional void in his life by increasing the affection that he so sorely needed.

I discussed details of Jacob's living situation: his room, the amount of time he spent with his dad and his dad's wife, and information about their daily and weekly schedule of activities. I learned that he had a small, cramped bedroom with little room of anything other than the main essentials. With Jacob's permission, I telephoned his father and persuaded him to agree to four points: first, to build a set of legs to raise Jacob's bed enough to allow for storage of toys and books underneath; second, to give Jacob a half hour of time each evening, reading him a story and listening to a report on his day; third, to allow him to contact his mother by correspondence so that he would know that she was still alive and was remembering him; and fourth, to stop all criticism of his mother in front of Jacob. Such criticizing puts the youngster in the middle of an impossible conflict of loyalty and never helps a child. Anyone who criticizes the stock he comes from cannot feel good about himself (Satir, 1988).

Accommodating Individual Children

Many worry that, if one student gets special privileges, others will make a request for the same benefits, but this concern generally is not well-grounded. If Johnny needs an amount of physical and psychic space for his idiosyncrasies, Jorge, Charmaine, or Paul do not need the same leeway necessarily and usually will not ask for special privileges if a sensitive teacher or counselor accommodates Johnny's needs. In schools, people generally believe that the "worker ants" will become complainers if a teacher singles someone out for special treatment. The simple answer for students is, "Johnny prefers standing up most of the day. If you too want permission to stand, come and ask me and I will give your request serious consideration." Another obvious tactic that applies to impulsiveness or to any other problem in this section is managerial. Creative curricular methods and classroom management strategies—cooperative learning groups, class meetings, and other "fun" approaches to learning—will forestall many behavioral problems before they mushroom into major differences.

Depressing and Withdrawing: Advantages for Teachers

Do you know anyone who pushes people away and then complains about loneliness? People do choose their emotional states. But even so, when you see a young child sitting in a closed and withdrawn posture, you should be concerned; when you find a minute, walk over to that desk, crouch down so that your eyes meet, and ask, "Is everything all right with you today, Margee?" If the child says she is feeling badly, perhaps you can suggest a time later in the day when the two of you will have a few minutes to talk. Counselors talk to children about a myriad of problems, but they lack two major advantages that teachers have: (a) the opportunity to personally engage students by interacting with them in the classroom where they spend so much of their time, and (b) curriculum that they can arrange into creative learning opportunities for their students. By choosing projects, students can work hard on something they are really interested in, gaining a sense of achievement and confidence. If a counselor suggests a project (e.g., keeping a journal about thoughts and feelings), the child may well regard it as a tiresome chore. Besides talking with their teachers about a problem, students can do a curricular project related to their worry and thereby express their needs and attain their goals. A shy child can team up with a more talkative one to audiotape a creative story.

Depressing Sometimes Makes Sense

Holding our emotions down by depressing these urges often helps us cap other strong negative feelings such as aggression and anger. Also, we can ask for help in socially acceptable ways, and we buy time to figure out what to do when we do not know what to do (Glasser, 1984). No human behavior is foolish in itself, and depressing or sulking may be a sensible choice of behavior until people either can regain control over their other feelings or pick a more rational action or attitude to help them get what they want. Many people are afraid of depression and withdrawal because of its power and the emotional backlash they invite when they choose to depress—all the pain and frustration turns back inside. Still the most common emotional upset, we must take depressing seriously. When children show us emotional withdrawal and somber spiraling, we should make opportunities to listen and explore their intentions. By spotting a more serious problem early enough, one can help children move out of the emotional tailspin. Once you hear the story, you probably will want to say, "I'm sorry to hear that you are not feeling positive right now. Considering what is going on in your life, I want you to know that I would be more worried about you if you were not depressed. Would you like to talk about finding some solutions to your difficulties?"

Choosing Loneliness

Feeling sad from time to time is normal and even healthy—and being depressed and feeling lonely are *not* necessarily one and the same. Both hurt and both serve a purpose. Depressing our emotions may prove an effective method of involving other people. As stated earlier, Glasser (1984, pp. 56-62) identifies four advantages of depressing: As a powerful emotion, depressing can (a) hold in check another powerful emotion, angering; (b) allow us to ask for help from others in a socially acceptable way; (c) excuse our unwillingness to do something more effective; and (d) gain powerful control. If you ask lonely children what is going on and what they want, they may not be strong enough to risk telling you candidly that the problem is lack of caring friends. Anyone may feel lonely, even in a crowd. You will read the hesitancy, the caution to show too much personal need; but if you are calm and positive, the child definitely will allow you to show your concern and support. Confidence will replace fear, and meeting at least one new friend who is helpful and accepting is the surest cure for a lonely child in school.

Solving Some Social Problems with a Bridge Club

Many schools do not address the needs of new students or transfer students, and making a smooth adjustment to the new school is often tougher for these kids than need be. I will never forget my first day in high school (ninth grade). I attended a very traditional school in St. Louis, some 300 miles from home. I noticed that the lockers had been manufactured in my home town of Aurora, Illinois and I blurted out to a fellow student who had the locker next to mine, "Hey, these lockers were built in my home town." His response: "So?" Setting up a small club for new students to their school, its facilities, and its students will not prevent rudeness, but such a group can be very useful.

Being accepted and liked is very important to any child, and a counselor (or teacher) can do much to guarantee at least a fair hearing for newcomers. In fact, if some careful planning goes into this, a school can serve two purposes: (a) making new students' assimilation smoother and (b) reminding current students of the rich resources they already have within their grasp. Everyone likes to show a new friend something of value. Five students can comprise each unit of the "bridge club"—perhaps an alienated student, two relatively new students, and two enthusiastic students who have been at the school for more than two years. Club members should be free either to arrange individual interviews with teachers or to set up discussion or lunch groups with small numbers of current students. Tours of the facilities, school, and neighborhood can be arranged along

with other planned activities. A buddy system works well with one student acting as a special pal to a new arrival. Colleges routinely do this in a variety of
ways: registration week orientation groups, Big Brother or Big Sister relationships, and student "dorm dons" or leaders (moving away from matrons and
house mothers) in each dormitory. But in college, *every* new arrival is expected
to be unfamiliar with the system. The need is just as great in elementary schools
where fewer regular orientation systems exist. A teacher or counselor must be
especially alert to introduce a new student to the class for the first time. Moreover, supervision is vital at the start. Otherwise, students resort to hazing and
other practices from the older British public schools, pledge weeks (which also
exist for the younger kids' private clubs), and similar traditional abuses.

Fearing

As adults, we all pay money to watch films that terrify us. In fantasy, most
people condone fear; but in real life, we generally avoid it at all costs. Whenever possible, we shield children from any cause for fear and we often chide
them for displaying even a little fright. A few years ago, a ring of men and
women conspired to hijack a school bus full of children along a major state
highway in central California. The kidnappers then *buried* the bus and its
human cargo for several hours while they tried to extort huge sums of money
from parents and the local school board. Fortunately, the crazy and daring
scheme backfired and, after 36 hours, all of the children emerged relatively
unscathed from the ordeal. We all know that children often enjoy scary experiences, as in daring their friends to sneak into a PG Slasher film. How often do
they naturally want to explore something dangerous like an abandoned mine
shaft or rickety old building, and they may take much pleasure later on in re-
hashing the close calls. In all these cases, though, the children are in control
and are calling the shots. When danger strikes suddenly, children and adults
automatically show genuine fear and make efforts to escape the threat.

Keeping Fear Alive: Perpetuating Terror

On the first anniversary of the Chowchilla incident, a newsman interviewed
some of the children: "You were kidnapped in the bus hijacking a year ago,
you still must be terrified." Watching this scene on television, I could almost
hear the children answer the interviewer's programmed expectation: "Okay, we
will." We have made a ritual, if not an art form, out of insisting that everyone
who ever experienced a traumatic event will analyze the trauma *ad nauseam*
and endlessly monitor their reactions to the miserable affair. Does implying
permanence of the trauma help survivors put aside a victim role and stop cling-

ing to their original primitive fear? What is wrong with the Chowchilla young-sters putting the gross nightmare behind them? What if they begin viewing the incident as an escapade and even feel a bit special for having undergone such a dangerous ordeal?

Overcoming Fear. In this society we *feature* victims, and we hinder the progress of all, especially children, who want to lay an evil experience to rest. In spite of social norms that insist on rampant lawsuits, permanent scarring, and even fearful traumas as invasive as sexual abuse can be resolved if a daughter and her family are willing to face the conflict head-on and put the problem behind them once and for all (Madanes, 1990). Posttraumatic stress disorder (PTSD) is a plausible explanation for bad experiences, but why turn a tragedy into a fixed 30- or 40-year emotional mortgage? Worse still is turning such a harsh label into a condition and making it a variable loan mortgage that sky-rockets in payments as the years pass. Relatively new psychiatric categories such as PTSD can help us see uncomfortable flashbacks and even nightmares as normal responses to earlier shocks, but such labels have a tendency to be-come real, take root in the culture, and assume a permanent life of their own. Long past an immediate basis for horror, a victim still may be sweating out a tragedy as if the event still were occurring. Presuppositions are part of lan-guage. A newsperson, insistent on conveying a "must" presupposition to the Chowchilla children on the anniversary of their days of terror, could have made a more therapeutic statement: "You must be happy that you all escaped. How have you used the experience to become stronger and make your life better?" A more neutral comment, of course, would be, "On the anniversary of your escape from the bus, what are your thoughts and feelings?"

Vietnam and PTSD. Vietnam veterans have carried far more than their share of society's confusion and scapegoating over that military quagmire, but the fact remains that if some veterans have resolved the moral conflicts and discarded the shame of that era, other veterans can do the same. Ellis proposed a change of wording from something such as "Ain't it awful that I have suf-fered" to something such as "That bad experience was terribly *distasteful* and *inconvenient*" and "I *would have preferred* avoiding such a crisis." "The war is over. I have my life and now I can choose to move on." This same hopeful attitude and alternative self-talk applies to alcoholism, codependency, adult child of an alcoholic (ACOA or ACA) status, adoption and foster care, and a dys-functional family of origin. Bemoaning the past and feeling helpless and alone can become a full-time job, if not a way of life. Standing around pawing the earth may make us feel less miserable for brief periods, but a healthier option to being hog-tied with regret is acknowledging the hurt courageously. Taking one formal occasion for sharing the struggle, the deep pain, grief, or betrayal with a friend or friends can bring a solid feeling of connection and community that everyone needs. Continuing the saga of sadness and earning a reputation as a whiner usually points to a dead-end path. Ultimately, only an outright rejection of the role of an isolated victim and a clear choice to find new enjoyment in positive relationships can bring true peace of mind to children and adults alike.

SUMMARY AND CLOSING REMARKS

In this chapter, we discussed 12 interpersonal problems ranging from shedding tears in all the wrong places to depressing, angering, and fidgeting out of control. To handle all of these difficulties, examples of tearing, remaining aloof, and fighting, appeared in a range of actual cases. Basic to all strategies for solution was an organizational scheme with several variations that teachers and counselors may adapt to their teaching or problem solving.

What helps with personal problems? Having two notions in mind can be very useful: (a) a problem-solving outline and (b) a conviction that one cannot force students to behave. Bribing students may work for the short-term, but this practice creates high and unrealistic expectations later as, more and more, a teacher must continue to draw carrots out of the hat to keep the hungry students motivated.

Problem Identification

Discuss matters with students in a safe setting, free of power struggles. A good starting point for almost all students is helping them figure out that they are in charge of their lives. No one else *can* be. Surprise the students with your understanding that you know (a) you cannot force them to do anything, and (b) you, as an adult, really hold all the cards. You can, after all, recommend that they go on the strange arrangement known as *home study*. Keep in mind that you can work with the families as well. See chapter 17 for ideas on family counseling and consultation methods.

BIBLIOGRAPHY

Bandler R., Grinder, J., & Satir, V. (1976). *Changing with families*. Palo Alto, CA: Science and Behavior Books.

Haley, J. (1987). *Problem-solving therapy* (2nd ed.). San Francisco: Jossey-Bass.

Madanes, C. (1981). *Strategic family therapy.* San Francisco: Jossey-Bass.

Madanes, C. (1984). *Behind the one-way mirror.* San Francisco: Jossey-Bass.

REFERENCES

Bateson, G., Jackson, D., Haley, J., & Weakland, J. (1956). Toward a theory of schizophrenia. *Behavioral Science, 1*(4), 251-264.

Beier, E., & Young, D. (1984). *The silent language of psychotherapy* (2nd ed.). New York: Aldine.

Catania, C., & Harnad, S. (Eds.). (1988). *The selection of behavior: The operant behaviorism of B. F. Skinner—Comments and consequences.* New York: Cambridge University Press.

Covey, S. (1989). *The seven habits of highly effective people.* New York: Simon & Schuster.

Dyer, W. (1991). *Pulling your own strings.* New York: HarperCollins.

Dyer, W. (1993). *The sky's the limit.* New York: Simon & Schuster.

Ellis, A. (1988). *How to stubbornly refuse to make yourself miserable about anything—yes, anything!* Secaucus, NJ: Lyle Stuart.

Ellis, A., & Harper, R. (1975). *A new guide to rational living.* North Hollywood, CA: Wilshire Books.

Featherstone, J. (1971). *Schools where children learn.* New York: Liveright.

Gibbs, J. (1995). *Tribes: A new way of learning and being.* Sausalito, CA: Center Source.

Ginott, H. (1976a). *Between teacher and child.* New York: Avon Books.

Ginott, H. (1976b). *Between parent and child.* New York: Avon Books.

Glasser, W. (1984). *Control theory.* New York: HarperCollins.

Glasser, W. (1991). *Control theory chart.* Chatsworth, CA: Institute for Control Theory, Reality Therapy, and Quality Management.

Gordon, T. (1989). *Teaching children self-discipline . . . at home and at school.* New York: Random House.

Haley, J. (1963). *Strategies of psychotherapies.* New York: Grune & Stratton.

Here's Looking at You, 2,000 Curriculum (2nd ed.). (1991). Seattle, WA: CHEF (Comprehensive Health Education Foundation).

Kohn, A. (1993). *Punished by rewards.* Boston: Houghton-Mifflin.

Lazarus, A. (1976). *Multimodal behavior therapy.* New York: Springer.

Liddle, H., Breunlin, D., & Schwartz, R. (Eds.). (1988). *Handbook of family therapy training and supervision.* New York: Guilford.

Madanes, C. (1990). *Sex, love, and violence.* San Francisco: Jossey-Bass.

Maultsby, M. (1975). *Help yourself to happiness: Through rational self-counseling.* New York: Institute for Rational Emotive Therapy.

O'Hanlon, W., & Weiner-Davis, M. (1989). *In search of solutions.* New York: W. W. Norton.

O'Hanlon, W., & Wilks, J. (1987). *Shifting contexts: The generation of effective psychotherapy.* New York: Guilford.

Palmatier, L. (1990). Reality therapy and brief strategic interactional therapy. *Journal of Reality Therapy, 10*(1), 3-25.

Palmatier, L. (1994). Changing symptoms by changing symptom patterns. In L. Litwack (Ed.), *Compendium of reality therapy journal articles, 1982-94.* Chapel Hill, NC: New View.

Powers, W. (1973). *Behavior: The control of perception.* New York: Aldine De Gruyter.

Powers, W. (1992). *Living control systems II.* Chapel Hill, NC: New View.

Satir, V. (1988). *The new people making*. Palo Alto, CA: Science and Behavior Books.

Watzlawick, P. (1983). *Situation is hopeless, but not serious*. New York: W. W. Norton.

Watzlawick, P. (1988). *Ultra-solutions*. New York: W. W. Norton.

Watzlawick, P., Beavin Bavelas, J., & Jackson, D. (1967). *Pragmatics of human communication*. New York: W. W. Norton.

Wubbolding, R. (1988). *Using reality therapy*. New York: Harper & Row.

Wubbolding, R. (1991). *Understanding reality therapy*. New York: HarperCollins.

Chapter 7

CHILD ABUSE AND NEGLECT: A GUIDE TO EFFECTIVE ADVOCACY

Lynn Loar

Editor's Note

One of the greatest duties teachers and others in education must fulfill is the responsibility to protect children from danger and harm. Spotting signals of abuse— emotional, physical, or sexual—is the first step in forming an effective advocacy position. Lynn Loar points out exact language readers will want to use in working with traumatized and abused children. Distasteful as is the idea that an adult in a position of trust would abuse a child, counselors and educators must put aside their personal feelings of disgust or anger and, in these cases, simply file the appropriate reports.

TEACHERS: NATURAL ADVOCATES FOR CHILDREN

Teaching is a thankless and difficult job. Not only are class sizes prohibitively large and resources strictly limited, but also teachers are asked increasingly to do much more than teach. Tears in our social fabric, economic strength, and family supports unfortunately have left the schools as the sole source of structure and stability for many children. Because of this singularity, teachers frequently are expected to assess and handle behavior problems; instill self-control and respect for adults in children who do not learn these at home; model and teach socially acceptable conduct and values that are not necessarily reinforced by the children's immediate family or environment; and monitor nutrition, health and hygiene, safety and welfare.

Incredibly, teachers routinely do this and more, usually as a matter of course. One will keep peanut butter and crackers in a cupboard for the child who does not get enough to eat at home; another will provide a notebook and pencils for the child who cannot afford to purchase school supplies; a third will offer tutoring after school and provide counseling as well. Such generosity is as routine as it is extraordinary.

The purpose of this chapter is to explain current child welfare policy and the statutory requirement for reporting child abuse or neglect in a way that will be useful to teachers and other school personnel. Awareness of the burden already facing educators makes me reluctant to ask that even more be done; however, because school personnel are often the only people outside the family with whom a troubled child will have contact, they are also the child's only potential source of help. Most teachers readily and willingly advocate for the needs of children in their care and are frustrated when they cannot obtain timely help for children in distress. To express my admiration for the work that educators do in a frequently thankless world, this chapter will suggest ways to be a more effective voice for those who cannot speak for themselves.

REPORTING CHILD ABUSE AND NEGLECT

Mandated Reporting

In most jurisdictions, adults who work in any responsible capacity with children are required to report suspicion or direct knowledge of child abuse or neglect to the appropriate protective agency. In a school setting, most employees —not just teachers and principals—are mandated. School bus drivers, crossing guards, playground supervisors, day care and after school recreation staff, library aides, lunchroom staff all are responsible for the welfare of children and are expected to keep a protective eye out for their charges.

Typically, both immunity and confidentiality are afforded mandated reporters. That means the reporter cannot be sued or sanctioned (either by the family in question or by the employer) for reporting. Usually, however, a mandated reporter can be fined and/or imprisoned for failing to report when he/she should have, especially if the child sustained additional harm as a result of that failure. The identity of the person making the report is not supposed to be disclosed in initial assessments and preliminary hearings. If parents deny all allegations and demand a full trial that rests solely on the information provided by one person, that person may be asked or subpoenaed to testify. Few cases receive a formal trial in which the reporter's confidentiality would be lost. In most cases, information is provided by several concerned adults, any or all of whom could have made the initial referral.

Reluctance to Report

Caring and responsible people hesitate to report their suspicions of abuse or neglect for any number of reasons. The following are a few of the more common concerns:

1. What if I am wrong? First, be assured that nothing automatically happens as a result of a report. Children will not be summarily removed from their homes; parents will not be whisked off to jail. Rather, a report pins down a specific time and set of circumstances in which a responsible adult with experience in working with children became concerned about the safety or welfare of a particular child and requested an assessment by someone skilled in evaluating allegations of child abuse and neglect. What happens next will depend on what that assessor finds. The immunity of the mandated reporter shields him/her from repercussions if the concerns cannot be substantiated or prove to be unfounded.

2. Parents have a right to rear their children however they want without government interference. Parents have considerable discretion in rearing their children, but this discretion stops short of willfully injuring or neglecting minors. Children also have rights, among them freedom from inflicted bodily harm and other types of abuse or neglect. In addition, they are entitled to food, shelter, clothing, basic medical care, and supervision.

3. What if the parent finds out I made the report? Although every practical attempt is made to keep the identity of the reporter confidential, parents sometimes do guess correctly who made the report. Take, for example, the parent who beats a child on the weekend, then lets him/her go to school Monday morning despite bruises on the face and arms.

If a child welfare worker or police officer then calls on the parent that same Monday to ask how the child got those marks, the parent likely will conclude that someone at school alerted the county welfare or police department.

If indeed you become worried about your safety at this point, you also must ask yourself how safe is it for the child to be alone with this adult. Parents who can muster a modicum of self-control become the embodiment of sweet reasonableness in the period following a report because they are aware they are being watched. Someone who cannot manage to behave well even under these circumstances may pose a real threat to the child's safety. Any threatening behavior by the parent should be reported immediately to both the child welfare and the police departments.

4. The child told me in confidence; I do not want to lose his/her trust. Children who disclose family problems take a considerable risk and are probably violating implicit, if not explicit, parental dicta by disclosing. The response the child receives will influence significantly his/her ability to trust the adult world in the future. Therefore, the recipient of the confidence must respond promptly and adequately. Two guidelines can be given.

First, *do not promise more than you yourself can deliver.* In other words, do not predict or guarantee what the social worker or police officer will or will not do; do not let the child think he/she can come home with you; and do not predict the future or make promises you may not be able to keep. Most children will be satisfied with remarks such as, "I am glad that you trusted me enough to tell me about the problem at home. I care about you and want to do what I can to help you. I am a teacher, and I need to ask for help from somebody who knows more about these types of problems than I do. I am not sure what he/she will decide would be most helpful, but I will continue to listen, to care, and to do what I can for you, and I will let you know about plans for your family if I hear about them before you do."

Second, *model responsible adult behavior.* Do not let the child's demand for secrecy control or constrain your behavior. In all likelihood, that child comes from a family that has difficulty setting limits, establishing and honoring boundaries, and delineating the roles and responsibilities of children and adults. Afford the child the opportunity to see a caring and capable adult take on a difficult chore in a timely and appropriate way. You may not be able to improve much in the child's home, but you surely can give the child the experience of observing decent and responsible adult behavior. The unspoken message that not everyone is abusive or irresponsible will resonate loudly for the child.

5. Hearsay. Reports are required whenever one becomes either suspicious or knowledgeable of child abuse or neglect. Because most instances of abuse and neglect occur in the privacy of the family's home, knowledge and eyewitness reports are rare. Rather, reasonable suspicion based on observation of indicators of abuse (e.g., marks), credible information provided by a member of the family or a third party necessitates making a report. For example, either an adult volunteering in the school library may observe something of concern and inform the teacher, or a child may confide in a teacher the abuse or neglect another child is experiencing at home. Assuming the information in either case suggests the serious possibility of abuse or neglect of a child, the teacher would be required to alert the appropriate protective agency upon hearing the concern from the third party.

6. What if the behavior involved two children? Child abuse must be reported when a child is being abused or neglected. The abuser's age does not affect this mandate. Abused children may victimize other children, and reporting such injurious behavior should make help available to both children and their families. (Under the heading of "Sexual Abuse" later in this chapter, point 6, Family Indicators, discusses in greater detail the difference between normal and abnormal sexual behavior among children.)

7. I do not want to report a colleague. A report must be made whenever a child's welfare is jeopardized. As with reports of familial abuse, every effort is made to protect the reporter's identity; however, allowing abuse to continue not only endangers the child but also undermines the morale and integrity of the staff.

8. I have made reports in the past and nothing (or nothing constructive) happened. The current child welfare system is in crisis. Caseloads have grown exponentially, especially in areas affected by cocaine and other illicit drugs, while services barely have expanded. The level of danger to a child needed to justify intervention may be much higher now, particularly in inner cities, than it was only a few years ago. As a result, frustration among service providers is widespread. Some therapists and physicians even have proposed a two-tiered reporting system in which

a privileged class of reporters would have considerable discretion in making reports and essentially would function in lieu of the court in overseeing an abusive family.

The fact that the present system does not work is clear. Fixing it is a better solution than building in compensatory stopgaps. Protective services caseloads need to be kept to manageable sizes, with workers given regular and capable supervision and training. Vigilante behavior on the part of frustrated mandated reporters only draws attention from the need to repair an overburdened child welfare system.

9. Summary. Failure to report suspected abuse or neglect condones and perpetuates the abuse or neglect. Furthermore, such failure says to the child who has confided in an adult that the trusted adult condones the abusive behavior. Reporting is an opportunity to show the child that someone cares, accepts responsibility, can set and honor limits, and can work within the system to try—regardless of outcome—to improve things for the child. One should not underestimate the significance to the child of observing integrity and of being given an alternative set of rules and standards.

WHICH COURT?

Cases pertaining to child abuse and neglect can be heard in a number of criminal and civil courts, each having a different purpose and, therefore, a different impact on the child and his/her family. Understanding the purpose of each type of proceeding will help advocates insure that the child does not get lost in the system without basic protection.

Criminal Court

Cases involving severe injury or death of a child, or cases having multiple victims, likely will be heard in a criminal court because the case does not hinge on the ability of a single child to testify and withstand cross-examination. Rather, the allegation typically will be supported either by medical experts or by a pattern of inflicted injuries or neglect involving numerous children. Many jurisdictions also require that a child be at least a certain age (typically approximately five) before being allowed to testify. This requirement is intended to protect small children from being traumatized by courtroom activities, but it also results in frequent failure to pursue cases involving young children, especially if the medical evidence is equivocal.

The focus of a criminal case is on the alleged perpetrator and the need to prove his/her illegal behavior beyond a reasonable doubt. The remedies available if prosecution is successful include county jail, fines, work furlough, community service, probation, or, in more serious situations, state prison and parole—that is, the temporary restriction of the abuser. The child participates to the extent that he/she can provide information leading to the conviction or exoneration of the suspect. In many venues, such children also qualify for reimbursement of therapy and other treatment through state-run victims of crime programs; however, the welfare of the victimized child is far from central in criminal court.

Civil Court

In several states, laws have been passed recently allowing victims to sue their abusers for damages, usually for therapy and living expenses while in treatment (e.g., the 1990 amendment to Section 340.1 of the Code of Civil Procedure in California). Much research has been presented to the legislatures about the phenomenon of dissociation in victims of severe child abuse and about how many survivors only begin to become aware of the severity of their past when, as adults, they have flashbacks or experience difficulty in intimate relations or upon becoming a parent (Gil, 1988, 1991; Putnam, 1989). Therefore, these laws tend to include a statute of limitations of three years after the victim becomes aware of abuse (usually measured from the victim's first disclosure in therapy) rather than after the abusive incident(s). As a result, incidents beyond the statute of limitations for criminal court still can be heard in a civil proceeding.

Additionally, the standard for proof in civil court, a preponderance of evidence, is not as high as for criminal cases. Thus, a victim might prevail in a civil suit even though a criminal case is not brought against the perpetrator. A victim may feel empowered and validated by a successful outcome in civil court. Poor families, however, likely will not benefit from these new laws because no provision for compensating victims beyond the resources of the perpetrator is provided. Appellate courts in California and elsewhere have ruled that homeowner's and other liability insurance may not be used to satisfy these judgments, but only the personal assets of the perpetrator.

Family Court

Family court addresses marital separation and divorce as well as custody, visitation, and support of minor children. Allegations of child maltreatment may be among the reasons a parent seeks the dissolution although serious (e.g., sexual) abuse is not higher among divorcing adults than in the general adult population. This is a setting, however, in which a child in need of protection may be overlooked due to a tendency by court personnel to attribute allegations of abuse or neglect to friction surrounding the separation.

Family court also hears cases involving the parenting responsibilities and financial support of children whose parents did not marry. These cases can come to the attention of family court when the mother either seeks child support from the father or requests Aid to Families with Dependent Children (AFDC) from the county welfare department. The failure of noncustodial fathers to pay reasonable support for their offspring is rampant, and a major contributor to the impoverishment of so many single-parent families. Few jurisdictions have sufficient staff to pursue nonpaying fathers, and, by definition, the mothers do not have the financial resources to use the legal system to coerce payment.

Juvenile Court

In many states, juvenile court is divided into dependency and delinquency divisions. In the former, the child is alleged to be the victim of parental abuse or neglect. In the latter, the child's behavior is itself problematic, and the involvement of the juvenile court usually begins when the child is arrested.

As a practical matter, dependency court usually hears cases involving young children; delinquency court typically hears cases involving teenagers. Young children are more vulnerable and dependent on their parent(s) for their survival and welfare and have minimal ability to protect or fend for themselves in the face of parental incapacity or cruelty. Even the extreme behavior of a young child generally is seen as reflecting on the parent's inadequacy in setting limits, eliciting good behavior, and imposing benign and effective discipline. Thus, a young child is readily perceived as needing protection from harm. When a parent cannot do this, the juvenile court and/or the county welfare department step in. They provide such services as parenting skills classes, individual and family therapy, drug and alcohol treatment, in-home support services (e.g., family care workers, housekeeping assistance) and day and respite care for the child/children. In extreme cases where these services are not sufficient to allow the child/children to remain at home safely, emergency shelter and foster care are provided along with a reunification plan that includes regular visits between the parent/parents and child/children, either supervised or unsupervised depending on the level of risk for the child/children.

Older children are thought to be better able to protect themselves and also more provocative—that is, responsible for a parent's excess or failure. When children reach their teen years, they frequently become more rebellious and less willing to comply with adult authority, especially when that authority has not been earned by honorable adult behavior. These children tend to come to the system's attention when their own behavior crosses societal limits resulting in their arrest. Delinquency court orders provide many of the same services as dependency court orders, except that the emphasis is now on the child's misdeeds rather than on those of the parents. Thus, various punitive restrictions (i.e., similar to adult criminal court) in the form of mandated programs and possibly restrictive housing (e.g., group homes, juvenile hall, other residential programs) are imposed on the child in addition to therapy and other treatment services. The parents may have no sanctions. A common misunderstanding is to see these various systems as separate and discrete. Rather, children who are seriously abused or neglected in early childhood and not given adequate intervention, protection, and treatment often will become difficult in their teens, triggering the delinquency system. Those who fail at this level will, in all likelihood, become clients of the adult criminal justice system. In summary, then, rather than three disparate groups (i.e., abused children, unruly adolescents, and adult criminals), each being dealt with by a different section of the legal system, what really exists is one group of people at three different ages and stages. The National Committee for Prevention of Child Abuse (NCPCA) reports indicate that at least 80% of convicted felons had an abusive childhood.

Juvenile court focuses on the child, exerting influence over adults only to the extent that they wish to be involved with that specific child. A parent who either fails to comply with court orders for drug or alcohol treatment or fails to participate in an incest offenders program may be denied access to the child in question. Because few cases of intrafamilial child abuse or neglect also are prosecuted in adult criminal court, usually no way exists to prevent that parent from refusing treatment, walking away from that situation, and then beginning or joining a new family and committing the same offenses with new victims. Even tracking histories of reported abusers becomes difficult because the cases are usually recorded under the child's last name, which with single parents is often that of the mother. Cross references, which would allow investigators to track unmarried or step-parents who use different last names and go through serial relationships seldom are kept. Few counties even have the funding to purchase computers that eventually could be used to cross reference half- and stepsiblings, maiden and married names, and aliases.

CHILD ABUSE OR NEGLECT:
EFFECTIVE AND RESPONSIBLE REPORTING

The Role of Mandated Reporters

Increasingly the policy of child welfare agencies throughout the country has been to promote family preservation through the use of preventive services and in-home programs to obviate the need to place a child outside the home. Children are bonded to those who care for them, whether that care is good or bad, and they experience loss, disruption, and anxiety when separated from familiar people and settings. Ideally, then, a child is removed only when the risk of remaining at home is substantially greater than the harm automatically, if unintentionally, done through removal. Moreover, courts usually order the return of children to their home as soon as parents can demonstrate progress (as opposed to resolution of problems) and promise that the child will be safe and have his/her minimal needs met.

This commitment to family preservation and rapid reunification is balanced by the demand that adults who work with children keep a protective eye out for their welfare and report suspicion or knowledge of abuse or neglect immediately to the appropriate protective agency (e.g., usually child welfare, juvenile probation, police, or sheriff). In contrast to the high level of suspected danger needed to justify the removal of a child from his/her home, reasonable concern about safety or welfare is enough to justify making a report to a protective agency. Most abuse or neglect occurs in private, so people who are not members of the immediate family more often suspect rather than know for sure (i.e., have witnessed the abuse). When responsible adults in the community become concerned, they likely are seeing only the tip of an iceberg whose depth they cannot fathom. They should request an assessment promptly from the appropriate child welfare program. Timely reporting may not stop parental abuse or neglect, but it can shorten the life of family secrets and reduce the damage these secrets do to the child.

Making an Effective Report

Remember that the report is sent to juvenile authorities who focus on matters affecting a child's safety or welfare. Do not begin by describing how ineffective or aggressive the parents are, as parent behavior has no necessary legal relevance to the child's safety or welfare. Instead, describe the current harm to the child, the likelihood of continuing risk, and whether the child is afraid, lacks good judgment about his/her safety, or has any special needs or handicaps that might limit his/her ability to protect himself/herself. Describe previous attempts to improve the child's situation and assess the parent's capacity and motivation to recognize and respond appropriately to the child's needs. In other words, subordinate the dysfunction of the parent(s) to the danger posed to the child, the necessary legal focus of the case.

Rather than reporting abuse in the following manner: "The child was slapped across the face during a family argument and has a bruise. The child said it was not the first time this happened," say the following instead:

> The child, 3 feet tall and weighing 45 lbs., sustained a blow to the head an eighth of an inch from the eye in the course of a family argument on (date). The child has received similar injuries in the past and is afraid of a recurrence. Due to the history of such abuse, the fact that it occurs during arguments when tempers flare and impulse control is apt to be poor, the child will continue to be at risk of reinjury without intervention. Attempts to provide guidance have been made by various school personnel: the child's current teacher, teacher last year, school counselor, school principal. All overtures were rejected by the parents. Therefore, protective services by the juvenile court are requested and seem needed to have the parents participate in services that would improve their control and ensure safety for the child.

Rather than reporting neglect in the following manner: "The parents use drugs, never take care of the child, and refused three requests for conferences," say instead:

> The child, age 7, comes to school tired, hungry, and inadequately clothed. He reports that no one prepares meals at home, bathes him, or puts him to bed. He is afraid when he is home alone at night and reports that this happens at least twice during the week as well as on weekends. He is increasingly inattentive and groggy in class, and his work is poor. It is likely he will fail the year. He has become argumentative with his peers, and they have begun to ridicule him because of his dirty and unkempt appearance. Three appointments were scheduled to discuss these concerns with the parents. Only the last appointment was kept, and the parents were unable to see any deterioration in the child's behavior or reason for providing a more stable home. Therefore, the child remains at significant risk because of the parents' inability to recognize the child's needs, much less respond appropriately and protectively to them. It is likely that at least some of their indifference to their child's well-being is due to drug usage.

Reports are expected to be made whenever a mandated reporter becomes aware of a dangerous or neglectful situation. Because abuse tends to be episodic —a child will have fresh injuries—knowing when to report abuse is more obvious than when to report neglect. Neglect, the continual failure to attend to the child's needs, is ongoing, so that timely and useful reporting is more difficult to do. Although one person should not report the same incident more than once, damaging behaviors that are repeated merit separate reports. In the example of neglect given above, if the child is neglected each weekend, a new report should be made every Monday morning documenting the neglect of the preceding weekend. Either an emergency or an enduring and compelling pattern of neglect is needed in the more overworked counties to procure intervention.

INDICATORS OF ABUSE AND NEGLECT

Physical Abuse

Physical abuse involves any nonaccidental injury. The seven points that follow present specific examples.

1. Shaking, often referred to as "shaken baby syndrome." Shaking, especially of an infant, can be extremely injurious and may cause mental retardation, epilepsy, convulsions, and/or blindness. As the child is shaken, the brain travels at a slightly different speed than the skull, causing it to bump against the bone. Swelling, bruising, and blood clots frequently result. Because the skull prevents the brain from swelling outward, the resulting pressure on the brain, optic nerve, and eye may result in irreversible damage.

    Shaking most commonly occurs with infants and toddlers. A parent may become frustrated with a baby who will not stop crying, or he/ she may have unrealistic expectations about when a child should be toilet-trained. Babies who have colic; are fussy or irritable due to a rash, teething, or illness; or were exposed to drugs prenatally are, therefore, at greatest risk. Indicators of shaking include fractures or bruises suggesting hand marks on the upper torso or upper arms (i.e., wherever the child was held while being shaken).

    One of the most severe types of abuse, shaking is also one of the most preventable. Parents are frustrated, exhausted, and want to stop the baby from crying. They even may want to hurt the baby but have hardly any idea of the severe consequences of shaking. Giving this information to people who will have the responsibility for babies and toddlers may encourage people to substitute less injurious behaviors for life-threatening ones.

2. Biting. Children are very oral and, in infancy, one of the chief ways they explore their world is with their mouths. Similarly, toddlers and small children may bite when frustrated; however, biting is an immature response that should be outgrown once a child has acquired language and several behavioral options to express anger and annoyance. An adult who bites a child—usually to show a child that biting hurts and should not be done—is acting on a very primitive reflex, showing regressed behavior and poor judgment. Moreover, he/she is unwittingly modeling biting for the child despite his/her desire that the child cease this behavior. This adult's abilities may be sufficiently impaired to warrant a professional assessment of mental capacity and responsibility.

3. Burns. As with bites, burns indicate disturbed and injurious behavior. An adult deliberately may burn a child after warnings about staying away from a hot stove or iron have gone unheeded. Cigarette burns and immersion burns (i.e., where an extremity is immersed in hot water) also occur.

4. Bruises and Other Marks. While usually less severe, bruises and marks are also more common. Injuries may be inflicted by a belt, switch, telephone or extension cord, fist, or a forceful open hand. Any corporal punishment that results in a mark should be reported. Spanking a child is permitted; injuring a child is not. The level of response protective agencies can make to reports of marks will vary from county to county and season to season (e.g., reports usually decrease during the summer and increase in the fall and spring as a direct result of a child's contact with teachers) but should be reported regardless of the anticipated response. At the very least, a record will be kept of prior injury if something worse befalls the child.

5. Inflicted or Accidental Injuries? Both children and parents may attempt to keep the abuse a secret within the family. A few guidelines for distinguishing between accidents and abuse are provided:

    • Does the explanation of an injury or mark make sense and correspond to what you see? A child who fell off a bicycle likely will have skinned arms and/or legs and accompanying bruises, not marks on the small of the back or upper arm.

- Where are the marks located? Accidental marks tend to appear on appendages, occasionally a forehead or chin. Inflicted injuries are found more often on the back, buttocks, back of the thighs, upper arms, cheeks, and eye.
- Is the child wearing long sleeves and slacks when the other children are in shorts and T-shirts or bathing suits?
- Is there a history of recurring or unexplained injuries?
- Are there frequent and/or unexplained absences from school?

6. A Child's Behavioral Cues. A child may demonstrate

- withdrawal or aggressive behavior;
- self-destructive behavior (e.g., head-banging);
- hypervigilance, extreme fear, or anxiety;
- bed-wetting;
- wariness of physical contact with adults or indiscriminate and clingy attachment;
- attention-getting, antisocial behavior such as fire setting, truancy, or stealing;
- fear of, overprotectiveness of, and responsibility for a parent, or drastic behavior change in the presence of a parent;
- speech or learning difficulties or other school problems; and
- running away, drug or alcohol abuse, prostitution or promiscuity, or suicide attempts.

7. A Parent's Behavioral Cues. Behavioral indicators by a parent may include the following:

- a history of abuse in the parent's childhood;
- use of harsh discipline, rules inappropriate to the child's age and development;
- description of the child as big, powerful, and perhaps as an equal who is challenging the parent;
- inflexible and unreasonable expectations of the child;
- judgmental or cruel; and
- abuse of alcohol or other drugs.

Sexual Abuse

Sexual abuse means the sexual use of a child. It does not involve touching necessarily, nor does the perpetrator have to be an adult.

1. Who are Victims? Children of any age can be victims of sexual abuse; however, sexual abuse most commonly begins when children are in elementary school although disclosures often are not made until children are much older. Girls are more likely to be molested in their own home—frequently in their own bed—by their father, step-father or other significant family member. Boys, on the other hand, are molested more often by someone known to the child but not part of the immediate family—a coach, baby-sitter, or Sunday school teacher, for example. Seldom are children forced by a stranger; rather they are encouraged and persuaded by someone they know and trust. Children with a disability are more likely to be molested than their nonhandicapped peers; they are more vulnerable, dependent, and less able to tell, run away, or refuse the advances.

2. Types of Sexual Abuse. Sexual abuse need not include touching. Someone may begin a sexual relationship with a child by asking to take photographs, possibly including nude or provocative pictures of that child, or by sharing pornographic photographs, television, or videocassettes of others engaged in sexual activities. Such visual materials serves to lower the child's inhibitions and teach the desired behaviors. Nontouching sexual abuse also can include exhibitionism (by either party), instructions that one will watch the other masturbate, insert objects into orifices, or engage in other forms of sexual activity. Although touching may progress to intercourse, at least as common are fondling and oral and anal contacts.

3. Differences Between Normal Sex Play and Abuse. Sexual abuse does not necessarily involve an adult preying on a child. It also can include an older, larger, or more powerful child taking advantage of a younger child. Normal sex play occurs between children of roughly the same age, size, experience, and capacity. These behaviors are consistent with the curiosity, attention span, and level of knowledge common to children of that developmental stage and level of experience. A certain amount of comparative anatomy and curiosity—especially at times of developmental significance such as toilet training or puberty—are to be expected. Unusual, however, would be either a nine-year-old attempting to sodomize a toddler or a pet or else a child who can describe accurately adult sexual behavior or who masturbates in public for hours despite being asked not to do this. Questions a concerned adult should ask include the following:

    *   Are these children equally matched in size, experience, and capacity?

- Are they engaging in activities that most children their age would know about?
- Are they demonstrating the frequency, intensity, and duration that they demonstrate in other activities?
- Is their behavior more driven than playful?
- Do they have knowledge beyond their years of adult sexual behavior?
- How did they acquire this advanced knowledge?
- Are they preoccupied, or terrified, by sexual matters?
- Are they sexually aggressive with other children or adults?

4. Physical Indicators of Sexual Abuse in Children. Physical indicators include the following:

- torn, bloody, stained underwear;
- pain, itching, or discharge in the genital area;
- bruises or lacerations in external genitalia, vagina, or anus;
- venereal disease (in mouth or throat or genital tract);
- sexualized behavior including excessive masturbation or inserting objects into orifices of self, playmate, pet, doll;
- significant changes in eating, sleeping, grooming, or toileting habits;
- a sudden change in relationships or academic performance;
- self-destructive or self-mutilating behavior;
- eating disorders, drug or alcohol abuse;
- running away; and
- suicidal gestures.

5. Behavioral Indicators of Sexual Abuse in Children. Behavioral indicators include the following:

- withdrawn or aggressive behavior;
- poor peer relationships;
- sexualized behavior;
- poor or distorted body image; and
- feelings of guilt, shame, or worthlessness.

6. Family Indicators. For sexual abuse that occurs within a family (i.e., incest), some typical dynamics include the following:

- a parent who was sexually abused as a child;
- a strained, overprotective or "special" relationship between the child and one parent, together with relative indifference on the part of the other parent;

- a child's reluctance to be alone with one parent, or appearing "bossy" or powerful with that parent;
- sexual remarks to or about a child by a parent;
- a child routinely sleeping in the same bed as the parent(s);
- failure by the parent(s) to provide timely medical care; and
- the existence of a "family secret."

Other common signs include the following:

- drug or alcohol abuse in the family;
- a distorted sense of the child's development, maturity, size, or capabilities;
- a parent's lack of appropriate emotional involvement;
- parental failure to afford privacy to the child;
- parental refusal to allow the child to participate in reasonable social activities;
- isolation of the family; and
- paternal dominance and role reversal between mother and daughter.

7. Indicators of Nonfamilial Sexual Abuse. Children whose guardians often leave them alone may be lonely and hungry for adult attention. These children may be particularly likely to respond to the interest and eventual sexual advances of an older friend, relative, or stranger; however, most children are manipulated easily when an adult in any position of authority makes requests. A child spending an inordinate amount of time alone with an adult, or a child who receives a number of gifts from an adult may be involved sexually as well.

   Physical and behavioral indicators in the child generally correspond to those listed above; however, the onset of these changes may be more sudden since the abuse is not part of the ongoing dynamic of the child's family. Therefore, the changes may be more noticeable.

8. The Power of Secrets. In both familial and nonfamilial cases of child sexual abuse, children almost always are enjoined not to tell, by implicit or explicit means. If a concerned adult does not assure the child that he/she will be believed and reassure the child about the likely realistic consequences of telling, seldom will a child volunteer the information. Again, the concerned adult must guard against making promises that cannot be kept and reassuring the child that "everything will be OK." A child's ability to trust is at stake—and this is a child who already has been betrayed by an adult who made promises.

The kind of reassuring statement that can be made honestly and will assist the child includes the following: assurance that the child will be believed, assurance that the adult will continue to care about and support the child by getting appropriate help for the problem, and assurance that the child was not at fault regardless of his/her level of participation in the sexual activity. Because children do not abstract well, they may be more able to tell about an injunction against disclosure (e.g., "Daddy said he would go to jail if I told anyone" or "the minister said no one would believe me") than about the sexual activity itself. Hence, if a child seems reluctant to talk about the problem, it may be more fruitful to ask the child what he/she is afraid might happen if he/she did tell.

Emotional Abuse

Emotional abuse encompasses the chronic and persistent verbal and psychological maltreatment of a child including rejection, humiliation, constant disparagement, and criticism such that the child's mental or emotional health and development is jeopardized. In deciding when to report suspected emotional abuse, seek a pervasive pattern of negative treatment and not just a few isolated incidents of verbal cruelty.

1. Physical and Behavioral Indicators. Physical and behavioral indicators in the emotionally abused child can include the following:

   - seeking out and being overly anxious to please adults,
   - viewing the abuse as warranted,
   - depression,
   - developmental lags,
   - hyperactivity,
   - aggressive or bizarre behavior,
   - withdrawal and apathy,
   - unprovoked yelling or crying,
   - poor sense of worth and self-confidence,
   - difficulty in sustaining relationships,
   - self-deprecation, and/or
   - sabotaging success.

2. Familial Indicators. Familial indicators include an adult who may have the following attributes:

   - is harsh and inflexible;
   - blames, belittles, ridicules, or berates the child;

- is cold and rejecting;
- fails to support, encourage, guide, or express the positive value of the child;
- scapegoats the child;
- has unrealistic expectations;
- is inconsistent and unpredictable;
- has a childhood history of deprivation or abuse;
- identifies the child as bad, or associates him/her with something or someone hated or of the wrong sex;
- seems uninterested in the child's problems; and/or
- does not recognize the child as a separate person with worthy wants, needs, and interests.

More extreme cases may include psychiatric problems or bizarre behavioral patterns that prevent the parent from relating to the child. Such difficulties sometimes manifest themselves in the parent's cruel, extreme, or bizarre punishment of the child.

Neglect

Neglect is the willful failure to provide the essentials for a healthy life: food, shelter, clothing, nurturance, medical care, and supervision. Neglect includes the following:

- abandonment,
- nonorganic failure to thrive or malnutrition,
- inadequate clothing or hygiene,
- lack of timely medical care,
- extreme lack of interaction and attention,
- permitting serious or dangerous conduct by the child, and/or
- failing to send the child to school or allowing chronic absences.

1. Physical and Behavioral Indicators of Neglect. The neglected child frequently may have one or more of the following indicators:

   - be dirty, unwashed, hungry, and inappropriately dressed either for his/her size or the weather;
   - seem listless or tired;
   - have chronic untreated medical problems;
   - show fearfulness or learned helplessness;
   - have speech and language delays;

- engage in regressive behavior (e.g., thumb sucking, rocking, head banging);
- be left for extended periods of time without supervision, be expected to care for or be cared for by a sibling;
- beg for or steal food;
- prostitute;
- abuse drugs or alcohol; and/or
- in the most serious cases, attempt suicide.

2. Familial Indicators of Neglect. The key parental indicators of neglect are the following:

   - abuse of drugs or alcohol,
   - a childhood history of neglect or abuse,
   - a long-term chronic or mental illness,
   - depression,
   - isolation, and/or
   - lack of interest in self and/or the child.

3. Environmental Indicators of Neglect. Environmental clues include the following:

   - a filthy, chaotic, unsanitary and/or unsafe household;
   - absence of nutritious food;
   - few if any toys for the child; and/or
   - heavy curtains that are closed during the day or blankets that are draped across windows.

4. Difference Between Poverty and Neglect. Unfortunately, many families live in abject poverty and cannot provide even the essentials for their children. Poverty should trigger a referral to resources for needed goods and services. Reportable neglect, on the other hand, is the willful deprivation or failure to provide the essentials of life to a child. A poor family will seek out a food bank and make as much food available to their child as possible; a negligent family will sell the child's food, exchange it for drugs, let it spoil on the shelf, or deprive the child of it in some other way. A poor family will child-proof their inadequate home and keep the child safe and supervised despite the paucity of resources; a negligent family will allow a child to play in unsafe or dangerous surroundings or will make a young child responsible for the supervision of other little children.

Discipline or Abuse?

Discipline means self-control and self-regulation. If a method is implemented benignly and allows a child to assess options and make increasingly self-reliant choices, it is discipline. Consequences—apart from dangerous ones from which the child should be protected—are learned through trial and error by the child with gentle guidance by the adult. Punishment, and its extreme, namely abuse, focuses instead on external controls. A punished child will obey if he/she thinks he/she is likely to get caught and the consequence is forbidding. Such compliance is exacted at the price of learning and hardly leads a child to develop the skills necessary to make safe and constructive choices throughout life, to regulate and defer impulses, or to build confidence in his/her own ability to make wise choices. In summary, punishment looks backward to the error, whereas discipline looks forward to application of the new knowledge.

EFFECTIVE RESPONSES

In order to have responsible adults involved, the following points are suggested.

1. Broaden Your Base. Ask others who come in contact with the child how he/she seems to them. Several responsible adults in addition to the classroom teacher likely will know the child: the bus driver (whose impression should be sought out and valued—who else sees the child both at home and at school and watches the child make the transition each day?), the playground aide, the librarian, the school nurse, or other specialist. If your school has access to the services of a social worker or psychologist, refer the child for an assessment.

2. Build a Network. Secure the assistance of adults who will be able to keep an eye on the child when he/she is not in school. Ask the county health department to send a public health nurse to the child's home to check on the child's welfare, hygiene, and safety. Almost any concern involving a child will affect his/her health, justifying such services. Child protective services will sense a graver situation if professionals tracking the child both at school and at home voice concerns.

3. Encourage Extracurricular Activities. Persuade the family to have the child participate in a recreational activity after school and/or on the weekend. This activity will reduce the time the child spends in the parent's care in a way acceptable to the parent, thereby reducing the time

the parent is responsible for the child and the attendant stress of that responsibility. Additionally, the parent unknowingly may learn some skills if paired with a more adequate parent, and the child can have the opportunity to interact with healthier children and adults while doing something enjoyable. Abused and neglected children often lack social skills to make friends easily and also may feel unworthy. Such a setting and a little extra encouragement can help a lonely child blossom socially.

Encourage the Child to Develop an Interest, Skill, or Talent

Dysfunctional families usually are very isolated and rarely expose children to the riches that their community and culture have to offer. Special talents go unnoticed or ridiculed. Children in such homes do not have the opportunity to taste, sample, dabble, try new things, or take up a hobby. Developing such an interest, however, is one of the best things a child in a dysfunctional family could do for a multitude of reasons. Having wider interests and competencies can help with the following:

1. Give a new, healthy identity (e.g., "I'm a gymnast" vs. "I'm the kid my parents wished hadn't been born.").
2. Provide a child a friendly and welcoming place to go.
3. Lead to a new group of friends. Even children whom others avoid at school have a relatively easy time making a friend in a specialized activity where the common denominator of the class tends to outweigh a child's idiosyncrasy. Frequently this group of friends will remain largely intact for years as they continue the lessons.
4. Present a child with a responsible adult friend who is apt to be good with children.
5. Open doors for a child that could lead to alternatives to following in the familial tracks. An interest in photography, for example, could lead a child to pursue a career in commercial art; an interest in judo could turn into both a lifelong hobby and a teaching career.

CONCLUSION

The author intends the preceding information as a framework that educators may use to become more effective advocates for needy children; however, anyone easily may become overwhelmed not only by the number of warning signs and possible indicators of abuse or neglect but also by the number of systems and their representatives that might have authority over a child. In this context, the most valuable thing an educator can keep in mind is the singular importance of treating children in a humane and respectful way. Whereas much else is beyond the control of any individual, the quality of the time one spends with a child is within that person's grasp. Children who sense that their teachers and other adult caretakers appreciate them, value them for their insights or observations, enjoy them for an amusing anecdote, and admire them for a special sensitivity will feel much better able to face any challenges on their path.

BIBLIOGRAPHY

Child abuse prevention handbook. (1988). Sacramento: Crime Prevention Center, Office of the Attorney General.

Finkelhor, D. (1986). *A sourcebook on child sexual abuse.* Beverly Hills: Sage.

Finkelhor, D., & Browne, A. (1985). The traumatic impact of child sexual abuse: A conceptualization. *American Journal of Orthopsychiatry* 55, 530-541.

Garbarino, J., & Garbarino, A. (1980). *Emotional maltreatment of children.* Chicago: National Committee for Prevention of Child Abuse.

Garbarino, J., & Gilliam, G. (1983). *Understanding abusive families.* Lexington, MA: Lexington Books.

Gil, E. (1990). *Children who molest: A guide for parents of young sex offenders.* Walnut Creek, CA: Launch Press.

Gil, E. (1990). *United we stand: A book for individuals with multiple personalities.* Walnut Creek, CA: Launch Press.

Kempe, H. & Helfer, R. (1980). *The battered child.* Chicago: University of Chicago Press.

Office of Child Abuse Prevention. (1991). *The California child abuse and neglect reporting law: Issues and answers for health practitioners.* Sacramento: State Department of Social Services.

Sgroi, S. (1982). *Handbook of clinical intervention in child sexual abuse.* Lexington, MA: Lexington Books.

Summit, R. (1983). The child abuse accommodation syndrome. *Child Abuse and Neglect: The International Journal. Pergamon Press, Ltd.,* 7, 177-193.

REFERENCES

Gil, E. (1991). *The healing power of play: Working with abused children.* New York: Guilford Press.

Gil, E. (1988). *Treatment of adult survivors of childhood abuse.* Walnut Creek, CA: Launch Press.

National Committee for Prevention of Child Abuse (NCPCA). (undated). *Fact sheet.* Chicago, IL: Author.

Putnam, F. (1989). *Diagnosis and treatment of multiple personality disorder.* New York: Guilford Press.

Chapter 8

SUBSTANCE ABUSE IN CHILDREN AND ADOLESCENTS: A FAMILY PERSPECTIVE

Kimberly Barrett
Sarah Rafton

Editor's Note

Teachers and school counselors are not licensed clinical social workers with dual training in community resources and psychotherapy. Treating drug abuse is both simple and a heavy burden. By understanding the social context of students' lives, educators can see how taking drugs makes some sense. Then, a counselor guides the family out of the mine field one cautious step at a time. As logical as this work may sound, however, counseling a family through a crisis with drugs is a serious responsibility and the professionals who provide this help need all the art they can master. What this chapter does is offer readers a transparent view of addictive problems in a context of relationships. No reader can be naive about drug abuse after reading this chapter by Barrett and Rafton. Case examples make clear the value of Adlerian parenting skills classes, strategic and structural family therapy, and multiple family counseling.

People who allow for induction in their lives do not stay the same. By experiencing an initiation rite on the topic of drug abuse and treatment, educators take a stand on spotting the trouble, sensitively referring the student and family to counselors who can make a difference, and being there for the whole family when they have "cleaned up their act." Reminding yourself that you do not have to become a drug counselor is probably an important step before reading this material. Schools cannot be all things to all clientele. They must rely on ancillary services in the form of community mental health, substance abuse treatment centers, community diversion programs, university-based community counseling clinics, alternative services for youth through local police departments, hospitals and clinics, and other agencies.

DRUG AND ALCOHOL ABUSE TODAY

Drug and alcohol use is commonplace among children and adolescents in contemporary society. An estimated three million American youths between the ages of 10 and 17 have substance use related problems (Dryfoos & Klerman, 1988). National survey results on drug use from the *Monitoring the Future Study, 1975-1992* (Johnson, O'Malley, & Bachman, 1993) indicate a 62% prevalence rate of tobacco use among teenagers and 90% report of alcohol use among high school seniors. Additionally, the study found significant increases in the use of marijuana, cocaine, LSD, stimulants, and inhalants among eighth-grade youth. The increasingly downward trend indicating that youngsters first use drugs at earlier and earlier ages demands an examination of use patterns as well as a delineation of the risk factors pointing toward such usage. Recognizing at-risk children is a first step in diverting them away from a path to substance abuse. The most critical period for intervention is still between the fifth and ninth grades (Office of Substance Abuse Prevention [OSAP], 1990). Moreover, according to a survey of Washington state adolescents, a majority of those students stated that drug education should begin in the fourth grade, if not sooner (Deck & Nickel, 1989).

Principal Drugs Adolescents Abuse

The main substances young adolescents use include cigarettes, inhalants, alcohol, and marijuana. A Washington state survey revealed that 12% of its sixth-grade students use cigarettes (Deck & Nickel, 1989). Given their accessibility, inhalants are just as popular as cigarettes among junior high-aged students, rating above cigarette use with Washington sixth-graders, at 13% (Deck & Nickel, 1989). Unlike alcohol or marijuana, inhalants are found easily in adolescents' homes and do not require purchase. Such innocuous household products as airplane glue, cleaning fluid, gasoline, lighter fluid, and even whipped cream become a means for youngsters to get high (Barun & Bashe, 1988). One of the primary causes of death among teenagers in the U.S. is drunk driving (Julien, 1992). Young people frequently take up marijuana early in their adolescence. One in six children will use marijuana by the time they reach seventh grade. Ninth-graders, however, are the most frequent age group to initiate marijuana use (DuPont, 1990).

Gateway Substances and Age. The aforementioned substances often are referred to as "gateways" to further drug use. The term "gateway substance" refers to those initial drugs that serve as the stepping stones to subsequent ingestion of more serious drugs and more frequent use. Therefore, detecting gateway drug use alerts educators and counselors to the risks and to practical steps they might take in preventing further drug use. Early childhood drug use is correlated with later use as well as with an increased probability for problem behaviors, including crimes such as drug dealing (Robins & Pryzbeck, 1985). Twelve- to fifteen-year-olds who smoke cigarettes, for example, are twice as likely to use alcohol, 9 times as likely to ingest depressants or stimulants, 10 times as likely to smoke marijuana, and 14 times as likely to use cocaine, hallucinogens, or heroin (DuPont, 1990). These are startling data. Moreover, 71% of males who started using marijuana at age 14 or younger are likely to initiate other illicit drugs by age 25, as opposed to only 9% of males who delayed first use of marijuana until age 21 (Kandel & Yamaguchi, 1985). In addition, recent epidemiological research has found those who first use alcohol at the age of 12 or 13 are far more likely to have problems with alcohol than those who initiate use at age 21 (OSAP, 1990).

The Real Culprit Drugs. Other findings about the influence of gateway drugs report age to be less of a predictor than *the particular substance* preteens and teens use. Kandel found that use of legal and available substances, such as the gateway drugs of cigarettes, alcohol, and inhalants, precedes the use of other more serious illegal drugs regardless of age (Kandel, 1975; Kandel & Faust, 1975). Whether age or legality is the chief predictor, both demographic factors recognize gateway substances as forerunners to more serious drug use.

Defining Adolescence

As predominant as is adolescent drug and alcohol use, definitions of adolescence vary (Varenhorst, 1988). Varenhorst defined adolescence as the years 12 to 22, subdividing adolescence into early, middle, and late categories. Early adolescence covers 12- to 15-year-olds (Varenhorst, 1988). Early adolescents, the most understudied segment of the entire adolescent population, are nevertheless the most vulnerable to drug exposure. They are also the least understood group and the most ineffectively served subset with respect to alcohol and drug use (Varenhorst, 1988). Generalizations about adolescents may discourage serious research about them. Often society discounts them because they are in transition, as if their problems represent only one of those phases. Besides dismissing them through this common misconception, myths exist that all adolescents are alike and that their growth patterns follow a predictable schedule (Lipsitz, 1977; Varenhorst, 1988). Framing adolescence as a time of moratorium invites greater understanding and tolerance from parents and others. The new perspective helps people see adolescents as legitimately engaging in socially tolerated experimentation (Varenhorst, 1988).

Family Context. Early adolescence brings a variety of emotional stressors and new challenges into children's lives. Families must confront new transitions in their dynamics as they learn to negotiate new developmental tasks and hurdles. New social and academic expectations arise with the onset of junior high or middle school. As these dramatic shifts are occurring, adolescents must develop independence, autonomy, and personal values (Kidwell, Fischer, Dunham, & Baranowski, 1983) often within an inflexible family atmosphere that does not accommodate and foster this maturation process.

Drug Abuse Is a Choice. Educators and counselors must examine young adolescents' first experimentation with drugs in the framework of new social pressures and growing complications in their lives at home. Add to these social and family dispositions, ethnicity, and biological factors and a new picture comes into focus showing all the possible informational pieces that may influence early drug use. Early drug initiation by adolescents involves a complex interplay of all these factors. Researchers can isolate no single factor as a determinant of drug usage; instead, many components interact to lead early adolescents to choose alcohol and drug use. Choice theory provides a possible explanation. The youngsters perceive themselves not in full control of some key parts of their lives and they mistakenly believe the path to meeting those important personal needs and regaining control is through drug use.

Attitudes Are Messages. As in all stages of human development, families play a critical role in young adolescents' lives. Parents hold a key position in influencing their 6- to 11-year-old children's values and standards (Rhodes & Jason, 1988). From age 12 onward, children naturally distance themselves increasingly from their parents. Though young adolescents are trying to break from parental closeness, parents still set a powerful example for them through their influence in two categories: example through attitudes, and example by their own use or abstinence (Kandel, 1980). Let's start with parents' influence of their children through their attitudes about substance use. A child's perception of permissive parental attitudes may be equal to or more important in influencing the child's substance use than the parents' actual usage. Parents hold certain beliefs and attitudes about drug use which adolescents my subsequently internalize as a part of their own value systems; thus, parental attitudes toward substance use influence use by children (Dishion, Patterson, & Reid, 1985; Jessor & Jessor, 1977; Kandel, 1980; Kandel, Kessler, & Marguiles, 1978).

Actions Speak Loudly. The second form of parental influence of children is through modeling. Because children and adolescents observe and imitate their parents' actions, children of parents who use drugs or alcohol are more likely to use these substances themselves than children whose parents do not indulge in drugs (Barun & Bashe, 1988; Dishion & Loeber, 1985; Dishion, Patterson, & Reid, 1985; Kandel, 1974, 1980; Needle, McCubbin, Wilson, Reinick, Lazar, & Mederer, 1986; NIAAA, 1984). Adolescents from families in which one or more members smoke, drink, or use drugs are more likely to use substances than adolescents of nonusing families (Needle et al., 1986). Parental use of hard liquor predicts adolescent use of hard alcohol, just as parental use of illicit drugs (i.e., other than marijuana) predicts use of illicit drugs by their children (Kandel et al., 1978). One characteristic of young problem drinkers is having parents who drink (NIAAA, 1984). Parental drug abuse is a distinct predictor for subsequent adolescent drug abuse (Kandel, Treiman, Faust, & Single, 1976).

Parental Supervision. Another parental factor influencing adolescents' drug use lies in parental monitoring and rule-making. Parents need to find a balance in their supervisory role because being either too strict or too lax may influence a child toward using (Barnes, 1990; Barun & Bashe, 1988). Moreover, specific parental rules against drugs are ineffective (Jessor & Jessor, 1977; Kandel et al., 1978). A Washington state survey found that parents commonly had knowledge and approved of adolescent drinking in their homes. At the sixth-grade level, 76% of alcohol was consumed in the adolescents' homes *with parental consent*; 11% of the alcohol consumption occurred in the home without parental knowledge. Thirty-three percent of eighth-graders reported consuming alcohol in their homes with parental consent, and 15% revealed that they used alcohol at home without parental consent (Deck & Nickel, 1989). Obviously, in the Washington cases, parental monitoring contributed directly to adolescents' use of alcohol. With respect to marijuana and alcohol, delinquent users have far less supervision than do nondelinquent users and abstainers (Dishion & Loeber, 1985).

Quality of Parent-Child Relationship. Yet another way in which parents have an effect upon young adolescent drug use lies in the interpersonal relationships of parents and their children. The degree of emotional closeness between parents and adolescent children is a factor determining adolescent drug use (Jessor & Jessor, 1977; Kandel, 1975; Kandel et al., 1978). At-risk adolescents often have parents who are not affectionate toward them (Barun & Bashe, 1988; NIAAA, 1984). Moreover, a lack of closeness between parents and children has been found to be a strong predictor for marijuana initiation (Kandel et al., 1978). The poorer the family relationship in general, the more likely an adolescent is to use drugs (Kandel, 1974).

Drugs as a Symptom of a Family's Communication Conflicts

Parents' personal marital and familial problems may spill over and influence early adolescents' drug use (Brook, Lukof, & Whiteman, 1978; Dishion et al., 1985; Tolone & Dermott, 1975). A family unit plays a crucial role in influencing adolescents to develop and maintain drug use. A decrease in a family's coping skills and a family's support networks influence adolescents' substance use (Barrett, 1989, paper submitted for publication). Baer, Garmezy, McLaughlin, Porkorny, and Wernick (1987) also pointed to deficits in a family's support systems as related to adolescent substance abuse problems. Many adolescents use drugs in order to distract themselves from family problems (Barrett, 1989; Haley, 1976, 1981; Stanton, 1979) or to help their families maintain a stable balance in their relationships (Madanes, Dukes, & Harbin, 1980; Stanton, 1979; Steinglass, 1987). A drug problem may serve as a stabilizer in the midst of many other family problems and may hold feuding parents together when they are considering a divorce.

Authoritative versus Authoritarian Parenting

Parents, however, *can* use their influence to decrease the chance that their adolescent will take up alcohol or drugs. As previously mentioned, parental modeling is very powerful. Parents may set a positive example for their children through moderate and healthy attitudes about alcohol and drug use. Beyond the parents' personal views about drug use, their particular disciplining methods are crucial in deterring substance abuse. *Authoritative* parents (i.e., competent people whose children find them credible) as opposed either to *permissive* or *authoritarian* parents, promote the conditions in which their adolescents may behave responsibly (Baumrind, 1987). Authoritative parents communicate, support, and enforce rules that parents and children have adopted mutually (Hawkins, Lishner, & Catalano, 1985).

Communicating Well. Parents who keep open their lines of communication with their adolescents can alter the rules that guide family relationships as changing conditions dictate. Thus, parents can create the conditions within which teenagers are unlikely to resent family rules or to resort to open rebellion. Genuine two-way communication is the best defense parents have against adolescent drug use. As Wills wrote, "The more a student was able to talk comfortably with parents . . . when he or she had a problem, the *less* likely the student was to be engaged in use" (1985, p. 66). Investigators have also found a positive correlation between parents' conventional behavior and adolescents' abstinence from drug use. The more religious, conventional, and traditional a mother, the lower the incidence of adolescent problem drinking and illicit drug use (Jessor & Jessor, 1977). Wills (1985) also found religion to be a successful coping tool for countering alcohol use. Close, supportive, and involved (but not intrusive) family relationships may protect children from the problem of drug use (Newcomb, 1995).

Parents or Peers. Supportive and authoritative parents can influence their children in acquiring sound coping skills and appropriate assertiveness (Kaufman, 1986) and, thereby, can assist the early adolescent in gaining a behavioral repertoire for handling the powerful pressures to come. Parental roles that accent caring involvement with their young children and adolescents can neutralize or reverse the impact of peer-related pressures to recruit new user-followers (Kandel, 1980). Adolescents who value closeness with their parents are less likely to dissociate from home in favor of associating with deviant peers (Kandel & Andrews, 1987).

The social norms governing peer relationships contribute strongly to risk of drug abuse and counselors must explore these silent forces. Thirty-nine percent of fifth-graders have reported experiencing peer pressure to use drugs and, by the eighth grade, this number had increased to 68% (Barun & Bashe, 1988). A *Weekly Reader* poll asked fourth- through sixth-graders why they smoke marijuana, and a majority acknowledged doing so in order to conform (Barun & Bashe, 1988). Adolescents' perceptions of their peer group's drug use is the strongest predictor of their subsequent induction into alcohol, marijuana, or other illicit drug use (Kandel, 1974; Kandel et al., 1978). Peers' self-reported use is also a high predictor of initiation into drug use (Jessor & Jessor, 1977; Kandel et al., 1978; Newcomb, Chou, Bentler, & Huba, 1988). Adolescents whose peers use drugs are more likely to use drugs frequently than those whose friends do not use (Jessor & Jessor, 1977; Kandel, 1973; Kandel et al., 1978).

Influence of Siblings on Drug Use

Siblings hold an important role in adolescent substance use. Older siblings have greater influence on the potential user than do parents (Penning & Barnes,

1982). Closeness in age and experience make a sibling a more likely model that a parent. Siblings possess a powerful combination of familial closeness in addition to peer-like influence. Perceptions of sibling use are predictive of a child's own use and attitudes toward substances (Clayton & Lacy, 1982). Children with older siblings who smoke are more likely to begin smoking than children whose siblings do not smoke (Murray, Swan, Johnson, & Bewley, 1983; Presson et al., 1984). In a sample of 9th- and 10th-grade students, adolescents with an older brother who used marijuana were more likely to use (Brook, Whiteman, Gordon, & Brenden, 1983). One study independently asked older and younger siblings about substance use. The older siblings' use was predictive of the younger children's use (Needle et al., 1986).

Other Social Forces

Beyond peers and one's family of origin, a variety of societal messages can influence the early adolescent's decision to use drugs. Television and movies glamorize drugs and alcohol and have a special appeal to youth between fourth and sixth grades (Barun & Bashe, 1988). The media expose children to the world of substance abuse by promoting positive associations in their advertising of each substance. The advertising and marketing industry has informed and influenced youth to a great degree by personalizing their pitches to kids and offering a two-for-one deal. Youngsters simultaneously can smoke a cigarette and make a defiant statement to parents and other encroaching adults. Media can portray products as "cool" and harmless, thus leading youth to use substances to enhance popularity (Kaminer, 1994). Young adolescents face a constant barrage of advertising that portrays a world filled with enticing images of substance use.

What goes on in an adolescents' environment is clearly a factor in the process of their initiation into substance use. No factor *makes* them choose drugs, but all the information—from parents, siblings, peers, and societal forces —collectively can become a very persuasive case. Ethnicity, for example, may also be a risk factor by association as both African-American and Latino cultures have specific elements that operate as influences toward substance use. Inner-city African-Americans, for example, draw from a variety of environmental factors to influence their choice to use drugs. Some aspects of family life itself may lead the way to drug use. An African-American child is four times more likely to grow up in a single parent household than a Caucasian child. Fifty-three percent of all African-American children are born to single mothers today (OSAP, 1990). Three in five African-American families experience disruption due to separation, divorce, or death (OSAP, 1990). The absence of a father leads to a variety of behavior problems for early adolescent males. They often experience a painful sense of loss of control and subsequently rejection in the school environment. Older men in the street culture exploit these youngsters' feelings of rejection and provide these abandoned and forlorn youths a sense of identity through crime. Poor education is a second environmental factor for young African-Americans with one half of African American elementary age children a full grade behind their Caucasian counterparts. Violence is another disruptive environmental factor for young adolescent African-Americans. Of two hundred Oakland families whom researchers interviewed, one in five families reported drug-related violence by one member of their immediate family or by someone in their community (OSAP, 1990).

Poverty and Drugs. Inner-city African-American children and adolescents also face psychosocial pressures affecting their use of drugs. A drug mentality is pervasive in inner-city America and, therefore, these norms affect all youths living there. Two salient mores of a drug culture are (1) trust no one and (2) anything is permissible (OSAP, 1990). Black children in inner-city neighborhoods internalized these modes of conduct into a value system as a primary method of survival. They have little or no faith in their chances for future economic or educational achievement in the mainstream (OSAP, 1990). In that context of limited alternatives and hopelessness, young people may view drugs as an appealing option. They may let the option loom large in their minds as a natural part of growing up (OSAP, 1990). The fast lifestyle and economic success that drug dealers flaunt also appeal to early adolescents whose lives are rather drab by comparison (Barrett, 1989). Sixty-six percent of such children in one survey reported drug dealing as an attractive way of life (OSAP, 1990).

Given the population growth of the Latino community, they are understudied when compared to urban African-Americans. Parental and sibling use is the best predictor for drug use among young Latino males who make up a large portion of the Latino community (OSAP, 1990). A disruptive family environment, including intergenerational difficulties, and cross-cultural conflicts, is a major risk factor among young Latinos (Szapocznik & Kurtines, 1993). The highest risks among Latino children are (a) children of users, (b) latchkey kids, and (c) children not attending school (OSAP, 1990).

Interpersonal Competence Provides a Shield. Do emotional or physical predispositions lead children to later drug problems? Social and environmental factors are outside children; physical and psychological disposition factors are internal. Skill deficits and poor social skills are predictive of later use (Dishion et al., 1985; NIAAA, 1984). Trouble expressing oneself and showing a lack of impulse control are also possible precursors of early adolescent substance use (NIAAA, 1984). These interpersonal liabilities and characteristics bring shame and negative self-appraisal due to failure and rejection (Barun & Bashe, 1988; Varenhorst, 1988). Lowered self-esteem leads children to isolation (NIAAA, 1984). Caught in this painful trap, the early adolescent then looks toward drugs for one of the following two reasons: to gain confidence and acceptance or to escape from misery (Barun & Bashe, 1988; Varenhorst, 1988).

Developmental Deficits. These behavioral deficits point to future behavioral problems. Erikson pointed out that those who are less confident in their self-concept and abilities in late childhood are at-risk for later maladaptive coping behaviors (1963). Little value is placed on personal achievement (Barun & Bashe, 1988; Kandel et al., 1978). Because these youths and their parent or parents appear to show no interest in school, they perform poorly. Discipline problems naturally ensue (Barun & Bashe, 1988). Huba and Bentler (1980) cited low tolerance of the law and rebellion as predictors of drug use. At-risk adolescents lack conventional interests, refuse to conform to adult or authority expectations, and increasingly show a higher tolerance for deviance (Jessor & Jessor, 1977; Kandel et al., 1978; Newcomb & Bentler, 1989).

A Drug Sequence Is Predictable. Using one or more gateway drugs is another warning sign to recognize among high-risk students. Kandel (1975) has organized substances into four stages. The first in this sequence is beer or wine, followed by cigarettes or hard alcohol. The third stage is marijuana and, finally, other illicit drugs (Kandel, 1975; Kandel & Faust, 1975). Using a drug in the early sequence is a necessary, though not sole, condition pointing to drug use in a later stage (Kandel, 1980). Therefore, counselors who interview at-risk students who are just beginning to toy with gateway drugs may succeed in deterring those adolescents from using more serious drugs.

Biological/Genetic Factors and Alcohol Use. Children in adoptive families have provided much evidence about biology's relationship to alcoholism. Adoptees with alcoholic biological parents have a greater tendency to alcohol abuse (Bohman, Sigvardsson, & Cloninger, 1981; Cadoret & Grath, 1978; Cadoret, Cain, & Grove, 1980). Children raised in adoptive families whose biological parents were *not* alcoholic did not show a tendency to alcohol abuse (Cloninger, Bohman, & Sigvardsson, 1981).

Collective Impact of All the Risk Factors. Counselors who start by reviewing the five preceding risk factors can focus on the interaction of all five contributors, because no investigator can isolate a single risk factor as causal.

NIAAA described the interplay of the many factors influencing adolescents' substance use as a cluster of initiating causes (1984). Although risk factors include disturbed family relationships, modeling of substance use by peers and adults, substance abuse also can occur in conjunction with depression, poor school performance, and low self-esteem (Rude & Horan, 1993).

INTERVENTIONS THAT WORK

School Counselors Are on the Front Line

Counselors must intervene on many levels when helping youth with substance abuse problems; however, America's current focus on addiction, the war on drugs, and various popular movements aimed at treating drug abuse and addictive disorders create a confusing array of possible treatments. Not every school counselor has special training as an addictions specialist, or as a family therapist, yet they are frequently the first professional who must provide help to a child who is using drugs. Additionally, schools frequently provide drug education and host family prevention programs. Parents may raise many questions about prevention and treatment during the course of a school meeting, or in the face of a crisis a child has related to substance abuse. Many professional staff members offering inpatient substance abuse treatment programs for adolescents now are working as consultants to schools. These consultants are providing drug education and assessment services that sometimes result in a questionable increase in pupil hospitalizations for suspected drug use. School counselors must make multiple decisions relating to recognizing and treating students' substance abuse problems. These decisions by counselors affect students, their families, and the school staff. Sometimes school authorities must set new school policy regarding outside intervention and resources. We strongly recommend, therefore, that school counselors keep informed on the current literature on at-risk youth that discusses and validates effective methods of diagnosis and drug treatment.

Does Drug Treatment Work? Outcome data on counseling effectiveness are extremely important although researchers have done relatively few such treatment outcome studies to date. Current reviews of the research and treatment literature are available free of charge through state branches of federal agencies such as the Office of Substance Abuse Prevention (OSAP) and the National Institute of Drug Abuse (NIDA). Also, many journals are available that are dedicated to experimental and clinical research on the topic of substance abuse in youth and families. By reviewing the reference section of this chapter, you will find an overview of these journals.

Comprehensive Assessment. When you decide to intervene with a young person presenting with a substance abuse problem, begin by increasing your understanding of the risk factors (i.e., parental alcoholism, financial hardship, lack of social support, and a high drug use peer group) that are specific to that particular child, family, and school and community group. Attention to protective factors, such as a family's positive closeness, parental concern, and a child's motivation to participate in hobbies or sports, are all significant in intervening successfully. Protective factors provide a positive foundation upon which counselors can build an intervention and must be an integral part of any assessment of an individual child, peer group, family, school, and social environment. Appraising the risks and the protective factors is essential in forming an appropriate treatment. Intervention can come in the form of family therapy, skill-based prevention programs for children and adolescents, and multiple family programs with both educational and treatment components. To illustrate the contextual nature of the problems that substance abusing children and their families face, we have included case examples that a school staff and mental health professionals may use to see how to assess risk factors and areas of family strength. Our intervention methods include such adjunctive treatments as recreation activities, teaming up with social service programs, and organizing community groups.

Choosing a Treatment. Parents and professionals currently confront a myriad of treatment programs for dealing with substance abuse. These options range from outpatient self-help groups to highly structured inpatient programs in hospital settings. Often these treatments espouse conflicting theoretical and philosophical positions. In an extensive review of treatment programs for adolescent substance abusers, Catalano, Hawkins, Wells, Miller, and Brewer (1991) stated that the superiority of specific components or approaches to adolescent treatment have not yet been demonstrated clearly and that relapse rates remain high. The authors urged a continued search for effective treatment methods based on rigorous evaluation. Additionally, professional counselors working in this field must balance their clinical practice with ongoing study of the literature and current research on treatment methods and outcome.

Problem as Metaphor

Systems or family therapy approaches view the problem of adolescent substance abuse in a family context, seeing a child's problem as a reflection of other family difficulties. To that extent, the problem is a metaphor that may distract from other serious difficulties while helping to maintain a balance in family relationships. Family problems may be internal, such as a marital problem, or may emerge through the interaction of internal and external stresses facing the family, such as unemployment.

Family Roots of a Troubled Student. Barrett (paper submitted for publication) cited a case example of a young Hispanic youth who repeatedly arrived at school in the morning in an intoxicated state and who frequently fought with Asian students. After meeting with the family, the therapist learned that the father frequently drank before going to work in the morning as an attempt to cope with stress he felt at his factory job. He openly told his son about his fear of continued layoffs due to the accelerated hiring of Asian workers and described interracial conflict as a continuous source of tension at work. The father's depression over his financial problems and his drinking created further problems between himself and his wife. This information puts the boy's troublesome behavior in a larger context—both as a metaphor of the larger family problem and as a distraction from marital tension that the parents had to put on hold as they united temporarily to help their son stay in school. Subsequent treatment in this case addressed the boy's problem in this larger context, touching on marital issues, developing coping strategies for dealing with stress and conflict, treating the father's drinking, helping the boy with school problems, and finding ways to address racial tension and employment practices in the father's job setting. The treatment plan fully utilized the family's strengths. The therapist emphasized all the positive aspects of the marriage and the genuine closeness and love that the family clearly exhibited. The father assisted his son in learning to relax in ways other than drinking by involving him in his hobbies of gardening and furniture restoration. The school counselor also worked with the parents in a cooperative effort to help their son to replace drinking with success in school.

Family Therapy with Drug Abuse

Gurman, Kniskern, and Pinsof (1986) cited structural strategic family therapy as having the strongest documented evidence in the research literature for the successful treatment of drug abuse. Lappin and Covelman (1986) and Tavantis, Tavantis, Brown, and Rohrbaugh (1986) described the successful use of structural family therapy with adolescent runaways and delinquents with substance abuse problems. Catalano et al. (1991) evaluated the effectiveness of several other family treatments and interventions with delinquent and/or substance abusing youth. Investigators found parents' participation in treatment meant fewer behavior problems during treatment and more often led to treatment completion. Structural-strategic approaches of family counseling were shown to produce higher rates of attendance and engagement in the therapy process than traditional (nonfamily systems) approaches. Catalano et al. (1991) listed structural family therapy, behavioral family therapy, and a combination of structural approaches as being the most promising methods for treating adolescents. A brief description of these three models follows.

Viewing Drug Abuse in a Family Developmental Context

Stanton and Todd (1982), Haley (1981), and Steinglass (1987) all emphasized the importance of assessing family developmental stages when working with substance abusing families so that a counselor can see the substance problem in relation to a particular crisis or hurdle in the life cycle of a family or one of its members. A 14-year-old girl, for example, lives with her single mother and older sister and develops a serious drug problem at the time her older sister is about to leave for college. Leaving home to attend college is a significant event for any family because it marks children's first serious step in leaving their family and, ultimately, leaving the mother to remain alone. If a woman already is isolated socially or depressed, having her children stay at home with her could be a source of support, providing her with a sense of purpose. A drug problem with her last remaining child may keep her busy with her duties as a mother for, perhaps, an extended period of time. Thus, the daughter's drug use may turn out to be more of a solution than a problem.

Multifamily Therapy Research. In evaluating the effectiveness of multisystemic therapy (MST) in treating drug abuse in a sample of 247 serious juvenile offenders, Henggeler, Borduin, Melton, Mann, Smith, Hall, Cone, and Fucci (1991) reported a greater reduction in substance-related arrests and soft drug use for youths assigned to MST treatment than for those who received individual counseling or conventional juvenile justice services. The MST approach is a form of family therapy that addresses child and family developmental stages, highlights the need for behavioral training and coping skills, uses a systemic or interpersonal approach to relationship problems family structure and parenting skills, and helps adolescents develop a sense of personal motivation and better capacity to handle peer pressure. This comprehensive model utilizes such community programs as schools, recreation centers, and social service agencies and, also, develops family support systems. Multisystemic therapy represents the broadest context of any therapy in globally addressing the complex problems and contextual layers often accompanying substance abuse problems.

A 13-Year-Old Girl and Drugs

Terri was a 13-year-old girl who frequently used alcohol and marijuana and was beginning to experiment with crack cocaine. She attended a public alternative school for youth with learning disabilities and severe behavioral problems. Although she had multiple learning disabilities, she frequently showed cooperative behavior and excellent school performance. Interspersed with these calm periods, however, were episodes of physical fights with other girls and sexually promiscuous behavior away from the campus at lunch time. Terri slowly improved her behavior at school through individual counseling that addressed her low self-esteem and the conflicts she created with her peers and teachers. She also gained social skills training to help her resist pressure to use drugs.

On a Monday morning, the school counselor received a call from Terri's mother, Ellen, saying that Terri had run away from home and had been gone since Friday night. The counselor met with the mother later that day to discuss Terri's history and current problems and to learn some details about the mother's personal life, family history, parenting style, and current interactive patterns within the family. Up until Terri's disappearance, the school had been unsuccessful in involving the mother in family counseling that the school had made available. The crisis Terri precipitated through running away provided the counselor at school with an opportunity to include Ellen in counseling in order to help Terri with her drug and behavior problems. The counselor learned that mother and daughter lived with Ellen's sister, brother-in-law, and their six-year-old child. Because the house was small for two families, Terri shared her mother's bedroom. The girl seldom saw her father who was remarried and enjoying a successful career in real estate. Despite his substantial income, he was lax in his child support payments. Ellen worked as a secretary in another real estate office and earned a low income. The mother described her relationship with her daughter as close and positive, and she stated that Terri's problems had started when she reached the fifth grade and began spending time with a group of "rough" kids in the neighborhood. Despite frequent fights, mother and daughter often went out to movies together and enjoyed weekend shopping trips and joint walks on the beach.

Ellen admitted setting few explicit rules or consistent limits for Terri regarding her behavior, curfew, and household chores. She attempted to manage Terri's disruptive behavior through anger and overt attempts at control, and, occasionally, she tried buying Terri new clothes as an incentive to behave well rather than as a reward for good behavior.

Ellen had no friends and no support system outside her family. She reported frequent conflicts between herself and her sister, and she said that Terri was jealous of the attention that the extended family gave her six-year-old cousin. Terri's jealousy and insecurity led her to fight with her aunt, which heightened family tensions. In later sessions, a pattern emerged that linked Terri's acting out to a conflict between her mother and aunt. Ellen turned to her daughter for companionship and emotional support during periods of conflict with her sister and brother-in-law, a role Terri obviously was not emotionally equipped to play.

After Terri returned home and once again went back to school, family counseling continued. Terri said that she had run away because "she couldn't stand it at home." She cried while she pleaded for her own room and complained about her mother's arbitrary use of punishment and inconsistent rules and limits. She hated the fighting in the extended family and said how hard she found it to watch her cousin getting new clothes and toys while she and her mother were so poor. She said that life was much more fun when she stayed at her friend's houses. Terri was very good at getting people to feel sorry for her in a first meeting and she, in fact, had enlisted the help of a friend's parents when she had run away. In a later session without Ellen, Terri discussed her worries about her mother's loneliness and her lack of a social life outside of the family.

The therapist assessed the risk and protective factors for Terri and her family as follows:

Risks. These included a lack of rules and consistent parenting skills, a high degree of family conflict with few problem-solving skills, continual financial problems, poor school performance, early drug use, and association with a peer group that used drugs heavily.

Protective Factors. Strengths included a strong and happy relationship between Ellen, Terri, and her maternal grandmother; Ellen's decision to work with her daughter in family therapy and to involve herself in her daughter's life at school by connecting with the school staff; a positive and affectionate relationship between Terri and Ellen; and skillful use of an open communication style despite periods of intense conflict, anger, and frustration. The school staff worked as a unified team, showing patience and persistence throughout the time of turmoil and supporting Terri and her mother.

Keeping Treatment Simple. Treatment with Terri and her mother addressed the risk factors when laying out the goals of therapy, incorporated the protective factors above, included work on Terri's symptoms and acting-out behaviors, and addressed the interactional patterns of the larger family context. Terri's runaway behavior served as a metaphor for the relationship between her and her mother and between her mother and her aunt. Family members alternated periods of extreme closeness with intense conflicts and emotional distance. Terri felt smothered when Ellen turned to her for support and companionship during periods of estrangement from Ellen's sister. When Ellen intruded emotionally, Terri ran off and turned to drugs as a relief. Sharing a room with her mother intensified the over-closeness in their relationship and was developmentally inappropriate since a young teenager has legitimate needs for privacy and free time to develop peer relationships. Terri's drug use and her association with a street gang provided her with breathing space from her mother and a false sense of independence, as described by Stanton and Todd (1982). The street gang provided her with friendship and nonrestrictive social support that gave her a sense of freedom and adventure not found in the depressive atmosphere at home. The school staff related Terri's sporadic drug use to her low self-esteem and her attempting to be included with an alternative family of peers rather than feeling completely left out.

The School's Role in Family Counseling

The therapist and school intervention team continued to work with Terri individually and also helped mother and daughter reach mutual agreement on consistent rules, limits, and household chores. Emphasis was placed on increasing the contacts between Terri and her mother and grandmother as this fostered more positive family relationships and created an appropriate distance between Ellen and her sister. The counselor taught Terri and Ellen conflict resolution and problem-solving strategies for dealing with family tension and rivalry. Therapy included private sessions with Ellen so that she could discover for herself the value of a social life and interests that were separate from Terri. She enrolled in art classes and joined a literature group at a local community center. Terri joined a youth program at the local YWCA, which simultaneously helped her to make new friends and avoid the streets on weekends. The counselor also helped Ellen find legal services in order to obtain regular child support payments. When the regular payments began to arrive, Ellen and Terri moved into their own apartment, and Terri had a room of her own. In a four-year follow-up, Terri had graduated from high school, was abstinent from drugs, had stayed out of trouble during her later high school years, and had worked in a student apprenticeship program at an auto insurance company where she was employed as a regular employee following graduation. Terri and her mother came to counseling over an 18-month span with occasional follow-up visits. After that period, Terri chose to continue regularly in counseling throughout high school.

Multiple Family Programs. Multiple family therapy that addresses family structure, organization, parenting skills, family communication, and sociocultural stress is a treatment for substance abuse that shows promise even with limited research and little clinical development. Many authors have called for further development of multiple family programs for substance abuse treatment, particularly with adolescents (Barrett, paper submitted for publication; Bartlett, 1986; Ellis, 1980; Friedman, 1989; Kaufman, 1986; Kaufman & Kaufman, 1979; Stanton, 1979; Stanton & Todd, 1982). They describe treating groups ranging from 3 or 4 to 10 or 12 families.

Counselors employ a family therapy perspective and treat issues of family coping, internal and external stresses, maladaptive family organization, negative family traditions, and intergenerational patterns of substance abuse. Gurman et al. (1986) have reviewed several multiple family programs including those that address more extreme problems and have concluded that these treatments have provided participating families significant benefits. Bank, Patterson, and Reid (1987) cited the use of parent training in delinquency prevention, and Friedman (1989) found that parent groups significantly reduced substance abuse and promoted improvement in clients' symptoms and family communication. Parent groups were as effective as individual family therapy in a comparative treatment design, and drop out rates were lower for the group approach.

Treatment Matches the Problem. Treating several families in a group can provide a forum that may be more productive than single family methods in addressing predominant family stressors and a family's sense of social isolation, confusion in family roles and organization, the developmental tasks of adults and adolescents, and sociocultural transitions in a way that may not be available through single family methods (Barrett, paper submitted for publication). Families with similar problems, such as a drug or alcohol abusing teenager, may feel less isolated as they share their common problems with other participants. Expressing the trauma and shame in an open forum breaks the monster's back and offers a support network of mutual encouragement. Additionally, families inevitably will model different types of strengths and coping skills that other group members can learn. Concurrently, they can see themselves through observing the problematic interactions of the other families. Many will find trying new parenting methods easier through the mutual support for change that they experience in a climate of group consensus. Parent education programs are the foundation of multifamily counseling. Training in effective parenting seems to be a natural complement to a family systems group approach that targets problems of adolescent substance abuse and behavioral misconduct. The typical regret from parents in these large groups is that they did not participate in a parenting group 10 years before their adolescents' drug crisis.

Initiating a First Multiple Family Group. Counselors recruit multiple family groups through schools, community youth service agencies, churches, and juvenile probation departments. Parents of various age groups can receive preventive counseling or actual treatment for common problems and/or concerns (Barrett, 1989, paper submitted for publication; Pentz, 1991). Parent groups are less costly than individual approaches, thus making counseling more affordable for agencies and families, although attending on a regular basis is sometimes a problem (Friedman, 1989). Serving food, coffee, and soft drinks; providing child care; and limiting the number of meetings in a treatment package may improve attendance rates.

Single Parent Father and Two Sons

The effective use of multiple family therapy comes through best in a case with a young father and his sons. A teacher's aide caught Simon, age 10, and his brother Zak, age 12, smoking marijuana on the school grounds of Simon's elementary school. Zak was in the seventh grade at a district junior high school and frequently cut classes so that he could hang around his younger brother's school during the day. Zak had been expelled from his neighborhood school for drug use and truancy and already had accumulated a negative record and reputation in his large, urban school district. The school counselor referred Simon and Zak to an adolescent drug treatment program in a nearby university outreach clinic where their father joined them for counseling in a multiple family setting. The father, who we will rename Pete, was young to have two pre-adolescents. His first son had been born when Pete was only 17, and Pete had been a single parent for about two years. The boys' mother had spent little time with them since she and Pete divorced. During the initial interview, Pete voiced his worries about Zak's school problems, which he felt were more important than the boy's drug use. He also stated that both boys were uncooperative with household tasks and that the house was messy and disorganized. He confessed feeling confused about ways of changing their household routines and developing more cooperation as a family since he was busy seven days a week. During the week, Pete worked in computers and on the weekends he played lead guitar with a modestly successful band. He frequently allowed the boys to stay up late with him while he practiced his music at home and also invited them backstage to spend time with the band at intermissions during his weekend gigs.

From Marijuana to LSD. Both boys reported frequent use of marijuana. Pete said that he allowed them to smoke at home, hoping that this would keep them from trying marijuana or other drugs on the streets. He described being a good friend to his sons and acknowledged setting few limits on their behavior. Simon was getting good grades at school, but he was beginning to spend his free time with older kids and admitted taking LSD a few times with Zak and his friends. Many of Zak's friends were 15 and 16 years old, much older than his peer group. Zak was on the brink of a second expulsion from middle school, which he said would be fine with him because the school was too far away from home.

Like Father; Like Sons. When the therapist asked Pete if he knew of any concerns his children had about him, he admitted that they frequently had expressed worry about the amount of cocaine he used while practicing his music in the house. The therapist then asked Pete if he also took his boys with him when he went out on a date with a woman. Pete showed surprise at the question, and stated, "no, of course not." The therapist noted that he shared a great many activities with his sons. Pete then said, "I understand what you mean; I'm doing too many things in front of the boys."

Father Hears the Fire Alarm. The therapist gained a commitment from both the father and the two sons to reduce or eliminate their drug use and helped Pete come to his own conclusion that abstaining from drugs himself was the best way he could help his boys become drug free. As Pete was not in treatment for himself, the therapist did not seek a court order to mandate abstinence (Miller & Rollnick, 1991). The father ordered his boys to stop smoking pot at home, promised to curb his own cocaine use, and declared that he would never again snort the drug around his sons.

Building on a Parent's Strengths. The therapist took care to note the positive aspects of all the relationships in the family and commented on the benefits of being a young dad with sons who viewed Pete as a great father. Furthermore, the family had a mutual interest in music that increased their sense of cross-generational connection. The counselor reframed the friendship between dad and boys as a protective factor and negotiated two new goals with Pete: (a) that he exhibit greater authority and firmness with his children and (b) that he learn some practical organizational skills. Six special risk factors emerged in this case: (a) the father's serious drug use; (b) the boy's early drug use; (c) Zak's conduct disorder and school problems; (d) underdeveloped parenting skills; (e) absence of boundaries in the parent-child relationships; and (f) the lack of a support system for a young, single-parent father.

Taking New Risks to Overcome Risks. Simon, Zak, and Pete agreed to join a multiple family therapy group with two other families. Children in the other two families had both parents at home but were struggling with the same problem of drug abuse. The two-parent families were especially supportive of Zak's dad because he was only 29 and was a single parent. Pete was especially helpful to another man in the group who was having continual conflict with his 18-year-old son. The group met weekly for four months and followed an Adlerian educational agenda: task-focused interventions and discussions on problem solving, improving communication, reducing stress, setting limits, applying logical consequences, encouraging one another's relationships in the family, and studying family development and the varying dynamics of substance abuse in families. Mothers in the two other families provided Pete and his sons with ideas for organizing the household, establishing routines, and dividing up chores. The group was mutually supportive as all the adults worked toward establishing clear rules, limits, and consequences with their children.

Playing a Father's Role. As Pete learned more about interpersonal boundaries, he became less a friend and more a father to his sons. The counselor was instrumental in Zak's conditional readmission to his home school, and the boy met the challenge by improving his attendance and drastically reducing his drug use. He began discouraging his younger brother from using drugs. Together, they joined the local Boys Club, which had developed a popular and effective after-school program for youth who had previously spent a lot of time on the streets. Pete soon reported a great reduction in his cocaine use and stopped totally three months after completing the treatment program. His band became more successful, and the multiple family therapy group joined together to attend one of his Saturday night performances. The MFT group also encouraged Pete to solve a work problem by requesting a promotion more assertively. He won the promotion and described feeling a new eagerness about going to work in the morning, whereas he previously had hated his job. Zak, Simon, and Pete began working together to organize a smooth running household, and both boys commented on their dad's increased happiness. The adult group members reported that learning parenting skills, studying educational material, and feeling the group support were three key elements in solving their family problems. All of the adolescents and preteens noted the value of a safe environment in which they could talk more openly with their parents and, thereby, improve their communication at home.

Skill-based Prevention Programs for Children and Adolescents

Pentz (1991) reviewed several types of school-based prevention programs that included drug education, self-management skills, training in resistance to peer pressure, and creating drug free school zones. She outlined four components of strategic prevention that children and early adolescents learned about at different times in their schooling. The first component of the strategic plan is primary prevention, including school-based drug education for students and their families. Pentz's research showed that primary prevention for all school children leads later to students' requests for information about pregnancy, family problems, and depression as well as parents' requests for post-treatment communications training. A second component is a brief, topic-focused group counseling program for which all students may register on prearranged school days. A third component is peer counseling and well-organized support programs for students with academic, social, or behavioral problems. A fourth component is a prevention-treatment link for identifying youth with drug problems, referring them for services, and helping recovering students successfully return to school. Pentz as well as Catalano et al. (1991) emphasized programs that successfully utilize active teaching methods from cognitive-behavioral and social learning theory approaches. Social skills training, changing norms and handling peer pressure, evaluating adolescent expectancies for drug and alcohol use, developing skills for stress reduction and seeking social support are all important program components that have been shown to reduce gateway drug use, to increase problem-solving abilities, and to diminish problem behaviors. Treatment success depends on a staff using practical, problem-solving approaches (Friedman & Glickman, 1986) that appeal to youth rather than relying on traditional methods that emphasize harsh confrontation or psychoanalysis.

Climbing Ropes Tests One's Mettle. When counselors supplement their family treatment with such recreational programs as Outward Bound or the Ropes Course, adolescents show positive results in improved school attendance, better behavior at home, reduced delinquent behaviors and drug use, and increased self-confidence and feelings of well-being (Catalano et al., 1991; McPeake, Kennedy, Grossman, & Beaulieu, 1991). Recreation programs often serve as adjuncts to counseling and therapy or are integral parts of structured treatment programs. These physical programs allow adolescents to experience a number of genuine inter- and intrapersonal challenges, thrills, and risk-taking behaviors that do not flow from drug use. In a wilderness environment, nature provides a set of inherent rules about safety and survival. Behaving responsibly and caring for oneself are integral components of maintaining a relationship with nature. McPeake et al. (1991) described nature as an authority figure that adolescents do not challenge. Teenagers do not encounter any locked doors, curfews, or power struggles with their parents while they are stomping around in the woods. By showing a respectful interdependence and by cooperating generously with companions and adult leaders, adolescents can earn safety and comfort.

CONCLUSION: TAKE HEART

School counselors may or may not be in a position to treat drug abusing students. Because of the costs, the complexity, and the lack of special training, most schools simply will not offer family counseling services; however, most parents want their children to succeed in school, regardless of their level of skill as parents or their degree of involvement with school activities. Drug abuse by children and adolescents predictably precipitates a crisis that warrants family involvement. Parents may be more open to working with a school counselor than a mental health or juvenile court agency. The school counselor thus may have a unique opportunity to provide time-limited counseling for a family that otherwise may not seek help from outside therapists. Helping children succeed in school is every educator's common goal, and offering family counseling with school-related problems can treat adolescent substance abuse, solve related family problems, and improve parenting skills. Counselors who cannot work with adolescents' problems in a school still must understand drug abuse and addiction in order to make an appropriate referral and to know how students and their families will handle treatment. School counselors also may seek a family's authorization to access information about their progress in treatment. Furthermore, counselors may serve as consultants or team members who coordinate the efforts and knowledge flow among a family, a student, a drug treatment program, and the other school personnel. Relapse prevention training is another important part of the recovery process that may occur at school (Meyers & Brown 1990a, 1990b). Addressing the total interactional context of adolescents' lives leads to optimal recovery.

BIBLIOGRAPHY

Arkin, E. B., & Funkhouser, J. E. (1990). *Communicating about alcohol and other drugs: Strategies for reaching populations at risk.* (OSAP Prevention Monograph 5). Rockville, MD: U.S. Department of Health and Human Services.

Barrett, K. (1991). Substance abuse treatment: solution or problem? *Family Dynamics of Addiction Quarterly, 2*(2).

Bohman, M., Cloninger, R., Sigvardsson, S., & von Knorring, A. L. (1987). The genetics of alcoholism and related disorders. *Journal of Psychiatric Research, 21*(4), 447-452.

Dishion, T. J., Patterson, G. R., & Reid, J. R. (1988). *Parent and peer factors associated with drug sampling in early adolescence: Implications for treatment.* National Institute on Drug Abuse: Research Monograph Series. Mono 77, 69-93.

Kandel, D. B. (1978, March). Similarity in real-life adolescent friendship pairs. *Journal of Personality & Social Psychology, 36*(3), 306-312.

Kandel, D. B. (1988). Issues of sequencing of adolescent drug use and other problem behaviors. In B. Segal (Ed.), *Drugs and society: Perspectives on adolescent drug use, 3*(1& 2). New York: Haworth Press.

Kaufman, E. (1985). *Substance abuse and family therapy.* Orlando, Florida: Grune & Stratton.

Orlandi, M. A., Lieberman, L. R., & Schinke, S. P. (1988). The effects of alcohol and tobacco advertising on adolescents. In B. Segal (Ed.), *Drugs and society: Perspectives on adolescent drug use, 3*(1 & 2). New York: Haworth Press.

Oyemade, U. J., & Deloris, B. M. (1990). *Ecology of alcohol and other drug use: Helping black high-risk youth.* (OSAP Monograph 7). Rockville, MD: U.S. Department of Health and Human Services.

Single, E., Kandel, D., & Faust, R. (1974, December). patterns of multiple drug use in high school. *Journal of Health & Social Behavior, 15*(4), 344-357.

REFERENCES

Baer, E. B., Garmezy, L. B., McLaughlin, R. J., Porkorny, A. D., & Wernick, M. J. (1987). Stress, coping, family and adolescent alcohol use. *Journal of Behavioral Medicine, 10*(5), 449-466.

Bank, L., Patterson, G. R., & Reid, J. B. (1987). Delinquency prevention through training parents in family management. *Behavior Analyst, 10*, 75-82.

Barnes, G. M. (1990). Impact of family on adolescent drinking patterns. In R. L. Collins (Ed.), *Alcohol and the family* (pp. 137-161). New York: Guilford.

Barrett, K. (1989). *Multiple family intervention with adolescent substance abuse.* Unpublished doctoral dissertation, University of San Francisco, California.

Barrett, K. (paper submitted for publication). *Multiple family intervention with adolescent substance abuse: A clinical perspective.*

Bartlett, D. (1986). The use of multiple family therapy groups with adolescent drug addicts. In M. Sugar (Ed.), *The adolescent in group and family therapy* (pp. 262-283). Chicago, IL: University of Chicago Press.

Barun, K., & Bashe, P. (1988). *How to keep the children you love off drugs.* New York: Atlantic Monthly Press.

Baumrind, D. (1987, June). *Authoritative parenting in the adolescent transition.* Paper presented at The Family Research Consortium Second Annual Summer Institute, Santa Fe, New Mexico.

Bohman, M., Sigvardsson, S., & Cloninger, R. (1981). Maternal inheritance of alcohol abuse: Cross-factoring analysis of adopted women. *Archives of General Psychiatry, 38,* 965-969.

Brook, J., Lukof, I., & Whiteman, M. (1978). Family socialization and adolescent personality and their association with adolescent use of marijuana. *Journal of Genetic Psychology, 133,* 261-271.

Brook, J. S., Whiteman, M., Gordon, A. S., & Brenden, C. (1983). Older brother's influence on younger sibling's drug use. *The Journal of Psychology, 114,* 83-90.

Cadoret, R. J. Cain, C., & Grove, W. M. (1980). Development of alcoholism in adoptees raised apart from alcoholic biologic relatives. *Archives of General Psychiatry, 37,* 561-563.

Cadoret, R. J., & Grath, A. (1978). Inheritance of alcoholism in adoptees. *British Journal of Addiction, 132,* 252-258.

Catalano, R. F., Hawkins, J. D., Wells, E. A., Miller, J. M., & Brewer D. (1991). Evaluation of the effectiveness of adolescent drug abuse treatment, assessment of risks for relapse, and promising approaches for relapse prevention. *The International Journal of the Addictions, 25*(9A & 10A), 1085-1140.

Clayton, R. R., & Lacy, W. B. (1982). Interpersonal influences on male drug use and drug use intentions. *The International Journal of the Addictions, 17,* 655-666.

Cloninger, R., Bohman, M., & Sigvardsson, S. (1981). Inheritance of alcohol abuse. *Archives of General Psychiatry, 38,* 861-868.

Deck, D., & Nickel P. (1989). *Statewide report on substance use among public school students in Washington.* Olympia, WA: Superintendent of Public Instruction.

Dishion, T. J., & Loeber, R. (1985). Adolescent marijuana and alcohol use: The role of parents and peer revisited. *American Journal of Drug and Alcohol Abuse, 11*(1 & 2), 11-25.

Dishion, T. J., Patterson, G. R., & Reid, J. B. (1985). Parenting practice in the etiology of child drug abuse: Implications for treatment and prevention. Paper presented to NIDA Technical Review Committee on Adolescent Drug Abuse: Analysis of Treatment & Research, Washington, DC.

Dryfoos, J. G., & Klerman, L. V. (1988). School based clinics: Their role in helping students meet the 1990 objectives. *Health Education Questionnaire, 15,* 71-80.

DuPont, R. L. (1990). *Stopping alcohol and other drug use before it starts: The failure of prevention.* (OSAP Prevention Monograph 1). Rockville, MD: U.S. Department of Health and Human Services.

Ellis, B. G. (1980). *Drug abuse from the family perspective.* Rockville, MD: National Institute on Drug Abuse.

Erikson, E. H. (1963). *Childhood and society* (2nd. ed.). New York: W. W. Norton.

Friedman, A. S. (1989). Family therapy vs parent groups: Effects on adolescent drug abusers. *American Journal of Family Therapy, 17,* 335-47.

Friedman, A. S., & Glickman, N. W. (1986). Program characteristics for successful treatment of adolescent drug abuse. *Journal of Nervous and Mental Disease, 174*(11), 669-679.

Gurman, A. S., Kniskern, D. P., & Pinsof, W. M. (1986). Research on the process and outcome of marital and family therapy. In S. L. Garfield & A. E. Bergin (Eds.), *Handbook of psychotherapy and behavior change: An empirical analysis* (pp. 565-624). New York: Wiley & Sons.

Haley, J. (1976). *Problem solving therapy.* San Francisco: Jossey-Bass.

Haley, J. (1981). *Leaving home.* New York: McGraw-Hill.

Hawkins, J. D., Lishner, D. M., & Catalano, R. F. (1985). Childhood predictors and the prevention of adolescent substance abuse. In C. L. Jones & R. J. Bahjes (Eds.), *Etiology of drug abuse: Implications for prevention* (pp. 811-830). Rockville, MD: National Institute on Drug Abuse.

Henggeler, S. W., Borduin, C. M., Melton, G. B., Mann, B. J., Smith, L. A., Hall, J. A., Cone, L., & Fucci, B. R. (1991). Effects of multisystemic therapy on drug use and abuse in serious juvenile offenders: A progress report from two outcome studies. *Family Dynamics of Addiction Quarterly, 1*(3), 40-51.

Huba, G. J., & Bentler, P. M. (1980). The role of peer and adult models for drug taking at different stages in adolescence. *Journal of Youth Adolescence, 9,* 449-465.

Jessor, R., & Jessor, S. L. (1977). *Problem behavior and psychosocial development: A longitudinal study of youth.* New York: Academic Press.

Johnson, L. D., O'Malley, P. M., & Bachman, T. G. (1993). *National suvey results on drug use from the Monitoring the Future Study, 1975-1992: Volume I. Secondary school students.* Rockville, MD: National Institute on Drug Abuse.

Julien, R. M. (1992). *A primer of drug action* (6th ed.). New York: Freeman.

Kaminer, Y. (1994). Adolescent substance abuse. In M. Galanter & M. D. Kleber (Eds.), *Textbook of substance abuse treatment* (pp. 415-433). Washington, DC: American Psychiatric Press.

Kandel, D. (1973, September). Adolescent marijuana use: Role of parents and peers. *Science, 181*(4104), 1067-1070.

Kandel, D. (1974). Inter- and intragenerational influences on adolescent marijuana use. *Journal of Social Issues, 30*(2), 107-135.

Kandel, D. (1975, November). Stages in adolescent involvement in drug use. *Science, 190*(4217), 912-914.

Kandel, D. B. (1980). Drug and drinking behavior among youth. *Annual Review of Sociology, 6,* 235-285.

Kandel, D. B., & Andrews, K. (1987, April). Processes of adolescent socialization by parents and peers. *International Journal of the Addictions, 22*(4), 319-342.

Kandel, D., & Faust, R. (1975, July). Sequence and stages in patterns of adolescent drug use. *Archives of General Psychiatry, 32*(7), 923-932.

Kandel, D. B., Kessler, R. C., & Marguiles, R. Z. (1978, March). Antecedents of adolescent initiation into stages of drug use: A developmental analysis. *Journal of Youth & Adolescence, 7*(1), 13-40.

Kandel, D., Treiman, D., Faust, R., & Single, E. (1976, December). Adolescent involvement in legal and illegal drug use: A multiple classification analysis. *Social Forces, 55*(2), 438-458.

Kandel, D. B., & Yamaguchi, K. (1985, August). Dynamic relationships between premarital cohabitation and illicit drug use: an even-history analysis of role selection and role socialization. *American Sociological Review, 50*(4), 530-546.

Kaufman, E. (1986). Adolescent substance abuse and family therapy. In M. Mirkin & S. Koman (Eds.), *Handbook of adolescents and family therapy* (pp. 245-253). New York: Gardner.

Kaufman, E., & Kaufman, P. N. (1979). *Family therapy of drug and alcohol abuse.* New York: Gardner.

Kidwell, J., Fischer, J., Dunham, A., & Baranowski, M. (1983). Parents and adolescents: Push and pull of change. In H. McCubbin & C. Figley (Eds.), *Stress and the family, Volume 1* (pp. 74-89). New York: Brunner/Mazel.

Lappin, J., & Covelman, K. (1986). Adolescent runaways: A structural family therapy perspective. In M. Mirkin & K. Koman (Eds.), *Handbook of adolescents and family therapy* (pp. 343-362). New York: Gardner.

Lipsitz, J. (1977). Growing up forgotten: A review of research and programs concerning early adolescence. Lexington, MA: D. C. Heath.

McPeake, J. D., Kennedy, B., Grossman, J., & Beaulieu, L. (1991). Innovative chemical dependency treatment and its outcome: A model based on outward bound programming. *Journal of Adolescent Chemical Dependency, 2*(1).

Madanes, C., Dukes, J., & Harbin, H. (1980). Family ties of heroin addicts. *Archives of General Psychiatry, 37,* 889-894.

Meyers, M. G., & Brown, S. A. (1990a). Coping responses and relapse among adolescent substance abusers. *Journal of Substance Abuse, 2,* 177-189.

Meyers, M. G., & Brown, S. A. (1990b). Coping and appraisal in potential relapse situations among adolescent substance abusers following treatment. *Journal of Adolescent Chemical Dependency, 1*(2), 95-113.

Miller, W. R., & Rollnick, S. (1991). *Motivational interviewing.* New York: Guilford.

Murray, M., Swan, A. V., Johnson, M. R., & Bewley, B. R. (1983, April). Some factors associated with increased risk of smoking by children. *Journal of Child Psychology & Psychiatry & Allied Disciplines, 24*(2), 223-232.

National Institute on Alcoholism and Alcohol Abuse (NIAAA). (1984). *Prevention plus: Involving schools, parents, and community in alcohol and drug education.* Rockville, MD: U.S. Department of Health and Human Services.

Needle, R., McCubbin, H., Wilson, M., Reinick, R., Lazar, A., & Mederer, H. (1986). Interpersonal influences in adolescent drug use: The role of older siblings, parents and peers. *International Journal of the Addictions, 21*(7), 739-766.

Newcomb, M. D. (1995). Identifying high-risk youth: Prevalence and patterns of adolescent drug abuse (research monograph 156). Rockville, MD: National Institute of Drug Abuse.

Newcomb, M. D., & Bentler, P. M. (1989). Substance use and abuse among children and teenagers. *American Psychologist, 44,* 242-248.

Newcomb, M. D., Chou, C. C., Bentler, P. M., & Huba, G. J. (1988). Cognitive motivations for drug use among adolescents: Longitudinal test of gender differences and predictors of change in drug use. *Journal of Counseling Psychology, 35,* 426-438.

Office of Substance Abuse and Prevention (OSAP). (1990). Stopping alcohol and other drug use before it starts: The future of prevention. (OSAP Prevention Monograph 1). Rockville, MD: Department of Health and Human Services.

Penning, M., & Barnes, G. E. (1982, July). Adolescent marijuana use: A review. *International Journal of the Addictions, 17*(5), 749-791.

Pentz, M. A. (1991). *Perspectives on drug abuse prevention.* Paper presented at the XXIII Banff International Conference on Behavioural Science, Banff, Canada.

Presson, C. C. et al. (1984). Predictors of adolescents' intentions to smoke: Age, sex, race, and regional differences. *International Journal of the Addictions, 19*(5), 503-519.

Rhodes, J. E., & Jason, L. A. (1988). The social stress model of alcohol and other drug abuse: A basis for comprehensive, community-based prevention. In K. H. Rey, C. L. Faegre, & P. Lowery (Eds.), *Prevention research findings* (pp. 155-171). Rockville, MD: U. S. Office of Substance Abuse Prevention.

Robins, L. N., & Pryzbeck, R. R. (1985). Age of onset of drug use as a factor in drug and other disorders. In C. L. Jones & R. J. Battjes (Eds.), *Etiology of Drug Abuse: Implications for Prevention.* Rockville, MD: National Institute on Drug Abuse.

Rude, S. S., & Horan, J. J. (1993). Substance use disorders. In R. T. Ammerman, C. G. Last, & M. Hersen (Eds.), *Handbook of prescriptive treatments for children and adolescents* (pp. 254-269). New York: Allyn & Bacon.

Stanton, M. D. (1979). Family treatment approaches to drug abuse problems: A review. *Family Process, 18,* 251-280.

Stanton, M. D., & Todd, T. C. (1982). *The family therapy of drug abuse and addiction.* New York: Guilford.

Steinglass, P. (1987). *The alcoholic family.* New York: Basic Books.

Szapocznik, J., & Kurtines, W. M. (1993). Family psychology and cultural diversity: Opportunities for theory, research, and application. *American Psychologist, 48*(4), 400-407.

Tavantis, T., Tavantis, M., Brown, L., & Rohrbaugh, M. (1986). Home based structural family therapy for delinquents at risk of placement. In M. Mirkin & K. Koman (Eds.), *Handbook of adolescents and family therapy* (pp. 343-362). New York: Gardner.

Tolone, W. L., & Dermott, A. B. (1975). Some correlates of drug use among high school youth in a midwestern rural community. *The International Journal of the Addictions, 10,* 761-777.

Varenhorst, B. (1988). *The adolescent society. Adolescent peer pressure.* Rockville, MD: NIDA, U.S. Department of Health and Human Services.

Wills, T. A. (1985). Stress coping and tobacco use in early adolescence. In S. Shiffman & T. A. Wills (Eds.), *Coping and substance abuse.* New York: Academic Press.

Chapter 9

DEPRESSION AND SUICIDE: INJECTING HOPE

James C. Park
Albert O. Boyd

Editor's Note

    This chapter is not about gruesome information for its own sake. Because bad things sometimes happen, teachers are better off being prepared. Suicide is a terrible act that leaves families and friends powerless and devastated. Often, many warning signs are available because, deep down, people do not want to eliminate themselves. To avoid missing the danger signs that children and adolescents sometimes signal, Drs. Park and Boyd have laid out a very practical framework for all educators and counselors. Moving from fear of engaging in discussion of a formerly taboo topic is the wisest move we all can make. The most significant step we can take in managing the problems that result from serious depression, self-alienation, and self-annihilation is to insure a clear place at school for each and every student. Valuing all students and integrating the marginal ones is the most important contribution we can make. Hope is the best antidote to pathos, angst, and the threat of premature death. Learning choice theory gives hope because students learn options to caving in to any dismal fascination.

CHAPTER OBJECTIVES

1. To point out the magnitude and tragic impact of student suicidal acts
2. To note the relative merit of various suicidal risk factors
3. To give a practical framework for assessing the immediate risk of suicide
4. To show how professionals in schools may effectively prevent a student suicide
5. To detail effective uses of community resources and prevention programs
6. To describe ways of managing the traumatic social outcome of a student's suicide

CASE STUDY: A STUDENT SUICIDE

We give the tragic scenario of a preventable suicide. At least a dozen people closely related to the victim failed to recognize the conventional signs the student displayed. Unfortunately, this story of an attractive 17-year-old high school student is true. We shall call this young woman Carol Jones, but we are changing her name and the names of all others in order to protect everyone's identity.

Carol had stunning beauty, brains, and a pleasing personality that manifested itself in the loving and caring way she treated her many friends. During the last few days of her life, however, Carol clearly had signaled, time and again, her plan to take her life. She initially wrote a poem for one of her classes wherein she expressed her feelings about ending her life in a very dramatic and irreversible way. Neither her teacher nor her peers paid attention to Carol's warning. Next, she made direct notations in her friends' yearbooks about her plan to kill herself. Finally, she began giving away her prized personal possessions to her closest friends. At any time during Carol's closing days when she publicly was threatening suicide, those close to her—teachers, parents, or friends—could have witnessed the real danger and obtained help for her.

Carol's boyfriend and lover, Bob, was a 17-year-old, employed, high school dropout. According to her mother, Carol was totally infatuated with Bob and believed that he reciprocated her affection. In the course of their relationship, she had become pregnant by Bob and underwent an abortion. Meanwhile, Bob became romantically involved with a 22-year-old woman and broke off his relationship with Carol.

On the day before Carol killed herself, she drove over to Bob's house in a desperate attempt to have him take her back. A neighbor overheard her say, "Don't do this to me, Bob! Don't do this to me." At that point, she showed him a 22-caliber pistol that she had taken from a cabinet in her stepfather's den. Bob took the firearm away from her and put it in a dresser drawer in his room. She then proclaimed to him that she was going to kill herself. Bob replied, "Go ahead; do it!" With Bob's disdain ringing in her ears, Carol drove away. Bob's disinterest in Carol was evident. His mother reported later that he had spent that night with his new girlfriend. Even at this crucial point, though, as little as a telephone call to Carol's parents, the school, or the police, could have sparked an intervention that would have helped Carol manage her deep despair.

During this period, Carol expressed her mental torment in another manner; she ran away from home. This gesture was a kind of practice suicide. In removing herself from her family, she metaphorically rehearsed cutting herself off from her lifeblood. She made certain, however, that her mother could find her easily. With the aid of the local police, her mother and stepfather tracked her down, but they seemed to misread her blatant call for help. Instead of offering her a helping hand and some tender understanding, they took a harsher path. They punished her by taking away some of her privileges, such as restricting her freedom to come and go from the house. Police officers familiar with Carol's plight learned of the parents' decisions to confine her and notified the community Youth Services Bureau. Counselors in that agency undergo training to read various signs of depression and to take appropriate action when they judge an adolescent's behavior to be particularly dangerous. A counselor telephoned the stepfather at home and volunteered to work with the family to find new avenues for Carol to solve her dilemma. The stepfather thanked the counselor but labeled the offer to help as unnecessary. He said the problem was under control. An immediate crisis counseling session would have been a useful forum for Carol to discuss her painful rejection. In that safe environment, she may have divulged her private thoughts about ultimate solutions to her anguish. A counselor surely would have recommended some action steps this young woman could have taken to relieve some of her distress and to connect her with a friendly support network. This hindsight, however, is all *coulda, shoulda, woulda.*

Who else could have intervened? Clearly, the teacher or school officials were in a position to know. Turning the clock back a few days, anyone can see in retrospect how a less tragic scenario was possible. With prior training in reading the warning signs of a potential suicide, the teacher who received Carol's poem could have alerted the appropriate helping agency.

If Carol's peers at school had received prior instruction, they also would have been aware of the typical warning signs that Carol was exhibiting in her cry for support. These red flags included her suicidal comments in the yearbook and her giving away her prized possessions to her friends. Any one of a dozen people were in a position to hear the alarm and to reach out and save Carol's life.

On June 12 of that year, at 3:34 p.m., Bob's mother came home from work and found Carol lying bloody and motionless inside Bob's bedroom closet. Carol had entered the house through the back sliding glass door sometime during the day when the family was not home. She poured herself a glass of brandy, drank it, took off her shoes, stood up inside the closet, put the 22-caliber Derringer pistol that she found in Bob's dresser drawer to her right temple, and pulled the trigger. Carol died as the bullet severed her brain stem.

Who would say that suicide prevention education is unimportant? Many young people see suicide as a solution to their problems. All of us in education and mental health must focus intently on one highly effective solution that is within our grasp. We need to create a program in our schools that accentuates more awareness of suicide, its warning signs, and how administrators, counselors, teachers, parents, and peers may intervene to save a precious young life.

SOCIAL AND POLITICAL CONTEXT
FOR SUICIDE IN AMERICA

Suicidal behavior is a major problem in our society. Overall, suicide is the eighth leading cause of death in the United States and the third leading cause of death for 15- to 24-year-olds (National Institute of Mental Health, 1986). The overall rate of suicide is increasing throughout the United States, especially among the 15- to 24-year-old group (National Center for Health Statistics, 1986). Each year in the United States, approximately 6,000 children and teens commit suicide (Greene & Keown, 1986). Suicide rates among 15- to 19-year-old youths increased by an alarming 400% from 1950 to 1977 (Eisenberg, 1984).

Each year in California nearly 4,000 suicides occur—that is, 11 suicides per day or almost one every two hours. Also, an estimated 400,000 nonfatal suicide attempts take place every year. Combined, this totals 404,000 suicidal behaviors a year—that is, more than 1,100 suicidal gestures each day or almost 50 per hour. The actual number of suicides are underreported by an estimated 10% to 50% (Jobes, Bermany, & Josselsen, 1986). When we consider cases of accidental drowning and single-vehicle accidental deaths—events not usually considered suicides—the number of suicides may be staggering (Braught, Loya, & Jamieson, 1980; Holding & Barraclough, 1977). The results of other studies showed that 3% to 7% of single-car vehicular accidents were in fact suicides (Jenkins & Sainsbury, 1980; Pokorny, 1975).

The main purpose of this chapter is to provide you with statistics about the magnitude of suicidal attempts and successes along with information that you can use to prevent students from injuring or killing themselves. Most suicides can be prevented (Murphy, 1985). Learning how to intervene in suicidal situations is at least as important as learning to use a fire extinguisher in a fire emergency. Both pertain to life and death situations. The more we know how to recognize suicidal risk early and provide emergency intervention, the more effective we all will be at reducing the number of suicidal behaviors.

This chapter presents information to school counselors, nurses, psychologists, administrators, teachers, and other school personnel about intervention strategies in situations where suicide is a real possibility. Additional information here will show you what to do about a student at risk of suicide until professional help arrives. Targeting this critical stage in a suicide risk does not mean that you would intervene only at the point of imminent danger of self-imposed death. The information in this chapter will help you recognize a risk as early as possible and to step in before a child or adolescent seriously exposes himself/herself to life threatening danger. The chapter does not provide information on conducting therapy to resolve the problems that might have first brought an at-risk student to contemplate suicide in the first place. An all-encompassing three-step policy is outlined in the following pages.

STEP I:
FORMULATE A SUICIDE PREVENTION POLICY

Most people, including teachers, counselors, nurses, and, yes, even psychologists, have difficulty dealing with death, dying, and, especially, suicide. The difficulty stems from a sense of helplessness in the face of a threat of suicidal death of a significant person in one's life. Frequently, individuals shield themselves from evidence of a possible suicide by denying the data and turning to avoiding behaviors as a means of coping with such stress. Carol resorted to these same shielding tactics—that is, she and others minimized the seriousness of the threat. People typically will rely on such platitudes as "everything will be OK" (Boldt, 1983). School district staff members are no different from most people in this regard.

In order to be precisely prepared for a particular suicidal threat, district professionals first may formulate a suicide prevention policy that they regularly update and explain to other staff members' parents. The key to protecting students and staff is to have an explicit policy with clear procedures that everyone may follow in any suicide situation (Sonoma Valley Unified School District, 1989).

School districts have become hypervigilant about their professional liability as a result of actual lawsuits over suicide. Although these legal issues are not settled completely and each case has its own individual merits, a 1985 federal court decision (Kelson v. City of Springfield, 1985) issued a ruling favoring parents' right to sue a school. The court decided that the parents of a young person who had committed suicide could rightfully sue a school because the student's death allegedly resulted from inadequate training in suicide prevention practices. We are not debating here the other side of this coin—the parents' responsibilities in assessing danger of lethality for one of their own children and in preventing a suicide. In light of such legal action as the Oregon case, all schools in California now must provide student and staff training in child and adolescent suicide prevention and must develop a suicide prevention policy (California Department of Education, 1987).

STEP II: ESTABLISH PROCEDURES
FOR PREVENTING SUICIDES

Your decision to act in the face of a genuine threat can make a critical difference in the life or death of a student. You can take life-saving action by applying the following procedures.

Recognize Common Warning Signs

A Student with Few Personal Resources. A student's resources include physical and emotional systems that a student-at-risk feels are helping, caring, or supportive. These social support resources may include other persons such as family, close friends, caregivers, and peer counselors; and groups and organizations such as church and scouts (Litman, Farberow, Wold, & Brown, 1974; Slater & Depue, 1981). Personal resources include a sense of hope for the future, coping skills, physical and mental health, confidence, esteem, and positive aspirations, which sometimes recede and appear as unavailable to a student-at-risk of committing suicide (Farber, 1968).

Prior Attempts at Suicide. A student with no prior suicidal attempts is at a lower risk than a student who has attempted self-elimination. If a student has attempted suicide at least once, the lifetime risk of dying by suicide is 10% to 15% (Murphy, 1985). Another researcher (Berman, 1975) reported that 35% to 40% of actual suicide victims had made prior unsuccessful attempts.

The rates of suicide among young people in California who have attempted suicide previously are 45 to 50 times greater than general population rates (California Department of Mental Health, 1988). Even if a student's suicide attempts do not seem serious to you, that person still may be at risk for suicide. We need to remember that any prior attempt, no matter how slight, is an attempt. Once people "break the ice" with a suicidal attempt, they may feel they have earned a special permission to complete the suicide at some time in the future.

Current Suicide Plans. The degree of planning and the specificity of details in an at-risk student's plan for suicidal death reflects the degree of lethality. This concrete planning of means, timing, and imagined post-suicide activities by survivors indicates how imminent the suicide may be. The more detailed the plans, the more likely a student has selected suicide as a solution. Such a decision provides a solution to the torture and, often, students then show a sense of peace and relief just before committing the act.

Detailed plans include a *method* of committing the act, a *time* to do it, and an exact *means* by which to do it (i.e., shooting with a gun, stabbing with a knife or slicing with a razor blade, ingesting some pills or other form of medication, hanging from a rope, or driving an automobile off a cliff). Carol's suicide plan contained a clear and tangible means: a 22-caliber pistol. Teachers become immersed in the many necessary obligations in and out of the classroom. Counselors too may notice what is right in front of their faces. Many people, professionals included, regrettably form the assumption that a written note always precedes suicide. Not true. Some slip silently away—without a formal good-bye.

Worrisome Changes in Behavioral Patterns. Although some of the following feelings and symptoms usually fall under normal behavior for students, we all need to be alert that some may be feeling hopeless and depressed to a suicidal extent. In the midst of a heavy feeling of depression, anyone could entertain the thought that life is not worth living. Discouraged students may not realize that depressing feelings are temporary and that they can do something about their miserable condition. Consequently, students fearing the danger of further loss and failure, or sensing a heightened notion of not belonging, automatically may turn to suicide for relief from their bind (California Department of Mental Health, 1988). Even though most self-respecting students mask these dark thoughts quite well, they may manifest their secret side through sudden changes in their behavior at school. The following changes in a student's behavioral pattern represent a few of the visible changes at school that responsible and caring adults may take as warning signs of potential suicide (California Department of Health Services, 1986):

- sudden changes in attendance and punctuality,
- decline in academic performance,
- abrupt inability to complete assignments,
- loss of interest and withdrawing behaviors,
- classmates report changed relationships,
- increasing aggression and irritability, and
- despairing demeanor.

Other symptoms may emerge as warning signs of potential suicidal intent. School officials, parents, and peers may become aware that the student is showing such classic signs of depression as sleep disturbances, loss of appetite, loss of weight, long periods of solitude, and deteriorating changes in appearance or cleanliness.

A particularly serious symptom of potential suicide is the making of "final arrangements"—that is, giving away prized personal belongings. In effect, the student has made or is executing a will when he or she gives away personal tapes, albums, compact discs, teddy bears, posters, and other possessions to close friends. The student also may say something directly or indirectly about suicide or death (e.g., reminiscing about a dead person, creating poems or artwork about death, or showing intense interest in themes such as death, dying, suicide, worthlessness, or hopelessness) (California Department of Mental Health, 1988).

Stress and Stressors. We all have some stress in our lives; challenges go with the territory. How we manage the stress is the key to our success or failure. People's reactions to stressful events (i.e., stressors) are very individualized. One person's stressor is another's energizer. Something you deem relatively minor—a boy and girl stop going steady—can become an overwhelming stressor in youngsters' minds. When a person experiences serious life stressors, suicidal thoughts sometimes may appear in a random fashion as one possible solution. Our creativity system is working overtime and constantly throwing ideas out that we can consider in living our lives. Suicide is one such random idea that pops up as a choice. When a sense of great loss is the main component of these stressors, the suicidal thoughts possibly could become suicidal actions (Teicher & Jacobs, 1966).

A person such as Carol, experiencing a break-up in a romantic relationship, may perceive the loss as much more than the separation from a loved one.

The student may see the incident as a catastrophe and feel the rejection as a total loss of value or self-esteem. Carol certainly felt utterly worthless without her boyfriend's acceptance and exclusive attention. In this sense, people do not kill themselves to inflict harm or to act self-destructively. They mostly are trying to close off the painful awareness they have that they no longer count for anything and, furthermore, cannot access any power by which they might regain some self-worth (Glasser, 1965, 1984).

The following life events or conditions are what most students probably would view as high stress challenges. As such, sometimes students may opt for suicide as a solution to their untenable position (Breed, 1967; Bunch, Barraclough, Nelson, & Sainsbury, 1971; Greer, 1966; Lester & Beck, 1976; Ramsey, Tanney, Tierney, & Lang, 1987).

- Parent or friend commits suicide or dies
- Student becomes victim of a crime
- Family member is seriously ill
- Parent abuses substances
- Parent remarries
- Student is dependent on alcohol and drugs (as Carol was)
- Student is In legal trouble
- Student runs away from home (as Carol had)
- Student witnesses a violent event
- Student moves to a new school
- Student gets a failing grade (or grades lower than A's)
- Student becomes sexually active (as Carol had)
- Student has inability to refuse sex
- Mother returns to work
- Student becomes victim of physical or sexual abuse
- Parents become separated or divorced
- Parent becomes unemployed
- Student has insufficient funds (poverty)
- Student feels peer pressures (real or imagined)
- Student is pregnant
- Student has sexual identity or preference conflicts
- Student experiences general frustration, fear
- Student has severe emotional or psychological problems
- Student experiences the loss of religious faith

Prepare Today for the Suicide Crisis Tomorrow

Examine your own feelings about suicide and suicidal students. Are you ambivalent and anxious about suicide? If so, welcome to the club. Being aware of your feelings helps you to prepare to act efficiently during a suicidal crisis. Denial could lead you to underestimate the seriousness of a suicide threat (California Department of Health Services, 1986).

Learn appropriate ways to talk about suicide with your students. Bringing up the subject with your students will not put ideas into their heads that they cannot control. Neither does open discussion of self-harm precipitate a suicide. These two fears are myths. Talking is not the problem. Not talking about suicide is the problem. Avoidance can create barriers that prevent students from getting the help they need (Lang, Ramsey, Tanney, & Tierney, 1987).

Prepare a network of internal and external resources. Talk with the people on whom you will need to rely in a crisis, for example, your school psychologist or counselor, the on-call medical emergency team at your local hospital, the crisis team at your city or county mental health department, the juvenile officers at your local police department, and the staff of a local suicide prevention center. Meet these people and tour their facilities so you will know what they offer and what their requirements are (California Department of Mental Health, 1988).

Evaluate the Suicide Threat

If one of your students has threatened suicide directly or indirectly or if you suspect suicidal intentions, take a risk assessment to determine if predictors of immediate risk are present. First make sure you have established some alliance with the student (usually teachers already have this). As the front-line evaluator, you must look for the three greatest predictors of suicide:

1. Current suicide plan,
2. Prior suicidal behavior, and
3. Lack of resources.

Do not rush through this area of assessment. Ask the following types of questions openly and directly:

- "Are you feeling unhappy a lot of the time?"
- "Is this feeling of unhappiness so strong that sometimes you think of killing yourself?"
- "Are you thinking about how you would do it?"
- "When do you think you will do this?"
- "How do you plan to do it?"

If a student clearly expresses an intention to commit suicide, one always should view this decision as *extremely serious*. The degree of lethality or the imminence of the suicide becomes even greater if the student has the following:

- a plan about *how* to commit suicide,
- a plan about *when* to commit suicide, and
- the *means* (gun, knife, pills, rope, vehicle, high place) to do it; ask where the means are located.

Do Not Keep This Information a Secret

Suicidal students often have very little self-esteem. Their fear of rejection may be equal to their fear of death. Sometimes they do not want other people to know they are feeling as though they want to die and, therefore, they want to keep these private thoughts secret.

- Do not keep a suicide plan a secret.
- Do not wait to notify the appropriate individuals.

Help the Suicidal Student

In a crisis, help the suicidal student in the following ways (Fisher, 1990):

- Ensure that backup and emergency service units (e.g., police, ambulance, fire personnel) are out of sight of the suicidal student.
- Listen patiently and attentively, responding with understanding and empathy.
- Ask questions that encourage expression of feelings or events leading to the crisis.
- Be nonjudgmental.
- Do not oversimplify solutions or make statements that triviaiize the situation.
- Avoid threatening gestures or flippant comments.
- Call in mental health professionals or anyone else who could possibly reach the troubled student.
- Suggest alternatives to suicide that can be made available to the student.
- Do not rush; take whatever time or steps are necessary to get help for the troubled student. (Beck, Resnick, & Littieri, 1974; Hoff, 1984; Motto, 1978; Robins, Murphy, Wilkinson, Gasner, & Kayes, 1959)

Design a Suicide Risk Assessment Form

The assessment form described below is intended to help you develop a suicide risk assessment format that is easily usable in determining the degree of lethality or the imminence of a student's behavior. Sometimes pulling out this resource sheet and going over it with the student is easier than avoiding the topic altogether.

1. Resources: List names and phone numbers of friends.
2. Prior attempts: Invite the student to give details about any prior attempt including the method, the people present, and any prior emotional stressors.
3. Current plan: What method does the student plan to use? Are the materials needed in the plan available?
4. Assess for other symptoms such as drug abuse or pregnancy.
5. Find out stresses and pressures for the student. What stresses/pressures does the student perceive that he/she is under from others?

By filling out this form with the student present, you keep no secrets and you form a better alliance. If the student is at low risk, you have a starting point to provide the student with ongoing help. If the student is at high risk, you have the document for the police, school resource officer, or other mental health professionals (Fisher, 1990).

Assess the Suicide Risk Factors

After filling out the suicide assessment form, use the following points system to evaluate level of risk.

Points	Warning Signs of Suicidal Intention
1	1. No resources (Alone?)
2	2. Prior attempts (Any?)
2	3. Current suicide plans (Available means?)
1	4. Symptoms (Hopeless, depressed, or suddenly euphoric?)
1	5. Stress (Losses?)

Total Points _____

1 to 3 = Low risk
4 to 5 = Moderate risk
6+ = High risk

Student's Name _____   Date _____

Evaluator's Name _____

Consider Suicidal Behavior as a Clue to Child Abuse

A final important consideration of any suicide intervention plan is to remain open to the possibility that a student considering suicide may be reacting to recent or past physical or sexual abuse. Physical and sexual abuse are clearly associated with self-destructive behavior in children. Abusive acts by parents are often immediate antecedents to suicide attempts, threats, running away, and other risk-taking behaviors among abused children (Green, 1978). These brutal experiences may be too painful and students may be too fearful to tell someone in authority. In the face of such a burden, they may turn to suicide as a solution to their overwhelming hopelessness. As a mandated reporter, you have an obligation to question the student and to report any reasonable suspicion of child abuse to a child protective services agency or to the police. In this case, you do not need to see bruises or other physical evidence to make such a report of your suspicion. Strictly speaking, suicidal behaviors are *ipso facto* potentially self-abusive in nature, and you must report such dangers. For the laws, definitions, obligations, and procedures for reporting suspected child abuse, consult the state laws that apply in your home area.

STEP III: ESTABLISH PROCEDURES FOR DEALING WITH A SUICIDE

If a suicide has occurred at your school, the students, staff members, parents, and people in the community need help to deal with their shock and grief. Volunteer counselors from the community and even the region outside the school zone can make an immense contribution to the school community at this time.

Designate One Person to Be in Charge

Usually, a district superintendent names the school principal as the primary person in charge of a crisis from a suicide. At least one additional leader or council of three with back-up authority should always be available to act if necessary.

Enlist Outside Assistance

School authorities who have been through a suicidal loss recommend that a resource specialist or team outside the school be predesignated to come in to help plan an emergency response. Mental health personnel can serve this purpose. Many schools have developed crisis response teams that are made up of professionals from the child protective services agency, the probation department, a police department, licensed private therapists, psychologists, county mental health department personnel, and church pastors and ministers.

Appoint One Spokesperson

When a suicide occurs, be prepared to receive telephone calls from parents, reporters, and community leaders. They all will want immediate information about the suicide. Requests for information must go to a single spokesperson who has accurate information about the suicide. Insist that no one else from the school provide formal public statements. The school principal and spokesperson first must discuss with the suicide victim's parents which details about the death will be available to the public.

Gather All Staff Members Together

After a suicide, your staff members will need factual briefing and a chance to discuss their feelings. It is not uncommon at this point to deal with grief by denying it and directing energy to caring for others. Thus, the following actions are suggested.

1. Time permitting, arrange to help staff members deal with their feelings of grief, guilt, or anger and prepare them to deal effectively with students. Provide for time off for anyone who clearly cannot be helpful to students during this shock stage and make sure that someone close to the needy staff member remains in touch with the person.
2. Some staff members may manage their reactions well enough but feel uncomfortable about discussing a suicide with their students. Respect their feelings and provide opportunities for students to receive this information from a licensed counselor. This information can be available in small group sessions.
3. Grieving and seeking to learn from the tragedy should be the primary focus of all the meetings. Looking for someone to blame or spending time talking about how "good" or "bad" the deceased student was should not be the topics. Recrimination has never proven a repository of valuable social healing.

Share Factual Information

Promptly sharing factual information with everyone is the best way to limit the spread of rumors. Prepare and distribute to all concerned a written statement about the death. Assure staff members and students that blaming is not helpful and that the school is committed to learning from the suicide.

RESOURCE OPTIONS

An important extension of any suicide intervention plan involves the consideration of individual and organizational resources available to you in dealing with students-at-risk of suicide. Coordinated efforts for suicide prevention require the orchestration of these resources and the relationships between them. In addition to your school counselors, the following three options can be utilized in your school district to form a comprehensive network toward preventing or reducing the incidence or duration of suicidal behaviors (California Department of Health Services, 1986):

24-Hour Suicide Crisis Intervention

This option provides 24-hour immediate support to students-at-risk of suicide. These resources are police, fire department, hospital emergency units, crisis lines, ambulance services, child protection services, mobile response units, and other 24-hour emergency accommodation centers. All professionals connected with the school must be particularly observant of potential resonating suicides because children often wish to understand the tragedy or to join a loved friend by following suit.

Longer-term Professional Care Options

You also have access to alcohol and drug abuse programs, family service centers, vocational and school counseling services, mental health programs, rehabilitation services, hospitals, youth centers, correctional agencies, and other professional caregiving and treatment services.

Other Community and Institutional Support Services

This option includes a community network of family, friends, employers, clergy, family doctors, teachers, self-help groups, and others.

BIBLIOGRAPHY

Beck, A. T., Kovacs, M., & Weissman, M. (1975). Hopelessness and suicidal behavior: An overview. *Journal of American Medical Association, 234,* 1146-1149.

Boldt, M., & Solomon, M. (1974). *Interim report on suicide. Phase 1: Youth suicide.* Unpublished report submitted to Alberta Social Services and Community Health.

Centers for Disease Control. (1986). *Youth suicide in the United States, 1970-1980.* Atlanta, GA: Author.

Durkheim, E. (1951). *Suicide.* Glencoe, IL: Free Press.

Englesmann, F., & Ananth, J. (1981). Suicide rating scales. *Psychiatric Journal, University of Ottawa, 6,* 47-51.

Goodwin, D. W. (1973). Alcohol in suicide and homicide. *Quarterly Journal of Studies of Alcoholism, 34,* 144-156.

Gottlieb, B. H. (1983). *Social support strategies.* Beverly Hills, CA: Sage.

Hendin, H. (1982). *Suicide in America.* New York: Norton.

Klagsburn, F. (1981). *Too young to die: Youth and suicide.* New York: Pocket Books.

Maris, R. W. (1981). *Pathways to suicide.* Baltimore, MD: Johns Hopkins.

Peck, M. L. (1982). Youth suicide. *Death education, 6,* 29-47.

Pfeffer, C. R. (1986). *The suicidal child.* New York: Guilford.

Sainsbury, P. (1982). Depression and suicide prevention. *Bibliotheca Psychiatra, 162,* 17-32.

School Climate Unit. (1985). *Youth suicide prevention school program.* CA: California Department of Education.

Stack, S. (1980). Region and suicide: A reanalysis. *Social Psychiatry, 15,* 65-70.

Turkington, C. (1986, November). Suit data show no need to panic. *APA Monitor,* 9.

Wilkinson, K. P., & Israel, G. D. (1984). Suicide and rurality in urban society. *Suicide and Life Threatening Behavior, 14*(3), 187-200.

World Health Organization. (1982). *Changing patterns in suicide behavior: Report on a World Health Organization working group.* Copenhagen: Regional office for Europe.

REFERENCES

Beck, A. T., Resnick, H. P., & Littieri, D. J. (Eds.). (1974). *The prediction of suicide.* Bowie, MD: Charles Press.

Berman, A. L. (1975). Self-destructive behavior and suicide: Epidemiology and taxonomy. In A. R. Roberts (Ed.), *Self-destructive behavior* (pp. 5-20). Springfield, IL: Charles C. Thomas.

Boldt, M. (1983). Normative evaluations of suicide and death: A cross-generational study. *Omega, 13*(2), 145-157.

Braught, G. N., Loya, F., & Jamieson, K. J. (1980). Victims of violent death: A critical review. *Psychological Bulletin, 87*(2), 309-333.

Breed, W. (1967). Suicide and loss in social interaction. In E. Schneidman (Ed.), *Essays in self-destructive behavior.* New York: Science House.

Bunch, J., Barraclough, B., Nelson, B., & Sainsbury, P. (1971). Early parental bereavement and suicide. *Social Psychiatry, 6*(4), 200-202.

California Department of Education. (1987). *Suicide prevention education.* Sacramento, CA: Author.

California Department of Health Services. (1986). *Suicides in California, 1980-1984.* Sacramento, CA: Author.

California Department of Mental Health. (1988). *The California Helper's Handbook for Suicide Intervention.* Sacramento, CA: Author.

Eisenberg, L. (1984). The epidemiology of suicide in adolescents. *Pediatric Annals, 13,* 47-54.

Farber, M. L. (1968). *Theory of suicide.* New York: Funk & Wagnalls.

Fisher, D. (1990). High school suicide crisis intervention. *FBI Law Enforcement Bulletin, 5,* 5-8.

Glasser, W. (1965). *Reality therapy.* New York: Harper & Row.

Glasser, W. (1984). *Control theory.* New York: Harper & Row.

Green, A. H. (1978). Self-destructive behavior in battered children. *American Journal of Psychiatry, 135,* 579-582.

Greene, J. W., & Keown, M. (1986). Depression and suicide in children and adolescents. *Comprehensive Therapy, 12,* 38-43.

Greer, S. (1966). Parental loss and attempted suicide: A further report. *British Journal of Psychiatry, 112,* 465-470.

Hoff, L. (1984). People in crisis: Understanding and helping (2nd ed.). Menlo Park, CA: Addison-Wesley.

Holding, T. A., & Barraclough, B. M. (1977). Psychiatric morbidity in a sample of accidents. *British Journal of Psychiatry, 130,* 244-252.

Jenkins, J., & Sainsbury, P. (1980). Single-car road deaths: Disguised suicides? *British Medical Journal, 281,* 1041.

Jobes, D. A., Berman, A. L., & Josselsen, A. R. (1986). The impact of psychological autopsies on medical examiners' determination of manner of death. *Journal of Forensic Science, 31*(1), 177-189.

Kelson v. City of Springfield. (1985). Oregon 767 F2, d 651, Oregon: Ninth Circuit Court of Appeals.

Lang, W. A., Ramsey, R. F., Tanney, B. L., & Tierney, R. J. (1987). *California suicide intervention training program: Organizer's guide.* CA: California Department of Mental Health.

Lester, D., & Beck, A. T. (1976). Early loss of a possible "sensitizer" to later loss in attempted suicides. *Psychological Reports, 39,* 121-122.

Litman, R. E., Farberow, N. L., Wold, C. I., & Brown, T. R. (1974). Prediction models of suicidal behaviors. In A. T. Beck, H. P. Resnick, & D. J. Littieri (Eds.), *The prediction of suicide.* Bowey, MD: Charles Press.

Motto, J. (1978). Recognition, evaluation and management of persons at risk of suicide. *Personnel and Guidance Journal, 56*(9), 537-543.

Murphy, G. (1985). Suicide and attempted suicide. In R. Michels (Ed.), *Psychiatry* (pp. 1-17). Philadelphia: J. B. Lippincott.

National Center for Health Statistics. (1986). Advance report of final mortality statistics, 1984. *Monthly Vital Statistics Report, 35*(6), 40-41.

National Institute of Mental Health. (1986). *Useful information on suicide.* Rockville, MD: Author.

Pokorny, A. D. (1975). Self-destruction and the automobile. In A. R. Roberts (Ed.), *Self-destructive behavior* (pp. 123-137). Springfield, IL: Charles C. Thomas.

Ramsey, R. F., Tanney, B. L., Tierney, R. J., & Lang, W. A. (1987). *A suicide prevention training program: Trainer's handbook* (3rd ed.). Calgary, AB: Authors/Canadian Mental Health Association.

Robins, E., Murphy, G., Wilkinson, R., Gasner, S., & Kayes, J. (1959). Some clinical observations in the prevention of suicide based on a study of 134 successful suicides. *American Journal of Public Health, 49,* 888-889.

Slater, J., & Depue, R. A. (1981). The contribution of environmental events and social supports to suicide attempts in primary depressive disorder. *Journal of Abnormal Psychology, 90,* 275-285.

Sonoma Valley Unified School District. (1989). *Administrative regulations regarding the district crisis team: Administrative response to a crisis situation.* Santa Rosa, CA: Author.

Teicher, J. D., & Jacobs, J. (1966). The physician and the adolescent suicide attempter. *Journal of School Health, 36*(9), 406-415.

Chapter 10

COUNSELING SEXUAL ABUSERS

Steven Eckert

Editor's Note

School professionals are not clinical social workers even though they probably could do a fine job at it with appropriate training. One of the most challenging problems educators must address is the damage sexual abusers and violent sex offenders have inflicted on children and adolescents. Knowing what therapists do with these sexual molesters and predators is better than hiding one's head in the sand and pretending that sexually offensive behavior stops at the school house entrance. Not only do some adults sexually prey on children, but also sexually abused children sometimes express sexual violence against other youngsters. Steve Eckert sensitively yet bluntly explains both the depth of this social taboo and a range of effective treatment methods. He also shows educators and counselors how to handle trouble when the problem rears its ugly head right where they work.

I have to confess that, as a licensed psychologist and marriage, child, and family counselor, I summarily excluded the idea of ever treating sexual deviates. I found their behavior too disdainful to offer them the kind of encouraging support all clients need in order to improve their lives. While not seeking a counseling specialty with this population, I now view many sexual offenders differently after reading Steve Eckert's substantive documentation and seeing his professional expertise. Perhaps Steve's best contribution will be shedding light that will increase readers' understanding and reasonable vigilance. I feel more compassion for young offenders who themselves have been violated sexually. I still struggle with conjuring up an accepting attitude toward the hard core adults who refuse to acknowledge any problem with their predatory style and sexually assaultive behaviors. Perhaps, though, we all can be more honest about the dangers and more assertive in protecting children and teens.

SEXUAL ABUSE COMES TO SCHOOL

"Girls these days complain too much," said the mother of a 14-year-old boy convicted of stalking, tackling, and forcing sexual contact on at least eight female victims.

You are counseling at an elementary school. A teacher is at your door with three seven-year-old boys. At recess, Allan and James pulled Johnny's pants and underwear off in front of other students. Alternatively, you work at a typical suburban high school and a female freshman, Gina, comes to your classroom after school. Her best friend just told her that two boys she had been flirting with forcibly pulled her sweater up yesterday in the parking lot during lunch and both touched her breasts. Gina promised her friend that she would not tell anyone about this incident—too shameful—and she begs you to keep the information a secret.

What would you do in these two situations? What are your options? What interventions are best for all involved? This chapter, along with chapter 7—Lynn Loar's article on (a) assessing and reporting child abuse and neglect and (b) advocating for the victims of abuse—will provide you with the necessary background and resource information to make appropriate decisions in situations similar to the ones above. This chapter describes the assessment and treatment of juvenile and adult sex offenders and, because these programs have produced little outcome data, the clinical cases given here either are anecdotal or come from the developing literature on this sensitive topic.

Sensitive Material: Caution to the Reader

Sexually offensive behavior is complicated. Sexual impropriety and abuse are offensive not only to the victim but also to all family members, friends, and acquaintances in the victim's and the perpetrator's lives. I want to advise readers at the start that many counselors and teachers may be exposing themselves to this rather direct material for the first time, and they will need to stay focused on the reality that (a) abuse occurs and that (b) as professionals working in schools, you likely will be responsible for intervening in cases of molestation and even more serious sexual assaults. Please take care of yourself while reading this material as it can, and perhaps *should,* be upsetting to the average person. Some readers even may find this material offensive. Studying the population of sexual abusers and discovering treatment methods from the mental health field can only strengthen a counselor's knowledge base and repertoire of skills for resolving dangerous threats to students. No one likes to acknowledge another aspect of this problem: at times, even adults within a school may be the perpetrators. All the more reason for counselors and other professionals to stay vigilant and to be forceful in identifying problems and taking the necessary steps when children are in danger.

Sexual Abuse Causes Serious Damage

Sexual abuse is harmful to children. The fallout from sexual abuse is a legacy of psychological problems that family researcher Cloe Madanes (1990, p. 53) described as a "pain in the heart" for both victim and offender. Although children sometimes show no signs of disturbances immediately following the abuse, many often experience and express the following symptoms later:

- flashbacks and nightmares;
- changes in their perception of others from "people are safe and trustworthy" to "people are dangerous and untrustworthy";
- depression (Milloy & Wilkes, 1990);
- feelings of guilt and shame;
- difficulty with adolescent and adult sexuality;
- increased risk of future victimization;
- dissociation (i.e., "spacing out"); and
- low self-esteem.

Sgroi (Batchelor, Dean, Gridley, & Batchelor, 1990) noted that "a victim's academic achievement may suddenly decrease, and then there may be a general withdrawal from peer relationships or school functions. In addition, a number of cases of aggressive or precocious behavior have been reported" (Sgroi, 1982, p. 122). Updated information regarding this behavior comes later in the chapter.

PREVALENCE

The level of research in the area of child sexual abuse has exploded in the last 15 to 20 years. Correspondingly, the level of research regarding adult sex offenders has increased; most objective information regarding juvenile sex offenders has been published in the last 10 years. Readers will notice that much of the information regarding the assessment and treatment of juvenile sex offenders represents an adaptation of the greater wealth of information generated from the study of adult sex offenders.

An International Problem

Sexual abuse of children has a long history. In ancient Rome, "the code of sexual ethics authorized young boys, as well as girls and women, to be violated, raped, and sold in prostitution and slavery. In ancient Greece, pederasty, or anal intercourse, was a central factor in the upbringing of boys. It had a deeply religious significance and was regarded as a normal precursor to marriage" (Ellis, 1933, cited in Barnard, Fuller, Robbins, & Shaw, 1989, p. 11). In modern American culture, the above approval of sexual abuse of children still exists albeit to a lesser extent. Social approval for adults to pleasure themselves at children's expense is shrouded in secrecy and, surprisingly, not necessarily on the fringes of American society. Sexual abuse transcends socioeconomic status levels even though convictions tend to apply to those from the lower to middle classes. Certainly, the United States does not sponsor traumatizing children sexually in the same way some other nations do. Many Latin American and Asian countries—most notably, the Philippines and Thailand—feature child pornography and prostitution of young boys and girls for domestic residents' use and for tourists' pleasure on a scale that probably matches ancient Rome and Greece.

America. Estimates of the annual incidence of child sexual abuse in the United States vary dramatically: from 123,000 cases reported nationally by the American Humane Association in 1985 (Barnard et al., 1989), to 375,000 confirmed cases (Sheaffer, 1986), to an estimated 2,000,000 incest only violations (James & Meyerding, 1977). Some professionals question whether the actual incidence of child sexual abuse is increasing or, given the recent level of education and attention to the painful subject, the rate of disclosure is finally closing in on the true rate of incidence. Unfortunately, most investigators concur that acts of child abuse are steadily rising (Finkel, 1987).

In a recent national study, Finkelhor, Hotaling, Lewis, and Smith (1990) found that 27% of American females and 16% of males are living victims of child sexual abuse. In an average classroom of 32 students, this frequency translates to eight or nine girls and four or five boys have been or will become victims of child sexual abuse by the time they reach age 18. Also, boys are less likely than girls to disclose their victimization—42% for females to 33% for males (Finkelhor et al., 1990). Russell (1983) found that less than 6% of female child sexual abuse victims ever reported these incidents to the police. Finkelhor (Davis & Leitenberg, 1987) found that only 35% report to anyone.

Reporting versus Convicting. Although reporting may be rising, only a minority of cases end in a tangible conviction. This dismally high failure to convict rate is often a result of an *accommodation syndrome* (Summit, 1983). This syndrome is a subtle but overwhelming psychological process of internal and external pressures to compel victims to recant their charges or qualify their disclosures by assuming responsibility for the abuse or by revising some aspect of the original report.

Case Example #1: Six-year-old Sammy

A school principal referred Sammy, age six, and his family to the general counseling program based on the first-grader's inability to pay attention in the classroom and on his aggressive behavior indoors and on the playground. Coincidentally, the police had just referred his 15-year-old brother for diversion counseling because of his fondness for graffiti. Moreover, a school counselor referred his 16-year-old sister for treatment of substance abuse and serious problems with her boyfriend.

During the intake interview with the family, the counselor asked each child in the presence of the entire family, "Has anyone ever touched you, without your permission, in your private areas?" Whereas the older children responded in the negative, Sammy revealed that, two or three times on the school playground recently, two eight-year-old boys had held him down, reached inside his pants, and fondled his penis while laughing at him. Upon this revelation—not surprisingly—Sammy's mother began to cry; however, her immediate comments *were* surprising:

> **Mother:** *Great. This is all I need. Why did you have to tell that? Are you sure? I don't need this.* (Sammy began to cry and look to his suffering mother for direction.)
> **Sister:** *Who did it?*
> **Sammy:** (reluctantly and still watching his mother) *Jimmy and Tommy.*
> **Mother:** *I guess you're gonna get those social workers in on this, aren't you?*
> **Counselor:** *Yes. We are going to need their help.*
> **Mother:** *You are always lying. Tell the truth.*
> **Sammy:** (picking up the underlying demand and beginning to accommodate his mother's injunction) *I don't know.*

Sammy learned an important lesson that day in the counselor's office. His mother had clarified for him and for his siblings the family rule: Don't tell the truth about sexual invasions or assaults because you could bring shame on your poor mother and her family. Worse, the authorities could come into the picture and who knows what danger to the family system they could bring. Would the family face bad publicity in the local newspaper, removal of a parent from the home, or jail time?

The Mind and Behavioral Pattern of Sex Offenders

Do sex offenders molest or rape once and never again? It is possible but not likely. Once the taboo is broken, the risk to reoffend is higher. A widely cited study by Abel, Becker, Cunningham-Rather, Rouleau, Kaplan, and Reich, using an incarcerated population, showed "adult offenders have reported an average of 380 victims" (National Task Force on Juvenile Sex Offending, 1988, p. 5). Research with convicted sex offenders indicates that 50% committed their first offenses during adolescence (Groth, Longo, & McFaddin, 1982). Deisher, Wenet, Paperney, Clark, and Fehrenbach (1982) found that adolescents perpetrate 30% to 50% of all child molestations and 20% of all rapes. All studies they reviewed were conducted by interviewing convicted sex offenders about their histories. Ageton (1983) conducted a confidential survey using a national probability sample of males aged 13 to 19. The rate for forced sexual assault including rape, incest, sodomy, and fondling was 5% to 16%, with the highest rate committed by 17-year-olds. At the time of this study, only 20 treatment programs existed in the United States (National Task Force on Juvenile Sex Offending, 1988)—a very large majority of juvenile sex offenders received no specialized treatment. "Adolescents currently being evaluated report an average of less than seven victims. Early intervention is clearly indicated" (National Task Force on Juvenile Sex Offending, 1988, p. 5). As of 1996, 1,000 programs treat juvenile sex offenders in the U.S.

Adolescent Offenders Pose a Serious Threat. We have always known that adult sex offenders are dangerous and we recently have learned that adolescent sex offenders are also dangerous. Prepubescent boys can get erections and physically penetrate female victims. Addressing sexually inappropriate behavior early in an offender's career is more effective than remediating it later. Early treatment is shorter and less expensive than adult treatment. In 1988, Prentky and Burgess (Marshall, Jones, Ward, Johnston, & Barbaree, 1991) calculated the cost to investigate a reoffense, prosecute and jail the offender, and offer minimal assessment and therapy to the victim. The estimate of costs provided by Children's Protective Services, police, courts, corrections, and hospitals amounted to $180,000 per victim. The average cost per family participating in one typical outpatient juvenile sex offender program in northern California is $900, whereas incarceration costs over $20,000 per year.

Early Treatment Is Best. Treatment prognosis is more optimistic with young perpetrators because personalities and behavioral routines of younger offenders are more amenable to therapeutic change. Offenders often psychologically pair acts and/or fantasies of sexual assault with sexual arousal and orgasm. These pleasurable physiological reinforcements are so powerful that a therapeutic cure is unlikely, particularly with adults who may have perpetrated many more incidents than younger offenders. Early intervention benefits everyone. The young perpetrators benefit as do the would-be victims whose lives are spared this pain if an effective intervention occurs early enough. Sexual behaviors have a way of serving as their own reward system and, naturally, the earlier counselors intervene, the better. Also, young boys who molest little children do not define themselves initially as sexual predators. At first, they may be reenacting behaviors they experienced as children when an older sex offender victimized them. If a therapist were to work with them early to see how they could resolve their hurt, confusion, and leftover fury, they might not go on to earn the identity label of *criminal sex offender.*

OFFENDER PROFILE

The profile of a juvenile sex offender usually includes some of the following:

- low self-esteem,
- feelings of inadequacy,
- poor academic performance in school,
- inability to trust,
- poor social skills,
- previous victimization by an older perpetrator(s),
- out of touch with personal emotional system,
- inability to feel empathy for others,
- exposure to adult models of aggression or intimidation,
- aberrant sexual fantasies,
- aggressive and antisocial behavior,
- dysfunctional family system,
- exposure to adult models of sexuality (e.g., pornography),
- inadequate or inappropriate sex education,
- skill deficit in managing impulsive urges, and
- denial or minimization of sexually offensive behavior.

These characteristic behaviors or traits typically comprise the criteria that define juvenile sex offenders in a clinical assessment, but most professionals will recognize evidence of these qualities or behavioral components in the general population of juvenile delinquents. Van Ness (1984, in Davis & Leitenberg, 1987) found that 41% of adolescent sex offenders reported histories of physical abuse or neglect compared with only 15% of a matched group of delinquents. Probably the most salient characteristic of a sex offender is a personal history of sexual abuse as a child. Comparing the previously-mentioned (Finkelhor et al., 1990) rate of 16% of child sexual abuse in the entire male population to the findings of other studies (Finkelhor, 1984; Groth, Longo, & McFaddin, 1982; Johnson, 1988), the rate of child sexual abuse for sex offenders is as high as 81%. The rate of disclosed child sexual abuse victimization for participants in the previously-mentioned California juvenile sex offender program is closer to Finkelhor et al.'s 16%, but the rate of physical abuse and neglect is over 50%.

Case Example #2: 12-year-old Conrad

A local small town police department referred Conrad, age 12, to the Juvenile Sex Offender Program after a six-year-old neighbor boy disclosed that he had orally copulated Conrad. Conrad's mother believed that something had happened but was unsure of the actual details because Conrad denied the accusation. When Conrad was six, a teenage neighbor boy held him down, forced Conrad to orally copulate him, and rubbed feces on his face. At the time of Conrad's own abuse, his parents reported the incident to the police, and the neighbor boy was arrested for his behavior. At age 10, school officials had referred Conrad for psychotherapy services due to his aggressive behavior in school, but he never had received counseling to help him with his own experiences as a victim of sexual abuse.

Case Example #3: 25-year-old Ronald

A staff psychiatrist at California's San Quentin Prison referred Ronald, age 25, to a Pilot Sex Offender Program. The medical doctor believed that the focused treatment program might be more beneficial for Ronald than the anti-anxiety medication that he originally had requested. Ronald's commitment offense was digital penetration of his 10-year-old niece's vagina and fondling of her breasts and genitals. He was accused, but not convicted, of other sexual misconduct counts with the same victim, and he also had been arrested at age 18 for sexual harassment of a 16-year-old ex-girlfriend.

Ronald's family background was unremarkable: His middle-class parents had remained married, he had two siblings, and there were no reports of serious family problems or prior arrests of other family members. Ronald had held a skilled union job before his incarceration and, although substance abuse was a significant problem for him during his teen years, his indulgence in drugs was practically nonexistent during his 20s. During treatment, Ronald remembered a 15-year-old neighbor boy forcing him to copulate him orally a few times. He remembered his perpetrator threatening him with violence if he did not comply. He decided to "put it out of my mind" and never disclose the molestation to anyone, fearing punishment and being labeled gay. Ronald left the prison on parole before disclosing other possible offenses against him, and he continued in post-incarceration outpatient treatment.

From Victim to Victimizer

The transformation of victim to victimizer is a common story of sex offenders. As people grow, they gradually develop a natural sense of mastery over their environments. Abuse of bodily integrity negatively affects this mastery. The natural process of healing implies regaining control by whatever means available. For juvenile sex offenders who have been sexually abused, the rationale is often simply, "Do unto others as has been done unto me." The younger the age of the perpetrator, the higher the likelihood of earlier sexual victimization to himself/herself (Johnson, 1988). For others, the causes may be more complicated. In a family with evidence of child neglect, for example, children may substitute sex play for the affection they craved but did not receive from their emotionally distant parents. Others may learn sexually aggressive behaviors from peers, parents, or the media. Some combination of the above profile factors increases the risk for a person to make the choice of offending sexually, but the only known correlate is a history of abuse or neglect.

Finkelhor (1986) has proposed a four-factor model in explaining causality of child molestation. Some features of this model are summarized below:

- Emotional Congruence. An offender has an "arrested psychosexual development," is emotionally immature, and identifies with the aggressor.
- Sexual Arousal. An offender has early sexual experiences, is aroused by pornography, and is aroused by children.
- Blockage. An offender has difficulty relating to peer-age females, has disturbances in adult romantic relationships, and has repressive norms regarding sexual behavior.
- Disinhibition. An offender's inhibitions may be reduced by alcohol abuse or by the failure of the incest avoidance mechanism (i.e., the taboo of father-daughter sexual contact).

Case Example #4: 50-year-old John

John is a 55-year-old married grandfather with a history of alcoholism. He received a state prison sentence after his conviction on charges of fondling his nine-year-old granddaughter and enticing her to orally copulate him while bathing together. John said that he generally feels more comfortable with children than with adults. His own grandfather molested him by enticing him to perform the same oral sex act that he persuaded his granddaughter to do for him. John explained that he had not had sex with his wife for over 10 years because of her medical problems. He reported that he was often under the influence of alcohol and/or marijuana during the molestations. His wife would send their granddaughter to the bathroom when John was bathing so that he could wash the girl's hair.

TYPOLOGY OF ADULT SEX OFFENDERS

Researcher and therapist Larry Corrigan (personal communication, October 25, 1989) pointed out the difficulty in rigidly classifying sex offender types because they often participate in a variety of offensive behaviors. Mark, age 17, for example, entered the Juvenile Sex Offender program for fondling the vagina of his two-year-old cousin on at least two occasions.

In the early stages of his court-directed treatment, he reoffended, but this time he followed a 14-year-old female acquaintance into the restroom of a fast-food restaurant and forcibly pulled down her blue jeans and panties to digitally penetrate her. Do we classify him as a rapist or as a molester? Here in an abbreviated version, Groth (1978; Groth & Birnbaum, 1979) answered this question and further delineates types and subtypes of adult sex offenders. This typology can be applied generally to juvenile sex offenders.

Defining Molestation

1. The offender approaches a potential victim with seduction and persuasion.
2. A passive and dependent behavioral style is the major pattern of molesters.
3. Offenses are generally progressive in severity.
4. Subtype: Fixated.

   - the offender's primary sexual orientation is to children
   - persistent interest and compulsive behavior

- pedophilic interests begin in adolescence
- male victims are primary targets
- little or no sexual contact with agemates
- delayed maturation

5. Subtype: Regressed.

- primary sexual orientation is to adults
- interest in children is episodic, and may be stress-related
- offender replaces a conflicted adult relationship with involvement with a child
- female victims are primary targets
- sexual contact with children coexists with agemate contact
- alcohol usage often accompanies the sexual offense

Defining Rape or Sexual Battery

1. The offender approaches in an attack or assault mode.
2. In the approach, the violator implies or directly expresses threat and intimidation.
3. The attacker employs aggressive and hostile actions.
4. The perpetrator uses sexual assault to display power in one of three ways: dominating, angering, and sadistic behaviors.

   A Subtype: Dominating Behaviors
   - a using absolutely whatever threat or force is required to subdue a victim
   - b assaulting a victim with premeditation
   - c preceding the attack with persistent and violent rape fantasies
   - d using instructional and inquisitive language
   - e selecting a victim by vulnerability

   B Subtype: Angering Behaviors
   - a using more physical force to subdue a victim than is required
   - b impulsively assaulting a victim
   - c using abusive language during the assault
   - d selecting a victim by convenience and availability

   C Subtype: Sadistic Behaviors
   - a eroticizing and ritualizing the physical force
   - b calculating and methodically preplanning the assault

    c alternating commanding and degrading words with reassuring and threatening words

    d selecting a victim by specific characteristics or a symbolic representation—usually complete strangers

Not listed in the above descriptors are noncontact sex offenses such as those who expose their genitals and peep into people's private living spaces. Most treatment programs separate the above two types of sex offenders, and even the subtypes, into separate treatment groups because rapists subtly intimidate other molesters in a counseling group. The Juvenile Sex Offender Program separates teenagers who molest from those who assault and also provides distinctive treatment for 9- to 13-year-old molesters. The San Quentin Sex Offender program currently serves only the regressed molester subtype.

ASSESSMENT

Before therapists and judges can make decisions about appropriate levels of treatment and punishment, a specialized psychotherapist must do a comprehensive assessment of the offender. The main purpose of this testing is to assist law enforcement and court personnel in their recommendations regarding prosecution, sentencing, conditions of probation, parole supervision, and placement in a diversion program while the offender is living in the community.

Prior to sentencing, a thorough clinical assessment is not possible. Therapy and court hearings do not mix well. Defense attorneys often insist that their clients maintain their denial of any sexual misconduct. Even after conviction and sentencing, an offender's statement regarding admission or denial must be considered in the context of other assessment information. In the two programs I am describing here, we do not press offenders for complete admissions of guilt and responsibility during the preliminary assessment. We expect the treatment group to handle that task if needed.

Level of Risk to the Community

After a juvenile sex offender comes our way, we immediately investigate the records as a first step in the comprehensive assessment. Having a copy of victims' statements on hand is crucial. We normally view these statements as highly accurate. The second step is a brief meeting with the adolescent and his/her family to have the parents sign all release of information forms. With parental authorization, the assessor gains information from school personnel, previous therapists, and other professionals who have worked with the juvenile. Education professionals are a valuable resource to the assessor in their ability to provide both subjective and objective information about the juvenile's daily behavior, peer relations, and academic abilities.

After this brief release signing meeting, a member of the treatment team interviews the juvenile and administers a battery of psychological tests. Currently, the Millon Adolescent Personality Inventory is the assessment instrument. Sometimes, others have conducted testing at the juvenile's school or at juvenile hall. The third step is interviewing the juvenile offender and his/her family. A subsequent section of this chapter contains more information on the interview when the victim is also a member of the juvenile perpetrator's family. The fourth step is either welcoming the newcomer to the Juvenile Sex Offender Program through the ritual of signing appropriate treatment contracts or recommending optional resources. Incarceration, of course, is always an option when the individual is unwilling to participate in the program. We do not meet with the families of the adult offenders at San Quentin state prison, but we do administer a comprehensive battery of psychological tests including the WAIS-R, MMPI, Rorschach, and the Multi-phasic Sexual Inventory.

The main objectives of assessment are to determine the level of risk to the community and the level of supervisory services we will recommend. Do we propose incarceration or probation for the juvenile offender? We give the assessment results to parents and to appropriate school personnel so that they can supervise an offender on probation adequately and protect all potential victims. Another assessment goal is determining the level and type of psychological services the offender will need. Do we, for example, assign a nine-year-old perpetrator to a group for offenders or victims? We consider at least 14 risk factors in reaching a decision:

1. Level of Admission. We recognize that feeling guilty can be a transitory emotion and depends on many factors. We first identify and evaluate any discrepancies between a victim's and an offender's statements. This discrepancy can be plotted on the scale shown here.

High Risk			Low Risk
1+	1	1	−1
		admission	admission
nonadmission	minimization	with justification	with guilt

We then ask offenders to self-evaluate the level of seriousness of their offense(s) on a scale of 0 (not at all serious) to 10 (very serious).

When offenders report low numbers on the above scale, they show little concern or understanding of the effects of their actions on the victim(s), and this low-level awareness automatically elevates their risk of repeating the offense.

2. Level of Coercion. How did the offender persuade the victim to comply with his/her instructions in the first place? Usual methods of pressure include bribery, threats, violence, and the coercive power that flows naturally from an age and status differential. A higher level of coercion indicates a higher level of risk.

3. Level of Consent. Finkelhor said that two conditions must prevail for true consent to occur. "A person must know what it is that he or she is consenting to and must have true freedom to say yes or no" (Finkelhor, 1984, p. 17). Children, by definition, do not meet these standards; teenagers often do not qualify either. If a low level of consent exists during the offense(s), early release of the offender poses a greater risk to the community.

4. Extent of Harm. Did the offender continue the abuse after the victim refused to participate? Did the assaults against the victim(s) follow a pattern?

5. Selecting a Victim. Was the offense a crime of opportunity or did the perpetrator premeditate the offense and stalk the victim?

6. Frequency and Duration. How often did the offending party sexually violate the victim? Exactly how long did each offense last: five seconds or five hours? Was the offense a one-time act or did the perpetrator commit multiple offenses over a long period of time?

7. Family Dynamics. (These will appear in greater detail later in the chapter.)

8. Type of Offense. (Please refer to Groth's types and subtypes under the "Defining Molestation" and "Defining Rape or Sexual Battery" sections earlier in this chapter.)

9. Fantasies. Does the offender admit to sexual fantasies preceding the offense? (In my experience with the assessment phase, the juvenile offender usually does not admit having had sexual fantasies prior to the offense.)

10. Arrest History. "Youths with at least one previous conviction of any type were significantly more likely to reoffend criminally" (Kohn & Chambers, 1991, p. 344). Youths with previous sexual offense histories should be considered higher risks.

11. Motivation for Treatment. Is the offender concerned about his/her behavior and does he/she want to learn to stop these illegal and abusive acts? What is the offender's previous experience with psychotherapy? What does the offender say about being in a therapy group with other sex offenders?

12. Substance Abuse. Was the offender under the influence of alcohol while offending a victim sexually? Does the offender have a chronic substance abuse problem? If so, we assign them to separate treatment for substance abuse.

13. School History. (Greater detail on this topic appears later in this chapter.)

14. Other Issues. Treatment specialists in the program take into account a variety of factors and stressors as they evaluate an offender's suitability for assignment to a group. Among the key criteria that inform the appropriateness of group work are personal victimization, age, emotional sophistication, neurological deficits, developmental disabilities, psychotic handicaps, and recent life challenges, such as recent losses through abandonment, divorce or death, and suicide risk. (See chapter 9 for assessing and handling suicide risk.)

Testing Methods

Most of the above information comes from self-reports and others' observations. Aside from psychological testing as an attempt to gain objective information about offenders, the *penile plethysmograph* can be a useful, if not controversial, medium in assessment of adult offenders. This device uses a sensor ring slipped on the offender's penis to monitor erection responses to pictorial stimuli. One use of the instrument is as a lie detector: deviancy is more likely when a picture of a minor child elicits arousal on the plethysmograph. As with polygraph devices, however, the absence of a physical response in the laboratory does not necessarily indicate that the alleged offender never has deviant arousal patterns. Another consideration is that an obvious confounding factor may be automatically present: The mechanical apparatus itself may serve as a sexual stimulant the moment an adolescent male feels it against his genitals. Finally, requiring involuntary clients to use this device raises significant ethical questions, particularly with adolescents. Ironically, the procedure itself may be another form of sexual intrusion; in this instance, the social control agency may be violating the sexual rights of the offenders.

SCHOOL HISTORY

Juvenile or adult sex offenders show a higher incidence of academic and/or school behavioral problems. One study reported that one-third of the offenders showed school difficulties beginning in kindergarten, and over 80% had experienced learning or behavioral difficulties during at least part of their school career. About one-half of the subjects had long-standing problems with teachers and peers (Awad, Saunders, & Levine, 1984; Fehrenbach, Smith, Monastersky, & Deisher, 1986; Kohn & Chambers, 1991).

In one study, only 55% of the adolescent sex offenders were on schedule in their grade placement (Fehrenbach et al., 1986). This means that almost half of the group showed no special problems regarding their grade placement. This finding that a large percentage of sexual molesters show no behavior problems in school may indicate they are trying very hard to keep a low profile in a public place. Many molesters desire to be quiet and alone, not wishing to attract the attention that school misbehavior usually brings. This information, however, corresponds to the problems in a juvenile sex offender typology. Lest any researcher become smug with this profile information, other researchers suggest, "Concurrent and past signs of behavioral and school disturbances are common in the histories of adolescent sex offenders, but no more so than in other delinquent youth who have never committed a sex offense" (Davis & Leitenberg, 1987, p. 425).

Abbot found intelligence not to be a significant contributing factor in adolescent sex offending behavior (Abbot, 1990). In their 1983 study, Tartar, Hegedus, Alterman, and Katz-Garris (Davis & Leitenberg, 1987) found no differences between adolescent sex offenders and other delinquents in academic performance and IQ scores.

FAMILY DYNAMICS

Incest is a family affair (Madanes, 1990). Even in families where only the perpetrator, and not the victim, is a member, the dynamics are quite similar to incest families. The most common trait appears to be denying or minimizing the offense. As with child victims, juvenile sex offenders appear to accommodate to the stress they feel through disclosure (Summit, 1983). A juvenile offender carefully notices how his/her family will react to his/her disclosure as the offender will need the family's support in this time of stress. The offender will look to his/her parents who also resort to fight or flight behaviors as they see a team of police and social workers on the horizon. Responses range from the *fight* of jury trials (usually in adult perpetrator cases) to *flight* into complete denial.

Therapists who connect with a family immediately after disclosure can join with the family as an advocate before denial and accommodation set in. Therapeutic work with the family is at least as necessary as work with the juvenile offender because the offender will deny the victim's accusations as long as the family does.

Revisiting Example #2

Conrad, age 12, who had compelled a six-year-old neighbor boy to copulate him orally, denied the extent of the molestation during the assessment and for a full year into treatment. His father refused to attend the conjoint parent group, excusing himself by stating that he could not take time off from his job at a warehouse. The treatment staff hypothesized that Conrad's father might have held the key to Conrad's admission of the offense, so they scheduled a special family therapy session.

Family Sticks Together. Conrad's father was a man who displayed rude bumper stickers on his pick-up truck but also coached his son's baseball team. As he had during the initial family assessment, the father complained about the police department for harassing his family with this matter of Conrad's arrest. The therapist shifted the discussion and Conrad's father then said that even though the police "acted like 'assholes' during the investigation," he agreed with his wife that "something might possibly have happened."

Father's Rules. The therapist asked the father, "Is it OK if Conrad tells the truth?" and the father replied, "Of course." The therapist then asked the father, if the truth were that the molestation did happen, would he be angry at Conrad for telling the truth. The father replied, "No." The father seemed to soften up with the therapist/counselor, which increased his resolve to continue the questioning. The therapist/counselor asked Conrad, "What would your father do if you were to say that you molested your neighbor?"

Father's Support. Conrad watched his father closely. "He'd be OK." Conrad's eyes darted between his mother's and his father's. He was testing the water and so far so good. The therapist also sensed the parents' silent permission to continue the questioning. "Would you tell me and your Dad—right here and now—if you did it or not?" The therapist felt that the odds were good enough for this gamble given the above line of questioning and the trust he had developed with the family. "I did it," Conrad replied. He felt safe enough to take the risk. His father let his eyes water. "Would you like to shake your son's hand for telling the truth?" asked the therapist. Instead of merely shaking hands, Conrad's father got up from his chair, quietly crossed the room, and hugged his son warmly. At his next group meeting, Conrad was able to acknowledge his offense and later successfully graduated from the program.

Family's Abuse History. Extensive abuse often characterizes families of juvenile sex offenders. Lewis et al. (Davis & Leitenberg, 1987, p. 422) found that 79% of a sample of incarcerated adolescent sex offenders had observed serious intrafamilial violence, as compared to 20% of a nonviolent delinquent group. Abuse exists also in the histories of the perpetrator's family members. Johnson (1988) found that, in 64% of the families in the SPARK program, one or more of the parents or grandparents had been physically abused, and 67% of these family members themselves had endured sexual abuse. Finkelhor et al. (1990) pointed out unequivocally that growing up in an unhappy family appears to be the most powerful risk factor for abuse.

Assessing Other Family Dynamics

1. Sexualized versus Repressed Family Context Continuum. As with the issue of consent, adults generally have enough knowledge and experience to understand the consequences of high levels of sexuality. Children, and, to varying degrees, adolescents do not fully understand the consequences of direct sexual involvement. Generational boundaries in some families often are blurred. Some of the participants in the juvenile sex offenders program reported watching their parents having sex, with the parents' knowledge. Others had the Playboy Channel available at home without supervision. Children imitate what they see or hear and sometimes act on parental injunctions. Take, for example, a father who continually tells his son, "Look at your sister; just look at that sexy body. Whoever gets her will be a lucky guy." This father may be setting his son up to act out his (the father's) sexual fantasies.

Conversely, with an absence of appropriate sexual boundaries in the offending family, repressed families may have overly rigid values regarding sexuality and other behaviors. Although children may be naturally curious, they may have little information about appropriate sexual behavior. When sexual behavior occurs in these families—particularly, sexually offensive behavior—the level of shame is very high, requiring the therapist to provide firm but gentle respect to all concerned.

2. Level of Family Isolation and Alienation. Abusive families are typically socially isolated as a natural protective mechanism to keep the outside world from knowing about the family's activities. Disconnected from conventional social networks, family members attempt to meet most of their social needs within their immediate family unit. Sadly, the more they turn inward, the more bound up they become in their own sexually inappropriate patterns. Sexually abusive families must learn to develop support systems outside their immediate boundaries, including reconnecting with their own extended family, finding new friends, and joining activity groups and self-help groups.

3. Dysfunctional Parental Relationship. The parental relationship is the key example that sets the tone within the family for other relationships in the family system. Often, poor communication, sexual dysfunction, or domestic violence characterize an offender's family. In families where a juvenile has committed a sexual offense with a high degree of violence, either the father or the step-father usually is intimidating. In families where juveniles have molested other youngsters, the fathers may be patriarchal but also either passive or passive-aggressive. These dynamics in parenting styles contribute to *mothers only* parent groups. Therapists and probation officers must develop special communicating skills to convince the fathers that attending the group would be worthwhile.

4. Inadequate Bonding. The histories of many juvenile sex offenders show much disruption in a family's normal stream of development. This disruptive pattern includes high levels of divorce and remarriage, parental substance abuse, and offenders receiving child care from relatives or foster parents. Sexual offenders identify with their parents significantly less than nonsexual offenders and nonoffenders (Levant & Bass, 1991). Families of offenders are often in a state of chronic crisis (sometimes called *burnout*), a condition that limits parents in their efforts to be available emotionally for their children. In the absence of the natural guidance and nurturing that the majority of parents offer their children, professionals must fill the void by offering extra casework services to these families.

5. Familial Lack of Empathy. Some parents of offenders show little concern or warmth for their son's particular victims or for general victims of sexual violence and intrusion. Parents' own experiences of abuse as children and the psychic numbing to which they resorted as they managed their own victimization at that time may explain their current emotional distance from their children and the emotional numbness they display. The opening line of this chapter is, "Girls these days complain too much." The juvenile offender's mother who made this statement explained that, when she was a child, her brothers sexually touched her and she was not affected by the fondling. When the offender and the victim both belong to the same family, evaluators always should assess first the victim's physical and psychological safety level because the perpetrator may be receiving more support in his/her denial of the crime than the victim is receiving for his/her immediate needs.

Also, like it or not, parent(s) may portray a high level of antisocial or criminal behavior continually, which offenders mentally register and subsequently copy. While these parents may say they want their sons to treat others with respect, their own behavior may model deceitful or even predatory relationships. Juvenile sex offenders from these families appear to be at a much higher risk for repeatedly offending than those from families with a history of socially responsible behavior.

6. Consequences. Are the parents able to administer and enforce appropriate consequences for serious sexual misconduct? Did the parent(s) actually administer appropriate consequences to their son/daughter for his/her abusive behavior in this instance?

7. Family Secrets. Who in the family knows about the offender's action? Do the offender, victim, and one parent collude to keep the crime a secret? The siblings probably are aware of sketchy details, at least, and should hear accurate information about the story as soon as possible. Is someone indiscriminately announcing information about the sexual offense outside of family boundaries? The family needs guidance and encouragement from trusted mental health and social service specialists in order to resolve their problem within their own family unit and not to face coercive pressures to defend themselves beyond the family's boundaries.

CHILD PERPETRATORS

Most children are naturally curious about sex—one human function from among many bodily functions that children learn to confront. Childhood sexuality is not inherently a pathological condition. Children's capacity for sexual arousal is evidenced by such normal behaviors as playing "doctor," such games as, "show me yours and I'll show you mine," and (contrary to the views of some religious sects) masturbation (Ryan, 1991). Yates said, "There is increasing professional and scientific agreement that sexual interest and activity among children is healthy and perhaps even salutary to later sexual functioning" (Finkelhor, 1984, p. 15); however, even children participate in sexually offensive behavior. Identifying and reporting children who offend sexually had been almost nonexistent prior to 1985. Assessing sexual abuse by children against peers or younger children is very dependent on assessing the levels of equality and consent in the relationships as well as determining the quality of threats and coercion. The literature on sexually abused children, children in play therapy, and emotionally and behaviorally disturbed children is rampant with accounts of sexually aggressive behavior. Many investigators in the field of sexual abuse have described these behaviors as *reactive* or *acting out,* and they have denied or rationalized the offending nature of the abuse. This shift in thinking from an earlier time is clearly reminiscent of our reluctance to see the development of sexually offending behaviors in adolescents. Less than a decade ago, society knew today's sex crimes as "adolescent adjustment reaction" or "exploratory and experimental" (National Task Force, 1988, p. 42).

Just as adult offenders have identified sexually offensive behavior in adolescents (Groth, Hobson, & Gary, 1982; Deisher et al., 1982), "many teenage offenders in therapy have been able to identify retrospectively, that their offending patterns of thinking and behavior were present as early as age five" (Law, 1987, cited in Ryan, 1991, p. 395).

Families of young sex offenders typically show significant levels of chaos or neglect. As a result of low levels of supervision and availability of parental nurturing, children often use the pleasure that sex play brings as a replacement for feeling emotionally bereft. The sexual activity is often a consensual behavior, but the first mutual act often leads to more abusive and damaging behaviors. Child perpetrators are more than twice as likely to victimize family members due to their lack of freedom in the world outside of home and due to their roadblocks in accessing other victims (Johnson, 1988). Boys most likely will be the victims of abuse by young offenders (Finkelhor et al., 1990). This behavioral pattern can follow a ripple effect resulting from the previously mentioned victim to victimizer process. Johnson (1988) found a high incidence (49%) of sexual victimization among young perpetrators and noted that the younger the perpetrator, the higher the likelihood of personal victimization. When assessing a suspected youthful sexual offender, an assessor needs to look at the following range of sex play behaviors and treatment options:

Sex Play Behaviors	Assessment	Treatment Options
1 normal play no coercion	1 brief assessment	brief education
1 advanced play no coercion	−1 full assessment	possible family or individual therapy
−1 sophisticated play no or low coercion (2 or more years difference in age)	1 full assessment	victim's group (Children United) legal interventions
1 sophisticated play high coercion (2 or more years difference in age)	1 full assessment	specialized treatment legal interventions

Legal Interventions

In order to evaluate and develop appropriate models of child and family sexuality, assessment specialists rely mainly on parent support and parent education in all of these treatment options. Furthermore, the law mandates legal intervention whenever an offender coerces another person into sexual behavior or whenever a parent is aware of the offender's own earlier victimization. The legal mandate will be discussed in greater detail later in the chapter.

CONFIDENTIALITY

Confidentiality is the cornerstone of all psychotherapy; however, in sex offender programs, prospective participants first must sign release of information forms that allow staff to discuss investigative information about the subjects, their progress in treatment, danger levels to the victim(s) or to the community, and the appropriateness of involving certain other professionals in the case. Most sexual abuse cases are complicated and require the cooperative participation of a variety of people from many disciplines who can work together. These agencies may include law enforcement, mental health, probation, children's protective services, schools, social services, penal institutions, and other social and educational groups. To provide a continuum of care to the offender and his/her family, a case manager coordinates the efforts of a team of professionals from all these different agencies.

Legal Limits on Teachers

As previously mentioned, sexual abuse occurs in a context of secrecy, shame, and poorly defined boundaries. The involved professionals must share appropriate case information in order to ensure that the secrecy that usually surrounds sexual assault does not remain a black hole that hampers the inquiry and destroys the therapeutic process. Holders of the disclosed information must be absolutely discreet in appropriately protecting an offender's, a family's, and a victim's confidentiality and dignity. Respecting confidentiality can create a bind that is particularly difficult for school teachers who naturally become part of a continuum of care team. They typically have more contact with young offenders than all the other professionals on the team. Teachers can offer valuable information regarding the offender's behavior patterns, peer relations, and academic performance as well as provide their best professional judgments about the offender's family. As with all members of the continuum of care team, however, teachers must restrict the information they pass along to the content parents have authorized them to divulge. Releases of information forms give green lights on selected information but also limit people in what they legally may discuss. Certainly, for teachers, respecting parental releases can cramp their style of talking openly with one another in the faculty break room about all students and their families. Sometimes, the freedom to share information informally appears to follow a code that guarantees teachers a sense of mutual support and personal survival. Sharing information too freely, however, can reduce juvenile sex offenders' trust in the therapeutic process. On the other side of the coin, juvenile offenders sometimes see the benefit of dissolving a conspiracy of secrecy into appropriate and respectful confidentiality and regain their trust in teachers and others responsible for their treatment.

The Law about Reporting New Disclosures

Counselors routinely encourage and expect both juvenile and adult sex offenders to make further disclosures of other sex offenses as part of the healing process. If the offender reveals new offenses against the same person whom he/she was convicted of victimizing, the new information remains confidential. The mandate to report does not apply in this instance because the victim already is receiving services and the offender and victim already have had their day in court. If there never has been a court hearing (i.e., diversion), then investigators and therapists will report new offense information to the police or to Children's Protective Services. Also, reports go to appropriate authorities if the offender discloses new victims who are still minors. Offenders learn about these limits of confidentiality before beginning the formal assessment and again before the formal treatment program begins.

When Partial Disclosures Emerge. Given the above legal guidelines, some offenders voluntarily admit to sex offenses but choose to withhold identifying information to prevent further legal action. Debate continues regarding the ethics of treatment under these conditions of nonspecific disclosures; therapists must decide on a case-by-case basis whether to continue the treatment that the offenders' vague disclosures have compromised. In my professional experience, sex offenders usually lack the interpersonal competencies and strengths to maintain the necessary motivation to stay committed to the sometimes stressful treatment process without the external pressure of the law.

TREATMENT

Historical Treatments

Over the years, methods for treating sexual predators have ranged from the physical treatments of psychosurgery, castration, and medication to one or more of the psychological treatments of psychoanalytic, family, cognitive-behavioral, and behavior modification approaches. Authorities have abandoned psychosurgery altogether. Also, castration has been discarded even though the success rate was probably high (Marshall et al., 1991). Medication, such as Depo-Provera, has shown mixed results and is, therefore, of inconclusive value. Dropouts from usage pose a significant problem (Marshall et al., 1991).

The Salutary Effects of Relapse Prevention

Pure behavioral approaches in the form of operant conditioning (including aversive therapy and negative reinforcement) have not shown long-term success because of the problem of maintaining nonoffensive behavior (George & Marlatt, 1989). The cognitive-behavioral approach of Relapse Prevention (RP) addresses the problem of maintenance and has become a central organizing treatment approach in many sex offender treatment programs. "Based on social cognitive principles, Relapse Prevention has a psychoeducational thrust that combines behavioral skill-training procedures with cognitive intervention techniques" (George & Marlatt, 1989, p. 2). The Relapse Prevention model is derived from the field of addictions, and therapists have applied these techniques to adult offenders because sex offense behavior has seemingly addictive qualities. Relapse Prevention also has proven appropriate with juvenile sex offenders but is less prominent than in adult programs. Treatment providers have received the Relapse Prevention model enthusiastically, but quantitative research on the effectiveness of Relapse Prevention with sex offenders is still developing.

Assumptions Underlying the Relapse Prevention Model

The Relapse Prevention model for treating sex offenders encompasses a variety of assumptions.

1. No known "cure" exists for those engaging in sex offending behaviors.
2. The treatment goal for most providers today is to reduce offenders' risk of relapse
3. Public policy states society's treatment goal as reducing the recidivism of offenders' assaults on victims.
4. The Relapse Prevention method requires the offenders' active cooperation and motivation to manage their own behavior.
5. Offenders can control and monitor their abstinence from sex offending behaviors.
6. Sex offense behavior is an initial problem of cessation and a subsequent problem of ongoing maintenance.
7. Although sexually assaultive behavior may have addictive qualities, the consequences of relapse are seriously damaging to victims.
8. Relapse should result in legal consequences that include legal intervention with offenders.
9. Relapses most often result from inadequate skills to cope with the urges to offend again.
10. Sex offending behavior stems from multiple factors. (As one offender at San Quentin described the assaultive pattern, "These behaviors do not come out of the clear blue sky.")

At each group session, a poster of the Relapse Prevention model is on display in a central location so that offenders may refer their behaviors to the graphic, cyclical model. Briefly, the Relapse Prevention model appears as the following:

```
+----------------------------------------------------------------------+
|                      Relapse Prevention Ladder                       |
|                                                                      |
|                 ABSTINENCE  <-------------------------------------+  |
|                   |                                               |  |
|  Normal Zone    SEEMINGLY UNIMPORTANT DECISIONS                   |  |
|                   |                                               |  |
|                 HIGH RISK SITUATIONS ------------> COPING RESPONSE-^  |
|                   |                                                  |
|  - - - - - - - - - - - - - - - - - - - - - - - - - - - - - - - -     |
|                 LAPSE                                                |
|                   |                                                  |
|  Danger Zone    ABSTINENCE VIOLATION EFFECTS -> COPING RESPONSE---^  |
|                   |                                                  |
|                 RELAPSE                                              |
+----------------------------------------------------------------------+
```

Abstinence Makes the Heart Grow More Self-Respecting

Bodmer-Turner (1990) referred to the above as the "RP Ladder," which spatially depicts a person who previously has offended and now is in a state of abstinence at the top of the ladder. As one progresses down the ladder, his/her risks increase, but he/she still retains the power to climb back up at any time and regain control. Offenders visually encode these behaviors as a cognitive map because the model is concrete and always available during every session. Offenders and group leaders regularly feature the Relapse Prevention Ladder during group sessions.

In the abstinence stage, an offender is in control, feels good about himself/herself, and is not offending. An abstaining offender also has a clear mental image or expectation of his/her continuing success. Paired with group discussions of abstinence as a goal are discussions of the privileges of social and non-incarcerated freedom, the joys of appropriate family relationships, and the satisfaction that familial respect engenders.

Apparently Irrelevant Decision. This part of the model is "the step in which one makes a decision that places himself in a situation where he is at risk to reoffend" (Nelson, Russell, Achterkirchen, & Michelli, 1987, p. 11). The decision to place oneself in jeopardy may appear rational at first glance, and offenders sometimes struggle to see stepping into this stage as increasing their risk. An example is the ex-drinker who makes the apparently irrelevant decision to go into a bar "just to get a pack of cigarettes," thereby physically exposing himself/herself to a high-risk circumstance. A more serious example of irrelevant decision-making is a child molester who cooperates with a neighbor who desperately needs a baby-sitter for her children (Nelson et al., 1987).

High-risk Situations. These refer to any situation in which one perceives a threat to one's sense of self-control. The threat is directly and inversely related to one's actual ability to cope or to control himself in the predicament (Nelson et al., 1987, p. 12). Factors contributing to this stage are negative emotional states (i.e., anger, boredom, loneliness), interpersonal conflict, social pressure, presence of a potential victim, and other conditions. A child molester who gives his/her five-year-old daughter a bath is in a high-risk situation.

Adequate Coping Responses. These are the steps that offenders take to avoid continuing down the ladder and to return swiftly to the top. Responses range from simple avoidance, to escape, to negotiating conflict situations (Nelson et al., 1987). Offenders could eliminate the risk by leaving the scene, calling a group member or leader, or asking another person to supervise if alone with a potential victim. They are, in effect, acknowledging to themselves and to the world that they must protect others from themselves. This awareness does not come easily and requires major responsibility for one's actions. Responses to threatening circumstances are not viewed as right or wrong, but as more or less effective in an offender's return up the ladder to the desired state of abstinence.

Lapse. This is the next step down the ladder, a stage in which a smoker or drinker "slips" and has a cigarette or a drink but immediately returns to abstinence. Given that the stakes are much higher, a slip for a sex offender is by definition an illegal relapse. "Just a little sex offense" is not a possibility. For sex offenders, however, a lapse may be defined as fantasizing a deviant sex act, viewing deviant pornography, cruising for victims, or simple physical contact with a child. This stage is particularly complicated when offenders combine lapsing behaviors with masturbation. Lapses should be expected. An offender who denies lapsing may pose an even higher risk as he/she does not even recognize that he/she needs specific strategies in order to handle this step in the danger zone of the ladder.

Abstinence Violation Effects (AVE) are the emotions and thoughts related to lapses. Lapses threaten offenders' abilities to control their behavior because of the immediacy of fantasy, pornography, or physical contact. The urges that emerge at this stage are powerful, and offenders can learn that these are "like a wave; just ride them out" (Bodmer-Turner, 1990). Offenders, however, can perceive the negative feelings these urges generate as too powerful for them, resulting in such negative feelings as, "I can't stop. I'll always be a molester. I can't control myself." They then denounce therapy itself and skid further down the ladder to relapse.

Any offender indulging in this negative self-talk does have one last chance, a second opportunity to use a coping response and to return to the top of the ladder to the safe haven of abstinence. When offenders recognize the thoughts and feelings of the Abstinence Violation Effect—which therapists reiterate almost *ad nauseam* during treatment—they could remind themselves, "I remember these thoughts and feelings. I can leave this danger situation now and return to abstinence and avoid relapse and the risk of a return to prison or to the juvenile hall." Relapse is at the bottom of the ladder: A sex offender has committed another offense, is at risk for more arrests, has violated his/her hard won sense of control and, most unfortunately, creates another victim.

Offenders receive training to deal with the normal zone stages in discreet ways of fine-tuning their lives. If being alone in a room with a child is high risk for the offender, he/she simply may call someone else to join the two of them. When offenders lapse, they enter a danger zone. In group therapy, we paint a very disturbing picture of this zone as a place of intense images of sirens and flashing lights, requiring immediate and emergency action.

Readers may ask, "How do you motivate offenders to follow the Relapse Prevention or any model? They don't really want to change their behavior, do they?" Some adult offenders clearly have absolutely no desire to change. These offenders are very high risks and the correctional system should remove them from the community for as long as possible. Other offenders clearly do not want to reoffend and are eager candidates for any treatment. Most offenders fall somewhere on the middle of this continuum: carrying some level of denial, recognizing that sex offenses may be harmful to victims, and understanding that treatment at least may keep them out of further trouble with the law. Juvenile sex offenders, almost by definition, are at least somewhat amenable to treatment. The question for society to answer is whether to treat this population in the community, in supervised residential placements, or in locked institutions. Legal sanctions are one means of helping offenders motivate themselves. This issue will be further discussed in the "Adjudication" section of this chapter.

Abstinence and Empathy. Another way offenders may improve their motivation to commit to abstinence is through the development of empathy for victims. Many offenders are so cut off from their emotional systems that they have little ability even to guess how their victims might have felt. Offenders who access their thoughts and feelings regarding their own victimization(s) have taken the first step in developing empathy for victims. With the information given earlier in this chapter, at least one victim of child sexual abuse will show up in a group of offenders. My groups usually have at least two, if not all, members who were victims of child sexual abuse. If a group member had not been victimized sexually, the dynamics of shame in his/her history of physical abuse or neglect are mobilized to help him/her identify the damage he/she may have inflicted on victim(s). Another treatment method is inviting child sexual abuse survivors to speak with offenders or using video-taped presentations to help offenders see the real life pain their behavior causes others.

Group leaders exhibit a great deal of empathy and support during this stage as (a) members often minimize the effects of their own victimizations, and (b) leaders should model appropriate empathy for the offenders to incorporate into their own behavioral repertoire. (As chapter 2 points out, emotional expression is a component of total behavior.) While in this stage of treatment, a group resembles a victim or survivor group; however, individual offenders still must recognize that each one of them must take responsibility for his/her choices in becoming a victimizer. Once most group members can show appropriate empathy for victims, they then can help the new members and members still in denial transform the cultural norms of the group to more open disclosure. The way they change the group norms from secrecy and self-deception to honest assertions and responsible confrontation is by showing forthright behaviors themselves and by exerting subtle peer pressure on newcomers.

Group Therapy—A Key

Group therapy is the core therapeutic model of choice for sex offender programs. This forum allows the re-creation of a safe family atmosphere, now with appropriate psychological boundaries, for members to practice dependency and affection in relationships that do not involve sex (Finkelhor, 1984). Group therapy is essential in breaking down participants' ability to hide behind the psychological mechanism of denial. This approach provides the support of "We understand; we've been there." This spirit taps the offenders' needs to belong and find acceptance, and it can be much more powerful than the mere expertise of a therapist. Having endured abuse and having repeated the abusive cycle is not, of course, a necessary requirement for performing effective counseling with offenders. In fact, since offenders are interested in learning how to stop offending, they can learn from those who know how not to offend others sexually as well or better than they can learn from former offenders.

Group Counseling Conditions. The tone of an effective group is both nurturing and confrontive. Group leaders should structure some specific time so that each member gets attention from the counselor and from the group members. Leaders also should present some structured or semistructured material to members based on the program's therapeutic goals. Group leaders use a very direct style with sex offenders, not a passive posture. Leaders encourage group members to claim ownership for the counseling process while offering special consideration for the offenders' age and the group's ability to confront the reality of their behavior.

Term of Treatment. As recommended by the National Task Force on Juvenile Sex Offending (1988), the period of treatment usually lasts for a minimum of one year and could extend to three or even five years. The reason sexual offenders remain in treatment so long is that the group counselor literally helps them reshape their basic cultural values about their relationships and the meaning of sexuality. Even after graduation from their first experience in a formal treatment program, most offenders see that they will need ongoing counseling and even group support for the rest of their lives. "Treatment within the Relapse Prevention model never ends. Sex offenders who believe they have successfully completed treatment are making an 'apparently irrelevant decision,' predisposing their own relapse" (Pithers & Cumming, 1989, p. 316).

Behavioral Goals. Two critical aims of the 19 goals in the Juvenile Sex Offender Program and of the 18 goals in the San Quentin Sex Offender Program are that offenders will disclose their own sexual victimization and display a *sincere empathy* for their victims. Other goals for offenders include *presenting detailed descriptions* of all their offenses and *accepting full responsibility* for these acts. Public admission means the sex offender gives an open apology, acknowledging personal guilt, and swearing allegiance to the conventional social norms that he/she has violated (Margolin, 1984). Although therapists have no sure way of knowing the full extent of the clients' offenses, the use of victims' statements, group members' divulging their versions of their experiences, group social pressure, group leaders' clinical skills, and awareness of statistical data on the widespread incidence of perpetration of these damaging crimes usually produce more accurate data than court reports offer. Offenders make these disclosures over time during the long treatment process as they develop a sense of trust in their therapists and in the program itself. They are much less likely to take risks in court and show vulnerability within the legal context where, in their minds, they see what they say as increasing their prison time and damaging them irreparably.

Reunification Therapy Sequence. If the family has separated by court order due to, for example, father-child incest—and both halves of the family subsequently wish to reunify—we strongly urge both the victim and the offender to participate first in separate therapies. Reunification would occur only after these two therapists agree to recommend family therapy. They would base this recommendation on three major factors: (a) the victim's readiness to reunify, (b) the non-offending parent's emotional ability to protect the victim, and (c) the offender's sincerity to adopt a new direction in his/her lifestyle as measured by progress in counseling. Professionals must supervise the family's initial meetings together.

Juvenile Abuse of a Sibling. With incest families in which a juvenile sex offender has victimized a sibling, few programs are more concrete and effective than the therapeutic and educational one that Madanes (1990) has developed. Her exacting 16-step method begins with everyone in the family openly admitting all details of the sexual abuse. Next, she requires the offender to get down on his/her knees and apologize directly to the victim in the presence of all family members. Once the therapist judges the victimizer's apology to be sincere, she asks all other family members to get on their knees to apologize to the victim for not protecting him/her. The family must find a powerful relative within the extended family system who is willing to serve as the victim's protector. Another crucial step in the total treatment plan is for the offender to provide significant restitution to the victim, such as putting money into a college fund. Finally, the perpetrator needs to forgive himself/herself in front of everyone and resume his/her role as a natural protector of the younger sibling. The therapist proclaims that the incest has inflicted "a pain in the heart" of the victim, perpetrator, and family members, and promises to keep in touch with the family after they finish with therapy.

Protection for Victims. Offenders often find that they may never have any contact with their victims and, in fact, a court order may decree such a separation ruling because of the psychological distress for a victim that such contact may impose. In such instances, we have offenders write a letter of apology to the victim that later may be mailed if the victim so desires or that is kept in the offender's file. Before graduating from the program, juvenile sex offenders also must apologize for the stress they have caused their immediate families.

Group Activities. Leaders specifically design group activities to increase offenders' awareness of their feelings, assertive skills, and their abilities in managing stress. These competencies or deficits in skills usually show up as problem areas when the group looks at the high-risk situations on the Relapse Prevention Ladder. To give readers an example of group counseling activities, "The Feelings Game" for juvenile sex offenders works well. In this exercise, group members simply list all the possible feelings a person *could* have. At the start of this exercise, we have seen many members who could not produce more than 5 or 10 feelings. One 17-year-old, for example, could list only "mad, sad, happy, and horny." A therapeutic goal is to increase offenders' identification of feelings that make them appropriately vulnerable so that they can recognize their emotional states and apply this information to the Relapse Prevention Ladder.

Relapse Prevention Ladder. Learning the Relapse Prevention Ladder arms offenders with a tangible method for reducing problematic behaviors as well as sex offenses. This training is particularly useful for incarcerated offenders because their risk to sexually reoffend is automatically lowered temporarily by their removal from potential victims. They, therefore, can practice Relapse Prevention skills along with other behaviors safely during this time.

Relationship Skills. Other therapeutic goals include increasing dating or marital skills, benefiting from substance abuse treatment, maintaining positive attendance and participation in a group, developing positive social groups to reduce isolation or antisocial behavior, learning accurate information about sex, increasing self-esteem, and, for adult offenders, improving parenting skills.

ADJUDICATION

In chapter 7, Lynn Loar explained when and why mandated reporters (including school personnel) should notify the police or Children's Protective Services if suspicion of child abuse exists. Reporting and prosecuting offenders early in their sexual deviancy leads to avoidance of sexual misbehavior and sexual violence so subjects can avoid an ingrained pattern and develop appropriate forms of sexual expression. Following these precautions obviously benefits potential victims, perpetrators, and society as a whole.

Case Example 5: A Star Turns Hostile

The police referred Levon, age 16, to the Juvenile Sex Offender Program for forcible sexual contact with a 14-year-old girl. He was his high school's star basketball player and, one day after practice, he met the victim in one of the school's empty hallways. Without her parent's permission to see him privately, she waited for him because she honestly liked him. After talking together for a few minutes, he pushed the girl against a wall and reached inside her bra and panties to fondle her. She wisely told a friend, who told her parents, who contacted the police.

School Leaders Look the Other Way. The police investigation revealed that the school assistant principal had received many reports already that Levon had engaged in sexually inappropriate behavior. These activities had included pinching female students' buttocks, fondling their breasts through their clothes, and reaching beneath the clothes of female students to touch their private areas. The assistant principal "counseled" Levon regarding these incidents on the recommendations of the basketball coach and the principal and released him even though the assistant principal personally felt that stronger disciplinary actions were needed. He jeopardized his position by violating the law that mandates a report of sexual assault.

Group Assault Plans. During the Juvenile Sex Offender Program assessment, Levon revealed that he and his friends often would look for a couple walking together, and he would approach the female and touch her breasts. When her male partner would defend her, he and his friends would assault the boyfriend physically. He revealed this information with pride and indicated that, although authorities, including his mother, probably would disapprove of this behavior, he doubted that consequences would be serious.

Early Detection Important. One obvious lesson is that, if Levon's behavior had been reported sooner, the school and the community would have had fewer victims. Even if some members of the school staff may have been unsure about the reportability of this case, a consultation, at the very least, was in order with Children's Protective Services (CPS) or the police. All an administrator, counselor, or teacher need do in reporting abuse or violence—or in checking out reportability—is telephone CPS or the police and say, "I know of a 16-year-old male student whom I observed doing such and such. What do you advise that I do?" The caseworker or police representative then can say, "This is a reportable offense." In this situation, you should do the following:

1. provide the police or the CPS identifying information on the victim(s) and perpetrator(s),
2. notify your school administrator that authorities are investigating an abuse report, and
3. not contact the students or parents whom you have reported until the police or CPS do their investigation.

Often Juvenile Sex Offenders See No Problem

These adolescents see no need for treatment because they do not label their predatory behavioral style as a problem. Adult sex offenders sometimes do self-refer but conveniently forget identifying information that would be crucial to making a proper report. Often these partially self-aware men drop out of treatment when they find the professional help becoming too stressful or expensive for them. Legal intervention helps waffling adult offenders motivate themselves to obtain treatment and to continue with the program. Legal intervention also makes clear to them that society does not condone their deviant behavior. Legal consequences represent an intervention that can be therapeutic to offenders after they attack someone sexually. If an offender engages in a deviant sexual act and faces no negative consequences afterward, the assault becomes its own reward.

Staying with the Program. The Juvenile Sex Offender Program encourages police departments, district attorneys, and juvenile court judges to prosecute and adjudicate young offenders (about age 10 and up) as opposed to diverting them from the formal juvenile justice system. Therapy is stressful for juvenile sex offenders and their families, and people under this pressure need the reminding presence of a probation officer to keep up their attendance.

Reporting Information. Offenders under age 10 generally need the supervision and support services of Children's Protective Services to continue their family's motivation in treatment. If the situation is incest, then counselors should make the report to Children's Protective Services. If the situation is intrafamilial, therapists should make the report to the police. Both agencies, in fact, cross-report to each other.

DATE RAPE

A study by Bergman (1992) showed that 15.7% of female high school students reported experiencing sexual violence, and 15.7% reported physical violence in their dating relationships. Almost one in four females reported severe physical and sexual violence, which "could indicate that violence between partners is an acceptable form of dating behavior that begins to occur as soon as dating starts" (Bergman, 1992, p. 23).

Disturbing Attitudes

The acceptance of violence while dating may begin before high school. The Rhode Island Rape Crisis Center interviewed 1,700 students in the sixth through ninth grades concerning their knowledge and attitudes about a variety of sexual situations.

More than half said a man had the right to have sex with a woman without her consent if: (1) she led him on, (2) she got him sexually excited, or (3) they had been dating a long time. About 30% of those students indicated that forcing a woman to have sex was acceptable under certain conditions: (1) she has had sexual intercourse with other men; (2) he is so sexually aroused that he cannot stop, or (3) she is drunk. (Ellerbee, 1991, p. 6)

Sexual Deviance Is Unspeakable. In the Bergman study,

A majority of the respondents told no one about the dating violence. Only 22%, in fact, disclosed the violence to someone, and all of them told a peer about it. In addition to disclosing violence to a peer, 4.4% told one or both parents, 1.4% told a counselor, 0.5% told a teacher, and 0.3% told a clergy person. (Bergman, 1992, p. 23)

Consenting to Sex. The William Kennedy Smith date rape trial provided an opportunity for massive social education about the subject of compelling sexual participation. A significant legal quandary with the issue of sexual coercion revolves around consent. The dating couple may be participating in some level of consensual sexual relations and, at some point during that process, one partner reneges on the original consent and the mutual understanding is no longer valid. For teenagers, most consensual experimentation is normal. Because adolescents still are developing their personal guidelines for mutual sexual involvement, switching from consensual sexual contact to nonconsensual contact can be confusing. As with child sexual abuse, victims are often afraid that others will blame them. (The victim's parents in the fourth case, for example, initially blamed her for staying after school for an unchaperoned meeting with Levon.)

Schools' Responsibility in Sexual Relationship Topics. Schools are addressing the matter of consent and coercion in personal relationships between the genders. Bergman (1992) suggested that teenagers are more likely to discuss this issue if someone asks them about it directly. Responsibility for openly sharing this information usually rests with the parents. Many schools provide the opportunity for group counseling, led by psychotherapists, guidance staff, or trained teachers, in order to allow a place for teenagers to discuss appropriate sexual behavior. Parental permission is a prerequisite, of course, and students should join the groups on a voluntary basis. The information coming out of the group process serves two functions: (a) to protect young men and women and (b) to educate young men and women. Group leaders must make members aware that either partner always has the right to decline, slow down, or stop sexual encounters. Each partner has the absolute right to say no to a sexual encounter and to feel safe.

Teachers' Role in Sex Talk. Teachers may choose to take a more indirect approach, particularly if the issue of sex education is politically sensitive in a particular community and if they structure educational programs into their curricula regarding violence in the media. Thomas Radecki of the National Coalition on Television Violence cited statistics showing that one out of eight Hollywood movies depicts a rape theme. A teacher, like a counseling group leader, will need to motivate positive peer pressure so as to influence the momentum of the discussion towards appropriate behavior. "Because they (teenagers) already feel driven toward independence, information regarding how others can influence them is helpful in encouraging them to resist the stereotypes and values placed on them by the advertising and media industry" (Bergman, 1992, p. 24).

RECIDIVISM

Do sex offender programs work? No method exists today to answer this question with complete accuracy. Given the level of secrecy attached to sex offenses, recidivism (i.e., rearrests for relapse), is the most common measure used. This measure is obviously flawed in that we know that a majority of sex offenses remain unreported. Also, published studies of treatment outcome are nonuniform in their methodology. For example, some sex offender programs may not include certain subtypes, as exhibitionists, in their treatment populations. Outcome information still is developing regarding specialized relapse prevention programs.

Adolescent sex offender treatment programs have a history of low recidivism rates. Recent statistics and preliminary outcome studies for juvenile sex offender programs are encouraging, showing lower rates of recidivism than results from typical programs treating sexual abuse. The record of adult programs has been less successful than the programs for teenagers. This discrepancy in outcome led to a recommendation in 1977 by the Group for the Advancement of Psychiatry (Pithers & Cumming, 1989) for incarceration instead of treatment. Since these earlier findings, however, adult sex offender programs using the Relapse Prevention model are showing signs of success.

1. The initial results from a highly controlled study conducted at California's Atascadero State Hospital, show a 20% recidivism rate compared

to a 32% volunteer control group rate and a 50% rate for offenders who did not volunteer to participate in the program (Milloy & Wilkes, 1990).

2. The Vermont Treatment Program for Sexual Aggressors showed a 4% recidivism rate during its six years of service (Pithers & Cumming, 1989). These results are promising.

CONCLUSION

This chapter highlighted the trauma of sexual offense, the need for rehabilitative programs for sex offenders, and the efficacy of such treatment. Unfortunately, sex offenses do occur, and professionals across all disciplines are working together to end the secrecy that has shrouded this topic for so long. In summary, the following statements may be made:

- The technologies for treating adult sex offenders are more promising than ever and now include individual and group therapies along with narrative (White & Epston, 1990), solution-focused (de Shazer, 1995, 1988, 1985; O'Hanlon & Weiner-Davis, 1989), and family system methods (Madanes, 1990).
- The implications for school teachers, counselors, and administrators demand that professional educators face this difficult challenge. Teachers must become competent in diagnosing trouble, assertive in making referrals of both victims and predators, and nonjudgmental and steadfast in their role as advocates for victims of sexual predators.
- Victims of various forms of sexual abuse and violence attend schools daily and have special needs that sensitive and responsible educators must accommodate.
- Victims of abuse are clearly at risk of becoming victimizers.
- Detecting all forms of sexual offenses early and making appropriate referrals can save vulnerable children from sexual assaults that can devastate them and their loved ones.
- Juvenile sex offenders are likely either to withdraw from age-appropriate social connections, to remain quiet, or to seek special attention by becoming a behavior problem.

Schools Face the Problem of Sexual Crimes

When sexually violated children act out in school, the professionals must monitor them and screen for inappropriate sexual behavior. Schools are probably the best place in which to provide preventive information about sexually offensive behavior. Therefore, school personnel who take the responsibility for educating themselves on this issue deserve much credit and sincere respect. One potential double bind for schools, however, is that these institutions either must offer appropriate services to abused children or run the risk of inadvertently contributing to institutional abuse (Roberts, 1986).

Schools Can Help

Ryan (1991) suggested that responsible and concerned adults can intervene in juvenile sex offender behavior in primary, secondary, and tertiary manners. Tertiary involvement is identifying and treating those who are already offending. Secondary intervention "requires specialized intervention with children in groups known to be at increased risk to develop sexually aggressive or deviant behavior" (Ryan, 1991, p. 393). Primary perpetration prevention requires changes in order to alter the "children's earliest learning experiences . . . in the family and the community at large" (Ryan, 1991, p. 393). As a fundamental social force, schools have the opportunity to impact children on all three levels. School personnel, especially counselors and administrators, have a special opportunity to reduce the impact of sexual victimization.

BIBLIOGRAPHY

American Psychiatric Association. (1994). *Diagnostic and statistical manual of mental disorders* (DSM-IV) (4th ed.). Washington, DC: Author.

Becker, J. V., & Abel, G. G. (1984). Methodological and ethical issues in evaluating and treating adolescent sexual offenders. Washington, DC: Draft Monograph to the National Institute of Mental Health (Grant #MH 36347).

Berliner, L. (1990). The human costs: Treating victims (doctoral dissertation). California Institute of Integral Studies. In C. D. Milloy & R. Wilkes (Eds.), *Washington State Institute for Public Policy.* Olympia, WA: Evergreen State College.

Gelman, D., Springen, K., Elam, R., Joseph, N., Robins, K., & Hager, M. (1990, July 23). The mind of the rapist. *Newsweek,* pp. 46-53.

Groth, A. N., & Loredo, C. M. (1981). Juvenile sex offenders: Guidelines for assessment. *International Journal of Offender Treatment and Comparative Criminology, 25,* 31-39.

Saunders, E. B., & Awad, G. A. (1988). Assessment, management, and treatment planning for male adolescent sexual offenders. *American Journal of Orthopsychiatry, 58*(4), 571-579.

Smith, W. (1988). Delinquency and abuse among juvenile sex offenders. *Journal of Interpersonal Violence, 3*(4), 400-413.

Sorenson, G. P. (1991). Sexual abuse in schools: Reported court cases from 1987-1990. *Educational Administration Quarterly, 27*(4), 460-480.

REFERENCES

Abbot, B. (1990). *Family dynamics, intergenerational patterns of negative events and trauma and patterns of offending behavior.* Unpublished doctoral dissertation, California Institute of Integral Studies, San Francisco, CA.

Ageton, S. (1983). *Sexual assault among adolescents.* Lexington, MA: Lexington Books.

Awad, G. A., Saunders, E., & Levine, J. (1984). A clinical study of male adolescent sexual offenders. *International Journal of Offender Therapy and Comparative Criminology, 28*(3), 105-115.

Barnard, G. W., Fuller, K. A., Robbins, L., & Shaw, T. (1989). The child molester: An integrated approach to evaluation and treatment. In J. G. Howells (Ed.), *Clinical Psychiatry Series: No. 1.* New York: Brunner/Mazel.

Batchelor, E. S., Dean, R. S., Gridley, B., & Batchelor, B. (1990). Reports of child sexual abuse in the schools. *Psychology in the Schools, 27,* 131-137.

Bergman, L. (1992). Dating violence among high school students. *Social Work: Journal of the National Association of Social Workers, 37*(1), 21-27.

Bodmer-Turner, J. (1990, March 30). Personal communication.

Corrigan, L. (1989, October 25). Personal communication.

Davis, G. E., & Leitenberg, H. (1987). Adolescent sex offenders. *Psychological Bulletin, 101*(3), 417-423.

Deisher, R. W., Wenet, G. A., Paperney, D. M., Clark, T. F., & Fehrenbach, P. A. (1982). Adolescent sex offense behavior: The role of the physician. *Journal of Adolescent Health Care 2,* 279-286.

de Shazer, S. (1985). *Keys to solution in brief therapy.* New York: W. W. Norton.

de Shazer, S. (1988). *Clues: Investigating solutions in brief therapy.* New York: W. W. Norton.

de Shazer, S. (1995). *Words were originally magic.* New York: W. W. Norton.

Ellerbee, L. (1991, September 1). What your kid doesn't know about rape. *This World,* p. 6.

Fehrenbach, P.A., Smith, W., Monastersky, C., & Deisher, R. (1986). Adolescent sexual offenders: Offender and offense characteristics. *American Journal of Orthopsychiatry, 56*(2), 225.

Finkel, K. C. (1987). Sexual abuse of children: An update. *Canadian Medical Association Journal, 136,* 245.

Finkelhor, D. (1984). *Child sexual abuse: New theory and research.* New York: The Free Press.

Finkelhor, D. (1986). *A sourcebook on child sexual abuse.* Beverly Hills: Sage Publications.

Finkelhor, D., Hotaling, G., Lewis, I. A., & Smith, C. (1990). Sexual abuse in a national survey of adult men and women: Prevalence, characteristics, and risk factors. *Child Abuse and Neglect, 14,* 19-28.

George, W. H., & Marlatt, G. A. (1989). Introduction. In D. R. Laws (Ed.), *Relapse prevention with sex offenders* (pp. 1-34). New York: Guilford Press.

Groth, A. N. (1978). Patterns of sexual assault against children and adolescents. In A. W. Burgess (Ed.), *Sexual assault of children and adolescents* (pp. 3-24). Lexington, MA: Lexington Books.

Groth, A. N., & Birnbaum, H. J. (1979). *Men who rape: The psychology of the offender.* New York: Plenum Press.

Groth, A. N., Hobson, W. F., & Gary, T. S. (1982). *The child molester: Clinical observations.* New York: Hayworth Press.

Groth, A. N., Longo, R. E., & McFaddin, J. B. (1982). Undetected recidivism among rapists and child molesters. *Journal of Crime and Delinquency, 28*(3), 450-458.

James, J., & Meyerding, J. (1986). The sexual abuse of children: Scandalous statistics. *American Journal of Psychiatry, 134,* 1381-1385.

Johnson, T. C. (1988). Child perpetrators-children who molest other children: Preliminary findings. *Child Abuse and Neglect, 12,* 219-229.

Kohn, T. J., & Chambers, H. J. (1991). Assessing reoffense risk with juvenile sexual offenders. *Child Welfare League of America, 70*(3), 333-345.

Levant, M. D., & Bass, B. A. (1991). Parental identification of rapists and pedophiles. *Psychological Reports, 69,* 463-466.

Madanes, C. (1990). *Sex, love, and violence: Strategies for transformation.* New York: W. W. Norton.

Margolin, L. (1984). Group therapy as a means of learning about the sexually assaultive adolescent. *International Journal of Offender Therapy and Comparative Criminology, 28*(1), 65-72.

Marshall, W. L., Jones, R., Ward, T., Johnston, P., & Barbaree, H. E. (1991). Treatment outcome with sex offenders. *Clinical Psychology Review, 11,* 465-485.

Milloy, C. D., & Wilkes, R. (1990). *Sex offender conference proceedings, Washington State Institute for Public Policy.* Olympia, WA: Evergreen State College.

National Task Force on Juvenile Sex Offending. (1988). A preliminary report from the national task force on juvenile sex offending 1988 [special issue]. *Juvenile and Family Court Journal, 39*(2).

Nelson, C., Russell, K., Achterkirchen, J., & Michelli, J. (1987). *Core relapse prevention group* (treatment manual). Atascadero, CA: Atascadero State Hospital, Sex Offender Treatment and Evaluation Project.

O'Hanlon, W., & Weiner-Davis, M. (1989). *In search of solutions.* New York: W. W. Norton.

Pithers, W. D., & Cumming, G. F. (1989). Can relapses be prevented? Initial outcome data from the Vermont treatment program for sexual aggressors. In D. R. Laws (Ed.), *Relapse prevention with sex offenders* (pp. 313-324). New York: Guilford Press.

Russell, D. E. H. (1983). The incidence and prevalence of intrafamilial and extrafamilial sexual abuse of female children. *Child Abuse and Neglect, 7,* 133-146.

Ryan, G. (1991). Perpetration prevention: Primary and secondary. In G. Ryan & S. Lane (Eds.), *Juvenile sex offending: Causes, consequences, and correction* (pp. 393-408). Lexington, MA: Lexington Books.

Sgroi, S. M. (1982). Family treatment of child sexual abuse. In *Handbook of clinical intervention in child sexual abuse* (pp. 241-268). Lexington MA: Lexington Books.

Sheaffer, C. I. (1986). The sexual abuse of children: Scandalous statistics. *Communiclue, 15*(3), 4.

Summit, R. C. (1983). The child abuse sexual abuse accommodation syndrome. *Child Abuse and Neglect, 7,* 177-193.

White, M., & Epston, D. (1990). *Narrative means to therapeutic ends.* New York: Norton.

Chapter 11

CHILDREN AND HIV: CONCEPTS AND STRATEGIES FOR TEACHERS AND COUNSELORS

Linda K. Brewer
Mary T. Parish

Editor's Note

Doctors Brewer and Parish have tackled a subject that strikes terror into everyone's heart—the dreaded and, up to the present, incurable AIDS virus and its traumatic effects in the lives of those carrying the disease and those who know the carriers. Fortunately, because of people such as these sensitive and committed writers, HIV also strikes compassion in the hearts of those who earlier knew only fear, judgment, and condemnation. Hope and a more human quality of life now can replace sensing only a putrid disgrace and hearing only echoes of jeering mockers. Today, HIV families can raise their sights to a more peaceful accommodation of the most serious health threat of our time.

Additionally, Linda Brewer and Mary Parish show teachers and counselors exactly how to relate to those afflicted with the disease. After getting over a false feeling of superiority and the critical thoughts that view AIDS as God's punishment of contempo-

rary residents of Sodom and Gomorrah, everyone needs to overcome irrational fears. Many still fear contamination by being in the same room or shaking hands with an AIDS patient. Embracing the ultimate truth that all humans are HIV positive in the sense that we all wear a mortality suit, is the key that unlocks our awareness that we are all members of the same community. Sufferers and nonpatients alike struggle with their common fear of loss of human relationships and death. The ever-present choice that we all have is to work at making the quality of our lives as beneficial and personally useful as possible.

The purpose of this chapter is to provide teachers and counselors with information and strategies for working with children and families who carry HIV disease. The particular scenario might be a child who is HIV-infected or a child whose parent or parents are HIV-infected. This chapter begins with a discussion of the HIV disease spectrum and how HIV may impact schools; later, matters of heath, behavior, and instruction for HIV-infected children appear along with issues surrounding HIV-impacted families. Next, we discuss issues important to teachers and counselors, counseling strategies, an exploration of death and dying issues, and cross-cultural implications. The chapter closes with a view of legal and ethical issues as well as universal health precautions. A list of resources and books for children about HIV can be found at the end of the chapter.

Our motivation for this chapter comes from years of working with HIV-infected people and watching their continuous struggle to integrate this disease into their everyday lives. We direct the information in this chapter to teachers, counselors, and school administrators who can work with families, children, and school personnel in a productive and holistic way.

HIV disease is viewed almost universally as a death knell that often causes people to live in isolation. Although adults may make a conscious choice to live alone, children almost never reach the same conclusion. HIV disease is transmitted by direct contact with infected blood and body fluids. Fear and anxiety associated with sexual transmission forces a thick shroud of secrecy to veil off those who either are infected or are associated with an infected person.

Encountering a student with HIV is not a situation that all teachers may face during their careers. In our experience, schools that have successfully integrated HIV-impacted children into the main population of students began planning and developing strategies for integration early in the disease history. Some school administrations have adopted a "wait and see" attitude, whereas others have adopted a more proactive approach. A proactive approach includes developing specific strategies that allow a smooth integration to occur whenever an

HIV family emerges. Examples of useful strategies are inservice education, information meetings, universal precaution training, and the development or adoption of an existing HIV curriculum.

The current trend of the disease indicates that the affected population is changing, and that, after gay and bisexual men in the United States, women are the next highest group infected with HIV. In 1985, 132 pediatric AIDS cases (age 12 and under) were reported of the total 8,661 cases of AIDS. As of December 1992, there were 4,249 pediatric cases of the total 253,448 reported cases of AIDS. This translates into 817 school-age children (ages 5-12) and 3,432 children under age five infected by this disease, a substantial increase during the past decade (Centers for Disease Control, 1993). The current trend is expected to increase as we approach the year 2000. These figures represent reported cases of AIDS, not HIV, which represents only a portion of people infected with the HIV virus. Only AIDS cases are reported to the Centers for Disease Control (CDC). The number of children impacted by HIV because of an infected parent is substantially larger than the above figures.

Children spend a major portion of their waking hours at school, and the quality of their lives and their ability to learn is tied closely to their relationship with their teachers, school staff, and fellow students. If the teaching and administrative staff are overly frightened by HIV disease, they cannot be completely available to children. One of the first steps to defusing and managing fear about HIV disease is to find out more about the medical spectrum and transmission of HIV disease.

THE HIV DISEASE SPECTRUM

The HIV virus is currently the sixth leading cause of death in the United States. Fortunately, the HIV virus, which is responsible for HIV disease, is not casually transmitted. The virus resides in body fluid, such as blood, semen, urine, and mucous. Since this virus dies quickly outside the human body, the virus needs to live in a body fluid in order to survive. The HIV virus can be transmitted, therefore, only when the infected fluid of one person comes in contact with body fluids of another person.

Once a person is infected, the statistical average before opportunistic infections develop in adults is 8 to 10 years. We talk, therefore, about an infected person on a disease spectrum rather than in absolute diagnostic terms. Two general components operate across the HIV disease spectrum. When people initially contract the HIV virus but are asymptomatic, we consider them to be in an infected but well state. Gradually, as their diagnosis changes to an opportunistic illness, they go from HIV-infected to a new classification of having Acquired Immunodeficiency Syndrome (AIDS).

Children are infected primarily through maternal transmission of body fluids or blood transfusions. An infected child may attend school and not manifest any symptoms of HIV disease. The child who is HIV-infected but asymptomatic appears as well as any other child. A child who is symptomatic should be considered a chronically health-impaired child.

Children with HIV infection typically respond poorly to treatment for bacterial infections. Teachers, as well as other school staff, should receive training in recognizing and managing the medical emergencies of these children. Depending upon their level of training, teachers and selected staff members may need to provide special services for children with this multisymptom disease.

Schietinger, McCarthy, Gillen, and Hammrich (1988) have proposed a framework to describe the impact of HIV/AIDS on a functional ability and disability continuum.

- apparently well: Children who have tested positive for HIV antibodies but require little or no medical treatment. They can attend school and participate in activities. The school psychometrist should assess for cognitive abilities, any neurological impairment, and motor skill delays.
- acutely ill: These children may have experienced an opportunistic bacterial or viral infection, chronic diarrhea, fever, or rash. They may be hospitalized or treated on an outpatient basis. After treatment, they return to school and often are able to participate fully.
- chronically ill: These children may experience relapses or receive a diagnosis of a new opportunistic infection. Some neurological impairment, weight loss, or impaired growth may be present. Concerns at this stage are similar to other chronic, progressive illness. School participation depends upon their ability to function adequately. If necessary, the school should implement home tutoring with the children's classmates and teachers maintaining continual personal support and connection.
- terminally ill: These children have a life prognosis of six months or less and most likely are unable to attend school regularly. Terminally ill children value continued care and attention from their classmates and teachers.

HIV-POSITIVE CHILDREN

Interacting with an HIV-infected child in the classroom can be both stressful and rewarding for a teacher or a counselor. A number of facets to this complex classroom situation become evident. The three main points fit into three categories: health, behavior, and instruction.

Health

If possible, teachers should view children with HIV disease who are asymptomatic as they see any other child in a classroom. The fact is, a teacher may not know that an HIV-compromised child is in the classroom. While asymptomatic children may appear well, they can be dangerously susceptible to any infections that the other students carry into the classroom. Chicken pox, for example, can cause severe illness and death. Exposure to measles, mumps, and rubella likewise can be very dangerous.

When possible, health services should be available at all school sites. After gaining the family's approval, school professionals should encourage these children to take as much responsibility for themselves as possible. This self-reliance also would extend to administering their own medicine. In order to recognize and manage emergencies, teachers and school staff deserve the best training. This special supervisory responsibility of those standing *in loco parentis* is not new with the AIDS virus. For years, teachers have handled children with hearing disorders, epileptic seizures, fainting spells from diabetes, bloody noses, and asthma attacks. Above everything else, teachers also must keep in mind that HIV children can participate in all school activities to the extent that their health permits and their family physician approves.

Behavior

The virus can create developmental disabilities. Central nervous system involvement in children, encephalopathy (brain dysfunction), appears to be related to the HIV viral infection rather than opportunistic viral or bacterial infections. Several studies (Fletcher, Francis, Pequegnat, Raudenbush, Borstein, Schmitt, Brouwers, & Stover, 1991; Brouwers, Moss, Walters, Eddy, Balis, Poplack, & Pizzo, 1990; Levenson, Kairam, Bartnett, & Mellins, 1991) have shown that a high percentage of children who are HIV-infected do have some developmental abnormality. These studies predict a downward trend in cognitive functioning as the organic disease progresses. Teachers and counselors need to understand common developmental stages as well as the natural progression of this disease because infected children begin to fall off the typical pace and lose ground. For this reason, HIV students need to be evaluated often as they may be eligible for special services for their learning difficulties.

Whereas a pediatrician may be the primary person who arranges developmental testing, the teacher, school counselor, and special education staff can be instrumental in collaborating with the doctor about a child's progress and need for special services. Children affected by HIV often demonstrate anxiety, depression, anger, or introverted behavior as they adjust to their disease status. Displaying these emotions clearly can interfere with the education of a child. Teachers and school counselors who maintain close contact with one another and with their students can treat behavioral problems early. Children need tangible opportunities to talk about their feelings and fears, lessons in recognizing when their energy drops and they begin to lose emotional control, and a chance to develop healthy coping strategies for those times when they are feeling out of control in the classroom.

Instruction

Under most circumstances, teachers should employ the same instructional patterns with HIV-infected students as they do with all other students. Teachers will find that they need to give special consideration for developmental delays that these ill children show. Brouwers et al. (1990) noted a decline in IQ as a consequence of HIV infection. When these students take Zidovudine (AZT), they recover their pre-treatment level of IQ. Brouwers et al. (1990) saw this restoration of their normative IQ as a function of their acquiring new skills and abilities through latent learning at a rate almost commensurate with that of their healthy peers. The HIV infection in these children, therefore, may interfere primarily with retrieving and expressing knowledge rather than acquiring knowledge and developing skills.

Absence from school can interrupt a particular classroom lesson or learning activity. Providing home instruction, of course, can minimize the amount of disruption of students' learning and help them achieve a smooth continuity of learning. This flowing stream of learning is important not only from an instructional perspective but also to cut down on children's feelings of isolation and unimportance. By continuing their learning at home, they can feel connected emotionally with their normal environment of friends and an involved teacher.

Overall, what seems paramount is to organize the same opportunities for HIV-infected children so they can see that they receive the same treatment as other children with chronic illnesses. At the same time, HIV-infected children benefit most when their social support network and the medical and educational teams are all aware of the stigmatization they must confront as sufferers of this disease.

FAMILIES AND HIV

The effects of HIV on a family are only now beginning to receive broad attention. Many families are burdened already with poor social support systems, discrimination, poverty, and lack of access to informed medical care. The effects of living with the socially stigmatizing illness of AIDS intensify all of the basic social and economic handicaps. Other negatives that go with an HIV diagnosis include learning to live with the uncertainty of the course of the illness; the strenuous effects on intimate relationships; living with a long-term but fatal illness; fear of disability and death; and the fear-ridden, judgmental, and distancing responses from others in society.

HIV may *infect* one individual, but the disease *affects* all family members. Noninfected children may feel their needs and concerns are of less significance and may be reluctant to ask for help. Schools, therefore, can help by giving friendly support to healthy members of a family as well as those carrying the infection within their blood stream.

A family with one or more HIV-infected member is a family with many types of stress: economic, social, emotional, and psychological. As mentioned, one of the primary problems facing families is the unique social stigma associated with HIV. Even though a strong educational campaign on AIDS occurs in some parts of the country, most people continue to fear HIV as earlier societies shunned those with syphilis, the black plague, or leprosy. Although this broad fear stems from primitive urges to survive, families on the receiving end of social ostracism learn to maintain a shield of secrecy about the disease. Their silence and sense of shame become major factors in their social isolation and lack of outside support. Their isolation from everyday interaction, in turn, increases the pressure upon all of the relationships within their family. Finally, the HIV diagnosis may effect more than one member of a family, thereby, exposing a family to multiple losses. Losses may include the following:

- loss of job and income,
- loss of friends and social support,
- loss of the support of other family members,
- difficulties in school,
- loss of health, and
- loss of home.

Ironically, this illness drives victims to self-imposed solitary confinement while simultaneously increasing their need to interact with many social services. Those with HIV rely on health-care facilities, foster care, and social agencies. Approximately three-quarters of the children with HIV come from African American or Hispanic American families. Families from these cultural groups often have fewer socioeconomic resources, more drug and alcohol related trouble, migration and resettlement issues, difficulty in accessing health care, and language barriers. For a general assessment of a family's need for social services, Brewer and Parish (1992) suggested the following questions:

- How many members of a family have HIV?
- What is the living situation of a family (e.g., nuclear family, extended family, foster family, single-parent family)?
- What other losses have been associated with HIV (e.g., home, family members, jobs, family support)?
- What are other major economic factors for the family?
- What is the age of the infected child or children?
- What are the ages of siblings?
- What is the health status of an infected child?

The nature of the illness itself presents stress because HIV is a long-term illness—to date, fatal—that manifests itself in different ways. No standard course of treatment has emerged, and the disease is unpredictable in both form and timing. The length of time between infection and display of symptoms varies from child to child. No clear markers define this disease and its course. These brutal idiosyncrasies complicate the interactions between a family and the community.

IMPACT OF THE DISEASE

Psychological

Often guilt associates with HIV transmission, especially when the transmission is between sexual or needle-sharing partners. Guilt is usually present and intensifies when a mother infects her own child. In the face of an HIV diagnosis, a family has a heightened sense of vulnerability and an overwhelming realization of mortality. Conflict is a frequent problem in any family where a member is chronically ill. The needs of an HIV-infected family member naturally take priority so that less attention goes to the physical and emotional needs of other family members.

Stress increases as extended family members become caretakers who themselves may be elders with their own health concerns and needs. The long-term nature of the illness can increase dramatically the level of stress that family members entertain. The fear of stigma invites families to maintain secrecy about the disease, and this silence can be especially difficult for children who are often in the dark about the true nature of the illness.

Financial

Families in which a member has HIV often face strained financial pressures and limited community resources. Families may encounter difficulty in finding adequate substance abuse programs, convenient medical care, suitable housing, adequate transportation, trustworthy child care or respite services, and appropriate psychosocial support services.

Families in Which a Child and at Least One Parent Are HIV-Infected

In this family, the child most likely has received HIV from the mother who may have become positive through injection drug use (IDU), through blood transfusion, or through sexual contact with a carrier. The child then acquires the virus in utero or during the birth process. Limited research exists on transmission of HIV through infected mother's breast milk, but such a medium is considered a possible transmission route. Stress increases when multiple members of the family are ill.

Surviving members have many concerns ranging from burnout among family and friends to the harsh toll that the multiple illness episodes exact. Multiple losses and gnawing stress pursue the family relentlessly. The siblings' or an uninfected parent's need for love and comfort often may go permanently unmet. Siblings of chronically ill children display a high incidence of behavior problems. In the event of the death of a parent, the surviving caretaker has the added stress of caring for both the infected child as well as healthy children. Treating each individual is a complex and intensive task of medical management because so many medical and nonmedical caregivers must be involved.

The following vignette describes an HIV family and the impact on all the members. Peter was an injection drug user who infected his partner, Rose, through heterosexual sex. Prior to a diagnosis in either parent, Rose gave birth to baby Joseph who was later found to be infected. When Joseph was six, his mother became terminally ill, spent several months in a hospital, and died. A year later, Joseph's father made appropriate arrangements for Joseph and then committed suicide. The little boy went to live with his uncle and aunt. He continues in school, having sustained the loss of his mother, his father, his home, and inheriting a lifetime of living in the shadow of HIV.

Many children with HIV—even those living with one or both parents—move into the foster care system because their parents simply are unable to care for them. Some social service providers have established special units for HIV-infected children and have been given special training and funding for those who participate in foster parenting programs for HIV-infected children and infants.

Families in Which a Child Is HIV-Infected

Needless to say, families and students impacted by HIV are especially challenging for school personnel. It is essential for teachers and counselors to identify their fears, frustrations, and anxieties and give voice to these threats and self-doubts. What are some of the deep issues and what particular strategies can educators use to cope with the needs of HIV students? Let us move on to a full discussion of these questions.

TEACHER AND COUNSELOR ISSUES

HIV infection is increasing in the general United States population and the chances of seeing an HIV-positive child or a child impacted by HIV continue to grow. As a teacher from Idaho recently reported, "the health issues for children in the classroom during the last 30 years have revolved around head lice and pinkeye. Even working with a student who was stricken with brain cancer has not introduced the level of complexity and stress as has considering the impact of HIV in the classroom." Counseling clients infected with HIV may be the greatest challenge facing teachers and school counselors today. Counseling clients with HIV disease requires the helpers first to grapple with the most contagious, debilitating effect: fear. Before teachers and counselors can offer others information, support, or empowerment, they need to confront their own fears and understand and develop an increased awareness of the importance of nonjudgmental support in the care of HIV-impacted children.

Overcoming barriers to fear and anxiety about dealing with children and families with HIV means assessing one's own fears and conflicts, knowing the facts about disease transmission and progression, resolving the conflicts, and getting whatever support is necessary. In the past, children have been infected primarily through blood transfusion. In the near future, we most likely will begin to see children becoming infected through heterosexual or homosexual activity or through injection drug use. This possible change in the transmission trends has been supported by a survey of 3500 middle school children in San Francisco. Fetro (1992) reported that 16% of all students (9% female and 23% male) reported they had engaged in heterosexual intercourse. Sexual behavior ranged from 11% in 6th grade to 19% in 8th grade. Thirty percent claimed they already had had sex with four or more people. Three percent already had contracted a sexually transmitted disease (STD). About one-half of these sexually active students (56%) reported using condoms. Because of this increasing sexual activity, early education is essential.

Families in Which Only a Parent Is HIV-Infected

The largest number HIV-infected children are those with an infected parent. Either the mother, the father, or both may have been infected through a blood transfusion, heterosexual or homosexual sex, or injection drug use. The following vignette describes a child whose homosexual father was infected with HIV. The father's illness now is affecting his son's ability to perform well in school.

Fred and Elena were married and had a boy, Simon. Two years later, after an affair with a man, Fred recognized that he was homosexual, and he and Elena separated and later divorced. Fred maintained financial support and contact with Simon. Eight years later, Fred discovered that he had HIV. At age 10, Simon now is coming to terms with his father's illness, which is compounded by the stigma associated with Fred's homosexuality. Simon visits his father but does not feel that he can talk to anyone at school about his situation. He has not told his friends about his serious worries. His schoolwork has become inconsistent, and he is falling behind his classmates. By now, his father has been hospitalized several times, and last week, while Simon was visiting his father in the hospital, a man in the next room died. Simon has been having nightmares stemming from his worries that his father will die.

Assess Your Position

As a first step in maintaining your own sense of mastery while working with HIV-impacted people, it is important to identify your feelings and concerns about the interaction you may have with your students and their families who are impacted by HIV. This self-assessment may include questions such as the following:

1. Are you afraid of contracting HIV?
2. Are you afraid that you will become too attached to a child who possibly will die during the school year?
3. Do you feel that working with a child or family impacted with HIV involves more work than what is expected of your peers and you resent the additional work?
4. Are you afraid of burnout?
5. Are you afraid that you may transmit the virus to your family?
6. Are your family and friends afraid of your working with an HIV-infected person?
7. Does your family ask you not to work with HIV-infected families?

If you have answered *yes* to any of these questions, then you may want to take time to develop your knowledge about HIV and begin to reduce your fears and the fears of your family and friends. Some parts of this chapter may help, and your local health department HIV program should have health educators available to increase your knowledge and allay your fears.

Coping Skills Strategies

People who do not resolve serious conflicts create stress for themselves that, in turn, can become emotional burnout if they do not learn to manage the stress well. Freudenberger (1980) was the first to use the term *burnout,* describing the phenomenon as the depletion of energy that health-care workers often experience. As Pines and Maslach have described (1978), burnout can occur in three phases. The first phase is noted by the presence of mild, short-lived, physical symptoms such as aches, muscle tension, and fatigue. Even in this early stage, individuals may dread returning to work on a daily basis. In the second phase, the symptoms are more regular, more persistent, and are more challenging to relieve. Individuals in the third phase experience chronic symptoms as they develop a most negative view of themselves and their work setting.

Coping well with these progressively worse binds involves both personal and professional coping strategies. "Taking one's work home" is natural as is wanting emotional support from significant and immediate others. Families and friends can be instrumental in offering such support. Fears and misinformation, however, may keep loved ones from communicating effectively under the strain of a stressing lifestyle. Many of the same issues that trouble a person in the throes of full-blown stressing patterns also concern the person's family. The best way to reduce the interpersonal barriers in these important relationships is to provide education and open communication to one's family and friends. As a result, those suffering in lonely silence will strengthen their relationships, be able to talk more openly with others, and gain the emotional support they crave.

Remembering that one is not alone is crucially important. Support groups for people impacted by HIV can be an excellent community resource. Stress reduction workshops with a direct focus on HIV can offer techniques for reducing stress generated by working with families dealing with a life threatening illness.

In caring for persons with HIV, teachers and school counselors confront circumstances outside their control. Somehow they must maintain their composure even as they confront the tangible possibility of death—at this time, an inevitable outcome of the disease. Witnessing young people dying is especially difficult. Educators who remember to take *good* care of themselves concurrently can make a big difference in the care and education of students impacted by HIV.

COUNSELING STRATEGIES
FOR TEACHERS AND COUNSELORS

Counseling students and family members impacted or infected with HIV may be the greatest challenge facing counselors and teachers today. Counseling issues in school range from concerns about heightened anxiety over HIV risk and immediate health problems to dealing with grief and death and dying issues for the student, family members, or friends. Counselors and teachers must inform themselves about HIV transmission routes, testing, and available school and community resources.

Since current social norms connect sexual orientation or activity with the disease, students and family members often bring their shame, guilt, and embarrassment with them into a counseling session. Because the disease carries the stigma of two and a half decades of discrimination, students may hesitate to speak openly and share their innermost feelings and questions. At a time when they need human contact the most, parents fear the discrimination and potential isolation they may face if they divulge secrets.

Elizabeth Glaser, the founder of the Pediatric AIDS Foundation, is HIV-infected herself and is the mother of two infected children, Ariel and Josh. Ariel died in 1990 at seven years of age and, as of this writing, Josh is still alive. In her book, *In the Absence of Angels* (1991), Glaser commented on the anxiety, hopelessness, and depression she experienced when Ariel was denied access to public school and how that experience translated into terror, rage, and profound sadness when it came time for Josh to attend school. Josh was accepted into a small private school after a mass education campaign by the school and local medical community. Nonetheless, Glaser relied heavily on the mental health counseling and support that both she and her husband, Paul, received during this most difficult period. Her story, along with stories of several other clients with school-age children, intensify the need to design counseling strategies that support HIV victims.

Common Responses

Regardless of each counselor or teacher's theoretical orientation, a uniqueness develops in the therapeutic relationship with clients affected by HIV. The nuances can be as simple as the location of the counseling to whether or not the student is touched by the teacher or counselor. The four most frequent responses in classroom counseling sessions are the following.

Denial. One of the major observations that professionals working with HIV-impacted students or their families note is denial. Refusing to acknowledge that a deadly disease has taken hold is a normal response and noninfected adult helpers should respect this position as long as such refusal does not interfere with the student's medical treatment. Children may encounter gross denial at home and among their friends. Watching out for signals that indicate the child's willingness to talk is important. Signals may be apparent in written work, drawings, or from the child's conversation. Teachers and counselors must be aware of their own tendency to hide behind a screen of denial about the student's immediate HIV condition or about some parts of their own lives and not impose their denial on infected children who want to talk about their condition.

Guilt. A child may entertain guilt. Often adults may not disclose an HIV diagnosis to children out of a fear of social stigma, but the youngsters may act in light of the unspoken tension they sense and automatically assume *they* are to blame for the family's unrest. Some families experience rejection from other immediate or extended family members and friends. This painful rebuff can lead to an increasing sense of isolation at the very time when family members most need full support and love.

Anger. Children with HIV may experience anger, envy, or resentment toward their parents, classmates, friends, health-care providers, teachers, and healthy siblings. They spontaneously direct these bitter feelings toward the people they rely on the most; however, children may not feel free to express these rancorous feelings and, consequently, may suppress their overwhelming ire. They may divert their frustration and anger through "acting out" eruptive behaviors.

Hope. "Be here for the cure" is one of the positive slogans about HIV disease. Sustaining hope is one of the major struggles families, friends, class-mates, teachers, and counselors interacting with HIV children must do. Staying hopeful becomes even more challenging as they experience the death of others in their clinic or medical settings.

Educators should encourage noninfected children or their siblings to seek out enjoyable experiences and academic achievement. Kubler-Ross (1974) ad-vised families facing a member's terminal illness to pursue their lives vigor-ously or they risk physical and emotional exhaustion prior to the relative's death. This sage advice is particularly true with HIV disease because the illness can be so long-term. Family members do best when they pursue their life inter-ests and benefit from counseling against "survivor's guilt."

Counselors need to delineate a theoretical base and define the boundaries and alliances that they believe they can tolerate in the relationship. In most counselor-client relationships, for example, the work is done in an office or at least in a neutral space. Because of the debilitating illness itself or victims' typical fear of identification, counselors must show more sensitivity in working with HIV-impacted clients in a less traditional manner. As with most students, HIV patients are more likely to engage in meaningful dialogue when they are comfortable and perceive a safe environment. Issues of previous childhood aban-donment and rejection often surface during counseling; thus, a counselor must make a tangible commitment to HIV children. This unequivocal commitment reassures the children and adds richness and depth to every session.

Interventions

HIV-infected students and families often need to utilize their counselor's social skills. People and institutions in some geographic areas across America discriminate so much against HIV students that finding appropriate resources for social support can be difficult if not impossible. Securing such support is often necessary, however, in order for counselors, social workers, social sup-port assessors, nurses, and housekeepers to carry out their roles fully. Counse-lors who keep their social service coordinating role to an absolute minimum and focus on ways to engage other support service personnel to help their stu-dent and family can be most productive.

Providing appropriate and useful support and counsel to clients means bracketing the sessions with a clear and concrete outline. One such framework is the *Tether Paradigm* (Parish, 1989), which encompasses the following points:

- establishing clear boundaries for working with clients (including students and any other family members),
- employing genuineness and reflective listening skills,
- relying on current information about HIV and the disease process,
- using effective reframing skills,
- conducting a needs assessment,
- recruiting social support,
- identifying current referral resources, and
- ending each session with a useful action plan.

The fundamental technique from the above list that seems both to foster practical work and to enhance emotional work is reflective listening. Showing empathy and support requires counselors to display genuineness as they reflect the students' intense feelings. Counselors need to resist the urge to alleviate all the student's pain with reflective listening but work instead to allow students to maintain their deepest feelings. Many of the authors' student counselees have mentioned their desire to express their intense feelings of anger, rage, hate, fear, and sadness and to see their counselor recognize and fully respect these resolute emotions. Because many students are experiencing "pure feelings," in the lexicon of choice theory, we have learned to sit quietly and capture their intense pain without substituting or supplanting their feelings in any form. In developing our joining and reflecting skills, we have relied mostly on Gendlin's (1978) practical suggestions. By adding reframing or cognitive restructuring suggestions, we noticed that students and their family members typically replaced their maladaptive thoughts or ideas with productive new thoughts, ideas, and opinions.

Special Needs

Special circumstances can impact counselors' work with HIV-infected clients. Whereas the following factors typically may not apply to students, these conditions may be common in the lives of HIV-infected parents. Often a history of substance abuse is at the top of the list of circumstances surrounding these clients. The prospect of facing a life-threatening illness may add additional stress to a client recovering from drugs. Understanding addiction and codependency can help these clients along with direct involvement with agencies providing specific services for alcohol and drug abuse. After a nonjudgmental explanation about how many HIV treatments interact negatively with alcohol and drugs, these clients often find this information a powerful incentive to transform their addictive behaviors.

Listed here are the American Counseling Association (ACA) (1990) guidelines for HIV and AIDS student support services. Children with HIV may need the following:

- advocates for appropriate educational services (i.e., special classes if needed, but regular classroom settings if the children are capable);
- counseling to address concerns of illness, issues of death or dying, stigmatization in a school setting, decisions to reveal HIV status, and social relationships including sports participation and dating;
- support with out-of-home placement when possible;
- counseling regarding illness of parent(s);
- opportunities to address concerns regarding medical treatment; and
- support with acute episodes of illness and their changing health status.

Children who have friends or family members with HIV may need counseling in regards to the following:

- emotional reactions to the disease such as fear, denial, loss of hope, and anger;
- concerns about the viability of the family unit;
- fear that others will find out about the infected person; and
- lack of support for the student's educational efforts.

Sexually active students (i.e., heterosexual or homosexual) may need the following accommodations or services:

- a confidential and nonjudgmental place in which to discuss concerns and to receive information about safer sex practices,
- referral for HIV testing, and
- referral for STD (Sexually Transmitted Disease) testing.

Students who are substance users may need the following services:

- a confidential and nonjudgmental place in which to discuss their concerns and to receive information about reducing risks in drug and sexual behaviors,
- referrals for HIV testing,
- referral for STD testing, and
- community resources for substance abuse.

Summary

HIV disease can seriously disrupt a student's living pattern, sharply reduce his/her self-esteem, and increase his/her social isolation. Those infected by the virus may be physically deteriorated and view themselves as ugly, damaged, and contaminated. Also, they may feel guilty for bringing this disease upon themselves or may be angry at a parent whom they view as a physical conduit for the virus. They may believe that their sexuality has betrayed them, if their sexual activity were the transmission route. Effective strategies for these remediating issues include respectful and genuine empathy, reflective listening, and cognitive reframing. Helping students deal with these issues and assisting them in obtaining adequate support services may allow them to transform their view from the end of their lives to the final stage of growth.

ISSUES OF DEATH AND DYING

Initial Preparation

In preparation for working with issues of death and dying, counselors need to be aware of their own fears and anxieties about their own mortality. Competent teachers and counselors begin with admission of their own fears and concerns about death and dying before they work with children with terminal illness. This same candid attitude helps people confronting terminal illness in their own family, but this experience is always more difficult because of the natural emotional linkages. Even in writing this section of the chapter, we two authors felt many personally painful issues surfacing for ourselves that we had to discuss and resolve before we could complete the chapter.

Fears Related to Death and Dying

We live in a society that denies the reality of death. The HIV diagnosis intensifies any latent fears surrounding death and dying in the general American culture. People neither routinely and openly acknowledge death and dying nor discuss these realities as part of their day-to-day activities. Children naturally experience losses in their lives, but too often adults put pain and sadness on the back burner or pretend that a death or other loss did not happen. Who among us experiencing a life-threatening illness would sense no fear of the unknown, the dying process, and the anticipation of loneliness, abandonment, and death?

Coping with a Wide Variety of Emotions

Teachers and counselors can help students express their feelings and perceptions. Expressing these troubling perceptual errors helps students decrease their sense of isolation and encourages them to participate actively in handling the difficult experiences they anticipate when losses take their toll and death comes to call.

Major fears of staff members who work with HIV-infected children include fear of contagion, death, and losing forever the one with a terminal illness. Working with a person or family of someone who is dying challenges our own unresolved feelings about our own mortality. Rando (1984) viewed loss as the central theme for both terminal illness and bereavement. Keeping in mind the following framework of concerns can be beneficial to most people dealing with imminent death and dying:

- developmental stage and previous management of loss;
- family structure—the more open and supportive, the better;
- clarity about their psychological needs and success in consistently meeting those needs earlier;
- cultural background, especially as those values impact the concepts of health and illness;
- religious beliefs related to illness and death;
- socioeconomic status and available resources; and
- medical and physiological condition.

CHILDREN AND LOSS

Losses for children with HIV can be considerable. One-third of HIV youngsters grow up in foster care settings, constituting a baseline loss of home and family and possibly multiple losses during their stays in various placements within the foster care system. Children experience loss of body functioning and privacy due to repeated medical interventions, loss of continuity of schooling, possible loss of one or both parents, and loss of friends whom they have met in clinics or hospitals during their diverse medical treatments. Many children receiving regular treatment in medical facilities likely will see their friends becoming ill and dying. Children experience frustration at their inability to perform daily living tasks—dressing, moving easily, attending school, and playing with friends. Accompanying these restrictions, they experience sorrow, pain, and desperate suffering. Children with an HIV-infected parent wonder what will happen when their parent becomes too ill to care for them or dies and leaves them to an empty future. Teachers and counselors can intervene best (a) by being aware of the range of possible losses, (b) by staying open to hearing about the terrible losses, (c) by encouraging students' full expression of their fears, and (d) by guiding students to do something tangible that will help them tap their competence and worth, and (e) by structuring a plan that will provide a more secure framework for managing the coming changes.

Developmental Considerations

Children understand illness, death, and loss in different ways depending upon their age and experience. Children under five years of age cannot distinguish the process of dying from the process of living as they view death as temporary (Tallmer, Formanek, & Tallmer, 1974). After age five, children develop an understanding of various parts of the concept of death in different stages.

Speece and Brent (1992) have evaluated several relatively distinct components in children's understanding of death. They are as follows:

- universality, defined as understanding that all living things die;
- irreversibility, defined as understanding that once something vibrant dies, its physical body cannot be made alive again; and
- nonfunctionality, defined as understanding that all life-defining functions cease at death.

Some children understand these three concepts by age seven, but most understand these notions some time between ages 5 and 12. In particular, most children take four years to go from a mature understanding of one key component (usually, universality—that all living things eventually die) to understanding all three key components. In Speece and Brent's investigation, nearly 80% of children understood the concept of universality by age 5. Neither gender, socioeconomic status, nor IQ alone accounts for difference in learning. Knowing a child's developmental age is important in perceiving his/her understanding of death. Awareness of these concepts also may be influenced by the child's own experience surrounding death. Children who have lived in poverty have had greater exposure to loss, death, and violence than children living in less difficult circumstances. Generally by 10 years of age a child has developed an understanding of the concept of death.

Death and Dying Issues

A major factor for anyone in the HIV disease spectrum is a sense of isolation. Unlike most illnesses, even family members of an HIV-infected person experience a great degree of isolation, fear, and stigma. Teachers need to be even more available to talk to children about these issues as HIV in this culture has been associated with death, dying, loss, sexual activity, and injection drug use. These topics will differ with each child and family according to stage of illness, age of the child, level of understanding, ethnicity, race, social status, and religious beliefs.

Death of Parent

Many studies exist on the impact of the death of a parent upon the development of children. Zambelli, Clark, Barile, and Jong (1988) identified several areas of concern for the classroom including (a) children's immediate reactions to loss, (b) subsequent behavioral patterns of grieving, (c) cognitive understanding about death, (d) impact of loss on conscious development, (e) impact of loss on academic and creative achievement, and (f) personality development. Van Eerdewegh, Clayton, and Van Eerdewegh (1985) reported that depression, falling school performance, and withdrawn behavior increased significantly in grieving children of both genders at all ages.

Prior experience will affect children's reaction to loss of a parent. Some children experience severe and persistent behavior problems. Elizur and Kaffman (1983) identified clinical symptoms that include overdependent behavior, fears, separation anxiety, night sleep disorders, discipline problems, restlessness, learning difficulties, eating disorders, aggressive behavior, and social withdrawal. These reactions tend to be more severe for children who are especially vulnerable and who lack adequate social support. Vulnerability may increase by losing the other parent, incurring additional losses due to migration and resettlement, experiencing multiple deaths in the family from other causes, and lacking a community that offers support.

Worden (1982) described four major tasks of the bereavement process.

1. accepting the reality of the loss;
2. experiencing the pain of grief;
3. adjusting to an environment in which the deceased is missing (This is particularly difficult if the loss is not acknowledged. The child may experience depression, helplessness, passivity, and fatalism); and
4. letting go of the deceased person and attaching to living people (Children with multiple experiences of loss may find this more difficult to achieve. These aspects are experienced in a circular fashion, and students will experience these stages in varying degrees of depth. The anniversaries of loss often trigger the need to reexperience these tasks).

Counselors and teachers can be present and supportive. Allow children their own individual style of mourning and be culturally aware of significant rituals and practices. Being patient, being predictable, and being persistent can aid young ones as they complete the mourning process (Rando, 1984). Confirm children's obvious experiences—that a parent is ill, that HIV is a difficult disease to discuss with others, and that none of these serous losses are due directly to the children's actions. Children can tolerate painful and sad feelings, especially when they are reassured that these feelings are appropriate, natural, and time-limited. Protecting children from their emotional pain is false support because this intrusion, while tempting, usually takes the form of devaluing children's experience.

MULTICULTURAL ENVIRONMENT

A concern for culture uniqueness is important in working classroom programs associated with HIV because the largest number of children affected by HIV come from cultural and racial minority groups. This section attempts to paint a wide brush stroke over a complex and multifaceted arena. Discussing fully the large number of varied issues related to cultural diversity in this small space is not possible. Teachers and counselors need to make their own rigorous attempts to understand fully the culture of the child who may be affected by HIV.

Cultural competence is an important factor in effective counseling. Cultural competence can be defined as

> a set of congruent beliefs, attitudes, and policies that come together in a system, agency, or among professionals that enable them to work effectively in cross-cultural situations. The word cultural is used because it implies the integrated pattern of human behavior that includes thoughts, communications, actions, customs, beliefs, values, and institutions of racial, ethnic, religious, or social group. The word competence is used because it implies having the capacity to function effectively. (Cross, 1988, p. 1)

Culturally aware teachers and counselors will respect and encourage the varying cultural backgrounds of the students entering their classrooms or counseling offices. These professionals keep in mind the historical factors that influence health services, such as racism, immigration, and resettlement patterns. In addition to the common acculturation pressures, a majority of immigrant groups also are handling such specialized stressors as war experiences and low socioeconomic status. One strategy for enhancing all students' cultural awareness and comfort levels is consulting directly with minority communities. This intercultural competence would include an awareness of the politics of AIDS and HIV.

Samuel Henry (1992) defined a multicultural environment as "one where multiple cultures exist, where knowledge and respect for many cultures predominate, and where an understanding of the interplay of cultures is . . . the basis of interacting with diverse persons and groups" (p. 1). Cultural factors operating in a school setting include the culture(s) of the classroom and school, the culture(s) of the family and a child with HIV, the teacher's culture(s), and the larger community's culture(s). Educators need to consider each of these cultural value systems when working with a family or child with HIV, as each component will either help or hinder the work they must all do together. Everyone has a culture and must come to know that personal culture in order to work competently and sensitively. Cultural elitism (i.e., the "our way is superior" syndrome) develops from a lack of understanding the diversity of others and from suffering from a debilitating blind spot in relation to one's own cultural biases. Cultural and ethnic differences may come from language, religion, socioeconomic status, immigration history, family values, sexual preferences, and gender roles. By the same token, the importance of family life, love, loyalty, friendship, concern for children, and spiritual beliefs also highlight the transcultural commonalties of personal experiences.

DISCRIMINATION AGAINST HIV VICTIMS

As important as ethnicity and culture are, social class is a major compounding factor in the history of pediatric HIV. Poverty, limited resources and options, greater exposure to the drug culture and violence, interactions with large bureaucratic institutions, and the struggle to maintain family life make dealing with issues of HIV more difficult.

The parent of an HIV-infected child may be infected himself/herself and, therefore, must cope with his/her illness as well as that of the child. Data reveal, in fact, that the mother is infected 85% of the time. Because this disease flourishes under conditions of injection drug use, poverty, and socially forbidden sexual practices, victims become social outcasts. They have a more difficult time accessing social services and remaining involved in their communities than those suffering from most other illnesses. Society's HIV-positive population is a contemporary throwback to yesterday's pitiful lepers.

The nature of this illness is infectious. Consistently interacting with the health-care system is essential. Poor families may have had few positive experiences with health-care systems, along with being historically undeserved by the medical industry. Limited services are available today for women and children with HIV. Even these scarce services are often scattered among many agencies. In the midst of this scattering among multiple agencies, parents of one or more sick children find accepting these minimal services to be time consuming, costly, and difficult to negotiate. Frequently, they harbor a high level of distrust about these social services and meager medical procedures. Most family members, teachers, and counselors simply cannot keep up with the rapidly advancing clinical knowledge of the disease.

LEGAL AND ETHICAL ISSUES

The legal and ethical issues surrounding HIV children and families are complex and require school officials to gain a careful understanding of all aspects of this disease. School policy and confidentiality are the two most relevant components among all the legal and ethical issues.

School Policy

Within school districts, local traditions, prejudices, and longstanding mores and practices reinforce the stigma of HIV, making it difficult for teachers and counselors to develop sensitive and open programs for students who are living with HIV. In a study of State Departments of Education, Hartwig and Eckland (1990) found that state administrators favor a conservative "wait and see" approach to developing a policy regarding children with HIV. By far, the most effective policy emerges from the collaborative efforts of a school board, a faculty, and a community. The model that San Francisco, California has used effectively is shown here as Table 11.1. Readers may obtain other examples of school board policy from the National Association of State Boards of Education listed in the Resources section near the end of this chapter.

Confidentiality

Confidentiality is the most important aspect of a school's plan to manage those carrying HIV disease. The overarching rule is *share information with no one without a written release of information from the family and, if appropri-*

TABLE 11.1
San Francisco Unified School District Policy
Regarding Students with HIV Infection

San Francisco Unified School District Policy P5143
Re: Students with HIV Infection

As long as eligibility for enrollment is consistent with other SFUSD policies and regulations, children with HIV (Human Immunodeficiency Virus) infection or diagnosis of AIDS (Acquired Immune Deficiency Syndrome) are encouraged to attend preschool, child care, and school unless the physician responsible for care of an infected child determines school attendance is not appropriate. Parents, foster parents, and guardians of children with HIV infection are encouraged to share the information with school personnel so that support can be given to the students and their families in addition to allowing the primary care physician to receive information about other infectious diseases in the school environment that might pose a threat to the health of the child with HIV infection.

As with all medical information, knowledge of HIV infection or diagnosis of AIDS will be strictly confidential and shared only with specific school personnel as indicated in writing by the minor's parent, guardian, or foster parent or by the student who is 18 years of age.

Knowledge of the presence of a student with HIV infection does not require special procedures for infection control. All San Francisco Unified School District Personnel are expected to be familiar with and to observe the guidelines published in the manual entitled "San Francisco Unified School District Infection Control Guidelines." The guidelines describe "Universal Precautions" to be used when handling all blood and *all* body fluids containing blood; that includes using latex gloves.

Existing Related Law: Health and Safety Code Part 1 of Division 1, Section 199.42. prohibits sharing information about AIDS or HIV infection except in specific circumstances. Existing law also requires that school districts inform employees annually (or more frequently if there is new information) about appropriate methods school employees may employ to prevent exposure to HIV and hepatitis B virus (Health and Safely Code Part 1 of Division 1, Section 199.81, Chapter 1.15).

Policy adopted by a unanimous vote of the Board of Education on 2/1/92 to replace the prior policy with the same number that was adopted in 1986.

San Francisco Unified School District
Health Programs Office 1512 Golden Gate Avenue
San Francisco, CA 94115 (415) 749-3400

Source: Copyright, 1992. Reprinted with permission of the San Francisco Unified School District.

ate, *from the student as well. A written release is valid only for the school* year *in which the disclosure occurs. School administrators must renew all re-* leases *each and every year.* School professionals always must clarify for whom or to whom any information is to be released, and they also must understand why such a release is necessary. All school officials must master their state's regulations covering confidentiality of HIV results. In California, disclosing a person's HIV status to anyone but the infected person is illegal. Several exceptions to confidentiality appear below, but these special circumstances are not likely to be present in a school setting.

Exceptions to Confidentiality

Although school authorities must use caution and consult with legal counsel and/or their superiors before acting on any of the exceptions, the following circumstances do allow for a breach of confidentiality.

1. Physician disclosure to sexual and/or needle sharing partners: Physicians may choose to disclose the HIV test results to the sex partners of their HIV-infected patients. Very specific regulations are in place regarding the procedures for making this disclosure.
2. Physician disclosure to medical record: A medical doctor may enter HIV test results into the patient's medical chart. Reviewing a chart for the purpose of disclosing HIV results without a patient's written informed consent, however, is illegal.
3. Disclosure to other health-care providers: Disclosing a patient's HIV status in the best interest of a patient is not a violation of confidentiality. The "best interest of a patient" includes a disclosure to those involved in the patient's care and treatment. "Health-care provider" under this exception has been interpreted to include licensed mental health professionals. Even in this instance, medical specialists need to obtain a voluntary written consent form from a patient before disclosing the information to other health-care providers and licensed mental health practitioners. No one may apply this exception to disclosure for the purpose of protecting other providers from HIV exposure.

The Tarasoff "duty to protect" case may surface as a confidentiality issue with school counselors in California, and similar statutes operate in other states. Analysis of *Tarasoff* (*Tarasoff v. Regents of the University of California,* 1976) and other related legislation indicates that the "duty to protect" mandate seldom compels a school counselor to disclose information related to an HIV-infected person in school.

Disclosure Procedures

The law defines the salient legal right in these circumstances as the right of an HIV-infected child to an education. According to current law, a school has no right to know the HIV status of any student, teacher, staff member, or administrator.

Disclosing someone's HIV status may occur in either a planned or unplanned way. The parents or guardians have discretionary rights to disclose the HIV status of a child to school officials. Conceivably, a child might disclose his/her HIV status accidentally, or one child might tell another who then relates the information to school officials, his/her family, or friends. Under these circumstances of a student's unintentional disclosure to one or more people at school, the authorities there should consult with the family of the alleged HIV-infected child and let the family determine what, if anything, they wish to do in light of the revelation.

Optimally, authorities may reveal a child's HIV disease only when doing so is in the best interests of a child and the family. If the school administration, staff, and faculty first learn that an HIV-infected child is in the school, they then can sponsor an information session with the parents of the other students. They also can initiate a collaborative and supportive environment in order to ease the whole student body toward disclosure. In several instances, schools have arranged for the child's pediatric specialist to confer with school personnel and also with the parents. Although arranging for a pediatrician to meet with students and staff is not a crucial step, most experts do advise school officials to invite the child's pediatrician to come to the school. Lastly, after they have informed the student body, the adult role models need to be clear about their special role. They work to provide a climate in which students feel free to ask their questions and make any comments. In the end, students show the HIV-infected youngster that they can be the same helpful friend after learning about the diagnosis as they had been prior to the information. The bottom line of the law for professional educators is respecting the privacy rights of students and families impacted by HIV. If school staff, administration, or faculty are unclear about any legal aspect of HIV confidentiality and exposure, they must rely on knowledgeable HIV consultants.

UNIVERSAL PRECAUTIONS AND HIV DISEASE

HIV is a serious disease and a public health crisis that merits everyone's awareness and concern. HIV disease has generated more alarm in both the medical and general population than any other disease in the last 30 years. Martin Fleidegger, a 19th-century philosopher, claimed that the root of all denial is steeped in a human being's fear of his/her own mortality. Whenever people couple their natural dread about death with the embarrassment of exposing intimate information about a disease that they contract primarily through sexual intercourse, they become terrified and irrational.

One way to combat one's fear and terror of dealing with HIV children and adults is through education. Most schools have yet to design inservice programs that lay out universal precautions. Optimally, school staffs—teachers, support personnel, and administrators—should become aware of universal precautions well in advance of accommodating an HIV-infected child.

The guidelines that the United States Centers for Disease Control (CDC) developed for universal precautions appear in their publication, "Morbidity and Mortality Weekly Report" (CDC, 1986). The guidelines suggest that health-care workers (HCW) reduce their risk of HIV infection by wearing latex or vinyl gloves. Such protection can prevent skin and mucous membrane exposure when directly contacting blood and other body fluids, such as urine or mucous.

Henderson, Fahey, and Willy (1990) documented support for health-care workers using universal precautions. Their research reported a minimal HIV transmission risk when workers used correct universal precautions. Corroborating this risk-reducing method, the results in Hadler's (1990) study indicated that the incidence of HIV in health-care workers was not significant when they used correct universal precautions.

School staff and teachers may not know the health or disease status of all the children in their care. For this reason, the precautions we list below are for everyone, regardless of one's knowledge of the status of the health condition of children in a school. In dealing with preschool children, care providers and teachers wisely wear latex gloves when changing diapers. They also must advise children not to share toothbrushes, because bleeding gums can transmit HIV-infected blood. Because school-age children often incur scrapes and cuts in schoolyard accidents, adults treating their physical injuries should use rubber gloves routinely and use bleach, diluted 1 part to 10 parts water, to clean soiled surfaces. In effect, one easily can see that all professionals and paraprofessionals must act as if everyone carries the HIV virus.

Sometimes a teacher or aide might not be able to put on gloves before treating an injured child on a playground. In these cases, the person definitely should avoid direct contact with blood. Once a child has received immediate care, teachers and care providers should use a disinfectant soap to clean their skin surfaces.

Biting seems to be a major concern for both preschool and school-age children. The risk of getting the HIV virus in this manner would exist only if the bite breaks the skin and causes bleeding and the infected blood finds a portal to enter another child's bloodstream. So far, no documentation exists of a case of HIV transmission from an infected child to another through biting.

Lastly, some children seal their friendships by becoming "blood brothers" or "blood sisters." The ritual involves the pricking of fingers, the mingling of the blood, and the professing of lifelong dedication and friendship to each other. Because infected blood transmits the HIV virus, parents and teachers should strongly discourage the initiation of blood-brother and blood-sister relationships.

Throughout the course of the disease, public health and government officials have claimed that the risk of transmission from a health-care worker to a patient is extraordinarily low, but not zero. Lightning strikes claim more lives each year than the HIV that health-care workers acquire, and the risk of being hit by a careless motorist on the way to a dentist's office is significantly higher than the likelihood of contracting HIV after arriving.

Despite the very low risk of transmitting HIV from one infected person to a teacher or school official, irrational fear of HIV is driving public policy and shaping the opinions of a precautionary public. People are understandably frightened by any suggestion that they might be at risk for contracting HIV. Again the best defense against irrational fear is education. Public Health departments that provide inservice educational training programs and other resources are listed at the end of the chapter.

RESOURCES

Organizations and Publications

1. American Federation of Teachers, 555 New Jersey Avenue, N.W., Washington, DC, 20001, (202) 879-4548.

2. American Red Cross, 17th and D Streets, N.W., Washington, DC, 20006.

   - *School Systems and AIDS: Information for Teachers and School Officials*—pamphlet.

- *Mi Hermano* (My Brother)—a 28-minute drama on video about the impact of AIDS on a family. The story centers around a Hispanic immigrant family that has that has lost a son to AIDS.

3. American School Health Association, P. O. Box 708, Kent, OH, 44240, (216) 678-1601.

   - Bradley, B. (1992). *HIV Infection and the school setting: A guide for school nursing practice.*

4. Association of Asian-Pacific Community Health Organizations, 1212 Broadway, Suite 730, Oakland, CA, 94612, (510) 2729436.

5. Centers for Disease Control National AIDS hot line (1-800-342-AIDS) —a 24-hour service for questions and information, also available in Spanish (1-800-344-SIDA) and for the hearing impaired (1-800-AIDS-TTY).

6. Child Welfare League of America, 440 First Street, N.W., Suite 310, Washington, DC, 20001, (202) 638-2952.

   - *Caring for School-aged Children with HIV Infection*—video ($59.95).
   - *Living with Loss: Children and HIV*—video ($59.95).
   - *The Courage to Care: Responding to the Crisis of Children with AIDS* —book by G. Anderson (Ed.) (1990).
   - *Serving HIV-infected Children, youths, and their families: A guide for residential group care providers*—book by G. Anderson (Ed.) (1989).

7. Hispanic AIDS Forum, 121 Avenue of the Americas, New York, NY, 10013, (212) 966-6336.

8. National AIDS Information Clearinghouse, 1-800-458-5231—provides information on organizations with AIDS resources, services, and printed material from the CDC.

   - Guidelines for Effective School Health Education to Prevent the Spread of AIDS—article in January 29, 1988, issue of *Morbidity & Mortality Weekly Report* (MMWR), *37*(S-2), 1-14.
   - Guidelines for Developing, Implementing, and Evaluating an HIV Education Program—article in January 29, 1988, issue of *Morbidity & Mortality Weekly Report* (MMWR), *37*(S-2), 1-14.

- Update: Universal Precautions for Prevention of Transmission of HIV, Hepatitis B Virus, and Other Blood Borne Pathogens in Health-Care Settings—article in June 24, 1988, issue of *Morbidity & Mortality Weekly Report* (MMWR), *37*(24), 377-388.

9. National Association of State Boards of Education, 1012 Cameron Street, Alexandria, VA, 22314, (703) 684-4000.

   - *Someone at School Has AIDS: A Guide to Developing Policies for Students and School Staff Members Who Are Infected with HIV—* book by K. Frazer (1989) ($10.50).

10. National Native American AIDS Prevention Center, 3515 Grand Avenue, Suite 100, Oakland, CA, 94910, (510) 444-2051.

11. The National PTA, HIV/AIDS Education Project, 700 North Rush Street, Chicago, IL, 60611-2571, (312)-787-0977—has articles on implementation of HIV education programs in PTA groups across the nation.

    - *HIV and AIDS Education: Planning Guide for PTA Leaders*—publication.
    - *AIDS Education at Home and School: An Activity Guide for Local PTA Leaders*—publication that is revised annually.
    - *How to Talk to Your Children and Teens about AIDS*—publication available in English and Spanish.

12. National Pediatric HIV Resource Center, 15 S. Ninth Street, Newark, NJ, 07107, (201) 268-8251—provides current information and resources.

13. National School Boards Association, 1680 Duke Street, Alexandria, VA, 22314, (703) 683-7590—has information on local district school policies addressing HIV education, an HIV/AIDS resource database, and other publications including training module/curriculum.

    - *Reducing the Risk: A School Leader's Guide to AIDS Education—* book ($5.00 plus shipping).

14. Pediatric AIDS Foundation, 2407 Wiltshire Boulevard, Suite 613, Santa Monica, CA, 90403, (213) 395-9051.

    - *Educating Our Children: How to Speak with Children 5 to 12 about HIV/AIDS*—video that presents a series of vignettes that teachers, counselors, and parents can model.

15. *Does AIDS Hurt? Educating Young Children about AIDS*—book by M. Quackenbush & S. Villarreal (1988) (Santa Cruz: Network Publications) that gives suggestions for teachers, counselors, and parents ($14.95).

Children's Books

Blake, J. (1990). *Risky times: How to be AIDS-smart and stay healthy: A guide for teenagers.* New York: Workman. For pre-teens, teens, and adults.

Hausherr, R. (1989). *Children and the AIDS virus.* New York: Clarion Books. Suitable for all children but directed towards children 5 to 9 years old. The book discusses transmission routes with sensitivity including same-gender sex. Ethnically appropriate. $4.95 paper, $13.95 hard cover.

Merrifield, D. (1990). *Come sit with me.* Toronto, Canada: Women's Press. Suitable for all children but directed towards children 4 to 8 years old. The book is ethnically appropriate and touches on issues such as the importance of support, friendship, and basic concepts of HIV. The book does not discuss transmission routes. $6.95 paper.

Schilling, S., & Swain, J. (1989). *My name is Jonathan (and I have AIDS).* Denver, CO: Prickly Pair Publishing. Written by a child with AIDS, this book covers personal experience, transmission routes, and precautions. Pictures and storybook for elementary level. Available in English, Spanish, and Vietnamese. $12.95.

Starkman, N. (1990). *Z's Gift.* Seattle, WA: Comprehensive Health Education Foundation. Suitable for all children but directed towards children 4 to 8 years old. The story focuses on a young boy's reaction to his teacher who is infected with HIV and how both the adults and other students react to the news.

BIBLIOGRAPHY

Ballard, D., White, D., & Glascoff, M. (1990). AIDS/HIV education for pre-service elementary teachers. *Journal of School Health, 50,* 262-265.

Dunkel, J., & Hatfield, S. (1986). Countertransference issues in working with persons with AIDS. *Social Work, 31,* 114-117.

Futrell, M. (1988). AIDS education through schools. *Journal of School Health, 58,* 324-326.

REFERENCES

American Association for Counseling and Development (American Counseling Association). (1990). Guidelines for HIV and AIDS student support services. *Journal of School Health, 60,* 255-259.

Brewer, L., & Parish, M. (1992, September). *HIV and children: Counseling issues in a multicultural setting.* Paper presented at the National Conference of Association for Counselor Education and Supervision, San Antonio, TX.

Brouwers, P., Moss, H., Walters, P., Eddy, J., Balis, F., Poplack, D., & Pizzo, P. (1990). Effect of continuous-infusion Zidovudine therapy on neurologic functional in children with symptomatic human immunodeficiency virus infection. *Journal of Pediatrics, 117,* 980-985.

Centers for Disease Control. (1986, February 7). Apparent transmission of Human T-Lymphotrophic Virous Type III/Lymphadenopathy-Associated Virus from a child to a mother providing health care. *Morbidity & Mortality Weekly Report (MMWR), 35*(5), 76-79.

Centers for Disease Control. (1993, February). *HIV/AIDS Surveillance Report, 6,*14.

Cross, T. (1988). *Focal point* (Vol. 3). Washington, DC: CASSP Technical Assistance Center, Georgetown University.

Elizur, E., & Kaffman, M. (1983). Factors influencing the severity of childhood bereavement reactions. *American Journal of Orthopsychiatry, 53,* 668-676.

Fetro, J. (1992). *Results of the 1991 middle school health survey.* San Francisco: San Francisco Unified School District.

Fletcher, J. M., Francis, D. J., Pequegnat, W., Raudenbush, S. W., Borstein, M. H., Schmitt, F., Brouwers, P., & Stover, E. (1991). Neurobehavioral outcomes in diseases of childhood: Individual change models for pediatric human immunodeficiency viruses. *American Psychologist, 46,* 1267-1277.

Freudenberger, J. (1980). Burnout: The high cost of high achievement. Garden City, NY: Anchor Press.

Gendlin, E. T. (1978). *Focusing.* New York: Bantam Books.

Glaser, E. (1991). *In the absence of angels.* New York: Berkley Publishing.

Hadler, S. C. (1990). Hepatitis B virus infection and health-care workers. *Vaccine, 8,* 24-28.

Hartwig, A., & Eckland, J. (1990). Policy issues concerning HIV-positive children: State education officials' opinions. *AIDS & Public Policy Journal, 6,* 91-97.

Henderson, D., Fahey, B. J., & Willy, M. (1990). Risk for occupational transmission of human immunodeficiency virus type II (HIV-1) associated with clinical exposure: A prospective evaluation. *Annuals of Internal Medicine, 113,* 740-746.

Henry, S. (1992). *Cultural diversity: A Samuel Henry information sheet.* Distributed at American College Health Association annual meeting, San Francisco.

Kubler-Ross, E. (1974). *Questions and answers on death and dying.* New York: McMillan.

Levenson, R. L., Kairam, R., Bartnett, M., & Mellins, C. A. (1991). Equivalence of Peabody Picture Vocabulary Test-Revised: Forms and for children with acquired immune deficiency syndrome (AIDS). *Perceptual and Motor Skills, 72,* 99-102.

Parish, M. (1989, October). *Counseling strategies for HIV-infected clients: A framework for change.* Paper presented at National Association of Social Workers, National Conference, San Francisco, CA.

Pines, A., & Maslach, C. (1978). Characteristic of staff burnout in mental health settings. *Hospital and Community Psychiatry, 29,* 233-237.

Rando, T. (1984). *Grief, dying, and death.* Champaign, IL: Research Press Company.

Schietinger, H., McCarthy, P., Gillen, M., & Hammrich, H. (1988). A strategy for educating health care providers about AIDS: The California Nurses Association's AIDS Train the Trainer Program. *Nursing Clinic of North America, 23,* 779-87.

Speece, M., & Brent, S. (1992). The acquisition of a mature understanding of three components of the concept of death. *Death Studies, 5,* 511-529.

Tallmer, M., Formanek, J., & Tallmer, J. (1974) Factors influencing children's concepts of death. *Journal of Clinical Child Psychology, 3,* 17-19.

Tarasoff v. Regents of the University of California. (1976). 17Cal. 3rd, 425, 551 P. 2d. 334, 131 Cal.Rptr. 14.

Van Eerdewegh, M., Clayton, P., & Van Eerdewegh, P. (1985). The bereaved child: Variables influencing early psychopathology. *British Journal of Psychiatry, 147,* 188-194.

Worden, J. (1982). *Grief counseling and grief therapy: A handbook for the mental health practitioner.* New York: Springer.

Zambelli, G., Clark, E., Barile, L., & Jong, A. (1988). An interdisciplinary approach to clinical intervention for childhood bereavement. *Death, 12,* 41-50.

PART III
CRISES AND SOLUTIONS—
INTERACTIONAL TRAUMAS

Chapter 12

HANDLING INTERPERSONAL PROBLEMS AT SCHOOL: IMPROVING RELATIONSHIPS

Larry L. Palmatier

Editor's Note

In the past, when students did not conform, school authorities' first reaction was to list ten ways they could pressure the students to follow the rules and fall in line. Faced with the high rates of students' disinterest, truancy, and desertion, those same authorities now find they must stop and ask what they may be doing to make school unappetizing. The problem may not be the entire school, of course, but, in some cases, only one particular teacher whom a student wishes to avoid at all costs. In any case, students will cooperate more willingly when educators show a more open attitude and do not focus on catching someone doing something wrong. In light of its ineffectiveness, why then does coercion so often head the list of favored tactics? What is the logic that adults use to help them frame most interactions as a power struggle? With alienated students, for example, or truants, or those who "fool around" when they do attend, simply suspend them. If a student is tardy too much, detain him after school to teach him a lesson. If he insists on avoiding behaviors, make relating with adults terribly unattractive by judging and criticizing the students who show only marginal interest.

Four tangible steps teachers could take would work almost immediately to break the cycle that leads to distance or conflict.

1. *Acknowledge the role the system plays in creating the problems and take the heat off individual students.*
2. *Demonstrate an encouraging and friendly attitude.*
3. *Show vulnerability instead of muscle; principals know they can always expel threatening students.*
4. *Create interesting curricular opportunities.*

ROOTS OF SOCIAL PROBLEMS IN SCHOOL

Teachers will tell anyone willing to listen that their biggest headache is a student whose rowdiness disrupts their classroom. Classroom nuisances and more serious danger go to the heart of this book's main theme for teachers: learning to be effective managers, especially of those students who choose to make trouble and cause discipline problems when, ideally, they should be working hard on projects they themselves see as important and high quality. Teachers' best hope for changing students' inappropriate behavior is by changing what they do. Sooner or later, students will see that a new quality is developing in the classroom and they will come to see their options for more useful actions.

Many students are obviously not satisfying their affiliation needs in the normal course of living—at home or at school. Their parents abbreviate the time they have for them because they may be too busy meeting their own needs, including the most basic need of surviving. Therefore, young people are fine-tuning their attempts to affiliate and their efforts show in the form of gang membership. This pervasive display of terrible loneliness is a serious social concern. One boy's story will not apply to all others his age, but the message of this student's tragic experience explains clearly how isolation tempts one to tune out anyone trying to befriend him. Linking up with a collection of similarly disenchanted peers can hold out the promise of a renewed sense of power and importance.

Some Key Essentials Students Need to Learn in School

Anyone fortunate enough to develop curriculum in schools would enjoy a *carte blanche* authorization to set the academic table for the eager diners. The following 10 competencies might rise to the top of a wish list.

- Direct Interpersonal Communication Skills and Assertiveness
- Negotiation Skills and Conflict Resolution
- Goal-setting Skills
- Thinking, Reading, and Computational Skills
- Managing Multiple Projects
- Concise and Creative Writing Skills
- Accessing Library Referencing Resources
- Using Computer Technology
- Group Communication, Multicultural Sensitivity, and Problem Solving
- Learning to Learn
- Knowledge of Sound Nutrition and Health Practices

A Young Man Learns to Share His Betrayal

A man had two sons, ages 14 and 16. One unfortunate day, both sons were in an automobile accident and landed in a hospital with multiple injuries. The insurance company dutifully extended a reasonable settlement on behalf of the two young men, and they gradually gained some solace in their payoff. After a few weeks, they even began enjoying a sense of security about the future when they abruptly discovered that their "found money" had vanished from sight. Who was the thief? Could the police find the rascal and bring him to justice? They learned soon enough who had committed the rotten act—their own dad.

How could they ever get over this vicious betrayal? Many counselors would say problems such as this knife in the back would take many years to understand, sort out, and resolve. Looking at the story differently, however, options appear that can be of immediate help and do not require an exclusive focus on the father's criminal behavior. The younger brother's counselor decided to check out Joe's willingness to retell his story in writing, even if he had to dictate the sad tale. The plan was for him to send the painful story to the sixth-grade children in an elementary school in a low income part of town. The young boys and girls in that other school would read about the father who ripped off his two sons' savings for college and then abandoned them and their mother. The students would get to know exactly what Joe had been through after the car accident.

Focusing on the Misery. The angry young man at juvenile hall found himself thinking only about his having been wronged. He built up a case in his mind of fear, hatred, and revenge against his dad. He was, in effect, living in his head and even plotting how to get even. He had not heard the adage on revenge—"start by digging two graves."

Refocusing on a Solution. When the counselor first suggested that Joe consider sharing his betrayal by writing 30 fifth- and sixth-graders who, in turn, would write 30 new endings to his story, he was slow to accept the plan. Every day for one entire month, he was to step outside of his day-to-day circumstances and read a new ending to his personal tragedy as written by one of the 30 children who had read his drama. Joe decided to give the plan a try. After receiving the new endings, he had a choice of sending the writers who joined with him in his bad experience two or three dollars as a token of his appreciation. The money was available in a small fund of donations that the juvenile facility had collected for such projects. Going on a window smashing spree conveyed his frustration but did little to give him a sense of personal control and peace. By sharing his misery with other youngsters, he too won a prize in the form of overcoming his isolation and loss. The essence of this solution was to invite a boy who felt grossly wronged to share his dad's betrayal instead of resorting to his immediate tendencies: fighting the battle alone and entertaining only more frustration and anger as time passed.

Perspective on Anger Management. Fury or anger is a perennial reaction to problems, and an old-time favorite emotion even for teachers at times. When examined through choice theory, fury is a choice for students when they are unaware of a better alternative or simply are unwilling to choose more rational behaviors in the face of the natural frustration most people would feel when their needs go unattended. Think about a time when you were really angry. Is your memory unpleasant? Glasser has stated often that only one psychological problem exists: people cannot get others to do what they want them to do. This is actually a more specific example of his general statement about psychological problems coming down to one point: a person wants something that he/she does not have. When it comes to anger, people report a certain amount of pleasure in openly expressing their fury, especially if the angry outburst worked to draw new recruits to their cause. Even psychotic breaks can be associated with heavy duty temper tantrums or expressions of serious fear.

Some trainers talk about anger management seminars as if anger were the problem. These same specialists refer to triggers that set angry people off as if the subjects have no control over their upset. Terms such as "triggers" and "anger-provoking situations" only reinforce people's excuse-oriented thinking about the powerful emotion of anger. The problem is usually the frustration of not having some key want or more general need, not the knee-jerk emoting the person might resort to routinely in an emotional stupor. Today, the matter of fury becomes compounded in light of students' common display of a strong sense of entitlement and personal rights. Teachers report feeling a pressure to perform or entertain their students and to cater to youngsters more so than in the past.

Pandering is probably too strong a word for teachers' attempts to meet the current demands of students, but teachers have reported a new sense of urgency in students' expressions of their needs. Some of the change can be attributed to a new level of candor in politics and in the media, which have inundated us with tabloid print and video. Some of this candor is not bad. Talk about AIDS, for example, and other sexually transmitted health risks is more open. Other topics may be less useful. The private lives of public figures, for example, and the political ills of education are well-known media topics. Students and their families and teachers must expose themselves regularly to larger doses of training in confrontational and assertive communication in one political war after another against drug abuse. A host of public and private programs designed to empower both students and the entire body politic take their turn as the focus for students. When adults in schools elicit students' opinions, therefore, the adults probably should not be surprised when children and adolescents express their views and appear to be demanding and even arrogant.

HANDLE THE PROBLEM AT HAND

Children who misbehave usually carry around a personal history of harshness or, at least, their share of tough experiences. Even someone generally regarded as a troubled child, however, often will relax physically during the first family counseling appointment. We might conclude that children's problem behavior is not the real heart of the whole family's complaint. Children's misbehavior is the most frequent complaint of other family members, however, and a counselor's first task is to work out a solution to the trouble staring everyone in the face. The label from the family therapy literature for the beacon signaling a family's distress, as Virginia Satir often described it, is the "person who wears the symptom."

Most often, a child or adolescent "wears the symptom" for a family, leading outsiders to conclude the child literally must volunteer for the role of convenient scapegoat. Or perhaps the child believes that, by assuming a serious problem himself/herself, the child can rescue certain family members or even the entire group. Madanes (1984) has described this phenomenon by suggesting viewing the symptom as a metaphor for the family's problem, and Minuchin and Fishman (1981, p. 18) speak of a "parentified" child. Also, some people assume that a problem kid is the broken or defective part of the system, and that everything will be fine if a counselor can just "fix" the child. Systems theory, however, takes a less judgmental position on this topic; blaming is unsuitable because any "problem" only sounds an alarm that the communication system has somehow gone awry. Other phrases that experienced counselors commonly employ for the most apparent point of difficulty in a family are "index person," "symptom bearer" (Minuchin & Fishman, 1981, p. 28), and the "identified patient," known simply sometimes as the I.P. (Boscolo, Cecchin, Hoffman, & Penn, 1987, pp. 108-109).

Children's Attempt to Solve Problems with Problems

Are children who work at cross purposes with adults smarter than we think? Perhaps they choose to act out in a conscious but reckless effort to become the medium through which the whole family finds needed help? Perhaps troublemakers typically visibly relax at a first meeting because they have managed to get their parent or parents some help in the form of a counselor and a counseling appointment. Experienced counselors do not emphasize the child's helpful role in this scenario too much (Haley, 1987; Madanes, 1984)—at least not during the first session. Even though the job of an I.P. is an important one to the whole family system, giving too much public acknowledgment and featuring the problem at a session might give the I.P. too much power and encourage him to move from sacrificing for the whole system to bullying everybody. When others comment on symptom bearers during a session and credit them for being instrumental in arranging family counseling, most I.P.s pay special attention.

Communication Principles to Guide Your Counseling

The communication principles that I apply in these short-term contacts with acting out children in schools are functionally compatible with the steps of reality therapy (see chapter 2) and also follow the methods suggested there as long as you bear in mind the fluidity of the approach. A counselor does not do therapy "by the numbers" and apply reality therapy in a cookbook manner (Wubbolding, 1988). These principles bear repeating and amplification.

- Listen to children's stories with no judgment or criticism.
- Identify for yourself what a student wants and doesn't have (i.e., where the pain resides).
- Connect the symptom (i.e., a futile attempt at a solution) to an unmet want.
- Convey your view that the problem behavior is understandable and makes sense considering the student's situation. (Salvador Minuchin [1981, p. 43] "normalized" the problem behavior, and the Milan group wrapped the presenting problem in a reframe of "positive connotation" [Boscolo et al., 1987, p. 5].)

- Ask children to evaluate the actual usefulness of the problem behavior.
- Permit children to experience the symptom—the painful feeling that comes when one tries to achieve something important and falls short.
- Suggest safe ways for a symptomatic child to express the dysfunction more openly (except, of course, for harmful acts, such as cutting into one's body).
- Find out whether the student would like to find a better long-range way to handle things. Create some optional things he/she can do in order to meet the frustrated want and, thereby, arm him/her with a practical plan to do something different in order to take control.

If the child's family is intact and willing to come in for a minimum of three meetings, hold out hope that a longer-term family solution may be possible if the family members are willing to put some energy into the effort and try some new directions.

BUZZY: A NEW KID ON THE BLOCK

A sixth-grade boy moved 2,700 miles across the country with his parents and enrolled in a K-8 public school in northern California. The school had a strong reputation for its positive learning climate and friendly teachers. Somehow the move was too much for Buzzy, and he managed to fight his way to four suspensions in his first few weeks at the new school. The principal asked me in my role as consultant to the teachers and counselors to meet with this young man and make suggestions that the school might use in helping this hostile fellow. I will describe our first meeting.

Looking for Strengths

Buzzy's mother first had to agree to drive him back to school on his day off, as he was enjoying his fourth suspension in five weeks. I started the conference by giving the floor to the mother and began with a series of structured questions. I wanted to set a positive tone and to assess the full picture at home and at school. The mother kindly cooperated in answering my questions, which I had jotted down during the 20 to 25 minutes it took the family to drive to the school.

1. What are Buzzy's strengths?
2. What are your goals for your son?
3. What would you like to see him change? (What exactly would you like to see him do?)

4. What does he do well right now in his interactions with other students?
5. If he succeeds, who would care?
6. Who else in the family has ever faced such a challenge?
7. How did that person handle the difficulty? (Or, if this is new: "So, Buzzy is a pioneer.")
8. Is it all right with you if Buzzy works things out in his way?
9. Who would be disappointed if Buzzy succeeded?
10. Who has more luck influencing Buzzy, you or your husband?
11. Do you and your husband agree on what your son should do?

After sitting with mother and son and hearing some very clear and supportive responses to my questions, I asked her if I could speak with Buzzy one to one. She quickly agreed and left the room. In my mind, Buzzy came out of this introductory phase very well because his mother had said that he was very talented ("like his father") and that he could do practically anything he set his mind to do. She described a massive family support network that extended almost blind faith to this boy. She specified what she wanted for her son in clear and reasonable language: to expect no more from others than from himself and to be courteous to others in his age bracket without giving in. She confessed that both she and her husband had high expectations for their 12-year-old son and that each of them carried a large stubborn streak. When Buzzy had come home with straight Cs on his report card, they told him to raise his grades and, as I discovered later from Buzzy, they literally showed him their own straight A reports.

Buzzy in the Driver's Seat

Mother left the room. I began by asking Buzzy to take his mother's chair if he wished. He volunteered that he agreed with much of what his mom had said about him, and he slowly opened up more and more during our 40-minute chat. His chief concern was whether or not his dad would allow him to go back to his former state and visit his best friend who recently had gotten into some trouble and had been arrested. In his head, he thought he and his friend back east were usually good for each other because "we kept each other out of trouble."

I used positive, solution-oriented language *a la* de Shazer (1995), Furman and Ahola (1992), and Cade and O'Hanlon (1993). Some of my comments were the following: Did you know that your mother was so positive about you? You strike me as a sensitive guy who has a lot of caring in his heart. What can you do to guarantee that your dad will *never* let you go visit your friend? His answer was, "Keep behaving like I'm doing now." He confided that his dad was most upset with him about his average grades. I soon learned, however, that he was hurting for a reason that was not obvious from the beginning of our meeting. I was searching for a toehold and asked, "Who knows you best in the whole world?" My expectation was to hear "My mom" or "My little brother," but he said something quite unexpected: "My friend back east." His name? "Samuel Jordan." He revealed that his friend, Sam, would start a sentence and Buzzy would finish it. He choked back his tears as he laid out a tender tale about himself and his best friend. I doubted that anyone at home or at school was aware of his personal dilemma. If he showed too much excitement about his new school and his satisfaction with the change in location, his dad might feel that he had made the adjustment and would no longer ask to travel back to his old haunts. He faced a classic double bind.

When I asked him about teachers he particularly liked and to whom he showed courtesy and a cooperative spirit, he named one of his six teachers. I decided I could be helpful to Buzzy if I addressed his unmet needs for love, belonging, and attention, social influence, and some good old-fashioned fun. His story about his private plan to earn enough money at home to make the flight back to Pennsylvania was both impressive and touching. He would ask his father to advance him the trip expenses and then pay back the whole amount by foregoing his weekly allowance money for as long as the repayment might take. Clearly, this boy thought a great deal. If only, as he said, he could show better control of his tendency to "mouth off," all would be well. My strategy was to pinpoint his unmet needs and to help him see that he probably could pick better actions to do if he wanted to feel better soon. He agreed that he was in a double bind: If I show too much satisfaction with this new geographical area, I may never be allowed to return home. At one time, he said, "My thoughts don't happen," showing his frustration and loneliness. He said that his mouth got him in a lot of trouble. Surprisingly, he said that he liked school but that it just didn't show.

My questions were simple and persistent: What are the advantages of having your dad on your back all the time? Are you willing to learn how to use your mouth differently so it won't get you in so much trouble? Do you mind if I telephone your dad and talk over a little plan that you and I can firm up together? How is the way you treat other kids different from the way your parents treat you? After a thoughtful pause, "Oh, it's not different," he said. "They expect me to be something I'm not, and I expect my friends to be something they're not."

In light of his parents expecting him to be something he is not, I asked him if he would go along with a little experiment. If I could get his dad to agree, would Buzzy be willing to get straight Cs for the rest of the academic year? This was a shocker to him because he already was getting all Cs. He said he could accomplish that mediocre level of achievement very easily because that is what he was getting currently. I told him he could go for higher grades if he wished; however, I wanted to ask his parents if they would be happy with straight Cs because I thought Buzzy was feeling too much pressure from his family to be somebody he was not. He fought me on my proposal that he maintain a C average and acknowledge to himself and to everyone else that he was just an *average* student. The more I spoke of his option to aim low while reserving the right to achieve as well as he could, the more he argued with me about how he could get As and Bs. He took back control over his schooling. We ended the conference with three specific plans Buzzy would work on in the next two weeks.

1. One of his teachers would give him a little spiral binding notebook and he would pull this out whenever he started a verbal spat with fellow students. In place of mouthing off, he would take a minute, sit down, and write down what his friend, Sam, would do to keep himself out of trouble.
2. In his favorite teacher's class, he would come up with a tangible curricular product and mail it to his friend back east.
3. With his parents' approval to aim low, he would have the option of shooting for straight Cs or doing better than average.

Later, I telephoned his dad and suggested that he and his wife discuss the third idea and decide if they were willing to implement this piece of the puzzle. I also talked with Buzzy's teachers and the school counselor about our meeting and plans. Some of my suggestions for the teachers' follow-up work with this student got lost in the cross fire of day-to-day demands of the classroom, and we missed a step or two here and there. Working out more complex situations in a school is difficult. Adding the variables of a family making a cross-country move, the student's limited skills in communicating with peers, and some marital conflict that gradually emerged makes this particular scenario a special challenge. In the end, Buzzy's parents split up, but Buzzy attended school for the next three months and incurred no new suspensions.

LATENESS

Many schools continue the practice of making a significant issue of tardiness. The main reason for this concern is probably tradition and established practices, because whenever a group of teachers discuss the topic, they always arrive at the same conclusion: report the lateness and record a note on the student's card. As mentioned in the preface, one otherwise enlightened school district has adopted a new policy about tardiness. The district has notified parents that not getting the car started in the morning is no excuse for tardiness. Furthermore, after three tardies, the child will be considered truant.

This approach to students and their parents puts the school's clientele on the defensive and asks them to motivate themselves to come to school and to arrive on time because of the threat of sanctions. An alternative to fear is to inject the notion of natural variance into the equation. How many teachers arrive late to school in the course of an entire school year? How about management? Everyone is late at one time or another in the natural course of living. By applying the natural phenomenon of variation to the matter of tardiness, the school would determine a certain number of late arrivals as normative, 5% for example. This would translate to 9 or 10 times in an entire school year that students could arrive late with no repercussions. Secondly, and perhaps a more important aspect, the teacher would get out of the role of behavior controller and shift that responsibility to students where it belongs. Students arriving late should place a check mark next to their own name on the lateness list. This changes the conditions of the classroom and replaces dominance with trust and personal responsibility.

TRUANCY

Many people still view truancy as a crime. Schools historically define truants as beggars or vagrants who shirk their duty and avoid work or school Truants are would-be students who are absent without leave. They are labeled "bad," "possibly dangerous," "will amount to little in their lifetime," and "probably are headed for criminal status." What happens to these students who refuse to come to school? Fortunately, many educators follow Deming's (1982) management model today and realize that truancy may say more about the school than about the students who refuse to attend the school. As schools share responsibility for problems with their students, they can fashion workable solutions to the problem of truancy and gain the state funding that accompanies increases in the average daily attendance.

Sit in Some Classes and Conduct a Poll

What would happen if counselors or administrators were to sit in on classes at their schools before telephoning truant students or sending letters home to parents? They could explain to teachers that they are trying to sort out students' logic for staying home and ask teachers' permission to conduct the class-visiting experiment. One good plan might have school leaders randomly attending classes for two to three days until they have a total of 12 hours of class experience in grades K-9. If possible, have several teachers do the same— sit in on one another's classes. This method of firsthand examination also can provide clues to the roots of the attendance problem by encouraging administrators to interview a random number of students who attend and those who do not attend school. Sit down over a bag lunch with a cross-section of students and ask them questions such as these:

- What brings you to school?
- Have you ever considered cutting or actually cut classes?
- If you generally miss school, what brings you on the days that you come?
- Do your parents know when you are not at school?
- When you stay home, what do your parents say to you?
- If you could create the ideal school, what would it look like?
- Tell me about your favoriate subject or about the teacher you like.
- Can you tell me three things I can do to help you want to be here?

Deming (1982) Saw 96% of Institutional Problems as System Problems

In the past, when students did not conform, the administrators' first reaction was to list 10 ways they could pressure the students to follow the rules and fall in line. With the high rates of truancy today, authorities now must stop and ask themselves what they are doing to make school unappetizing. The problem may not be the entire school, of course, but only a particular teacher or two whom students wish to avoid at all costs. In any case, students will cooperate more willingly when educators show a more open attitude and do not focus on catching someone doing something wrong.

Counselors as Police. Recently, a school counselor told me that the school district's principals had asked all secondary counselors to resume playing the quasi-administrative role of dispensing detentions and issuing suspensions. The order from the central office was for them to return to the "Dean of Discipline" role, a 300-year throwback to "Ye Olde Deluder Act" and thrashing children who do not recite the Lord's prayer in proper Latin. Why does *coercion* so often head the list of favored tactics in institutions commissioned to educate? With alienated students, for example, or truants, or those who "fool around" when they do attend, the logic so often is simply to suspend them. If students are tardy too often, detain them so that they are late to their next appointment. If these malingerers insist on avoiding school, punish them by sending them home. The private logic in this "might makes right" practice is send students home often enough and they somehow will land back in school willingly. These common disciplinary actions and the underlying rationale are senseless in light of the goal: to encourage greater school attendance and interest in learning. The more time students spend at home, the more distant from school they feel and the more difficult returning to school becomes. Everybody knows that a student develops competency to go to school by attending and experiencing successes day after day.

Winning the Power Struggle. When we remind ourselves that many educators are worried about losing the power struggle and prefer to frighten students because of their potential for taking the law into their own hands, we can understand why schools come down so hard on truancy. By examining policies on truancy, a counselor, administrator, or teacher can discover what actually works and what adds no improvement. The principles that apply to this problem fit a quality school model and, if the school puts these new practices in place, students will want to be there.

A Case in Point: No Place in the Educational Inn

Tim was an eighth-grader who seldom attended school and, when he did show up, he looked hesitant and out of place. When I met him during my first year of teaching, I decided that setting the Tims of the world apart and blaming them for a school's failure contributed to a vicious circle. The school's job was to teach students in such a way that they would want to learn more. To reach Tim and others like him, I sent out 180 letters to the parents of all of my seventh- to ninth-grade students, thanking them for a chance to meet their sons, daughters, or grandchildren. Many became instantly defensive, assuming the worst because they had received the dreaded note from the teacher. After all, their experiences with past communiqués from school had been predominantly negative. I feel sure that Tim's mother waited before opening the envelope. As things turned out, she did open it and apparently was delighted to learn that a teacher had taken the time to show an interest in her son. I heard from other teachers that this positive contact with truant Tim and his family was a first in their recollection. She did not actually come in, but she did take the time to send me a personal note canceling our appointment. She apologized that she could not meet me in person owing to jury duty and added, "This is the first time anyone said anything good about Tim. Thank you. Signed: Tim's

Mother." I probably never will forget Tim and his caring mother, a single parent whose face I never saw.

How Does a Label of Truancy Help Anyone?

I still do not think of truants as bad and conniving. I see them as possibly scared, alienated, one-down, and insecure. I picture these students as loners who probably worry more than their share and may lack a solid base at home. If you imagine yourself in the shoes of a young person afraid to come to school because he feels unwelcome and unsure, what action would you initiate to help yourself overcome those feelings of separation and fear? In *Self-esteem and the Quality School* (1987), Greene addressed the truancy issue and a solution to this problem in a continuation high school for dropouts or potential dropouts. Briefly, they took the lead and formed small "A-teams" (attendance teams) of students and at least one adult from the school. These groups went directly to the homes of students who chose to sleep in and miss school altogether. Each visit to a stay-at-home student's quarters emboldened them further to solve this problem at the source, and some of their tactics contained the element of surprise.

Do Teachers Cause Dropouts?

A Utah researcher (Barton, 1974) conducted a fascinating study of students who had dropped out of regular public schools and enrolled in an alternative continuation high school. Her study, undertaken as a doctoral dissertation, asked one simple question: Do teachers cause dropouts? The investigator asked all of the 132 students in the continuation high school to name a teacher from their former school whom they liked and for whom they were willing to work. The questionnaire included a follow-up: "Would you have stayed in that school if all your teachers were like the one you singled out for special mention?" Almost all the adolescents in the study listed at least one teacher they liked and in whose classroom they were willing to work hard. Only a few left the question blank. As you can imagine, students also had the opportunity to list the names of any teachers they wanted to avoid and whom they did not particularly like. For this negative category, every student wrote down a minimum of one name, with most listing three to five "bad guys."

The doctoral candidate then asked the students to describe what the teachers in each group had done, pro and con. Students said that the "thumbs-up" teachers maintained a positive attitude and were congenial toward them. Also, those teachers were creative, sponsored interesting activities, and encouraged students to participate actively and even to talk about their own learning activities. In short, the teachers who would have kept these dropouts in school, if you can believe the students, did not hide behind their roles and their subject matter and showed no fear of their students.

On the other side, students described the "negative" teachers as distant, unfriendly, cold, and sometimes punitive. They never shared a laugh with their classes. They did not seem interested in the students but spent much energy on classroom discipline and inhibiting spontaneous activities on relevant topics under study.

Every District Should Experiment with Faculty Choice

Both groups of teachers then filled out a personality profile and met individually with the researcher for a brief interview. At this juncture in the study, in order to retain an unbiased methodology and to respect the participants' confidentiality as much as possible, the researcher worked through a third party who was unaware of the students' ratings for each teacher. The assessment of teachers' attitudes, personalities, and teaching styles produced sharply distinct composite scores, according to the category the dropouts had assigned. Although no one could test the students' claims that they might have remained in their original schools if more of their teachers had been friendly toward them, educators fortunate enough to launch a new school or a new program know the pleasure of hand-picking a staff and selecting only teachers who have good track records in managing for quality. Such quality schools do not exist on a large scale yet, but the few models that are operating have a negligible number of true failures or dropouts. How about giving students a choice about their teachers and giving faculty members choices about the kind of school they want to work in for the year? Baseball allows teams to trade off their apparent "misfits." Why can't the educational enterprise encourage cautious teachers who prefer to teach in a back-to-basics program to shift themselves out of a school that embarks on innovative programs? A staff that commits to the quality journey ought to minimize the roadblocks and avoid the trap of *one-upping* fellow teachers who prefer more conventional practices. Contiguous school districts may consider forming a consortium among themselves and provide teachers with more mobility and no penalties. Everybody wins in this supra-district solution to an ongoing problem. The negotiating parties can include a clause to protect themselves from any school "dumping its bad apples."

Handpicking a Faculty: Every Administrator's Dream

I know of only one school in the U.S.—Huntington Woods in Wyoming, Michigan—where a superintendent authorized an elementary school principal to take over an empty building and hand select the entire faculty. That principal, Kay Mintley, now holds the honor of directing a school that William Glasser officially has designated the first Quality School in the U.S. What an experiment! Imagine school districts applying the notion of choice on a large scale. Teachers would need assurances that they would not be left out in the cold, of course, but the educators need large scale opportunities to build a total school staff by choice. Central office staffs follow the principle of choice. Superintendents have more choice than building level administrators about dismissing marginal workers. A football coach enjoys wide managerial prerogatives. Usually coaches are not straddled with undesirable assistant coaches. Hiring and firing happens all the time in sports—in and out of schools. Management in private business certainly follows the notion of maximum maneuverability. In public schools, little mobility occurs once a teacher is settled into a district. While retaining the advantages of job protection that tenure provides, districts could allow teachers to bid on the particular schools they would like to join and on the grade levels they would like to teach.

Interdistrict trades would make this notion even more interesting. With the inevitable implementation of school vouchers that will permit parents to choose their children's schools, the clientele will be voting with their feet. Why not encourage teachers ahead of time to make the necessary adjustments to accommodate the market place? Schools with an emphasis on basic skills can gather teachers who devote their attention to this orientation. Schools proposing other goals can announce their unique vision of schooling to the community-at-large, and to the parents, in particular, and begin to recruit like-minded teachers. Teachers then would apply for a position by making a case for their moving to a particular school. Some believe this simple idea of teachers' interdistrict mobility and choice will not work soon because schools are mainly in the business of *controlling children's lives* and not out to remove the barriers to students making their own responsible decisions (Glasser, 1993).

Attending School May Represent a Break in Family Tradition

One final consideration about truancy is in order. Thinking about avoiding or bypassing school as a metaphor for students' home lives may produce some useful clues to their motivation. Aside from the notion that a child's problem may be representative of a family's struggle (Madanes, 1984, pp. 86-87), Boszormenyi-Nagy and Spark (1973) earlier developed a similar idea of multigenerational effects within the personal units called families. The main effect these contextual theorists describe is an unwritten code of multigenerational loyalty. They see conflicts resulting from family members' attempts to recreate fairness and to balance out the family ledger (Nichols, 1984, pp. 200, 222). If the parents of certain students did not succeed in school they themselves may carry conflicting attitudes or competing intentions about school. Perhaps to succeed in school is to be disloyal to one's own family and the family's tradition. In this light, such students may regard school attendance as cooperating with the enemy. Graduating on schedule could threaten a student's sense of family ties and continuity over time—no small price to pay. Truancy may seem a viable strategy to meet the competing demands, a tactic Beier (1984, p. 15) labelled an "adaptive compromise." The decision to attend and avoid school simultaneously plays out this conflict.

Like Father, Like Son: Breaking the Cycle

Some students, of course, come to terms with their parents' stated or implied expectations and enjoy their success at school. Others may attend but make enough trouble to satisfy their parents' need for loyalty: "I graduated, but I hated every minute." Some families just do not care. The best advice I know in these conditions involves two steps.

1. Ask the parents about their educational goals for their children and for public permission for their children to succeed at school.
2. Deal with the students in front of you and stop worrying about a miserable home life or a disintegrated family. You have the students from time to time, at least, and you can work out a plan for the days they are at school.

Sometimes we can get away with practically anything as long as we are willing to pay the price for countering family tradition. One father came to a counseling session at school with his son but stood for most of the hour until the supervisor dropped by and asked the father to describe his feelings about his own schooling. He replied that school to him was always bad news and that he still felt nervous about dealing directly with any professional educator, especially a teacher. The counseling supervisor told him that his explanation shed a great deal of light and that, if he felt that uncomfortable, he could remain standing until they finished their meeting about his boy. This posture would allow him to teach his son to remain tentative about his own schooling and give dad a chance to dash out if he felt fearful. You can guess what the father did next. Hearing acceptance and understanding from a school figure, the man calmly sat down and rested his case. Those of us working in schools forget, it seems, how much authority teachers wield for good or ill, what a lifetime effect their choices can have on students and families alike, and how simple the alternative behaviors are that could improve students' lives immensely.

DE-PUPILING THE DEFIANT STUDENT

A pupil is a traditional passive learner who has sat through enough systematic cajoling to decide to forfeit any earlier intentions of pursuing quality (as such) in any school. The process of de-pupiling is really a systems strategy to transform the norms that affect learners' behavior by persuading them to transform their thinking back to their first contact with the school and willingly regain their primal motivation to learn. In the process of helping your students regain their initial enthusiasm, you will probably simultaneously adjust the norms affecting your own role as a teacher or counselor. These steps take valuable time, so you first have to answer the question: is the extra strain worthwhile? Details about the six-step de-pupiling process appear below.

Is Smiling before Christmas Allowed?

Begin your deliberations by looking over your entire academic year. In most states the school year is approximately 180 days, spread over four nine-week quarters and totaling 36 weeks. This holds for year-round school schedules as well, but breaks are intermittent throughout the year and not concentrated in the summer time. During those 1,260-odd hours of contact time with students, you will spend a great deal of physical, emotional, and intellectual energy working toward goals that you value. If you had a voice, would you choose to make your life easier during most of that time?

Experienced teachers who have managed to convert pupils to learners report that the most difficult portion of the academic year is the first three-week block. They find they must continue to concentrate their efforts on a few more students for another one or two months. After a quarter of consistent exposure to a clear, fair, and friendly teacher, a class of students usually will stop playing pupil, start taking more responsibility, and become more self-directing. All of this effort pays off even more in a quality school because, as time goes by, the teachers do help students shift the cultural norms of the place. Many counselors and teachers have used the following plan, adapted from Palmatier (1976), and modified for this chapter. First, we will examine the classroom context—showing the conditions of the schools that encourage students to remain mostly passive in relation to educational goals—and, later, turning to specific instances of inappropriate students' and teachers' behaviors that keep students one-down and still very much in a power seat as they dare their teachers to teach them anything.

Three Learning Styles

Students seem to learn in one of three styles: dependent; independent; and dependence and independence pushed to their extremes, where they meld as defiance. Picture these extremes forming the bottom ends of a tight little horseshoe rather than the opposite ends of a horizontal linear continuum. The extreme versions of both dependence and independence manifest as defiance because students can use either one to engage a teacher in the power plays of helplessness or confrontation; in either case, the students are defying authority. Counselors and teachers need to accommodate each of these unique learning patterns, first by noticing the learning style of each student and then by arranging appropriate curricular conditions and an emotional atmosphere so that all students can gain a quality learning experience.

Dependence. The majority of students are passive learners who lean the full weight of their dependency against their teachers. The passive students then demand, in a way, that teachers control their behavior through a system of coercive threats and the extrinsic manipulation contained in such tactics as behavior modification (Kohn, 1996). The dependent pupil is typically well behaved in a regular teacher's class but enjoys a certain amount of "fooling around" when a substitute teacher fills in. Working with administrative support, teachers who team up with counselors can wean these students systematically from their neutral and dependent learning styles by providing them with structured assignments and gradually introducing a choice of two or more options for fulfilling an assignment. Eventually, these passive pupils can learn to make active choices and become responsible for directing their own lives at school.

Independence. Independent learners do best when they have the resources they need and the time to delve into those materials as they pursue their chosen topics. Educators naturally take pride in the independent learners that appear in their classrooms, although they may find it difficult to admit that the students do not really need a teacher for most learning. A suitable strategy for these natural scholars is to work out learning contracts with them, set up periodic consultation times, engage them in leadership roles in cooperative learning groups, and stay out of their way.

Defiance. The third category is dependence or independence pushed to a logical extreme, resulting in defiance. Overly dependent students beg teachers to determine their behavioral and academic norms. When given a choice, of course, teachers usually prefer passive pupils to aggressive or hostile students; but either defiant extreme produces anxiety, irresponsible tantrums, or demanding behaviors. One of the most effective and appropriate strategies with these students—usually about three to five pupils per classroom, but sometimes many more—is to become very personally involved with them and counsel them with the problem-solving techniques of reality therapy. The principle of solving school problems *at school* applies to this group of pupils.

Eliminate Coercion from Your Interactions with Students

Start by ridding yourself of the conventional parental roles that restrict you to playing the monitor of pupils' behavior. Read *The Quality School* (Glasser, 1992) and discuss the book chapter by chapter with a trusted fellow teacher or group of teachers, a counselor, or a principal. (If your principal says this idea is ridiculous, begin looking for another job site.) Follow these book discussions with an invitation to a peer to come into your classroom on two or three separate occasions to watch you interact with children and give you feedback on your style. If you are a teacher, consult with teachers or follow these four practices.

1. Provide an involving curriculum.
2. Establish personal rapport.
3. Create conditions that ensure personal involvement for all students.
4. Reexamine the conventional role you play as a teacher or counselor.

The De-Pupiling Process Step by Step

The first four procedures above usually remedy any faults within the context of schooling; the seven suggestions that follow directly affect the behavior of defiant and uncooperative students. You will need to spend the first part of the school year showing your students how you are not playing a role of old-time disciplinarian or boss.

1. Talk to your students often and personally. Confront those causing problems with an objective description of their behavior; ask about their ideal wants, if they could have anything; and elicit their decision to change.
2. Offer a one-week period of probation during which you require the students who are in hot water to meet you at the door of the classroom before you begin teaching for the day or class period; they then must tell you *their* plan for the day or class period.
3. Write a personal letter to any student for whom the first two steps have not worked. Keep the note brief and use formal school stationery; give students an option of showing the letter to their parents. Keep a copy. This letter will come as a surprise to the students as will the option of keeping the letter to themselves. This last tactic often proves the turning point for the better in your relationship with students who may have come to expect school authorities to work on them through their parents. If you show them the courtesy and trust to work out a problem on their own, they often will muster the energy to use the opportunity. If they do not decide to resolve the problem themselves, perhaps they

see some advantages to your contacting their parents and to their remaining directly involved with them. We all know how a problem can sometimes serve as a solution (Beier & Valens, 1975).

4. Telephone the students at home. If you still are having trouble from some students, call them at home with another surprise contact; but *do not talk about school or any behavior problems.* The student will not expect this tactic and such an *asocial technique* will turn the corner for you as the student begins thinking: "My teacher called—the one I'm giving all that trouble—and she didn't even mention my detentions or messing around." The telephone call works because you send an unexpected message and do so warmly (Beier & Young, 1984).

5. Send a letter to the students' parents or guardians expressing your concern and suggesting either an exchange of detailed letters or, preferably a three-way conference with parent, child, and teacher if he/she wants to attend. More than likely, you will have worked things out by now; but if you have not jointly resolved the problem with the first four steps, you must persist. Think of the negotiation sequence as an airplane takeoff; you are three-fourths the way down the runway and have gained liftoff speed. Why stop now? Your payoff—basking in a minimum of 27 weeks of pleasant interactions among your students or counselees—is definitely worth the initial investment of time. Students will tend to be much easier to work with, especially if they have recognized a problem in the first place.

6. If the student is a danger, withdraw the student from class, either to work under special supervision or to participate in ongoing counseling, preferably within a family setting. Readmit the youngster to the regular class only after another three-way conference. Various names have emerged for these conferences—such as IEP, Individual Educational Plan, or SST, Student Study Team—but the idea is to provide the student with a fresh start and all the resources possible to assure success.

7. Withdraw the student from the school entirely and seek an alternative learning environment that will meet personal and academic needs.

Clarity and No Meanness. In today's quality school, every educator stresses the intrinsic merit of the curriculum and knows the futility of browbeating young minds into ingesting content that students will find valuable only if they choose. "Time-out" rooms, for example, are used only as a last resort and are a temporary feature during the four- to five-year transition to quality school status. De-pupiling works best as a strategy if everyone makes a common commitment to find solutions to all problems that arise, meeting the challenges head on as they appear. Assertiveness is at the heart of most of the new programs for the enhancement of students' self-esteem and of programs designed to improve curricular fare. The fundamental change that makes the new programs especially effective is a transformed learning climate, which develops when the relationships within schools undergo a qualitative shift from oppression and domination to trust and true freedom. Quality, in this sense, is everything!

FOUR FOOLPROOF FORMULAS
FOR FOSTERING FRUSTRATION

Four conditions that almost always create a painful awareness for people are (a) unmet expectations, (b) unfinished tasks, (c) unexpressed communication, and (d) thwarted intentions. Our automatic choice in the face of these experiences is typically frustration and stress. Students always believe they have solid reasons for feeling frustrated or angry. They also may lack the communicative tools for expressing their frustrations and presenting their needs clearly and directly to somebody who can do something about their predicament. Teaching students to say forthrightly what they want and helping them succeed at no one's expense is the essence of good counseling.

Teachers, too, suffer from the same frustration when they feel thwarted in their goals. Handling frustration more directly is something teachers can learn, as many already have. One of the characteristics of a quality school is the forthright communication that occurs at all levels. Candor and responsibility are definitely the norm. To reiterate, the four conditions that always lead to the familiar frustration signal that we all experience as an "urge to behave" (Glasser, 1995) are unmet expectations, unexpressed communication, unfinished tasks, and thwarted intentions. The common element in all of these conditions is discrepancy or dissonance between what we want and what we perceive ourselves having at any moment—choice theory at work. When we do not have what we want, we entertain frustration.

Unmet Expectations

When we have a picture in our head of what we expect and other people have a different picture, we have set the stage for discomfort and frustration. Conflicting prior assumptions almost always cause miscommunication, and we could save ourselves much grief if we immediately convey our expectations of someone. In this way, our interaction does not lead to unmet expectations and frustrations for both sides. In an inservice course, if you tell exactly what you want, and what you expect, you are being fair to yourself and your instructor.

Few people would start a formal association with a professional therapist, lawyer, or accountant without first negotiating an agreement. The best-trained professionals all begin with negotiating goals and mutual intentions. On a personal level, we lower the chances of conflict when we talk over with our family what each member expects in regard to organizing regular routines and schedules, cleaning up, planning a vacation, arranging a party, selling a house, or moving to a new area.

An example of an unmet personal expectation is not knowing something we believe we should know. Knowledge is power. Everybody knows this axiom intellectually. When we conduct a computer-assisted survey of the literature and track relevant research in a matter of minutes, we earn a special thrill that comes from the process of discovery and control. If you ever studied harder than a friend and then supplied the technical information to your classmate as you both prepared for an important test, you know the special feeling of command and control. The opposite is also true. When we do not know something that we think we should know, we experience a pain signal. If we lack knowledge in an area we consider out of our realm or beyond our ken, we feel less frustration because we do not have an expectation that remains unfulfilled.

Unfinished Tasks

How about unfinished tasks? We all know that toting around a mental "to do" list and reaching the end of the day with an intact list can be a foolproof formula for frustration. Shortening the list and aiming at completing fewer tasks or putting more realistic completion times next to the tasks will minimize or eliminate our need to frustrate when we do not complete all the tasks within an allotted time frame. People who specialize in confusing motion with progress drive their lives with the fuel of an insurmountable workload that never dwindles. Then they complain about their condition. I would call this a "Sisyphus complex." After rolling the boulder up to the top of the hill a few times and watching it slip out of our grasp, observers might conclude that the boulder pusher has something to do with the cycle.

Unexpressed Communication

Probably more ulcers develop from withholding communication than from any other discrepancy because we choose to remain silent when we are burning to say something. Many of us, teachers included, choose to sit on a message we believe we should deliver and prefer to fume silently rather than say something directly to someone. We put off expressing communications and make a hundred excuses as we rationalize that the message might hurt someone's feelings, might be too hard to say, or might not be helpful anyway. Meantime, we relay the message to others. Troublesome problems result from unclear and inadequate communication that requires someone to say something directly to someone who does not always want to hear the message. We could handle 50% of the confrontational challenges and conflicts through appropriate training and the practice of assertive "I" statements (Gordon, 1989). "I want to know if you think I am trying to bother you." Many people bottle up key communications for years, refusing to tap and express these tough messages. Doing so will lead to a lighter step, a happier heart, a clearer sense of self, and more satisfying interpersonal relationships.

Blocked Intentions

Unlike unmet expectations, which reside somewhat passively in our heads, we also can develop noble plans, set out to accomplish those ends, and encounter opposition. If we weigh all the data and still decide to open a business, run for public office, or campaign for a greener earth or animal rights, we still may be frustrated. Even if we limit our expectations and allow for a certain amount of organized resistance, we still do not want our intentions to go completely unfulfilled. When we see our goals as especially noble or altruistic, we can be even more frustrated when we see those goals thwarted. Solutions are difficult to find in this arena, but we certainly will do better if we remind ourselves that we are not the center of the universe and maintain regular contact with a group of friends who do not share our convictions at the same high level. (Politicians, for example, who generally take themselves too seriously, often become mean spirited and surround themselves with "yes people.") They often become the butt of pundits' columns and the objects of scorn in talk show hosts' monologues. The trouble with enjoying power struggles is that the activity becomes a game and turns into a never ending circle.

HANDLING FRUSTRATIONS WELL

When we are out of control, we use our natural urge to behave as a means of regaining control. We will modify and realign our expectations, finish the loose ends that constantly tease our brain and drive us until we finish the open-ended tasks, deliver the stuffed and unexpressed messages we have chosen to hold in, and study the topics we should know until we gain mastery. These are rational and responsible methods for taking charge of our lives in key areas.

Unfortunately, many people go through life carting a head full of dissonant baggage and choose many solutions that only serve to recycle themselves through the loop of ineffectiveness. The answers chosen by those folks are called "ultra-solutions" because these solutions are often worse than the original problems (Watzlawick, 1988). One such example of an ineffective pattern is a young man who developed a reputation for being almost blindly angry—we might call him the "angering specialist."

The Adolescent Blamer

This story is about a boy who was driving his life with the fuel of fury. A counselor in a juvenile hall reported the case of a 15-year-old boy who insisted on staying "mad at the world," thus driving back everyone who might have helped him. He could not figure out how to meet his need for acceptance and belonging. Therefore, he drove even harder to cover his painful realization that no one really cared enough about him to come close and tolerate his constant belligerence. In some form, this boy must have met his need for power, because he was able to get others to stand helplessly on the sidelines and watch him infuriate. One day a counselor somehow made contact with him—even very closed people periodically let their guard down—and she suggested that he take some of his impressive energy and turn it in the direction of a creative project to get his message across. She told him he could destroy the product after finishing it, show it to her, or do whatever he chose to do with his work. She was trading off on their relationship. If they he were willing to trust her enough to take a risk, her suggestion might pan out with this student.

A Teacher Touched by an Angering Specialist

Surprisingly, the angry boy went to work and created a fascinating and impressive piece of work, a collage to depict his own character from all sides. His inclination was to give it to someone who would appreciate it, especially after all of the positive compliments he received when he showed it to other residents of the hall. He finally gave it to a teacher who was about to go on maternity leave. She was so touched by the collage and the boy's sensitive statement as he presented his gift to her that she cried, and in her tearful response, he could see that he had touched another human being deeply, connecting emotionally for once through tenderness and not through anger. He mattered to someone who got his message on his new frequency and appreciated him for himself. For once, he had gone outside his self-imposed hostility and created a positive relationship that mirrored his identity back to him and helped him practice being vulnerable.

Naturally, all fury cannot be handled so neatly, but most problem symptoms do encase vulnerabilities in a protective coating. Different behaviors can invite different reactions and create opportunities for different relationships. This student took a risk and stepped in the direction of life without anger. He literally "collaged" his way to a personal connection and brought a new focus to his life through a pictorial swirl.

Physical Offenses: Creating a Social Impact

One of the most common physical problems that single a student out is body odor. Body odor can be touchy because many adults are conditioned to say little or nothing about a topic this personal. Kids usually will tell fellow students how much they stink and then keep a distance from them. The offenders themselves are skittish too and may be overweight or have some physical problem. Still, when youngsters come to school dressed for the mud yard or smelling of urine or other obnoxious odors, we owe them the courtesy of a private but direct message. Often these students are defensive toward those at school who may believe they need a bath, a change of underwear, or an update on oral hygiene. Counselors and teachers know that kids often do not share their scruples in the area of body presentation and descriptive language. Take nicknames, for example. "Hogshead" and "Ratboy" are seldom happy titles, but some children have been known to thrive on "Snake" and "Fat Albert" even as the adults cringed from the sidelines.

Family Influence. Children who present themselves as physically offensive also may be carrying a long family tradition of sloppiness and poor taste. Taking the time to speak with an individual student sometimes works miracles in conveying the honest truth about a disheveled and unkempt student's impact on the school community. When these one-on-one conversations do not lead to an improvement in a given student's general appearance and aroma, a counselor might telephone the parents or guardians and request a direct conference on the matter of their children's appearance and fragrance rating. Be prepared to see a parent dressed in either extreme—either too casual or too dressy a look, complemented by excessive paste on the face or a lot of eyeliner.

Novel Solution. One father accepted a counselor's invitation to meet, complaining about his children's messiness at home and especially about their disturbing habit of leaving "floaters" in the toilet. Interpreting this habit and the father's charged response as an attempt to send dad a message, the counselor asked for the father's permission to talk separately with his children. The counselor elicited an agreement from the children to flush the toilet but to leave behind other bathroom "surprises" for dad that he would find pleasant. They themselves suggested a note of appreciation, a pleasant smelling flower from their yard or nearby field, a colorful stone—all placed on a little note card and marked "just for Dad." Who knows? Maybe all along they were trying to get him to take time to stop and smell the roses.

Back to a Schoolroom. Sometimes keeping a mirror handy for students to look in privately and do an informal self-rating on their looks and readiness to appear in public will help sensitize them to possibilities for improvement. I supervised a counselor meeting with one young girl (probably in third- or fourth-grade) whose normative condition was filthy. The counselor asked the girl to look in a mirror and rate how close she was to her personal ideal of looking good. Meeting daily before school for a week, the student improved her appearance and hairstyle each day. The counselor remembered to warn the girl not to change too fast as experience shows that resolutions for improvement and personal reforms work best when they are taken slowly (Watzlawick, 1988; Erickson & Rossi, 1981). Quick abandonment of a symptom is known in the therapy field as a "flight into health." People make a counseling appointment and then suddenly make all the changes they had been putting off for months or years.

BIBLIOGRAPHY

Amatea, E. (1989). *Brief strategic intervention for school behavior problems.* San Francisco: Jossey-Bass.

Chance, E. (1985). *An overview of major discipline programs in public school since 1960.* Dissertation Abstracts International, Vol. 46, No. 08-A.

de Shazer, S. (1985). *Keys to solution in brief therapy.* New York: W. W. Norton.

de Shazer, S. (1988). *Clues: Investigating solutions in brief therapy.* New York: W. W. Norton.

Glasser, W. (1986). *Control theory in the classroom.* New York: Harper & Row.

REFERENCES

Barton, F. (1975). *Do teachers cause dropouts?* Unpublished doctoral dissertation, University of Utah, Salt Lake City.

Beier, E., & Valens, E. (1975). *People-reading.* Briarcliff Manor, New York: Stein and Day.

Beier, E., & Young, D. (1984). *The silent language of psychotherapy* (2nd ed.). Hawthorne, NY: Aldine Publishing.

Boscolo, L., Cecchin, G., Hoffman, L., & Penn, P. (1987). *Milan systemic family therapy.* New York: Basic Books.

Boszormenyi-Nagy, I., & Spark, G. (1973). *Invisible loyalties: Reciprocity in intergenerational family therapy.* New York: Harper & Row.

Cade, B., & O'Hanlon, W. (1993). *A brief guide to brief therapy.* New York: Norton.

Deming, W. E. (1982). *Out of crisis.* Cambridge, MA: Massachusetts Institute of Technology, Center for Advanced Engineering Study.

de Shazer, S. (1995). *Words were originally magic.* New York: W. W. Norton.

Erickson, M., & Rossi, E. (1981). *Experiencing hypnosis.* New York: Irvington.

Furman, B., & Ahola, T. (1992). *Solution talk.* New York: W. W. Norton.

Glasser, W. (1992). *The quality school.* New York: HarperCollins.

Glasser, W. (1993). *The quality school teacher.* New York: HarperCollins.

Glasser, W. (1995). *Control theory chart.* Chatsworth, CA: The William Glasser Institute.

Glasser, W. (1998). *Choice theory: Redefining our personal freedom.* New York: HarperCollins.

Gordon, T. (1989). *Teaching children self-discipline . . . at home and at school.* New York: Random House.

Greene, B. (1987). *Self-esteem and the quality school.* Kings Beach, Lake Tahoe, CA: Quality Training Associates.

Haley, J. (1987). *Problem-solving therapy* (2nd ed.). San Francisco: Jossey-Bass.

Kohn, A. (1996). *Beyond discipline: From compliance to community.* Alexandria, VA: ASCD.

Liddle, H. Breunlin, D., & Schwartz, R. (Eds.). (1988). *Handbook of family therapy training and supervision.* New York: Guilford.

Madanes, C. (1984). *Behind the one-way mirror.* San Francisco: Jossey-Bass.

Minuchin, S., & Fishman, H. C. (1981). *Family therapy techniques.* Cambridge, MA: Harvard University Press.

Palmatier, L. (1976). Can the counselor improve school discipline? *School Guidance Worker, 31*(6), 41-45.

Satir, V. (1988). *The new people making.* Palo Alto, CA: Science and Behavior Books.

Watzlawick, P. (1988). *Ultra-solutions.* New York: Norton.

Wubbolding, R. (1988). *Using reality therapy.* New York: Harper & Row.

Chapter 13

COUNSELING CHILDREN FROM FOSTER FAMILIES: CHALLENGES FOR SCHOOL

Sherry Tennyson

Editor's Note

Sherry Tennyson writes about the plight of foster care kids whose lives are battered by stormy violence and abuse, culminating in tragic loss—parental abandonment. The author writes from her own personal experience as a therapist for these foster children. She highlights the range of circumstances that they endure and shows educators and counselors exactly what they might do to help the children.

A bad home does not cause bad kids, but most children and adolescents from brutal homes do not come by positive living skills automatically. They need to learn to find solid footing, set useful goals, and create some predictability for themselves. They almost always will have difficulty orienting themselves in relationships outside their natural affiliation with mother and father. The interim counselors, social workers, and educators are more successful when they normalize these children's human responses to trauma.

Many social service professionals working with children in foster placements use an endless stream of labels for the children, all of which are harsh terms. One psychological construct in the discussion is impulsivity, a psychoanalytic term that veers 180 degrees from a choice theory feedback model. A more benign view of impulsivity— a pathological term—is an interactional explanation. These children do not misbehave because of some mysterious inner compulsion deep within their souls but because they are planets spinning out of orbit in a family constellation that has thrown them to the cosmic wolves.

Under circumstances of a disintegrated family of origin or unknown parentage, almost everyone's confidence and sense of identity naturally would be shaken or practically ruined. We might say that these kids are timeless. Circumstances outside their control have snatched their childhood away from them or, at least, seriously delayed that phase of their lives. They need help forming a tangible vision of the future because their pictures of the past appear as drab collages of danger and disdain. They may see school as a constraint, not an opportunity.

The best contributions any professional can make under these conditions is to help these psychological orphans connect with a trustworthy adult, specify some new hopes and plans, reclaim their lives, and enlarge their quality worlds by creating or co-creating some specific plans and alternative outcomes. We can help them create new stories about their lives and their futures. We can work with them to fashion new families and new connections.

FOSTER CHILDREN:
BEGINNING IN A STATE OF POWERLESSNESS

Children in the foster care system take into account a number of social, emotional, financial, legal, and educational factors in forming their perceptions of themselves and their accomplishments. The number of children in foster care in America increased from 275,000 in 1988 to 429,000 in 1994 (Mech, 1994), and, of that number, 55% were under the age of 13. Many of these children remain in care until they emancipate at the age of 18, and less than 20% of the adolescents will return to their families (McFadden, 1989). Children in foster home care placements often are referred to as "nobody's children." Gil (1982) noted that parental abuse and neglect was the reason for nearly 50% of foster care placements in California. Few of these children leave their natural families by choice or because of their own behavior.

Overview of the Foster Care System

Working with children in foster family settings requires a counselor's understanding of the multiple psychological issues that affect these children.

Unlike children growing up with their biological families and natural home environments, foster children regularly move to unfamiliar environments that too often have unstable living conditions. Oftentimes, these children grow up without a sense of control and power over their lives. Instead of enjoying a feeling of choice, they carry pervasive feelings of abandonment and rejection from biological family members, and a feeling of discontinuity and inconsistency in everyday living. Outside professionals, laws, and regulations control the lives of foster care children through a court system that determines "what is in the best interest of the child." Legal authorities and welfare agencies decide to leave these children with their biological families or to remove them from their own homes. Once placed in the foster care system, social workers and caretakers become surrogate parents who sometimes conflict with the natural families. These outside interventions disrupt these youngsters' familiar home environments and school routines. Finally, foster care children have no control over the critical decisions affecting their entire lives that adults make about them.

LEGAL ISSUES OF CHILDREN IN FOSTER FAMILIES

Originally, child rights advocates viewed the removal of children from their biological family settings as a temporary solution and not a long-term and permanent living arrangement. In recent years, however, the number of children authorities have removed from their biological families and placed in foster care settings has increased greatly, due mainly to changes in child abuse reporting laws and lengthier periods in care. Extended care has included large numbers of foster children remaining in placement until they emancipated. Physical, sexual, and emotional abuse, neglect, drugs, and alcohol are all factors that lead to children's removal from their natural families and receiving placements in a foster care setting with a legal guardian, with a foster family, or in a group home. For many children and adolescents, living within the foster care system becomes a permanent condition. Lutsk and Parish (1977) found that 46% of all children placed in one region in the state of Connecticut had been in care six years or more. Fanshel and Shinn (1978) noted that 36.4% of children in their sample remained in care at the end of five years. Unfortunately, many children and adolescents live in the foster care system permanently.

During the 1980s, the child welfare system addressed two principal objectives: (a) preventing out of home placement and (b) achieving some semblance of permanence when out of home placement was deemed necessary (PL 96-272: the Adoption Assistance and Child Welfare Act of 1980). Children in foster care have numerous adults in their lives: the biological family (e.g., parents, brothers, and sisters) social workers representing the agency that assumes responsibility for the child, and the foster family along with family values and culture. In addition, therapists step in when a child requires therapy. Social workers and administrators implement many day-to-day decisions that laws and regulations mandate.

When a court legally removes a child from the home of the biological family, several alternatives for an out-of-home placement arise. All of these alternatives address the specific needs of a child or youth and may range from highly restrictive placements to settings requiring minimal supervision. Children in foster homes present different emotional behavioral educational, and social needs. In many cases, extended family members, such as grandparents or siblings of the parents, may obtain official certification to care for the child. The next level of care is a residential group home. Children placed in group homes may seek less personal involvement, thinking that forming a relationship with a parent figure may cause them only more hurt and anger. They may, therefore, display mainly aggressive, destructive, or cruel behaviors toward any adults they encounter. Professional staff members evaluate trouble and help foster children find solutions. They also provide the children with a structured environment and useful activities that will allow them to resolve their own problems and increase their independence (Zeitz, 1969).

Children in foster care interact with numerous adults on a daily basis, beginning with the biological family that may include parents, brothers, and sisters; extended family members, including grandparents, uncles, and aunts; social workers representing the agency that assumes responsibility for the child; and the foster family along with their unique family values and culture. In addition, other participants may include therapists (when the child is in therapy), tutors (when the child needs additional academic assistance), court appointed lawyers (to protect the interest of the child), and concerned adults from the community and at school.

CHARACTERISTICS OF CHILDREN IN FOSTER CARE

Berrick, Courtney, and Barth (1993) reviewed the characteristics of children in the foster care system.

The great majority of the children in the foster care system have always come from poor, minority homes (Mech 1983; Shyne & Shroeder, 1978). African-American children, in particular, have consistently been overrepresented in the foster care population (Olsen, 1982; Pelton, 1989). Other studies indicate that children in foster care have higher than average rates of emotional disorders and physical disabilities (Maza, 1983; Schor, 1982). Hulsey and White (1989) studied and maltreated children placed in group homes and a similar group of children who remained with their families. The maltreated children showed more problematic behaviors than the children who remained with their biological families; however, the instability of the children's home environment provided better prediction of behavioral disturbances. In Fitzharris' study (1985) of 10,000 children in residential care in California, results showed that dependent children exhibited many problems including impulsivity, aggression, truancy, sexual acting out, lying, and delayed social development. Fanshel, Finch, and Grundy (1989) noted sever behavioral problems among children who had seen numerous placements in contrast to their peers placed in more stable placements. Almost one third of Fanshel and associates' sample were behind their age-appropriate grade level, and a significant minority of children and adolescents attend special education classes to meet their challenging educational needs (Whitaker, Fine, & Gasson, 1989). (Berrick et al., 1993, pp. 454-455)

FAMILY OF ORIGIN

Previous research studies supported the finding that natural parents had an impact on the child's behavior while he/she was in foster care. Fanshel and Shinn (1978) found that (a) children in foster care were at risk of losing contact with their biological parents as they remained in care for longer periods of time, (b) parental visiting of children in foster care was a strong predictor of reunification, and (c) parental visiting enhanced the well-being of the child.

Their results indicated that biological parents who frequently visited their children, in comparison with biological parents who infrequently or never visited their children, favorably affected their children's gains in intelligent quotient scores and measures of emotional adjustment. The children with more frequent contact also obtained higher scores on measures of responsibility and agreeableness, and received more positive ratings by their classroom teachers. In addition, Fanshel and Shinn noted that children who had frequent visits were more likely to remain in placement. They found that 66% of the children who had no visits soon after placement were still in care five years later, compared to only 28% of those children who had had the maximum number of visits.

EDUCATIONAL ISSUES
FOR CHILDREN IN FOSTER CARE

The importance of education for foster care children calls for special emphasis. In general, these children experience numerous educational problems and barriers. The number of children who remained until they aged out of the system or turned 19 or 21 years of age—based on individual state foster care regulations—increased in the latter half of the 1970s. During this long period, these children experienced multiple home placements, especially those in group home settings and those moving from one home to another or to relatives' homes. These placements occurred, on average, five times during the child's time in care. Numerous changes in placement also may affect school placements. Children who are already uncertain in the new home setting find that changes in school are another setback in their educational growth and achievement.

Hahn (1994) administered the *Test of Adult Basic Education* (TABE) to 200 New York state foster care youths between 16 and 19 years of age in order to investigate the basic skills levels of these youths. The results showed that youths in care needed additional services in the area of educational skill. His findings showed that the average reading comprehension for the sample was at the seventh-grade level; 58% had reading levels at or below the seventh-grade level, and only 20% had reading comprehension skills at the tenth-grade level or above. The mean score for math was the grade equivalent of 6.53, and half of the study sample had math scores at or below the fifth-grade level. The Westat study (1987) found that only 34% of the black 18-year-olds in the study had completed the 12th grade, whereas nearly 60% of all southern African Americans complete high school or obtain equivalency degrees.

Timberlake and Vriend's (1987) assessment of the psychosocial needs of youths about to leave foster care showed that one-quarter needed academic remediation and demonstrated shortcomings in such areas as self-control, managing home and school learning demands, and peer and adult relationships. Youths in foster care were less likely than youths not in the foster care system to be at normal grade level by age. Only 30% of these youths were in grade 12 by age 17 (Gershenson & Kresh, 1986).

Gil and Bogart (1982) interviewed 100 children between the ages of 8 and 18 in the San Francisco county welfare system. This investigation allowed children in foster homes and group homes the opportunity to express their perceptions of the care they received, to state why they thought they were in care, their expectations for the future, and suggestions for improving the system. Though the study was not designed to compare the foster care setting and the group home setting, the results illustrated differences between these settings according to the children's perceptions and experiences. Foster care children displayed higher levels of self-esteem (though below the standardized norm) and had reported more opportunities for interpersonal relationships with friends, more positive family relationships, and a greater sense of personal belonging and privacy. This study also revealed that foster care children had very serious educational needs. The researchers reported that many of the children interviewed could not read the questionnaire with comprehension or write intelligible responses. Foster parents also reported their frustration at being unable to obtain the specialized care and tutorial services they felt the children needed.

CLASSROOM IMPLICATIONS

This section describes the issues confronting a foster care child in a classroom setting. When a child goes to a foster home, the new parents and the professionals work together to stabilize and normalize the child's new home environment. Placing children in school will give them a solid academic environment in which they can succeed. Yet the remaining ties with the biological parents and family, the effects of neglect and abuse, the harsh jerks and traumatic shoves along an otherwise typical growth and developmental pattern, and the foster care system with its cumbersome rules and stuffy regulations are all major factors that professionals need to understand in assessing a child's academic functioning and classroom behavior. Teachers, counselors, and social workers must evaluate constantly the emotional, psychological, and social needs of a child and provide the appropriate interventions as the foster care child's needs appear.

Understanding the impact of abuse and neglect of all types is critically important. Professionals also need to recognize the manifestations of abuse on a developing child's emotional, social, and educational status. Children from abusive families adopt defensive behaviors to protect themselves from further abuse. In her book, *Foster Parenting Abused Children*, Gil (1982) listed the following behaviors abused children may exhibit:

- denial of reality—a refusal to face facts, constant fighting, and questioning;
- rationalization—making an excuse or explaining something that the child did or felt;
- displacement projection—placing blame for what has happened onto everyone else, including the complaint, "It's the teacher's fault";

- reaction formation—doing the opposite of what he/she is feeling; and
- mourning pains—at the time of placement, feeling grief and sorrow, similar to the death of a parent. The mourning process has four stages:
  denial—"It can't be; this isn't really happening."
  anger (and victimization)—"Why me?"
  depression—"Things will never be the same; I'll never be happy again."
  acceptance—"Finally, I can see some options again."

Many children enter care after being physically abused or neglected. They then tend to manifest these painful experiences in the classroom environment. Gil (1982) described conditions that may appear as the following.

- Learning disabilities—Children who suffer from emotional trauma may find it difficult to achieve in school. In addition, children who have been severely neglected by under nourishment may have growth lags that cause difficulty with learning tasks.
- Speech impediments—Some children may have difficulty communicating and speaking due to the horrors of abuse.
- Memory delays—Some children may forget their next tasks.
- Hearing problems—Some children may have hearing problems.

Failure in the classroom can definitely have lifelong effects on children in foster care. Barth (1986) reviewed studies of former foster care youth who had emancipated themselves from the child welfare system. Educational problems were pervasive in this population and less than 50% of the youths who left care had completed a high school diploma or a GED. Many of them would never enter advanced school programs, and many were several grade levels behind their peers in math and reading capabilities. For the child in foster care, everyday stressors more seriously affect behavior in the classroom and in the home. After returning from negative visits with parents who were intoxicated, became abusive again or did not show enthusiasm for these much anticipated reunions. These children may express their frustration, rejection, and painful sense of alienation through outbursts in most social settings, including the classroom.

EFFECTS OF ABUSE:
EMOTIONAL NEEDS AND COUNSELING ISSUES

The key task for professionals working with foster care children is to help them learn to take more effective control over their behavior and actions. As they complete simple small tasks, their self-respect and confidence improve. Positive and consistent personal involvement from a responsible and competent adult help the children feel good about themselves. The more control and responsibility they sense, the better their chances at future successes. Trust is the most crucial factor in counseling foster care children because they often either have lost or never developed a bond of trust with their natural parents.

Long-term, destructive, unpredictable, and abusive treatment invite children to see themselves negatively. Foster children need time and help in making a successful break from their biological families and these damaging patterns. They need constant reassurance that foster care is not punishment and that they are not bad people. These children benefit, and many even thrive, from consistent validation that they are valuable human beings. A history of numerous unplanned events and dramatic changes in living arrangements and educational settings results, of course, in an unstable and inconsistent environment. These changes interfere with essential and consistent connections with caring adults, as typical of normal growth and development. Self-confidence and a healthy sense of self-worth develop within secure and affectionate family settings. When children involuntarily abandon their dysfunctional biological family, they watch their sense of self and the interpersonal role that had given them personal meaning shatter before their eyes. Generally, in these chaotic conditions, they become confused, uncertain, and furious. Living with the label "foster child" is a continuous reminder that they belong nowhere and with no one.

Gootman (1993, pp. 15-18) reviewed abused children and their behaviors in a classroom setting.

Behaving Aggressively. Abused children often act aggressively, pick fights, and rarely hesitate to hit others when angry.

Hurting others without seeming to care. Some children hurt others and do not seem to care that they have inflicted pain. Many children are hurt so often that they finally close off their minds from feeling.

Deliberately annoying others. Some children deliberately provoke or annoy the teacher or classmates by tapping on desks, dropping pencils, constantly interrupting, and going out of their way to disobey. Because they view their environment as unpredictable and never know when someone suddenly will strike out at them, these children try to overcome their sense of powerlessness by staying in an attack mode. They deliberately provoke others: "I will misbehave so that I will be in better control and, at least, know exactly when I will be punished."

Being Hypervigilant. Abused children have to remain constantly on guard because abuse, by definition, occurs capriciously. These children have taught themselves to remain fearful, suspicious, and mistrustful—always on the lookout for potential dangers.

Dissociating Themselves. Some of these children may become trance-like, appearing forgetful and frequently daydreaming in school.

Fearing Failure. Some children may give up before trying. They may cry and even tremble when facing a new lesson or activity.

LEARNED HELPLESSNESS
AND FOSTER CARE CHILDREN

The experience of living in the foster care system reminds children and adolescents of their familiar sense of helplessness and their long-standing hopelessness. Moving from one house to another is almost always beyond children's control and is seldom what they want. Zimmerman investigated depression among foster care children, following Seligman's learned helplessness model.

> The learned helplessness model of depression as applied to the children in foster care provides a theoretical model for explanation and intervention on both the individual and environmental levels. From an explanatory standpoint, children entering foster care usually come from less than optimal home environments. In many of their situations, they were powerless to affect the negative outcomes of neglect, abuse, or their environments were too chaotic to produce any recognizable sequence of action and consequence. It can thus be anticipated that many children entering care have come from helplessness-inducing environments. As a result, their perception of causation or of response-consequence may not be well-developed or may be developed in a distorted fashion. They may not view themselves as responsible for any action or able to produce any good effect. Or they may hold themselves to be the cause of their events that, in reality, had little to do with them. These cognitive distortions, in turn, limit their interpersonal problem-solving skills and impair their ability to learn from new experiences. (Zimmerman, 1988, p. 42)

Unfortunately, for foster care youngsters, their prior living experiences with their biological family have not always provided the foundation for these children to flourish. With limited educational problem-solving skills, these foster children take challenges in an academic setting and turn them all into failure. Choice theory points to a genuine alternative to learned helplessness. Children can learn that they have the power to achieve, to make changes, and to be highly successful in the classroom.

Selin (1978) pointed out that many children who have been in abusive family settings present learning difficulties and problems that may interfere with emotional growth and development. These children may present the following problems in the classroom setting:

> **Impulsivity:** Impulse-ridden children (i.e., kids who have experienced the loss of parents or who feel cheated by life's blows) cannot put faith in the future because their past has been so bad. These children cannot see how school can be useful in the future. We might say these children are timeless. Circumstances outside their control have snatched their childhood away or, at least, seriously delayed it. They need help forming a tangible vision of the future because their pictures of the past appear as drab collages of danger and disdain. They see school as a constraint, not an opportunity. Impulsivity is a psychoanalytic term that veers 180 degrees from a control theory model.
>
> **Learning blocks:** A traumatized person may be aware that certain experiences, when called to mind by specific stimuli, become too painful to bear. Words such as mother, baby, or family, for example, may evoke a blank response in the mind of one who had suffered maternal deprivation.
>
> **Common behavioral defense:** Children in foster care may use their current living situations to reenact their feelings of rejection, anger, and frustration. Littner (1978) identified three typical defenses:
>
>> **A sour grapes defense:** The student constantly criticizes the teacher. "You're no good, teacher, and you have nothing to offer that I could possible want; therefore, I don't have to worry or be concerned about losing your love." Even sports fans, once burned by a cold and calculating owners' group or a short-sighted players' association, will keep a safe distance to avoid being taken for granted or flipped on their collective ear. Children in foster care have every imaginable reason to be cautious and self-protective.
>>
>> **A withholding defense:** "I'll withhold from you whatever you want from me, so that then you'll angrily demand it from me, and this will reassure me that you are still interested in me, though you plan to leave me or give me up." The child may refuse to do his homework, follow rules, or participate in classroom activities. A translation of this reenactment language of the psyche is, "Kids can do only what they know to do." If abuse had been their norm, they naturally repeat the conflict even if this pattern serves them poorly.

Another common behavioral choice for children in foster care is testing the emotional waters warily by checking to see if adults will become emotionally involved through anger, if nothing else. Later, after passing stringent tests, teachers, counselors, and others may manage to reach out and touch one of these children.

A first rejection defense: "I'll reject you before you have the chance to abandon me." This includes running away, truancy, and unexplained absences from class. Running off also makes sense to a child whose control over life s somewhere between marginal and nonexistent. This active expression of reluctance is easier to channel and transform than the message of withdrawal and despair. Such truant children are taking steps in their best interests and voting with their feet. Resourceful helpers can find ways to reach them. (Selin, 1978, pp. 246-248)

Children will attempt to re-create abusive environments that they see as predictable, if not safe and comfortable. The adults in their lives need to help them change these harmful and unproductive behavioral patterns.

DISRUPTIONS IN CARE

Being placed in foster care brings additional academic complications for children. For many, moving to several foster placements is the norm. Abrupt changes in home placements also may mean abrupt changes in educational placements. The foster care records may be fragmented, and incomplete educational records may complicate the child's placement in appropriate classes and educational programs. Numerous changes in home placements have led to outdated individualized educational plans or undiagnosed learning problems. Appropriate home placements are a priority for these children, yet, often in the course of placement, children may go from one school to another in the middle of the school year. In some instances, schools may transfer these children to out-of-county school districts. The county schools may not always provide similar services, so the children end up in holding patterns waiting for records from their previous school programs.

These disruptions in academic services affect children's ability to adapt and learn, and many begin viewing the school environment as hostile, confusing, and frustrating. Johnson, Yoken, and Voss (1995) investigated perceptions of children in the foster care system. The findings illustrated that these children experience multiple changes at every move. In the investigation of the foster care system, only 4 out of 59 children, ages 11 through 14, had remained in the same school they had attended prior to their placement. Forty-eight percent felt that their new schools were better than their previous schools, 25% responded that the new schools were worse, and 25% said that the new schools were much the same as the former. Slightly over half of the children reported that changing schools was very challenging, especially because making new friends and getting acquainted with new teachers was so difficult (pp. 966-967).

DISTRESSING CHALLENGES

Because foster care children have many others nearby, some of their interactions at home may affect their classroom behavior. Ugly visits with biological parents or other family members who ignore scheduled appointments predictably leave children feeling helpless and worthless once again. For want of viable new actions, these children may then return to entertaining their old standby emotions—anxiety and anger. Conflict and other stressors at home—for example, another child being removed from home or a new one moving into the house—need attention from a competent adult who has time to give to the children. Children seldom have advance notice that they may be making a change in their geography and living patterns. Involuntarily moving from house to house increases children's feelings of helplessness and being out of control. Keeping scheduled court dates and visiting lawyers and social workers are not always welcomed activities and can appear as further demands to foster children.

Relationships with foster parents are never static. Some children feel guilty living elsewhere and "loving" would-be replacement parents. Therefore, in their anguish over their parents' choice to abandon them, they inevitably put their foster parents to intense testing. They may interpret these events in such a way as to justify their feelings of futility and may feel free to act out in aggressive and hostile actions in the classroom. After taking in all of these emotional twists, and not successfully managing their discouragement, they enter school with many distractions. Unable to concentrate on their studies and the challenge of making new relationships in the classroom, they opt out. They may choose to withdraw or become hostile and aggressive to cover their miserable sense of themselves and their lot.

Payoffs for educators working with these children include the bond and satisfaction that occurs when helping at-risk children. Just as they begin responding emotionally and openly take to learning, they may have to change their home placement yet again. These random changes seldom allow for children to find any positive closure at the school site, to say good-bye to friends or teachers, or to complete assignments.

CLASSROOM STRATEGIES

Gootman (1993) suggested 10 basic strategies to counteract the unproductive behavior and help the abused child increase his/her self-esteem in the classroom setting:

> Model appropriate and positive behavior for the child to learn and
>   imitate;
> Redirect behavior that is hurtful and harmful to other children;
> Help the child acknowledge pain and other feelings;
> Teach the children to express anger in words rather than actions;
> Teach problem-solving skills;
> Establish routines and a predictable, stable environment;
> Set fair, meaningful limits and consequences;
> Provide opportunities for choice and decision-making;
> Help children find an area of interest and expertise;
> Because honest, sincere, positive feedback is a basic need for
>   every human being, focus on the positive side of children's choices
>   through recognition and encouragement. (pp. 18-19)

Working with the caretaker is essential in order to achieve educational success with children. Consistent support at home and guidance with academic activities can increase children's self-confidence and feelings of worth.

SUMMARY: FOSTER FRAGMENTATION

All children in the foster care system are at risk of educational failure. Schools are either unaware or unable to track these children because of the discontinuity in their home lives and school placements. Educational systems have several programmatic recommendations that can increase foster care students' success. When schools, caretakers, and agencies that are responsible for children's welfare all work together to coordinate their services, they can ensure appropriate resources. Teachers who role model positive behavior, who help students learn to apply problem-solving skills, who provide opportunities for successful accomplishments, and who offer involvement and encouragement for activities that help students succeed will find satisfaction in their work. Clear communication is necessary. When a specific staff member who is familiar with the educational system is able to stay with a particular child and maintain the student's academic records as he/she moves from one home to another, future success is on the horizon. Lost records and incomplete files are part of the problem for those sincerely intending to provide comprehensive academic services.

Because harsh family interactions, abuse, neglect, and crises affect the personal and educational development in foster care, professionals may find this review of the numerous psychological and social factors that affect foster children in schools to be especially useful. Losing almost all power to make decisions and to control one's life results in a numbing sense of helplessness and poor academic functioning. In this frame of mind, children do not appear strong enough to want to achieve academically. They remain aware of a nagging question: "If I work real hard in school, who will care?"

All professionals will be successful to the extent that they effectively remove barriers to students' regaining as much control as possible. An enhanced sense of control will translate immediately into more confident children who create more tangible goals, tap a higher level of self-respect, and cooperate more willingly in the classroom. With teachers, counselors, and placement workers pooling their energies, they may help foster care children eliminate these powerful negative feelings and make better choices.

BIBLIOGRAPHY

Barth, R. P. (1990, October). On their own: The experiences of youth after foster care. *Child and Adolescent Social Work, 7*(5), 419-440.

Fanshel, D. (1975). Parental visiting in foster care: Key to discharge. *Social Service Review, 49,* 493-514.

Fanshel, D., Finch, S., & Grundy, J. (1989). Foster children in life-course perspective: TheCasey Family program experience. *Child Welfare, 68,* 467-478.

Festinger, T. (1982). *No one ever asked us: A postscript to foster care.* New York: Columbia University Press.

Fitzharris, T. L. (1985). *The foster children of California: Profiles of 10,000 children in residential care.* Sacramento, CA: California Association of Services for Children.

Hulsey, T. & White, R. (1989). Family characteristics and measures of behavior in foster and nonfoster children. *American Journal of Orthopsychiatry, 59,* 502-509.

Maidman, F. (Ed.). (1984). *Child welfare: A source book of knowledge and practice.* New York: Child Welfare League of America.

Maluccio, A. N., & Fein, E. (1985). Growing up in foster care. *Children and Youth Services Review, 7,* 123-134.

Maza, P. (1983, December). Characteristics of children in foster care. *Child Welfare Research Notes,* p. 1.

Mech, E. (1985). Parental visiting and foster placement. *Child Welfare, 64,* 67–72.

Olsen, L. (1982). Services for minority children in out-of-home care. *Social Service Review, 56,* 572-585.

Schor, E. L. (1982). The foster care system and health status of foster children. *Pediatrics, 69,* 521-528.
Shyne, A. W., & Schroeder, A. G. (1978). National study of social services to children and their families. Washington, DC: Department of Health, Education, and Welfare.

REFERENCES

Barth, R. P. (1986, May). Emancipation services for adolescents in foster care. *Social Work,* 165-171.

Berrick, J., Courtney, M., & Barth, R. (1993). Specialized foster care and group home care: Similarities and differences in the characteristics of children in care. *Children and Youth Services Review, 15,* 453-473.

Fanshel, D., & Shinn, E. B. (1978). *Children in foster care: A longitudinal investigation.* New York: Columbia University Press.

Gershenson, C., & Kresh, E. (1986). School enrollment status of children receiving child welfare services at home or in foster care. *Child Welfare Research Note #15.* Washington, DC: Office of Human Development Services.

Gil, E. (1982). *Foster parenting abused children.* Chicago: National Committee for Prevention of Child Abuse.

Gil, E., & Bogart, K. (1982). Foster children speak out: A study of children's perceptions of foster care. *Children Today, 11,* 7-9.

Gootman, M. E. (1993). Reaching and teaching abused children. *Childhood Education, 70*(1), 15-19.

Hahn, A. (1994). The use of assessment procedures in foster care to evaluate readiness for independent living. *Children and Youth Services Review, 16*(3/4), 171-180.

Johnson, P. R., Yoken, C., & Voss, R. (1995). Family foster care placement: The child's perspective. *Child Welfare League, 24*(45), 959-974.

Lutsk, B., & Parish, E. (1977). *Foster children: Does custody insure security?* (mimeographed). Hartford, CT: Junior League of Hartford.

McFadden, E. J. (1989). Maltreatment: Obstacles to successful emancipation. In A. N. Maluccio, R. Krieger, & B. A. Pine (Eds.), *Preparing adolescents for life after foster care: The central role of the foster parents* (pp. 163-186). Washington, DC: Child Welfare League of America.

Mech, E. (1983). Out-of-home placement rates. *Social Services Review, 57,* 659-667.

Mech, E. V. (1994). Preparing foster youth for adulthood: A knowledge-building perspective. *Children and Youth Services Review, 16*(3/4), 141-146.

Selin, M. W. (1978). Why many placed children have learning difficulties. *Child Welfare, 56,* 243–248.

Timberlake, E. M., & Vriend, M. J. (1987). Psychosocial functioning of adolescents in foster care. *Social Casework: The Journal of Contemporary Social Work, 68,* 214-222.

Westat, Inc. (1987). *A national evaluation of title IV-E foster care independent living programs for youth, phase 1, final report, volume 1.* Washington, DC: Department of Health and Human Services, Office of Human Development Services, Administration for Children, Youth, and Families.

Zeitz, D. (1969). *Child welfare: Services and perspectives* (2nd ed.). New York: John Wiley and Son.

Zimmerman, R. B. (1988). Childhood depression: New theoretical formulations and implications for foster care services. *Child Welfare, 65,* 37-47.

Chapter 14

REDUCING CROSS-CULTURAL CONFLICT WITH CHOICE THEORY

Bruce Peltier

Editor's Note

With all the current pressure to be politically correct, educators and counselors have little room for having any fun in the arena of cultural diversity. Everything is for keeps and humor is not permitted. Obviously, what we all need to do is relax and talk to one another across cultural lines. Creating a climate of trust and a sense of shared vision would do much to help resolve the conflicts in the intercultural domain.

Peltier has moved the dialogue to a lowest common denominator by applying choice theory to the topic of cultural diversity. By superimposing the choice theory constructs of basic needs, Peltier shows how all people carry a value system and all strive for the same human goal—to meet their needs for love, power, fun, freedom, and survival. Because all living beings—mosquitos included—live from the inside out and not vice versa, this cybernetic theory helps explain differences and conflicts as well as paths to reconciliation.

Periodically, I see graduate students from overseas studying choice theory and, convinced that their own culture is unique, they may reach some interesting conclusions.

Take the example of a culture that places very stiff restrictions on the behavior of individuals through its system of extended family and strong social controls. They decide that everyone else in the world can be free to make choices except people from their culture. Choice theory applies to all living beings, they say, "except Chinese," or "except Ethiopians," or "except Egyptians." The theory applies not only to all human beings but also to all living creatures. We never want things from the outside in; only from inside out— even when the want is to please our elders.

Solutions in the area of intercultural conflicts exist! Schools do not have a very extensive record of resolving conflicts of any type. Educators have traditionally laid down the law as a way of smoothing the troubled waters. This posture may interdict a crisis, but does not lead to permanent peace in the learning place. Inviting students together in small groups and implementing choice theory in discussions with them will gradually lead to a transformation with the entire student body. Talking openly about deep-seated intercultural strife is one of the most beneficial tasks school leaders can sponsor. Outside experts may help initially, but school people themselves can do this! When those who work in schools confront differences—in behavior, rule-keeping, communication styles, economics, social status, and culture—they can educate in the fullest sense of the word as they create a safe, mutually respectful, and open learning environment. Now, onto a formula for success in the arena of transcultural communication.

AMERICA: A CHALLENGING POTPOURRI
OF DIVERSE VALUE SYSTEMS

Over the past generation, our world has rapidly grown smaller as more and more people and ideas appear to share it. In *The Shrinking City,* author Lawrence Fixel (1991) remarked on the changes many Americans felt:

> It is time to acknowledge openly what has already been verified by a number of independent sources: *our city is shrinking!* And this in spite of all efforts, . . . to further various "expansion" programs. These include raising the permissible height for new structures, as well as extending the city limits. . . . As for the reaction of our citizens, it is varied. Some still insist nothing has changed. (Fixel, 1991, p. 45)

Our city is indeed shrinking, and to insist that nothing has changed will do little good. The same is true at all levels of society above and below the city, from the entire world down to a single neighborhood or schoolroom. Moreover, as populations grow and move from place to place, people now share space with those who look, speak, or act differently—that is, with other cultures or races. Nowhere is this situation more obvious than in schools, especially in areas with a large number of recent immigrants.

The California school system offers a good example, for few states or areas have had to absorb so many newcomers in recent years. As an indication of strain and frustration, the voters of California recently approved a ballot initiative that many view as harsh and desperate: refuse educational and medical services to all illegal aliens and their children. Although nothing is actually shrinking, a stroll down the halls of many American schools can seem like an international experience, as if the whole world's children have shown up for school that day. Americans cannot remain culturally isolated any more, no matter where they live or learn. As populations grow and shift, people increasingly must share space with others who look, speak, behave, and think differently. Shrinking comes to mind because the world seems to have closed in on all of us; McLuhan and Fiore's (1989) global village is here!

More than half a million children whose parents were not born in the United States now enter the California school system *each year.* The old majority (i.e., white with European roots), an increasingly irrelevant term, is soon to be a statistical minority (Ponterotto & Casas, 1991), yet many teachers and counselors conduct business-as-usual with regard to race and culture. Most Americans maintain that our school system is not segregated (and we need not *force* desegregation), that the passing of time generally results in progress, and that this is the best darned country on earth. If so, what's all this nastiness about drive-by shootings, drug-selling kids with beepers, middle school gangs, astronomical drop-out rates, and teenage pregnancies? And what does all of this chaos and violence have to do with schools, reading and math, and teacher-student relationships?

This chapter considers the cross-cultural future of education and counseling in the United States and outlines approaches to healthy school interaction based on principles from the book, *Control Theory: A New Explanation of How We Control Our Lives* (Glasser, 1984). Although this book is ostensibly intrapsychic (because the author explores the mental processes by which individual people set goals and learn to become happy and unhappy), its principles can be used to guide cross-cultural interpersonal experiences. *Control Theory* (Glasser, 1984) presents a mental health theory in a self-help format, so that the lay public can learn ways to take charge of its own mental health and interpersonal relationships. Glasser's book presents fundamental views of the human experience, and this chapter translates and applies these views to the problems and opportunities presented by the shrinking of the educational world in the mid to late 1990s.

What follows is based on the premise that mixing people together is ultimately *good* and that such human blending generates greater potential and more positive outcomes than when people remain isolated in their traditional racial, cultural, and ethnic communities. Forging a pluralistic society is apparently not something people do easily, judging from the history of social interaction in the United States, or from the warring among various ethnic groups of Yugoslavia and Chechnya and the continuing splintering of the former Soviet Union. But, if Americans choose the goal of international tolerance and interracial harmony, becoming multicultural is not something to be avoided or endured in the way that some approach the eating of broccoli. Competence in diversity cannot be viewed as cleaning the garage, flossing teeth, raking leaves, or starting a physical fitness program. Cultural mixing can be exciting and enriching, but, as with most things, the experience depends on one's attitude. Appreciating others' value systems and eventually thriving in a multicultural environment require an adventurous spirit that can lead to viewing strangers and outside things as stimulating *opportunities* for new thinking and action. Unfamiliar situations may force us to reconsider what we know and even who we are. As common as it may be, reluctance to be multicultural represents a withdrawal from life, a fearful decision about self and other humans, a retreat to old and familiar ways that used to work in an old environment. In some U.S. school districts, reluctance to be multicultural is a long-standing way of life that served as a norm for generations. Difficulties reflect the reluctance of the community that surrounds the school.

The advantage, of course, in remaining the same is that one can feel safe in the familiar ways—nothing to bother, nothing to harm, little to risk. The choice to stay put might have been viable in some places as recently as 10 years ago, but now the world is shrinking so dramatically and so rapidly that we just cannot go back to yesteryear. Drive around the United States; satellite dishes are popping up in rural areas like seedlings in spring. The latest hairstyles are beamed in from New York and the newest dance steps come into farmhouses directly from L. A. As they say, you can run, but you cannot hide.

Conflict is inevitable in this time of social transition, but we can make conflict productive or counterproductive depending upon our strategies, skills, and willingness. If adults in school can handle discord well, they will have a powerful new force in their hands. Conflict is normal and regular. Children see chaos and trauma all around them, often in glorified forms, where super-heroes save the day by standing up to violent conflict with great regularity. Children possess little real power, and guns or larger-than-life heroes offer them a taste of importance. On TV, violence seems exciting, dramatic, and fun. Children see conflict in their families and communities and may bring family ideas to potential school conflicts. Children of any age view disharmony from their unique cultural perspective, and, therefore, the meaning of conflict varies widely from one American subculture to another, most of it filtered through the medium of television.

From the perspective of choice theory, to avoid becoming multicultural is to choose misery. Oddly, such a choice may seem a sensible option, all things considered. As Glasser noted, "choosing misery almost always makes good sense at the time" (1984, p. 53). But such a choice inevitably results in negative experiences and feelings, simply because that choice pretends a homogeneity about life that no longer holds true. In fact, the world has never been culturally homogeneous, but many Americans have lived in a situation that provided the *illusion* of a world dominated by one culture.

Glasser has emphasized that people always are acting on the difference between the mental pictures they have of the world and their conclusion that those pictures are not being met. He also believed that people have enormous choice in the pictures that drive their behavioral systems and of the behaviors they use to match pictures and satisfy needs. Difficult as changing pictures may be, reframing, paradoxical suggestions, and clinical hypnosis are all powerful counseling techniques that can help people perceive their worlds differently. "Remember that of all the pictures, the only one that cannot be changed or removed is the picture to breathe" (1984, p. 234). The territory Glasser described is vast; clearly, we can choose to be multicultural.

CHOICE THEORY: A REVIEW

Glasser has proposed, first and foremost, that people exercise choice in everything beyond organic functioning. Without embarking on a journey through the psychotherapeutic literature of the past century, we must note that such a position is controversial, in part because this view of reality puts pressure on people to perform and to take responsibility for their own personal happiness. No excuses are permitted, and a long review of one's personal and family history does not substitute for the need to make hard choices and difficult changes in present-moment behavior. Glasser has turned nouns into verbs, implying that we are actively *doing* the things that many mental health practitioners and patients consider disease states. Depression becomes people depressing themselves. Anger becomes the behavior of angering. Doing sadness or crying are interpersonal performances. People choose these behaviors as part of a strategy to get what they think they want, as expressed in Glasser's pictures. Pictures are manifestations of five basic needs common to all humans who develop such pictures in order to meet their basic needs. We all exercise choice as we attempt to get what we think we want. Control is an important variable in the equation. Control itself is not an innate *need* but rather a mechanism for meeting inherent needs. We are all driven by our needs, and our ability to control life depends on how well we think we meet those built-in needs. We strive to enjoy the picture of being totally in control and sometimes we strive for that sense of control in unhealthy ways.

> Our lives, therefore, are a continual struggle to gain control in a way that we satisfy our needs and not deprive those around us, especially those close to us, of satisfying theirs. Easy as this is to say, and logical as it sounds, very few of us realize how little attention we pay to this claim in practice. . . . [M]uch of our pain, misery, and insanity, as well as many of the chronic illnesses we suffer, are our personal battles to gain control of people around us. (Glasser, 1984, p. 44)

In a repertoire of human behavior that includes doing, thinking, feeling, and physiology, Glasser has emphasized *doing* as the most central method people have for controlling their lives and getting what they want. He used the analogy of an automobile with each of us in the driver's seat of our lives. The front wheels are doing and thinking, and the rear wheels symbolize feeling and bodily functions. We can change what we do and steer our lives in a different and more satisfying direction by working on the front wheels. Changing how we feel directly is a harder task because feelings follow action.

Five Basic Needs that Drive Us

Glasser's five basic needs combine to make up the basic human motivations in this model. These needs are of two types—primitive (or physiological) and higher order (or psychological). Both types are genetically encoded in the brain. The needs are as follows:

A Primitive Physical Need. Our most basic need is to survive. This need, which includes reproduction (hormonal sex), is modulated by the "old brain" and the involuntary physiologic systems. We take care of this fundamental need automatically. Although we may assume that all children have their survival needs taken care of outside the school setting, this assumption is no longer viable because many children come to school with serious unmet physical needs for security. Some have only minimal food, clothing, and shelter.

Psychological or Higher Order Needs. The need to belong, to love, share, and cooperate is common to us all. This generic need for love and support is more complex than the need to maintain body safety, but love is critically important in Glasser's model, as he noted in *Control Theory* (1984, p. 9). Every day people kill themselves because of the pain of loneliness and separation.

Power and Competence. The need for power is another complex need that both adults and children possess in a school setting, and throwing one's weight around can directly counter the need to belong. Humans constantly assess where they stand in relation to others, and different people bring different perceptions into the school building. The need for power must be met in some satisfactory way, or problems will result. Power is also control, and a teacher can use choice theory to smooth over many power difficulties.

The Need for Freedom. Adults often do not comprehend how students perceive school as a prison. Differences in perception between teachers and students are responsible for many problems in education today. Adults know that children must prepare for the future whereas children know that they would rather be meeting other, more pressing immediate needs. Children do not feel free when compelled to attend school, keep quiet all day, and stay busy with their work. And, of course, different children are aware of different levels of freedom as a result of their experiences in the larger culture.

The Need for Fun. Glasser feels that fun is a basic need, and if not met, one's life falls apart. In a cross-cultural educational setting, fun and enjoyment become a pathway to real multicultural learning and living. Through humor we can expose our vulnerabilities and connect with others in powerful ways.

Misery Can Become a Friend

In Glasser's model, humans feel miserable for one of several specific reasons. First, "miserying" or "doing misery" is an effective way to avoid angering by managing anger and keeping it under control. Sooner or later all healthy children realize that anger ceases to work very well and that the side effects of "furying" are not worth the benefits. People also may choose misery to gain sympathy. A common alternative to anger is to become depressed instead, and counselors treat depressing and angering people differently. Many people are uncomfortable when others are miserable and will do what they can to help. Misery can be used to manipulate others. For young people, especially, feeling miserable and getting others to help can seem the best way to avoid any real effort or action, a way to sidestep the hard work required for a good life. If we adopt misery and practice using misery for a while, we may find that this choice of behavior works so well that it becomes an automatic response and we decide that this is the only way to live.

The "misery strategy" relies heavily on blaming, a widespread human tendency to attribute life's difficulties to someone or something else. "They" are to blame for my troubles. A different cultural group can make a perfect target for such blame: "I can't get what I want because of *them.*" Schools are fertile grounds for the tendency to pin the cause of our self-pity and misery on others.

Conflict as Problem and Promise

Effective people know that sharp interpersonal differences can lead to both positive and negative outcomes. Therefore, they seek to control and manage disagreements rather than avoid or welcome them too aggressively. Obviously, conflict can decrease productivity, in school or elsewhere, depending upon how pervasive it becomes and how people handle it. We can view much conflict as having a basis in group membership (such as clique or neighborhood or race). Active tension can be unpleasant, although some children and adults derive a good feeling from fights, sometimes because they are used to fighting, and sometimes because they thrive on conflict and see it as a sign of strength. Often negative attention—contention—is better than no attention at all. But conflict strains everyone and, worst of all, conflict wastes time and energy. In a school, constant disruption can ruin day to day activities and generate bad blood. Excessive turmoil can warp the real purpose of a school and absorb resources that could go into teaching and learning.

Drawing on Allport's (1958) original description of five levels of negative action that racial prejudices generate, Sherman (1990) has described the predictable manifestation of the first four levels in schools. They are (a) *antilocution,* the verbal expression of ill feelings toward other groups and their members; (b) *avoidance,* students spending time exclusively with members of their own racial group; (c) *discrimination,* overt and covert action against students on the basis of race or cultural background; and (d) *physical attack,* assaulting others physically and attacking their property.

Direct conflict also can have positive results, though at a high price (Frederickson & Kijek, 1980). The most obvious benefit of interpersonal tension is that many previously hidden or whispered feelings can surface, be examined, and get resolved. Open conflict produces a powerful opportunity to change bothersome aspects of interpersonal and institutional life, as long as the process of conflict itself does not cause lasting damage. In the face of tension and open battle, people feel pressure to clarify their ideas and differences and thereby gain new understandings of themselves and others. Conflict necessarily creates a search for new solutions—very often solutions that have previously been discarded. Conflict can get the juices flowing, stimulate interaction, and provide the challenging discrepancy to motivate people to get involved. Few things are worse for a floundering school than apathy and avoidance.

Even though much of what choice theory has to say about conflict is intrapersonal—related to the ways that people experience their own internal conflict—Glasser has had something to say about the sources of interpersonal strife. In his model, conflict starts when pictures do not match, and, of course, the pictures that direct one person in this scenario are sharply different from the pictures in the minds of others. When two or more people have conflicting pictures, they share no mutual satisfaction. Instead, they see their pictures as mutually exclusive and attempt to control others in order to get what they want. Thus, behavior and its outcomes are still a matter of *control* (i.e., humans attempting to control life), only this time it is the control of others and avoidance of counter control that is the strategy. Glasser has noted that conflict is inevitable and difficult but still insists that turmoil is a better choice than passive acceptance or misery.

Sources of Conflict. When applying any theory to cross-cultural situations, one must guard against the tendency to blame the victim. In many school systems and situations, students who are in the minority or students who came into a system last are blamed for any new problems. In a way, this attitude makes sense: these problems were not evident before the new students arrived. One way to avoid the trap is to view cross-cultural conflict from four viewpoints: (a) think of the larger culture outside the school district or system; (b) think of the culture of the school system or the school itself; (c) consider the culture of the school staff, the administrators, teachers, and counselors; and (d) do not forget the cultures of students involved in actual observable disagreement, and imagine how they might feel.

A larger cultural perspective can help us see how cross-cultural differences happen and how difficult such conflicts are to resolve. Unfortunately, American society seems intrinsically racist. The U.S. was built to some degree on the exploitation of the most recent and poorest immigrant group and particularly on people of color. Although the doors and shores of the United States are, in theory, open to all immigrants, newcomers may or may not feel really welcome. Some districts around the country have done their best to avoid the difficult task of desegregating their schools for the past 35 years. In those schools that have not avoided mixing students together, genuine desegregation has not always happened. Often, same-race students still find themselves huddled together in classrooms, stairwells, and lunchrooms. In fairness to schools, this cultural clustering accurately reflects the cultural practices of the larger society.

Today most Americans still insist that students speak English when they are in American school buildings, no matter what language they speak elsewhere. Often traditional neighborhoods that feed into public schools are themselves segregated, particularly in large urban centers, making it difficult for schools to be multicultural at the most basic level. Urban schools are often the only places where students come in contact with culturally diverse peers. At 3:00 in the afternoon, everybody disappears into essentially segregated neighborhoods, often to speak a different language, eat a different cuisine, and live a different way.

Racism, of course, is not unique to the U.S., and foreign-born children may well do worse in the schools of other countries. Children of every country have had difficulty when they found themselves in some sort of minority in a classroom. But the U.S. maintains an espoused philosophy of freedom and openness to all who enter and desire participation. On paper, Americans guide their lives by a mandate to do better, to include, and to integrate. But too often barriers prevent real desegregation. New and different students are sometimes surprised when they encounter the prejudices of their schoolmates, not expecting such a thing in the U.S. and not being accustomed to bias and mistreatment in their local neighborhoods. But school children themselves, especially adolescents, are predisposed to prejudice and are known to be hard on one another (Glock, Wuthnow, Piliavin, & Spencer, 1975). Even when schools are desegregated by law, most are not truly integrated in a deep sense. Students in the minority often become exquisitely sensitive to differences in treatment, to subtly negative attitudes, and to inequities. Thompson, Neville, Weathers, Poston, and Atkinson (1990) have documented something they call the "racism reaction" that African American students bring to the classroom from the world outside, an attitude that includes the expectation that they will be treated inequitably.

The deeper social and political sources of cross-cultural conflict cannot be solved at any school. Teachers and counselors cannot do much in their everyday work to make a difference at the national level, but they can educate themselves and speak the truth about the reality of race and culture in their country. The ways that school staff handle racism in the larger culture directly influences the culture of the classroom and school building. Clearly, educators themselves must deepen their own accurate understanding of how cultures work, especially when their values and practices diminish the values and behaviors of people from other cultures.

The culture of a school system and even a school building is obviously an important contributor to the conditions that make for harsh differences among students, and school personnel can greatly influence aspects of those cultures.

Difficult as it may be to acknowledge, teachers and counselors themselves may have to resolve their own differences and cultural conflicts if they wish to improve things for students. School staff, especially counselors, cannot afford to withdraw and become what Wrenn (1962) and Pedersen (1991) called "the culturally encapsulated counselor." A system cannot improve its functioning or adapt to changing times and still stay the same. School populations need to be desegregated and integrated at both the formal and the interpersonal levels. This shift takes planning and hard work on the part of school leaders, requiring them to give extra time and to be willing to challenge entrenched patterns, problems, and habits. Teachers and counselors do not determine the cultures of their students, but they can acknowledge and use those cultures to educate. The home culture of a child is the most important reference point for all education and counseling. To ignore that value system or diminish its importance is, at best, to waste available educational leverage and, at worst, to oppress youngsters in the teachers' care.

The Situation at Present. School administrators often find ways to avoid conflict instead of dealing with it or taking advantage of it. They perceive racial problems as "hot" and try to ignore these knotty issues. Administrators can sidestep confrontation by creating an accommodating style in the system, bolstered by rubbery boundaries and studious avoidance of direct communication. Administrators, for example, can use language that puts out fires but fails to encourage authentic change. A recent review of 40 years' worth of education journals by Westbrook and Sedlacek (1991) revealed a great deal of attention on condescending euphemisms rather than understanding and accurate concern. Nice-sounding phrases such as "culturally deprived" and "culturally different" have served to humiliate in an attempt to ameliorate. Staff then can associate with other staff and with students on a superficial level or on trivial subjects. School leaders can structure interactions to minimize events that might spark an open struggle. Such scheming may not produce explicit conflict but does nothing to produce healthy outcomes either.

APPLYING CHOICE THEORY IN SCHOOLS

Starting from Glasser's fundamental premise about humans, cross-cultural problems are solvable insofar as they result from human *choice.* We choose to create or at least to accept the conditions that result in painful differences. Many people resist any suggestion that they can control multicultural forces or environments; the thought is especially uncomfortable at a time when educators are facing such difficult conditions. Claiming some control and tackling intercultural pressures head-on is a better choice than avoidance, which serves to maintain the problem. A good first step is to accept the idea that human choice is involved in school conditions and that educators can choose to do better regardless of the conditions. No one has ever shown that adopting a victim mentality ever does any good.

Working with Glasser's Basic Needs

When mediating direct interpersonal conflict, remember Glasser's first need. As students and teachers enter a school building, they all embody a need to survive. They have a precoded genetic obligation to survive, both physically and emotionally. Because students are young, they are in the early stages of developing effective coping strategies. Staff members feel the same need for survival, perhaps in a more sophisticated way, because they are more aware of threats to the basic survival need. They are concerned about the survival of their career, their image, and often their physical well-being. Conflict often represents a clash between perceptions about survival. Mainstream students and school personnel somehow cannot understand and appreciate the importance of survival to new arrivals. Nonwhite students can be particularly sensitive to threat (i.e., based on their earlier negative experiences in the larger society) and to the way that white teachers deal with them. Conflict erupts among students because the behavior of one group is usually perceived as a threat to the survival of another group. This tension cannot be tolerated for long and even may appear inevitable, as noted earlier.

The Need to Belong. The need for closeness may be difficult to spot in the middle of an active dispute, but it can emerge from long-standing, smoldering resentments or insecurities. When active conflict breaks out, remember that one person is frustrated and may simply want to be accepted, to be liked, to belong, and has not yet succeeded. Hurt often turns to anger. Some people organize their entire personality and their typical behavior patterns around a fear of abandonment. Many people immediately reenact earlier experiences of rejection and see potential abandonment everywhere.

The Need for Power. The need for power and control is often behind active conflict. In the service of personal power, students can find ways to exercise their need to influencing others through cross-cultural strife. Students are at different ages and stages with regard to power needs, and they have had widely different experiences with the powerful people who are models within their own families and cultures. Imagine the differences in attitudes about power between the child who grows up with successful parents who feel powerful and secure, and the child whose parents lack even a minimal social impact at work. Students are astute observers of the power in all relationships, especially those in their own family and community, and some students may use an absence of real power at home as a motivation to make trouble at school.

The Need for Freedom. Students must somehow discover ways to assert their need to feel free. In schools where students are not free and where they are subject to bald coercion, they must work very hard to create a single opportunity for the exercise of free choice. They must follow rules they did not set. The very structure of a school, with its schedules, assignments, and system of top-down authority works against complete freedom for anyone, and students are almost always at the bottom with little chance to gain approval to do what they wish. Adults constantly direct them to do what they do not feel like doing and always to make a transformation from childhood to adulthood, whether students like it or not. If children were permitted to do whatever they felt like doing in today's schools, disaster would quickly follow. So the natural tension between control and freedom makes the school a caldron of potential conflict. Teachers know this, and those educators who survive best factor power into a dynamic energy that can fuel learning in a positive way. Students' efforts to assert freedom and independence must not be crushed. Those basic needs must be nurtured and channeled, putting teachers and counselors into a role of tugboat to a large, beautiful, and often clumsy ship.

The Need for Fun. Students and teachers must have fun, one of the absolute requirements of education. What is life worth without fun? But fun may be the hardest need to satisfy, for what is fun to one group may mean misery for another. Conflict is an essential part of life too, but even bitter battling becomes nasty and inflexible without a larger context of fun, humor, and looseness. A positive atmosphere for such fun comes from holding a larger perspective that the human experience, at its base, is ridiculous. We are born into a world we did not create, to parents we did not choose, and we just do not seem able to control the very things we think most important. Life might go as we want from time to time, but something always comes along to remind us that we are not really in charge. If we do not laugh, we might be tempted to cry. When teachers take the attitude that laughter is preferable to tears, classroom arguments become more manageable. When they figure out what students regard as real fun, much of the classroom battle is won. When teachers convey that everything (including themselves) is always serious and important, they inject rigidity and phoniness, creating an atmosphere that is at once both numbing and explosive. That point of view contains no leeway. When people with different perspectives clash, they need room to find a new equilibrium. When we acknowledge that we are all a little silly, we generate the space to breathe, and the *room* we need to acknowledge others. A major concern in this area of enjoyment is that what is fun for one person can be humiliating to another, but the bottom line is that humor in a climate of trust and support allows us to be vulnerable and helps us grow.

Mental Pictures

Another important component of choice theory, and Glasser's own way of explaining any conflict, is his metaphor of pictures.

> But when we start out, none of us knows what we want; we only know we desperately want something—so we scream, cry, pout, or thrash about randomly to try to get it. The way we learn what we want is: When what we do gets us something that satisfies a need, we store the picture of what satisfied us in a place in our heads. . . . This means that we store in our personal picture albums the pictures of anything in the world that we believe will satisfy one or more of our basic needs. (Glasser, 1984, pp. 20-21)

To understand a person using choice theory, we must cipher the pictures in that person's head, specifically in their Quality World. These are not just images or memories, but goals for life, and they dictate the micro and macro strategies a person selects in making moment-to-moment behavior choices.

Each of us brings a unique set of perceptions or pictures to the school building and to interpersonal interactions. The very concept of different cultures presupposes different sets of mental pictures and accompanying attitudes. Each of us thinks that our pictures represent the truth, and each of us is liable to fight for them. People want others to acknowledge and respect their pictures. Adults often dispute the pictures of children or assume the existence of only one standard set for all youngsters. Adults can learn valuable lessons about themselves and others if they do not simply shrug off children's reports of their own reality. Such open explorations help students learn how humans work, think, and feel. Others' worldviews are wondrous and should not be diminished or discarded. Chronic conflict is often the result of a perception that one's pictures are threatened. These pictures can become powerfully embedded in the brain if one thinks that others are trying to change them or steal them away. When teachers take the time to explore their students' pictures, dysfunctional pictures can be adjusted or discarded by their owners. Learning about the pictures of students from other cultures can give teachers great insights; conflict itself opens the door to a learning laboratory about students' unique ways of seeing the world. Behavior that appeared to be automatic can become the subject of introspection, and this personal evaluation can result in a rational behavioral choice that enhances one's self-esteem.

Choosing Misery

Students who are depressed and too quiet put experienced teachers on alert because such withdrawn behavior often means that the students are avoiding strife and not resolving their differences. Passivity can mislead school staff (as well as parents) who mistakenly may suppose that they are successful in managing the student body. Teachers often prefer passive and withdrawn students over those who act out because they know they can ignore the "flat" students and isolate and handle the "rowdies." Adults in and out of schools seek at all costs to avoid wild and out-of-control behavior. The sad reality, though, is that many of the students who choose quiet misery over open battles do not always stay in school. They often follow their vocal activist friends to prison. When the adults in schools notice a student withdrawing and becoming emotionally flat, they have a duty to intrude, provide a friendly ear, and perhaps to make an immediate referral to a counselor.

Educating is not for the faint of heart. By nature, schooling means change, and change is a rough-and-tumble enterprise. Learning means continually adding new pictures as well as changing the ones that are no longer useful. Such a process means a bumpy ride for most people. We do not easily give up what we already know. Educated people, by definition, are cognitively flexible and ready to consider each new situation on its own merits. Tidy schooling does not foster this tendency. Intellectual flexibility results when teachers encourage reasoned disagreement while demonstrating their own assertiveness. Teachers can encourage students to disagree with them, and they can model effective ways to debate. One way to facilitate this emphasis on flexibility is to expose students to examples of sharp and weak debaters in the media—for example, political pundits, national talk show hosts, and spokespersons for various causes and movements. They can encourage students to take each other on and can facilitate healthy interaction when students challenge one another. An "I'm right and you're wrong" statement is the hallmark of ignorance. Educators must find ways to foster healthy answers to challenges, for this is one of the best opportunities for learning that a school can provide.

From Glasser's perspective, many students choose misery to dodge a harsher form of conflict. They choose to feel sad, ill, or bummed out as a way to manage anger and keep that bitter feeling under control. Why avoid anger? Because of a general perception that one would lose all control and the result could be devastating. Students may have seen the terrible impact of anger in their own homes—perhaps in a dangerous situation—so that even anticipating anger legitimately frightens them. Children may have encountered so much anger that they are simply sick of it. Conversely, they may have learned that anger is bad or dangerous because they grew up in a family that allowed no overt expression of anger. Children from such families are often clueless about expressing their own feelings; thus, they shut down and become spectators of the world of human interaction. They incorporate a television version of conflict, where disagreement is settled with fists and guns, and they cannot even imagine themselves engaged in such a process. Anger threatens survival.

Misery is a way students can get attention in school and broadcast their needs to anyone who will listen. Perhaps they can also manipulate innocent bystanders without resorting to a direct show of force as others look on, too dazed to mount a respectable challenge. Whether students bring these tactics from home or discover them in school, miserying is not a path to useful learning. Often students choose misery to avoid a difficult or taxing activity; but one lesson of adulthood is that life and learning require effort, perhaps *enormous* effort. Humans naturally and normally avoid difficulty, and an ambitious child stands out as an anomaly among peers.

Glasser also figured out that students choose misery to control others. Children may have learned this power play at home or from friends in or out of school. Teachers and counselors must thwart this strategy, insisting instead that students face their conflicts and learn to handle them constructively, rather than passively, hoping that they will vanish or that others will come along and fix their problems. School is a good place to learn alternatives to misery, and school professionals bear the burden of teaching this lesson through example and involvement.

Choice, Responsibility, and Conflict

As might be expected, applying choice theory to the issue of cross-cultural conflict requires that sooner or later all students take absolute responsibility for their own behavior, feelings, and thoughts. They must learn first to act directly on behalf of their personal needs, as expressed by their own unique pictures, and then to notice the needs of others. Counselors must peacefully and effectively assist teachers to ensure that students learn to meet their needs. No one can be allowed to block the process or subvert the striving of students who act on their own interpersonal problems. In the cross-cultural arena, however, complications are sure to emerge. For one thing, we all have stereotypes and resentments, acknowledged or not. These predispositions influence our pictures and the ways we perceive the behaviors and motives of others. Student prejudices play a huge and often subtle role in the face of a cross-cultural explosion.

Administrators, teachers, and counselors who intercede in cross-cultural arguments or battles must first *acknowledge* the role of cultural stereotypes in the interpersonal environment of the school and not turn a blind eye to racism as some schools have done. Denying that negative attitudes toward race have any significant role in students' relationships is part of a long American tradition. Fearing outside critics who might find fault if a teacher acknowledged stereotypes or prejudice in the daily life of the classroom seems to encourage a pretend-world that promotes lying and avoidance in the face of stress. Teachers, students, counselors, and administrators need to work out their own prejudices and overcome fears of stable and ongoing cross-cultural relationships. When it comes to understanding our perceptions of race and our attitudes toward people different from ourselves, we never arrive; we continue to seek to discover.

Basic Conflict Management Skills: Mediator versus Arbitrator

Educators sometimes collude with students to avoid dissension because they themselves are not comfortable with any form of cross-cultural tension. They can replace their undying commitment to avoiding cross-cultural conflict with efforts to manage these harsh collisions so that students learn from the negative experiences. Good conflict management can turn a problem into an opportunity for growth. The fact that the cross-cultural aspects of any situation tend to complicate things highlights the importance of basic conflict management skills. (See chapter 18 on conflict management.) Helping conflicted parties examine differences and similarities in their respective pictures is a key skill in conflict resolution.

In any active conflict, counselors first must decide whether they will act as mediator or arbitrator. In fact, school managers may require teachers and counselors to take each of these roles from time to time. A *mediator* is a third party to a disagreement who helps conflicting parties reach a mutually acceptable position or agreement. An *arbitrator* is someone who listens to positions, gathers information, decides what the eventual resolution of the conflict should be, and imposes that decision on the conflicting parties. One essential difference in the two roles is that the mediator is more likely to deal with the perceptions, pictures, and irrational and emotional reactions of the parties as he or she acts to help the parties understand each other. An official arbitrator must hear and understand accurately the perceptions and positions of all parties but is especially responsive to the administrative and structural needs of the classroom and school system in reaching a decision. Of the two roles, mediation seems the more likely to be informed by choice theory.

Counselors and Teachers as Mediators

To make strife and the resolution of conflict a learning process, counselors and teachers can help in the following specific ways.

1. Lay groundwork for communication between parties. Ideally, communication is continuous in the school environment but can be enhanced when active conflict breaks out. It must be clear that all parties will be respected throughout the process, and all parties must be encouraged to listen and reconsider perceptions. A breather sometimes can help to de-escalate tension or hostility but is seldom a long-term solution. Eventually, counselors must deal with conflicts and issues in real time, not just for brief moments in hallways or on breaks. They must also establish ground rules for interaction and discourage escalating behaviors.

2. Help the parties accurately define issues and perceptions. Most teachers possess the skills to do this critical work, provided they are willing. Teachers must not discount any perceptions even in the midst of a real dispute but must help the combatants to be specific and accurate if they are to resolve the problem. Obviously, school staff need to remain in a reasonably neutral role. This can be especially difficult in cross-cultural situations, because each of us communicates from our own cultural and racial perspective. Most likely, the student who comes from a cultural perspective different from the mediator's will feel resentment and insecurity during the process.

3. Help conflicting parties express their anger and frustration by clarifying their feelings. Sorting out confusion, defensive behaviors, and harsh feelings requires that teachers understand emotions and their function in cross-cultural conflicts. Educators must identify, respect, and accept the feelings of those in a conflict. Past hurts and misperceptions can be aired and modified or left behind.

4. Moderate communication. Once the groundwork is laid, the mediator can help students speak and listen to each other. Simple things like helping each person speak his or her mind, complete all thoughts, and listen to each other can make a significant difference in cross-cultural misunderstanding. Teachers can ensure that each person gets to speak without interruption. Explosive comments and impulsive statements can be analyzed, understood, and defused so that they can be additional tools for learning instead of damaging forces.

5. Help maintain a balance of power. Power in schools is out of balance right from the start. Teachers, then, must take an active role in establishing a level playground for the healthy resolution of conflict. Students are keenly aware of their relative social status and one problem

with conflict in the school is that students rarely possess equal interpersonal power. Adults need not agree with student perceptions but
can use their higher status to listen to those in lower positions. They
can apply their weight as adults to balance the equation in a realistic
way throughout the system.

6. Moderate the content of discussion. An adult third party also can bridge
   the irrationality and strong feelings that may accompany cross-cultural
   strife. All school personnel can mediate fights and can help parties move
   from absolute positions to more moderate and realistic ones. Teachers
   can adjust their own pictures, and when they make these changes, they
   will see the other group as more rational.

7. Modulate the tension. An optimal level of tension for effective resolution exists in any dispute. A teacher or counselor can help maintain the
   most productive amount of tension. Conflicted parties must feel enough
   tension to be motivated to work toward resolution but not so much that
   they act out of rage, frustration, or passive acceptance. Conflict resolution does not work very well when parties feel too little tension, give
   up prematurely, and then resent the outcome later. When tension is too
   high, mediators can work on less loaded side issues, modeling the appropriate expression of humor. When tension is too low, a mediator
   can remind students of the seriousness of the situation or of potentially
   important outcomes.

8. Provide problem-solving skills. Counselors can work with teachers to
   suggest problem-solving strategies that students have not yet learned.
   Adults generally know more about diverse options for solving problems, and teachers routinely are watchful of their students' special concerns. Why not reach out to students on a topic they are constantly
   monitoring within their Quality World—the matter of surviving without danger or threat?

Establishing the Best Milieu

Teachers can take steps to enhance a cross-cultural classroom and move
toward more healthy relationships among students, staff, and students. A healthy
environment increases the possibility that any future conflict will contribute
positively to the learners. Continuous growth is obviously preferable to a crisis-
oriented mentality.

First, adults will succeed to the degree that they are in agreement with the
approach they adopt. Teachers can present the goal of a healthy cross-cultural
atmosphere in such a way that each person perceives potential benefit. Everyone's life gets better, more interesting, more realistic, more varied, and more

connected to others. As in most things in life, success depends on the attitudes of the players and their ability to keep the experiment from becoming a chore and a bore. Cross-cultural immersion of all adult staff in the school can be enriching, especially if it includes relevant one-on-one exchanges across cultures (Mio, 1989). To make sure these ventures do not become intimidating, teachers themselves can establish them on a person-to-person footing. Any time the approach seems a sacrifice or plain hard work (i.e., to take care of those unfortunate "others"), the plan is likely to fail, even if the new program appears to succeed at first. Some will resist, and some will have trouble viewing a multicultural atmosphere as better. Some will be inclined to protect the status quo, feeling threatened by change and difference. In Glasser's model, their picture is crucially important, for many fear that they will somehow be worse off in an enhanced multicultural environment. When the power structure of a school is truly invested in healthy cross-cultural change, the staff can deal with any resistant faculty members. When the principal and superintendent are not behind the idea of a healthy cross-cultural environment, the task is obviously more difficult for the staff.

In fact, some schools find that, when they include *all* adult staff in the process, they receive unexpected benefits such as what happens when custodial staff and security staff make rich contributions to a positive racial atmosphere. People in those positions can act as informal mentors and models for effective cross-cultural behavior. Imagine the influence that a perceptive janitor can have on a hallway fight if he or she has been up and down those same hallways day after day, interacting casually with students, especially when students know that the janitor has no vested interest in disciplining them. They get to see what students are like when teachers and principals are not around. Security personnel often *really* know what is going on in the building and in the surrounding neighborhood and can establish ongoing, informal relationships with students. They usually have a better feel for the emotional and racial atmosphere and relational temperature of a school building. Select them carefully and include them in planning and training so that they know that their role is unique and valued. Counseling staff are important players, too. Cross-cultural issues and approaches can be central to all that they do, and the cultural background of each student must be seen as an asset. Individual teachers can establish individual relationships with students who are powerful figures in the informal social structure of the student body.

Effective teachers are willing and able to handle cross-cultural problems at the level of the classroom, of course, but this requires more than their consent and enthusiasm. Teachers may require additional training. When a classroom is suddenly quiet for no apparent reason (i.e., when the norm for that classroom is noisy), a smart teacher is ready to call attention to the process and knows when to push long enough to find out what is going on. When students scuffle or make verbal attacks on each other, competent teachers are able to intervene in a way that keeps a class on track and provides a learning experience for combatants and observers alike. This is not easy.

Racial slurs and cultural disrespect cannot be ignored because these overt violations of school and societal norms have been known to touch off major crises. Students also will test teachers to see where they stand on this issue and will adjust their own behavior and values according to teachers' statements and actions. When one student uses a racial slur, culturally adept teachers know when to turn the incident into a learning lab, when to discipline the offender, or when to do both. A series of case examples of the ways that teachers have handled vexing cross-cultural experiences in the classroom are reported by Shulman and Mesa-Bains (1990).

A second principle is that adults must tell the truth about race and culture. Facing this reality is not easy because the truth is rarely pretty or easy to discern. Students can tell when adults are committed to honesty, and it makes everything in the classroom go better (Kottler, 1992). This means, for example, that teachers find a way to tell the truth about their own experiences and their own private pictures, that they are blunt and honest about the cross-cultural aspects of the lessons they present, and that they tell the truth when they describe how the world and the local community works. Naturally, teachers and counselors have to learn the multicultural aspects of their subject matter. Teachers may have to adjust the lessons provided by textbooks when they are not accurate or when they do not tell the whole story about a racial group or a particular historical event. Models for such teaching and training are available in the literature at present (Anderson & Cranston-Gingras, 1991; Byrd & Constantinides, 1986; Christensen, 1989; Garcia & Wright, 1989; Pedersen, 1988, 1991; Sue, 1991). Teachers also can learn new ways to reach students whose optimal learning style derives from a different culture.

Third, every school and district would benefit from the establishment of a working plan to enhance the multicultural atmosphere. A comprehensive plan could attend to numerous areas in the system such as employment patterns, assignment patterns (of teachers as well as students), allocation of resources, lesson planning, text selection, inservice workshops, theme days and the handling of holidays, the involvement of parents and local members of the community, and special training that students could take. Such training must begin early in the educational process, as there is evidence that multicultural approaches can be effective as early as the preschool years, as soon as children are capable of concrete thinking (Ponterotto, 1991). Many systems already have such a plan, and some follow it slavishly. It is best done in a cooperative way, avoiding contention and bringing cross-cultural aspects of the school into the general planning of education. Obviously cross-cultural conflict is more liable to be a healthy, ongoing process when the racial make-up of the teaching staff bears some relationship to the racial makeup of the student body and community (although this does not ensure success). Other steps school leaders can take include choosing textbooks carefully for their multicultural value, implementing a fair discipline policy, and involving students and teachers in setting reasonable rules so that they feel some influence over the norms that affect them. Finally, a school will be healthier if students and staff will not tolerate stereotyping or inequity in power or the allocation of resources.

A comprehensive multicultural plan includes a peer mediation system. When there is a conflict, one of the early steps in resolution can require formal peer involvement. Complainants appear before a board to state their claim and make their case. If they feel offended, they can present the offense in front of a trained board of peers who can hear all parties, sort out the details, and help them work out an acceptable solution. The school system can provide peers with appropriate training that can have a ripple effect on others in the student body. Peer mediators can hold a position of prestige in the school community, and the views and cultural perspectives of all school groups can be represented on the board. Thus, when one student accuses another of, for example, the theft of his jacket, he could bring the matter in front of the peer board before it smolders too long or explodes into a nasty cross-cultural event involving many more students. When a student imagines that another stole his or her boyfriend or girlfriend, he or she can discuss the matter openly in front of a panel of peers, and all parties can contribute to the discussion. A similar group of representative peers can examine all matters of school turf.

The ways that students are "tracked" in a school can be examined as part of this plan. The African American student who is troublesome to a teacher cannot be placed into a program for the emotionally disturbed as a solution. Stereotyping is so easy to do in schools, and when students are, in effect, resegregated, stereotypes harden.

Lastly, a clear code of conduct can make a significant difference. Explicit expectations, written down and discussed, provide guidelines that everyone can follow. All parties in a school can have input to the code so that they will be able to feel a sense of ownership. When behavioral expectations are made clear, conflict and bad feelings can be avoided. Students need a forum for discussion and examination of the behavioral code.

Choice theory, a cybernetic (i.e., automatic or self-propelling) description of cognitive processing, directly applies to cross-cultural relationships and conflict in a school. *This theory can be taught to students.* In this model, people choose their thinking, feeling, and behavior, including the misery they display. Choice is based upon a perception of basic needs as filtered through pictures held dear. When a person examines and accepts these needs and wants, peace can prevail. People also can take pictures out of the picture album and put in new ones. Educators struggling with intercultural conflict can create a new vision of harmony. School professionals make the mental picture of harmony a reality when they take an active role in mediating the natural conflicts that derive from the competing needs and pictures perceived by two or more people. Cross-cultural conflict can become an asset in the educational process of all Americans. Nothing related to cross-cultural counseling is particularly simple or easy to do, but at the minimum, race and culture need to remain priority topics. School can become an effective, low-risk place to prepare youngsters for the inevitable cross-cultural interactions and conflicts they will encounter as adults in a rapidly shrinking world. Although some schools do well in these areas, if creating multicultural harmony were easy, all schools would be models of cross-cultural accord. Even as society demands more from teachers than from the general citizenry, state legislatures cut school funding and other resources. The twin threats of discouragement and alienation lurk in the academic hallways and teachers' lounges of many of America's schools today; withdrawing to pictures of the past is not a viable option.

REFERENCES

Allport, G. (1958). *The nature of prejudice.* New York: Addison-Wesley.

Anderson, D. J., & Cranston-Gingras, A. (1991). Sensitizing counselors and educators to multicultural issues: An interactive approach. *Journal of Counseling & Development, 70,* 91-98.

Byrd, P., & Constantinides, J. C. (1986). *Teaching across cultures in the university ESL program.* Washington, DC: National Association for Foreign Student Affairs.

Christensen, C. P. (1989). Cross-cultural awareness development: A conceptual model. *Counselor Education and Supervision, 28,* 270-287.

Frederickson, K., & Kijek, J. (1980). *Crisis events: Developmental potential.* New York: School of Education, Health, Nursing and Arts Professions, New York University.

Fixel, L. (1991). The shrinking city. In G. Boyd (Ed.), *Unscheduled departures* (p. 45). Santa Maria, CA: Asylum Arts.

Garcia, M. H., & Wright, J. W. (1989). Communication and multicultural awareness: An interactional training model. *Journal of Counseling and Human Service Professions, 3*(2), 29-39.

Glasser, W. (1984). *Control theory: A new explanation of how we control our lives.* New York: Harper & Row.

Glock, C. Y., Wuthnow, R., Piliavin, J. A., & Spencer, M. (1975). *Adolescent prejudice.* New York: Harper & Row.

Kottler, J. (1992). Confronting our own hypocrisy: Being a model for our students and clients. *Journal of Counseling & Development, 70,* 475-476.

McLuhan, M., & Fiore, Q. (1989). *The medium is the message.* Portland, OR: Touchstone Press.

Mio, J. S. (1989). Experiential involvement as an adjunct to teaching cultural sensitivity. *Journal of Multicultural Counseling and Development, 17,* 38-46.

Pedersen, P. (1988). *A handbook for developing multicultural awareness.* Alexandria, VA: American Association for Counseling and Development.

Pedersen, P. (1991). Multiculturalism as a generic approach to counseling. *Journal of Counseling & Development, 70,* 6-11.

Ponterotto, J. G. (1991). The nature of prejudice revisited: Implications for counseling interventions. *Journal of Counseling & Development, 70,* 216-224.

Ponterotto, J. G., & Casas, J. W. (1991). *Handbook of racial/ethnic minority counseling research.* Springfield, IL: Charles C. Thomas.

Sherman, R. L. (1990). Intergroup conflict on high school campuses. *Journal of Multicultural Counseling and Development, 18,* 11-18.

Shulman, J. H., & Mesa-Bains, A. (1990). *Teaching diverse students: Cases and commentaries.* San Francisco, CA: Far West Laboratory for Educational Research and Development.

Sue, D. S. (1991). A model for cultural diversity training. *Journal of Counseling & Development, 70,* 99-105.

Thompson, C. E., Neville, H., Weathers, P. L., Poston, W. C., & Atkinson, D. R. (1990). Cultural distrust and racism reaction among African-American students. *Journal of College Student Development, 31,* 162-168.

Westbrook, F. D., & Sedlacek, W. E. (1991). Forty years of using labels to communicate about nontraditional students: Does it help or hurt? *Journal of Counseling & Development, 70,* 20-28.

Wrenn, C. G. (1962). The culturally encapsulated counselor. *Harvard Educational Review, 32,* 444-449.

Chapter 15

STREET GANGS: COPING WITH VIOLENCE IN SCHOOLS

Morgan Peterson

Editor's Note

Gangs can be a security blanket to insiders and a source of terror to outsiders. Young and not so young have resorted to affiliating in suprafamily clusters to meet their personal needs and to find protection from a society that harbors increasingly dangerous elements. Members often meet all of the basic psychological needs in a gang—love and belonging, power and competence, fun and diversion, and freedom from social oppression, fear, racism, and even family domination. Gangs seem to afford young people a chance to enhance their personal and social power. Knowing this may create a challenge for us because I believe that most people hear the word power and immediately think abuse of power. If educators can figure out how to provide appropriate ways for students to express social influence, the need for reckless and destructive gang members' behaviors subsides.

Having worked in various professional fields—police, detective, social work with juvenile delinquency, and now educator, consultant, and psychotherapist—that have brought him face-to-face with this sociological dilemma, Dr. Morgan Peterson taps a long history of experiences and literature in presenting the story and suggesting solutions. He traces the development of ganging behaviors in America, highlights some of the tragic consequences, and points to management strategies that teachers, counselors,

381

*and school administrators may employ in making schools safe and even quality learn-
ing places. Readers no doubt will vary in their own personal experiences with the gang
problem in schools. Some may see this paper as too mild, whereas others may say that
they wish their problems were this mild.*

*This chapter depicts some serious gang activities. Not all schools currently face
extreme violence. Some do not directly observe students wearing colors to school or
flagrantly toting weapons into the classroom, but most educators do confront other kinds
of gangs and all have firsthand experience with the more subtle cliques. Some of these
groups also might present vicious long-term effects on young children whom teachers
are trying to teach. This less violent type of gang may be more prevalent in the younger
grades and teachers may still be able to influence their students to find alternatives to
danger and acting out behaviors. To one degree or another, today we all have to add
some counseling and some clinical social work skills to our professional repertoires.
We also need to tackle the problem of gangs as a team of educators and not as correctional officers or lone sheriffs. Keeping in mind that no one can empower another
person—only remove the barriers to their empowering themselves—let's take a look at
this serious problem for schools.*

THE GANG PROBLEM

The radio boomed in my ear, "Shooting at 24th and Broadway; person down;
possible gang fight." I hit the switch, and the red lights and siren pierced the
quiet night. I threaded my way rapidly through traffic thinking, "This is the
fourth gang-related shooting this weekend." Two victims had been innocent bystanders; all had been kids.

Arriving at the scene, I found a 13-year-old girl hunched over the body of
a boy who appeared to be 11 or 12. The girl sobbed, "Please, help my brother,
Jesús; he has been shot." The ambulance arrived at that moment and I gently
eased the girl away from her brother. She buried her head in my chest and
cried. The paramedic checked the boy's eyes for any sign of life and felt for a
pulse, but with a sigh of resignation, confirmed the obvious. Jesús was dead!

I took Jesús' sister, Stella, home to her mother and, as I had done many
times before, informed a mother that her son was dead as a result of a shot, we
thought, fired by a rival gang member. The mother, Teresa, cried, of course,
but she seemed to convey a sense of fatalism. Teresa wanted to talk. This evening was not the first crisis that had happened in the family, and tonight would
probably not be the last. Pedro, a brother, and Nacho, a cousin of Teresa, had

been killed in a drive-by shooting in the past. Teresa said that Jesús was 11 years old and had been talking about being in a gang since he was seven years old. His older brother, an uncle, and a cousin currently were active members of the "29th Street gang," and up until 10 hours before his death, Jesús had been a member of the gang's auxiliary (a part of the gang for younger boys, ages 7 through 10). You see, Jesús had been initiated into the gang just 10 hours before he was killed.

I observed this incident firsthand while I was a member of the San Francisco Police Department. I am not suggesting that teachers join a law enforcement agency, but I do think knowing the real world context for many children today will help teachers be more realistic in their efforts to be supportive friends and effective teachers and managers. Another point by way of background is that gangs are not new. History is filled with documentation on prison gangs, thieves' guilds, pirates' clubs, criminal secret societies, the Mafia, and the sinister tong hatchet assassins. The issue here is what can a school do to protect itself and to create opportunities for all students to engage in quality learning.

Thousands of gangs exist: Crips, Bloods, Rolling 60's, Bounty Hunters, Wah Chings, Locos, and La Arizona, to name only a few. Total membership exceeds a million gang members in the U.S. Members range in age from 8 to 55, with an average age of 17 to 18 (L. R. Price, 1989). These new groups, often a substitute for a disintegrated or marginal family, roam the halls and grounds of schools at all grade levels and, later on, sullenly fill the dank cell blocks and exercise yards of jails, juvenile halls, and prisons. They wear distinctive colors on their bandannas and jackets, develop code words and hand signals, and intensify their rebellion whenever any authorities try to control their behavior. In choice theory terms, gang members are desperate to gain a sense of belonging, power, and the security that comes from affiliation. In the elementary, middle, and junior high school levels, lonely, frightened, and alienated youngsters are flocking to the personal security and tangible identity that gang membership affords. We need to help these kids find safety and peace in the security of an accepting classroom climate that encourages them to display appropriate personal power, academic competence, and social influence.

GANGS AND POWER

Power in this world can come from guns, from money and other material resources, and from learning and knowing (Toffler, 1991). Naturally, in a book about schooling, I will emphasize power as competence in an educational setting and draw from Glasser's (1986) work, *Control Theory in the Classroom*.

Power is defined as coming from *choosing* one's friends and one's classroom lessons. Power's source is internal by definition because if someone else passes it over, that person holds the real power. Children best develop a sense of power within a noncoercive context where a learner finds little need to engage in power struggles with dominating adults. Instead, the boys and girls and the young men and young women are testing themselves and enjoying the discovery of self as they exercise the power within (Glasser, 1984).

Gangs cannot be viewed as a uniform or homogenous social concept. Modern gangs typically organize themselves around behaviors and themes that set them apart and allow them to make a special statement. Some gangs are clearly "social" where the members are mostly interested in the social aspects of group behavior—fun, security, and friendship. Such party gangs concentrate narrowly on drug use and sales while foregoing most other delinquent behavior. By contrast, a power-oriented gang engages mostly in violent crime and abstains for the most part from drug use. The organized street gang, like organized crime at the adult level, is involved in heavy crime as well as drug use and sales. Members of a typical street gang engage in violent behavior in order to establish control over crime and "sales" territories (Fagen, 1989). Their attitude reflects a primitive human urge—the meanest and vilest person has absolutely no fear of evil as he/she walks nonchalantly anywhere in the valley that he/she likes.

Basically there are two types of urban areas that are gang prone. The first is the transitory neighborhood, which is characterized by rapid population change with diverse cultural populations living side by side and in competition with one another (Bernstein, 1964). This pattern may shift as particular neighborhoods throughout urban America make the transition to more economic stability, but the general pattern still applies today in many inner-city war zones.

The second gang area is the stable slum, a run-down community where population shifts have slowed down and patterns of behavior and traditions have developed over a number of years. Working with gangs and initiating change there is more difficult because tradition and structure have become so deep-rooted, and because harsh violence is the root system of these members' lives. Belonging is critical. *People will belong* even if they choose to belong to a gang that purports to be separate and not belong to society.

Gangs must add new members constantly—a relatively easy process given the ecological and environmental patterns that exist in gang-prone neighborhoods. A never-ending supply of youths emerges as admirers of older hoodlums and gangsters whose violent and rapacious lifestyles appear so attractive to the younger ones. The young nobodies apply for membership and are readily accepted into the fraternity of somebodies. New recruits start off with low status in the gang, reflecting their inexperience and their need to learn the ropes. They pay their dues in one way or another, work their way up through the ranks, and gradually affirm their unconditional allegiance to the gang, further alienating themselves from society's mainstream. Gang affiliation and training almost always discourages any bonding with schools; indeed, signing into the gang fosters open disdain for the conventional educational process itself. The average school fails in the battle for fealty, provides insufficient and unclear goals, and makes normative schooling behavior a sign of weakness and failure. Like a fungus, delinquency and gangs proliferate in this milieu.

Prison gangs need to recruit members, and the young in these gang-prone neighborhoods are prime targets. The prison gangs provide what the schools cannot: power, a sense of belonging, and positive self-esteem. The prison gangs in California actually began in the California Youth Authority (CYA) at the Duell Vocational Institute in Tracy during 1957 and 1958. The first gang was the Mexican Mafia, comprised of individuals from many different local gangs throughout the state. The next identified prison gang was formed in 1965 at Soledad, California. This gang was called La Nuestra Familia and was formed to compete with the Mexican Mafia in criminal activity and to protect inmates who were Hispanic but not members of the Mafia. The two gangs actually were recruited geographically—the Mexican Mafia from Southern California and La Nuestra Familia from Northern California. The next prison gangs to form were the Black Guerrilla Family (BGF) and the Aryan Brotherhood (AB). Both these groups appeared as "special interests" in the mid-60s, organized to engage in criminal activities as well as for self-protection from other groups.

Many young people look up to and admire all of these gangs. In fact, many of the kids in neighborhoods where gangs are commonplace aspire to become members of known prison gangs, emulating the gang in dress and grooming and often using graffiti to show their loyalty to the "first team." CYA wards as young as 15 years old were quoted as saying, "When I get old enough, I'm going to be a Familiano [i.e., a member of La Nuestra Familia]. I will do what they ask me" (Castaneda, 1988, p. 5). Many of these youths have relatives who are prison gang members. Common responses to the question, "Where did you hear about prison gangs?" include "My brother is an NF member," "My cousin is a member of the Mexican Mafia," and on and on. A stretch in prison provides the "college degree" for an aspiring gang member. Viewed in this light, the prison represents a larger *system problem*. Even as the correctional institution tries to protect society from dangerous felons, the effect of defining prison residents as bad and powerless is to encourage more social impact than they might otherwise have.

When members of prison gangs gain their release, they generally return to their old communities, where they become folk heroes for the local kids. They have buffed up their muscles in the prison workout facility, and they show no fear. Prison gang members then use the young kids and their gangs as runners and agents to commit crimes (Castaneda, 1988).

Hispanic kids have gangs with which to identify (i.e., Mexican Mafia and La Nuestra Familia), and other groups or minorities seem each to have their own gang model to emulate. White youth gangs such as L.A.'s Supreme Power sometimes correspond to the Aryan Brotherhood that operates in prison. Some members of the CRIPS, the most powerful out-of-prison black youth gang, identify with the prison-based Black Guerrilla Family.

Let's take an example from the streets. I first saw Felix slumped in a chair nervously strumming his fingers on the table in the interrogation room. His cropped hair was neatly groomed and held down by a hair net. He was wearing an oversized white T-shirt, neatly pressed brown Big Ben slacks, and slippers. On his left arm was a tattoo EME (i.e., the initials of the Mexican Mafia). "Aren't you a little young to be a member of the Mafia? What are you, about 11 years old?" Felix glared at me, "I'm not Mafia yet, but when I'm old enough, I will do anything they ask of me so that I can be a member. El Bandido, my friend, is EME, and I've sold dope and pulled burglaries for him. Other members of my gang do the same for the Mafia."

La Nuestra Familia (NF) uses kids (ages 12 through 17) in their protection racket. The youngsters harass the targets through vandalism, robbery, and burglary. The NF offers protection from these acts for a monthly payment. The rationale for using kids is to avoid losing soldados (soldiers) to the pigs (police)—not to lose manpower. Kids this age are also very vulnerable to a suggestion and an influence they respect; it is not difficult to obligate the kid to the gang and to the Familia. When a youth has reached this stage, he/she is ready to be schooled and put to work (Castaneda, 1988).

HOW SERIOUS IS THE GANG PROBLEM?

Many Americans may not know that we are a nation at war—a silent, brutal, and uncivilized war in the streets. In the past six years 2,133 young persons (those reported) have been killed because they were members of gangs. In 1989, in Los Angeles, there was approximately one murder of a known gang member every 17 hours. Gang-related violence there has soared with attempted murder up 58 percent, assaults up 25 percent, robberies up 12 percent, and attacks against police up 131 percent. Gang membership in Los Angeles alone is over 100,000, which is three times the figure for 1980 (A. Price, 1989).

The problem of gangs has exploded in most major cities and is now pretty much out of control (Abadinsky, 1990). Authorities are simply unable to cope with the current situation because they are outnumbered, outgunned, and usually outsmarted. Business and the private sector in general are indifferent. To a large degree, churches are uninvolved and community service agencies have not developed any effective antigang programs to counsel potential recruits. The best that can be said about the efforts made to date to control the violence is inappropriate and futile (Empey & Stafford, 1981). What is more, funding for prevention measures is always in short supply.

Perhaps what keeps every responsible group distant and ineffective is the absence of a clear idea, a consensus, on what should be done. Practitioners in the field debate the value of any hard-line approach. A San Francisco city recreation superintendent stated, "There are some traditionalists out there who say we are taking too light a hand with these thugs, but it's the get-tough law enforcement approach that I feel has not worked." Others who have taken that military approach have not been successful. In Oakland, California, for example, stern police measures have resulted in a record number of homicides" (Associated Press, 1990, p. B3). We have a sense of how impossible fighting guerrillas can be, whether in Vietnam, Eastern Europe, or urban America. Another view of the solution was presented by San Francisco Police Captain Timothy Hettrich, formerly in charge of a unit that focused on street gangs. He stated in an article for a local Bay Area newspaper that, "Once we took off the titular heads [arrested] of some of these street gangs and put them in jail, then the other programs could work" (Associated Press, p. B3). Either or both of these gentlemen could be right or wrong; however, programs have a much better chance of working when a consensus emerges on the cause or etiology of gang behavior.

Over recent decades, researchers have produced a myriad of theories endeavoring to explain gang and delinquent behavior. Short and Strodtbeck (1965) conducted a three-year study on delinquency and the gang process in Chicago. They first collected data on 16 gangs ranging in size from 16 to 68 members totaling 598 boys (of whom 464 were black youths belonging to 11 of the 16 gangs. The same researchers later collected additional data on another 12 black and 10 white gangs. These and other researchers found that gang members were almost exclusively from the lower social and economic classes (often minorities), alienated from mainstream society, lacked fundamental social or interpersonal skills, had limited verbal proficiency, and even appeared to be below average in cognitive development (see also Bartol & Bartol, 1989). Considering these deficiencies, a school setting makes it apparent that these youngsters would be totally powerless. No child will stay long by choice in a place where he/she is powerless, especially when compelled to spend time with an alien, coercive, distant, and suspicious adult.

Over the years, many social researchers have developed theories on the causes and cures of youth gangs and delinquency. Writing in a standard text on criminology, Edwin Sutherland (1939) summed up the opinions of the 1930s (and hence of the crime-ridden Roaring 20s and Great Depression era). Sutherland felt that young people learn criminal or antisocial behavior in the same way that they learn responsible, law-abiding ways—by following the example of what they see around them. If they see glorified depictions of violence and deceit, and if gangsters or con men appear to be successful, kids are likely to regard those models as the way to achieve success. If "nice guys finish last," a child obviously has far less reason to grow up as a nice guy. "Only a chump believes what he's told and follows the rules." In the language of 1970 to 1997, this attitude is simply being "streetwise" or "street smart." Unfortunately, children must more vigilantly avoid abduction, recruitment by drug pushers, and even falling naively into the pornography trade. We might note that Sutherland's model (as well as the popular culture of the time in movies, magazines, and songs) did not emphasize racial or ethnic identity as a factor causing the existence of gangs and criminals. Instead, the major emphasis was on social and economic differences—on haves and have-nots.

Sutherland's views fit in surprisingly well with William Glasser's (1984) version of choice theory. What are Sutherland's model of emulation and striving to fit in if not an earlier explanation of Glasser's basic needs (especially the needs for belonging and worth or power) and the attempts to satisfy them? Glasser's ideas are, together with Sutherland's, an excellent guide for coping with gang behavior and violence in the schools. Children, even the very young, do not imitate the bullying "cool" guys' spiteful or violent behavior because they are inherently rotten. These children have their own needs; if these are not met, the children look for actions that will meet the needs. Kids do not play coercive power games because they want to; they see other kids having fun and meeting their needs by the same tactics, and they want to be like those other children.

In the era of *Blackboard Jungle* and *West Side Story*, Cohen (1955) maintained that lower-class male delinquency was the result of very limited opportunities for youth in an economic wasteland to gain access to the mainstream of middle-class society. This exclusion resulted in painful frustration and rage.

Lower-class kids became keenly aware of their inability to achieve a respected status because they had not been educated to the norms of the middle class and were in the dark about the proper behavior they needed in order to get ahead— "Hey, teacher, where do we put the finger bowls?" Later on, Miller (1958) disagreed with Cohen's contention that delinquency was a reaction against middle-class standards and values and instead viewed delinquent behavior as an adaptive compromise in order to gain success *within* the confines of lower-class society. He argued that the primary motivation of those engaging in delinquent behavior was a desire to realize the values of their own lower-class community and not an act of defiant action directed against so-called higher classes. Miller's gang theory hinged on two important social ingredients that were taken to characterize lower-class culture—female-dominated households and single-sex peer groups.

Block and Neiderhoffer (1958) suggested that gangs provided a mechanism for bridging the gap between the freedom of childhood and the responsibilities of adulthood—a duty many have shrugged off on the schools. At some time in their development, all young people frighten themselves with the concept "adult status." Later, when young people seek help from adults and that assistance falls short, they naturally turn to their peers for support. Thus gangs sometimes emerge by default.

Cloward and Ohlin (1960, p. 78) felt that "pressures toward the formation of delinquent subcultures originate in the marked discrepancies between culturally induced aspirations among lower class youth and the possibilities of achieving them by legitimate means." In other words, even though lower-class adolescents (mostly males) seek the American dream, legitimate avenues are not available. In their own eyes, they are held back by certain forces, such as a lace of parental support and encouragement for education, or racial and class discrimination. Many poor young people, reflecting on their situations, are likely to find few opportunities for a better future and feel trapped in their positions on the bottom rung of the social ladder. Giving-up is an inappropriate option and is always perceived by peers in the slums as weakness—a "chicken" way out—so lower-class youths typically resort to illegitimate ways to succeed. Once they make it clear that they will challenge social values and practices, they usually find someone to agree with them. Presto, a gang!

All these theories set a context for delinquent and gang formation or behavior and conjecture on the various circumstances that come into play in the development of an individual gang member—but only as an abstraction, a blank persona. The gang member, according to these theories, is someone from a lower socioeconomic background, alienated from mainstream society, lacking in fundamental social or interpersonal skills, and possessing limited verbal and cognitive skills (Short & Strodtbeck, 1962). He/she learns the delinquent behavior by the same process that all learning takes place (Sutherland, 1939). The formation of a gang could be the result of frustration and anger brought on by the inability of lower-class youths to reach out to mainstream, middle-class society (Cohen, 1955).

America's so-called underclass will, of course, always be subject to harsher punishments and blunter social rejection. Perhaps we ought to raise some questions about gangs and social class. Why do citizens not refer to a college fraternity or sorority as an upper-class gang? Why are fraternity pranks and vandalism passed off as youthful high jinks (possibly because they or their families can cover the monetary loss), while the same actions perpetrated by a "street gang" have the guilty ones hauled into court as delinquents? Why have so many fraternities been banned from college campuses? What about tales of upper-class thrill killers? For a long time, sociology as such had no place for upper crust associations of choice: these were not "gangs"; they are "sets" or "crowds" and, as such, not a proper subject for analysis of society at large. Analysts, beware: the elite become part of the mass culture as soon as that gang becomes part of mass communication.

Because affiliating with a gang is a critical step in realizing the goals or inner needs of lower-class and "minority" society (Miller, 1958), young people habitually build a gang identity in their teens as they try to span the gap between childhood and adulthood. A structured gang with its own rules is more likely to form when adult support is inadequate (Block & Neiderhoffer, 1958) or as a way to aid lower-class youths in meeting the needs of a consumer society when legitimate means are absent (Cloward & Ohlin, 1960). At the center of the pressure less wealthy children feel in the transition to adulthood may be the advertisers who are busy fostering a demand for certain products. Gang members have been known to kill for a pair of selected brands of tennis shoes. Government control on cigarette advertising to youth may be controversial but is a step in the direction of advocacy and resolving a system problem of over-hawking consumables.

George H. Kelly (1963) spoke of mental constructs as cognitive representations of the environment. As cognitive systems, these ideas about the world are our best efforts to make sense out of the internal world in everyone's head. Often these mental constructs do not work too well for us and we find ourselves getting into trouble. When these nebulous theories are applied to specific gangs or groups we must test these notions empirically to determine their usefulness. Would identifying valid theories of gang and delinquent behavior help us develop programs that would increase all students' chances of succeeding in society? If we found some effective alternatives, could we, thereby, decrease the need for gang activity?

Comer (Lee, 1990), the Maurice Falk Professor of Psychiatry at the Yale University Child Study Center, said the following of high school gang members in New York's Bedford-Stuyvesant District:

> The way these children behave is a function of economics, social experiences and generations of a caste system. Academic life is not meaningful or useful to them. Unless there is some understanding of the magnitude of the problem and why it occurs, there will be no progress in changing the behavior. (Lee, 1990, p. 7)

Gang behavior appears most often in lower socioeconomic areas where many people hold themselves in an alienated posture in relationship to the larger society. Operating on the premise that gang activity thrives on the conditions of a self-imposed sense of alienation and anxiety, the educator, counselor or teacher has a new set of tactics to deal with the problems.

WHAT TO DO ABOUT THE GANG PROBLEM

Everyone implicitly believes that if the home and neighborhood are dysfunctional and chaotic, the school should be a model of function and discipline. Currently, two divergent views exist about the roles schools play. One view is based on the assumption that American schools are viable and healthy institutions but are called upon to deal with a group of unruly, predelinquent, and delinquent youths. The other picture portrays the schools as being fundamentally implicated in delinquency because of various shortcomings and inadequacies within the American educational system. This latter argument also contends that schools exacerbate students' adjustment problems because they fail to satisfy their reasonable needs (Gibbons & Krohn, 1991). The specific needs in question here are the needs to belong, achieve, and have a sense of worth by feeling needed and important within one's family, peer group, or class.

Personalizing the School

The schools could go a long way in creating the conditions for students to fulfill their basic needs by making school more relevant and by facilitating students in experiencing a sense of belonging and achievement. If a school district or administration is apathetic or does not have the necessary funds to initiate innovative programs, individual school staff members can make a huge difference by showing students that they care.

Special Community Programs

Teachers and school administrators could enlist the support of local businesses in encouraging local celebrities and public figures in providing positive role models for the students. Many local police departments have programs that encourage youngsters to participate in cadet programs. These programs provide education relating to the laws of the state, city, and country. There is also pragmatic instruction pertaining to the Constitution and the Bill of Rights. The cadet programs also provide a source of employment for the students because the police department hires the cadets for special events.

Teachers need to stay informed of the programs available to students in their neighborhoods. One such program, which I selected for its longevity and effectiveness, began in Denver in 1973 and continues today as Project New Pride. In only its second year, Denver's New Pride had received national recognition by being chosen as a model program by the Law Enforcement Assistance Administration. Project New Pride works with youths 14 to 17 who have committed two or more serious offenses (felonies). They provide alternative schooling, jobs, and individual and family counseling. A teacher who identifies a student at the first stages of trouble at school might consider a referral to a program such as New Pride.

New Pride takes an holistic approach. The program believes that the needs of the total child must be met. Close supervision and counseling are imperative in identifying and understanding each youth's deficiencies. A counselor participates in all aspects of the young person's life, and the counseling relationship continues to be important during a 6-month follow-up period when the counselor works closely with the public school system and family to monitor the kid's gradual separation from the project to ensure that the desired behavior changes have occurred (Seidman, 1985).

Researchers have described special programs to resolve the problem of vandalism.

> An early indication of the presence of gangs in schools could be an increase in graffiti and other types of vandalism on campus. Many school districts hire security guards, employ guard dogs, install sensing devices and utilize other expensive security devices in the hope of reducing graffiti and vandalism.

The foregoing are all external controls, and to the student, they emphasize the already perceived oppressiveness of the school environment. The South San Francisco School District in northern California has devised a plan for students to control vandalism. The plan is called the "$1 Per ADA Program." This program establishes a fund at the beginning of each year for every school in the district, equal in dollars to its average daily attendance (ADA) for one day. As the school year progresses, the total cost of vandalism for the year is deducted from the funds, and all the money remaining is used for school improvements. The improvements are chosen by a committee of students with faculty advice. The results have been impressive; the cost in school vandalism fell from $40,000 to $7,000 during the program's first year. The rationale for the program, according to an administrator, is to "give students a more concrete concept of the cost of vandalism and get them involved in stopping it." (Kratcoski & Kratcoski, 1990, p. 159)

NEEDS THAT GANGS FULFILL

Neighborhoods in which gang activity is common share many ecological characteristics, including a high proportion of economically deprived residents. Economic disadvantages alone, however, do not appear to account for high rates of gang activity. When poverty and low income are accompanied by social isolation, these two factors are most likely to result in gang delinquency if those conditions are accompanied by low social integration (Gibbons & Krohn, 1991). It appears that the key to controlling the proliferation of gangs and gang influence in neighborhoods is increasing the level of social integration in those neighborhoods. In other words, showing residents how to obtain "a piece of the pie" legitimately and directly is an alternative to gang violence.

Educators in New York City schools are attempting to increase their students' level of social integration by enforcing strict dress and weapons codes and these measures appear to be having a degree of success. In the Bedford-Stuyvesant High School, for example, students know they had better leave their gold jewelry and their removable gold tooth jackets at home if they are to continue traveling in those circles. In many New York City high schools, students also are submitting regularly to metal detector searches for weapons. Sadly, many feel it is only a matter of time before every school will be undergoing such a thorough criminal prevention protocol. In prohibiting weapons at school or in establishing rules about a proper standard of dress, administrators see themselves closing the gap between the laws of the outside world and the regulations students must follow. A principal of Wingate High School in Brooklyn,

C. Ben Dachs, has said that, even though he was leery about installing a metal detector, he has observed a dramatic and continuing improvement in attendance and test scores since the school elected to use such equipment.

Aida Rosa, the principal of Public School 30 in the South Bronx gave all students in her school the option of wearing uniforms. After many of the students accepted the dress code, Rosa said, "with our uniforms we have created a sense of unity, a sense of feeling good about ourselves. No matter what I do here as principal I will never be one of the schools with the top reading scores in the district, but I think the uniforms have made a tremendous difference" (Lee, 1990, p. 7).

Gottfredson (1986) implemented Project PATHE (Positive Action Through Holistic Education) in seven schools in South Carolina with a primary focus on reducing delinquency by increasing students' stakes or payoff in appropriate behavior, compliance, of conformity. The keys to the program are the following:

1. strengthening students' commitment to school;
2. facilitating their success in academics;
3. increasing their attachment to role models in the education community;
4. increasing their participation in school activities; and
5. encouraging their sense of social competence, belonging, and usefulness (i.e., meeting their basic needs and thereby gaining a sense of real power).

The project sought to provide practical resources so students could develop in a positive direction. To achieve these goals, each school created teams of staff members, students, parents, and community members and provided the teams with special training in initiating changes and revising school policies to accommodate such changes. In so doing, the school leadership utilized all segments of the community in the school improvement programs (Gottfredson, 1986).

Starting in the fall of 1991, Milwaukee initiated the first school for black male students only. This school was formed because of a belief in some African-American communities that conventional schools have failed the young black male. Such exclusive schools may represent a desperate solution for a desperate situation: thousands of black males are dropping out of school and accepting lives of desperation, permeated with criminal activity, gang membership, drug abuse, and continued unemployment. This destructive pattern is a commentary on more than nonresponsive schools, of course. Many black adolescent males face the same dilemma some young people of other races experience: little nurturing and guidance from a structured and caring family and a limited social support network.

Although these newly segregated all black schools represent a radical attempt to remedy a critical situation, these social and educational experiments may provide a model for educators serving the needs of deprived black youth. In defense of this radical decision to operate an all black male school, Joyce Mallory, a Milwaukee school board member, has stated, "The skills kids need to be successful in mainstream America are not based on whether they sit next to a white child."

Reverend George Clements, a black priest working at Chicago's Holy Angels Catholic Church believes that the public school system has failed black youngsters and advocates that blacks should establish their own schools and reinvigorate their churches. He also thinks that African-American schools and churches can instill a new level of morality in young black people that no other institutions can match (Lunner, 1991). Attitudes may change after these schools and churches prove their effectiveness in changing young African-American males' attitudes about themselves, partially measured by their later success in integrating themselves more easily into the larger society.

MULTIPRONGED SOLUTION TO THE PROBLEM OF GANGS

In her investigation of adolescent males' perceptions of their family environments, Donna Greco (1994) compared the family environments of so-called "gangbangers" with their nondelinquent and nongang peers. In her causal-comparative study, 53 male delinquent, gang-affiliated adolescents and 43 nondelinquent, nongang adolescents completed two standardized instruments designed to assess their perceptions of their family environments. The Analysis of Family Environment Scale (FES) (Greco, 1994) indicated that delinquent gang-affiliated adolescents perceive their families as less involved in intellectual and cultural pursuits and also in social and recreational activities than their nondelinquent peers' perceptions of their families. The Family Violence Scale (FVS) (Greco, 1994) showed that a significantly greater number of gang members had parents who had been gang members. Also, gang members reported a significantly higher exposure to violence within their families. Besides living in dangerous family systems, and, in contrast to the comparison group, gang members also indicated coming from larger families with more gang members, lower incomes, and a stronger public interest in religious beliefs and symbols. Taking all of this into account, the final recommendations in Greco's study include the following solutions to the gang problem.

A   Provide family therapy with three aims.
   a   Interdict, as early as possible, the father's violence against the mother and offspring;
   b   Break, conclusively, the transgenerational cycle of ganging and criminal patterns; and
   c   Encourage family members to adopt new recreational and cultural activities.
B   Implement group counseling in schools on a large scale in order to accomplish the following.
   a   Model appropriate trusting relationships,
   b   Teach and practice new social skills, and
   c   Ensure academic success as a way of gaining a valid sense of power and competency.
C   Put in place community based programs to do the following.
   a   Enlist respected athletes to guide gang members away from delinquency,
   b   Transform delinquent adolescents' deeply held religious values as a source of leverage to lead them away from a ganging family tradition, and
   c   Feature alternative gang-free lifestyles that can open new and productive careers.

On the topic of the last point—alternative careers—the school might work collaboratively with other community agencies to create well-organized travel and study programs. These trips could introduce those students most at-risk for a criminal lifestyle to the panoply of human trauma and intensive social needs throughout the country and the world. Also, many predelinquents possibly could make major qualitative changes in their lives by exploring a career in such medical specialties as EMT and paramedical training. In this way, the school becomes proactive in guiding the youngsters into actual fields of danger and excitement but with a rescuing and life-sustaining thrust rather than a destructive and tragic bent.

SUMMARY: WHAT ELSE SCHOOLS CAN DO

Although the educational system did not create juvenile delinquency and gangs, schools may be able to play an important role in reducing the problem and preventing further deterioration. In the long run, gangs will be completely unnecessary in a quality school. One major role of a school is socialization—learning appropriate attitudes, beliefs, values, and behaviors—and juveniles spend the bulk of their day in school. Many believe that schools serve as screening devices that discourage certain students from succeeding academically, encourage a sense of alienation, and compel these needier students to consider dropping out of school, joining a gang, and engaging in delinquency. Responsive schools today are providing alternatives and additional learning opportunities to those students not attuned to the traditional mode of education. The whole thrust of the quality school is creating options and creating the conditions for withdrawn students to empower themselves. Finding alternative paths to curricular credit and signing up for remedial courses in subjects such as English and math are only first steps a school can take to acknowledge its role in students' decision to quit. Schools need to overhaul their plans for accommodating students who do not fit the profile of conventional, willing (albeit passive) learners. Hawkins and Weis (1980) viewed the schools' role in delinquency prevention as going beyond academic and intellectual development. They suggested providing such educational options as better skill training and taking a more active role in students social development by teaching civil and criminal law. The authors called for more student input on the educational process and urge schools to utilize student leaders to exert peer pressure on delinquency prevention. They pointed out that student leaders should not be merely academic leaders but also leaders of various social groups so that they exert influence on those students who traditionally are left untouched by superior academicians in the student body.

No one would disagree that something must be done and done soon. An average of 3,878 young people drop out of school daily with an estimated one million leaving every year. Eighty-two percent of all prison inmates in the United States are school dropouts. We all must act together to create a quality school community.

BIBLIOGRAPHY

Bynum, J. E., & Thompson, W. E. (1989). *Juvenile delinquency: A sociological approach.* Needham, MA: Allyn & Bacon.

Gossens, D., & Anderson, J. (1995). *Creating the conditions.* Chapel Hill, NC: New View Press.

Siegel, L. J., & Senna, J. J. (1991). *Juvenile delinquency: Theory, practice & law* (4th ed.). New York: West.

REFERENCES

Abadinsky, H. (1990). *Organized crime* (3rd ed.). Chicago: Nelson-Hall.

Associated Press. (1990, May 5). Bay Area gangs. *San Francisco Chronicle,* B3.

Bartol, C. R., & Bartol, A. M. (1989). *Juvenile delinquency A systems approach.* Englewood Cliffs, NJ: Prentice Hall.

Bernstein, S. (1964). *Youth in the streets: Work with alienated youth gangs.* New York: Associated Press.

Block, H. A., & Neiderhoffer, A. (1958). *The gangs: A study in adolescent behavior.* New York: Philosophical Library.

Castaneda, E. (1988). *The prison gangs influences on youth gangs.* San Jose, CA: Gang Investigators Association.

Cloward, R. A., & Ohlin, L. E. (1960). *Delinquency and opportunity: A theory of delinquent gangs.* Glencoe, IL: Free Press.

Cohen, A. K. (1955). *Delinquent boy: The culture of the gang.* New York: Free Press.

Empey, L. T., & Stafford, M. C. (1991). *American delinquency: Its meaning & construction* (3rd ed.). Belmont, CA: Wadsworth.

Fagen, J. (1989). The social organization of drug use and drug dealing among urban gangs. *Criminology, 27,* 633-669.

Gibbons, D. C., & Krohn, J. (1991). *Delinquent behavior* (5th ed.). Englewood Cliffs, NJ: Prentice Hall.

Glasser, W. (1984). *Control theory: A new explanation of how we control our lives.* New York: Harper & Row.

Glasser, W. (1986). *Control theory in the classroom.* New York: Harper & Row.

Gottfredson, D. (1986). An empirical test of school-based environmental and individual interventions to reduce the risk of delinquent behavior. *Criminology, 24,* 705-731.

Greco, D. (1994). *Adolescent males' perceptions of their family environments: A comparison of gang-affiliated delinquents and unaffiliated non delinquents.* Unpublished doctoral dissertation, University of San Francisco.

Hawkins, J. D., & Weis, J. G. (1980). *The social developmental model: An integrated approach to delinquency prevention.* Seattle: University of Washington Center for Law and Justice.

Kelly, G. A. (1963). *A theory of personality: The psychology of personal constructs.* New York: Norton.

Kratcoski, P. C., & Kratcoski, L. D. (1990). *Juvenile delinquency* (3rd ed.). Englewood Cliffs, NJ: Prentice Hall.

Lee, F. (1990, March 11). The region: Can a change of rules alter young lives? *The New York Times,* 7.

Lunner, C. (1991, May 23). Separate schools for blacks urged. *Marian Independent Journal,* 14.

Miller, W. B. (1958). Lower class culture as a generating milieu of gang delinquency. *Journal of Social Science, 14,* 5-19.

Price, A. (1989, August 10). Youth toll in gang violence. *Los Angeles Times,* 34.

Price L. R. (1989). *Gangs in schools: Breaking up is hard to do.* Malibu, CA: Pepperdine University, National School Safety Center.

Seidman, P. (1985). (brochure). Washington, DC: U.S. Department of Justice, Office of Juvenile Justice and Delinquency Prevention, 1-7.

Short J. F., & Strodtbeck, F. L. (1965). *Group process and gang delinquency.* Chicago: University of Chicago Press.

Sutherland, E. (1939). *Principles of Criminology* (3rd ed.). New York: J. B. Lippencott.

Toffler, A. (1991). *Powershift: Knowledge, wealth, and violence at the edge of the 21st century.* New York: Bantam.

Chapter 16

DEATH AND CHILDHOOD GRIEF

Jan Francis

Editor's Note

Few topics can be more heart wrenching than helping children handle their grievous losses. Jan Francis draws from her training and experience as a licensed registered nurse and, in the last few years, as a licensed marriage, family, and child counselor. She has extensive experience and success with families facing terminal illness and ultimate loss.

My own conviction on this topic is that none of us can really prepare for the death of another person. We can only prepare ourselves to face up to that part of us that dies when someone close to us passes away. In my mind, we are fortunate that children are much more resilient than adults and even more resilient than adults think children are. Teachers and counselors need to draw upon their deepest sense of humanity and their most vulnerable selves in helping children learn to accept all manner of losses. The loss may take the form of a divorce, a parental runaway, abandonment by other caregivers, death of a pet, death of a parent or sibling, loss of classmates, or some other devastating experience. Jan Francis provides the formula for being there for a child in tragic circumstances.

HELPING 5- TO 14-YEAR-OLD CHILDREN MANAGE THEIR GRIEF

The purpose of this chapter is threefold: first, to explore how death and life-threatening illness affect children and young adolescents emotionally; second, to give an overview of children's possible overt reaction to death and life-threatening illness, given their age and experience; and third, to offer suggestions and activities for helping children work through their losses. I specifically have featured working with 5- to 14-year-old children.

Grief includes a wide range of physical and emotional responses that can vary with individual children, depending upon the nature of the lost relationship, the way the death occurred, and the attitudes of the adults surrounding the child. Children may be facing the loss of a person, a pet, or even their own catastrophic illness. The death of someone important to children may have occurred suddenly, through accident or disease, or from long-term chronic illness. Many factors can affect children's success at saying their own good-byes and at accepting the finality of death. Some complications are the unexpectedness of the death, children's physical distance from the loved one, emotional avoidance, and the discouragement they hear from adults about the death. Children's style of coping and their progress toward recovery from any loss also will be influenced by their own level of development and by their already established coping skills.

Children or young adolescents who face devastating losses with no previous understanding of the natural life and death cycle will be poorly equipped to recover their equilibrium successfully through a normal grief process. Again, we can see that teachers are in an excellent position to serve their students' emotional needs as well as their academic ones. Teachers can introduce the topics of death, loss, and grief in their ordinary classroom lessons and can monitor and support a grieving child effectively. I will begin this chapter with a look at the most visible types of problems and continue with practical suggestions to aid in the natural healing process. Besides including the research and practical ideas of many investigators and therapists, I mostly will draw from my own ideas and case examples, going back to 1980 when I first worked in a hospice program. For many years, I also have been in private practice as a psychotherapist.

LOSING A LOVED ONE

Approximately one and a half million children in the United States lose one or both parents by the age of 15 (Lehman, Lang, Wortman, & Sorenson,

1989). This statistic indicates a large number of potentially grieving children, but this information also illustrates the loneliness of the grieving child in a school population where the majority of children have not experienced the impact of losing a parent to death. After all, the 1.5 million figure represents only 5% of our children in the United States. Donnelly (1989) pointed out that another 1.5 million people under the age of 25 will die from suicide, homicide, accidents, or illness. Because siblings will survive many of these people, the number of bereaved children is very substantial. In addition to bereavement, catastrophic illness (i.e., facing a sure threat of imminent death) can cause grief also and, if children ignore or do not notice the grief, they will most likely develop more serious problems. In one study, almost half the children in the survey who were surviving cancer had varying degrees of adjustment problems (Koocher, in Tull & Goldberg, 1984)

The Life Cycle Includes Dying

A teacher who introduces the topic of death and dying in the classroom often finds that many children have already been thinking in this area—a vitally important topic to them. Research has shown that approximately 80% of children think about death and have some death-related fears (Schaefer & Lyons, 1988). Studies also have shown that bereaved children who cannot resolve their grief early on sometimes experience complications later. In various studies of children needing psychological help in psychiatric hospitals, clinics, or guidance centers, researchers found that 14% to 50% of the subjects, depending on the study, had experienced a childhood bereavement (Fox, 1984; Rafael, 1983). Another study of bereaved siblings coming for psychiatric care, some as much as five or more years after a death, showed that the children had characteristic symptoms: guilt, depressive withdrawal, self-punitive and accident-prone behaviors, fear of death, distorted ideas about illness and the medical community, and difficulties in cognitive functioning (Rafael, 1983). The children most deeply affected by the death of someone close are the younger children who lose a mother and adolescents who lose a father (Schaefer & Lyons, 1988). Several independent researchers also have suggested that the death of a father may be associated with later antisocial behavior (Rafael, 1983; Osterweis & Townsend, 1988).

One teacher tells of a 12-year-old girl whose eight-month-old baby sister died suddenly. Within one month, the preteen child gained 90 pounds and by the end of the year had added 125 pounds, eventually bumping her total weight to a massive 350 pounds! "Prior to her sister's death, she had functioned well at her grade level. Within two years, she was functioning four grade levels behind, was tested, and made eligible for Learning Disabilities services. School systems are often not aware of the impact of grief on children" (Donnelly, 1988, p. 164).

Researchers agree that unresolved childhood bereavement affects adult life through physical and psychological health problems. Some studies even suggest that a direct link may exist between adult cancer and childhood loss (Rafael, 1983). According to Kastenbaum (1981), children who have lost a parent, in comparison to nongrieving classmates, tend to be more submissive, dependent, introverted, maladjusted, suicidal, and prone to such behavior as shoplifting or petty theft. Usually, those same children will perform less adequately in cognitive functioning (Kastenbaum, 1981; Rafael, 1983) than they did prior to the loss. In school, grieving children obviously need special notice by teachers in order to adjust successfully and to recover from their losses.

Grieving Is a Natural Behavior. Grief itself is not the problem. Rather, grieving, an open expression of one's heartache and emotional pain, is a familiar path to healing, for grieving is a natural behavior in any human loss. We are concerned here, however, with the very real problems that develop from stifled and denied emotions, conflicting or false information, and the general indifference many grieving children meet in the faces of adults around them. Thus, unattended and repressed grief is the problem, causing a wide variety of symptoms and maladaptive behavior, as many teachers can testify from observing their students' behavior.

Although teachers have no control over events in their students' home lives, noting some of the potential problems can be useful in order to gain a better understanding of the interventions I suggest later in this chapter.

LIFESTYLE DISRUPTION

Bereaved children's lifestyle is often disrupted by changes in their home environment, usually through role changes and/or the added stress a family must manage even though they already carry a heavy burden with their existing problems. During a family member's illness, the home routine may change due to the necessity of caring for a sick person. Adults may ask children to make many changes: keep voices lowered, avoid noisy play, and even restrict their spontaneous laughter. If the ill person is hospitalized, the home routine is usually altered further to accommodate hospital visits and medical appointments. A dying family member becomes the center of attention, often at the expense of the children's ongoing needs (Kastenbaum, 1981; Rafael, 1983).

In sibling death, a surviving child's life changes in several ways. First, over anxious parents may restrict the surviving children's activities unreasonably so they can get control over their fear of losing another child (Lehman et al., 1989). Second, the once-familiar role of brother or sister becomes the role of bereaved sibling, and the child no longer knows exactly what the parents expect (Kamerman, 1988). Remember, in losing a sibling, a child often loses an ever present companion and confidant (Donnelly, 1988; Rafael, 1983).

In many cases, the death or life-threatening illness of a family member overloads an already disturbed family where financial resources and support networks are limited (Rafael, 1983). Studies correlating childhood bereavement within unstable homes, unpredictable care, and inconsistent routines show an increase in the possibility of a negative long-term outcome for bereaved children (Osterweis & Townsend, 1988).

EMOTIONAL ABANDONMENT

Children may feel emotionally abandoned even in stable homes when parents become absorbed in their own grief following a family member's death. Parents are often emotionally and physically exhausted, anxious, and preoccupied, with no surplus energy for attending to their children (Schaefer & Lyons, 1988). When children experience the death of a sibling, they simultaneously sustain at least two losses—losing a sibling to death and losing parents to absorption in the death (Donnelly, 1988; Schumacher, 1984). Prior to a death, many siblings have been observed to respond negatively to the ill sibling owing to the parents' concentration on the illness, which, in turn, increases any surviving children's sense of guilt during bereavement (Kubler-Ross, 1983; Rafael, 1983).

After a death, adults outside a family sometimes ask children how their parents are doing, overlooking the children's own grief as if their sense of catastrophe were invisible or nonexistent (Rosen, 1986). In a series of interviews with teenagers, teachers sometimes mistakenly revert to calling a surviving sibling by the name of the deceased child; and they sometimes insensitively compare the child to the dead sibling, perhaps commenting that the survivor is doing as well as the sibling did (Donnelly, 1988). In one case, a 15-year-old boy described the effects of his older brother's accidental, or possibly suicidal, death.

> When he died, it changed our whole life. My mum and dad never got over it. They wouldn't talk about it. "It was such a disgrace," they said. . . . I was so confused. The kids at school avoided me for awhile. I didn't know what to say, and they didn't either. The teachers would always be comparing me to him, though, and they'd say, "You're getting on well—like your brother." But I got the message that I wasn't really as good as him. (Rafael, 1983, p. 153-74)

The Double Void: Death and Silence

Well-meaning parents, teachers, and other adults may inadvertently set up a "no talk" rule in their effort to shelter children from the painful truth about death or illness. Catastrophically ill children, for example, are often aware of the possibility of dying (DeSpelder & Strickland, 1987; Kastenbaum, 1981), but everyone they meet tries only to reassure them instead of letting them talk about their illness (Hinton, 1972). Roles often reverse in these cases as children attempt to shelter their parents and teachers from the children's own awareness of their illness (Kavanaugh, 1985). Almost 40% of high-school seniors in one survey responded that when they were children, they never heard anyone in their families discuss the subject of death directly. Another 26% of high school seniors said that only occasionally did they hear anyone superficially mention death (Carroll, 1985). Krell and Rabkin speculated that three types of children come from families where a conspiracy of silence predominates: children who live in fear of what may happen to them, children emotionally smothered by parents who fear losing them, and children who become substitutes for the deceased (see Hansen, 1984). Studies have shown that children suffering catastrophic illness must learn the truth about their diseases or they develop inner fears about their inability to understand the state of their health and may act out in their frustration (Kavanaugh 1985).

Parents losing a spouse often experience personal conflicts over a partner's death and may then have difficulty discussing their loss with their children (Kastenbaum, 1981). Most experts agree, however, that children can sense something is wrong (Kavanaugh, 1985; Schaefer & Lyons, 1988). Children see stifled tears or hear a denial that a parent was crying and may learn to deny their own sense of reality. They come to reason that a loved one did not hold emotional value, and begin to feel guilty for the unexplained pain they sense in others (Kavanaugh, 1985), or they feel humiliated and believe they "don't count" (Schaefer & Lyons, 1988). Jackson (1978) noted that although parents keep information from children, they may hold a funeral where other parents attend and the information thereby leaks down through classmates. The fact is that bereaving children often have their first real talk about their loss with a trusted teacher.

In some cases, parents and teachers may believe children do not comprehend the situation and, therefore, do not have feelings needing attention; or, as in the death of a pet, adults may not see the loss as a legitimate bereavement (Kamerman, 1988). Children inadvertently may reinforce these inaccurate assumptions by seeming to go back easily to normal pursuits (Kastenbaum, 1981); however, children do comprehend at their own level of development. In one incident relayed to me, the father of two preschoolers died unexpectedly. The mother took the children to the hospital to see their father's body, cried openly in front of them, answered questions, and talked about her husband's death with them. She later reported that both children are aware that their father is dead and is not coming back. The three-year-old does not ask age-typical questions such as, "When will Father return?" Instead, he has become 'father before' and 'father after' (death). In another family I know, a seven-year-old's mother told her and her brother to play in the back yard while the adults in the family attended their father's funeral. The two children tried to find a way to climb to the top of the wooden fence in order to see their father for one last time across the field at the nearby church.

In some families, children already feel a deep emotional abandonment long before any actual death or illness. Rafael (1983) pointed out that, in families specializing in finding fault, everyone recognizes guilt as a powerful tool for keeping children in line, and making them feel guilty is a common form of punishment. A death in such a family creates even more anger and hostility, and parents often find a scapegoat among the more vulnerable family members. This practice reinforces a child's normal tendency to feel guilty about the death. On the other hand, the general rule in emotionally avoidant families is to guard against growing too close in order to protect oneself from the pain of any loss. When a death does occur, the grief that families express seems to have little depth, and the family and bereaved children quickly and busily go back to work and school. Children may feel a death intensely, but they also know that their parents cannot accept their profound feelings or offer them comfort (Rafael, 1983).

Finally, when a dying family member is in the final stages of disease, that person may encounter loss of mental ability and memory as a part of the symptoms. The dying person whom the child previously turned to for love, comfort, and assurance no longer recognizes or appreciates the child. Children in this circumstance may experience a twofold loss: the loss of the relationship with the dying person and also the loss of family stability in seeing family members become angry, frustrated, and withdrawn, perhaps to the point of choosing hospitalization for the dying person as a way to reduce the problem (Buckman, 1988).

Children will not recognize easily the problems coming from disrupting a familiar lifestyle and from experiencing emotional abandonment associated with an illness or death. Children, in fact, may see any one of these traumatic symptoms as a part of their normal life. A teacher or counselor, however, will see children's unspoken reactions to the above situations in uncharacteristic or exaggerated behavior in the classroom. A child who must struggle with grief and loss usually behaves differently in the classroom and schoolyard besides carrying secret emotions and responses. The range of these "invisible" possibilities is discussed in the following section. Suggested interventions, helpful approaches, and therapeutic activities appear later in the "Helping a Grieving Child" section of this chapter.

INVISIBLE SIDE OF CHILDHOOD GRIEF: PAINFUL SIDE EFFECTS

A bereaved child may experience many emotional reactions that remain hidden simply because the child lacks the vocabulary or developmental understanding to express them. Sometimes the child does not have a clear awareness of his/her feelings, and the fact that they are not expressed overtly can make them all the more powerful. In addressing the needs of any child, a teacher needs to be aware of some of the possible responses buried within. Here are a few of the major ones.

Anger—At a Specific Person or Group

Some typical targets of anger include the dead person for leaving the child, the family or physicians for not telling the child a person would die or for not being able to stop the death, and God for causing the person's death (Grollman, 1978; Schaefer & Lyons, 1988; Schumacher, 1984). It is natural for surviving children to feel anger and betrayal as well as jealousy and unfairness, and talking about these feelings is healing (Carroll, 1985; Kubler-Ross, 1983).

Horror

Fears also develop in many forms. Children may fear that they caused the death or illness in their family through wishful thinking or by being too hard to handle (Anthony, 1972). By the five- to nine-year age group, children usually are concerned greatly over who will be their primary caretaker as they realize that if one parent is vulnerable to death, perhaps the other one will die too (Anthony, 1972). The child may question whether anyone would even care if he/she died, especially in cases where parents will not show grief in front of their children. Carroll (1985, p. 150) reported that "fear of being forsaken is more of a concern for most children than grief itself." Other fears include going to sleep (because the children have been told that death is like sleep); fear of the dark and unseen danger; fear of being alone; and even fear of God because God "took" the person (Bertman, 1984; Kastenbaum, 1981).

Schaefer and Lyons (1988) pointed out that children in the five- to nine-year age group usually want a more detailed explanation about a person's death, such as clarifying the difference between a minor, a serious, and fatal illness. Children may become preoccupied with morbid thoughts and become fascinated by the idea of death. Unable to understand their own fears, they may find a scapegoat in fearing an eccentric stranger, an authority figure, or a neighborhood animal. Often, too, they exhibit an inability to make decisions and show more dependency than usual. Nightmares are common among some children, and sometimes panic attacks occur. In all these cases, youngsters need reassurance that everything will get better, and that hope is still alive and well. In the face of any death, especially within a family, children often think they too will die. When a brother or sister dies, surviving children may think they will die after reaching the sibling's age (Donnelly, 1988). Thus, adults need to reassure surviving siblings that they are separate human beings and that what happened to the deceased will not happen to them (Carroll, 1985).

By 8 to 12 years of age, bereaved children, more than any other age group, tend toward fearfulness, phobic behaviors, and some exaggerated fears for their health. They become more acutely aware of death as a personal possibility and may search their body for symptoms of disease. They become afraid of even minute aches and pains or anything associated with death. In these cases, allaying the death-related fears should come before dealing directly with the grief itself (Rafael, 1983).

Catastrophically ill children may fear they, too, will die, as they see other hospitalized children dying all around them from the same disease or injury they have (DeSpelder & Strickland, 1987). Their fears magnify as they mourn the deaths of fellow hospital patients (Hinton, 1972). Fearing painful medical treatments is common. One young patient I observed made this fear more endurable by planning a large party to celebrate the end of the treatments.

Guilt

Another hidden symptom of grief is feeling guilty. Most studies agree that, sometime after age five, as children's conscience begins to develop, guilt becomes one of the most common reactions in childhood bereavement (Carroll, 1985; Rafael, 1983). With a sharpened sense of conscience, children may feel responsible on all fronts. Helpless, yet duty-bound to bring a grieving parent or parents back to a place of stability (Schaefer & Lyons, 1988), they may take on a compulsive kind of caregiving and a facade of self-reliance (Donnelly, 1988; Rafael, 1983). They may feel guilty for surviving the death, for feeling angry toward the deceased, for forgetting ordinary things about the person, for loving the deceased so much and yet not enough to save him, and for any relief they might feel because of the death (Grollman, 1978; LeShan, 1978; Schumacher, 1984). Conley (1984) talked about a 14-year-old girl whose best friend suffered a spontaneous brain hemorrhage and died while the two were fiercely competing in a game of volleyball. The girl blamed herself for the death because of her aggressive play that day. Although she attended the funeral, she was unable to go up to the casket and look at her friend: every attempt left her crying and guiltily retreating. Six months later she dropped out of sports and then out of school. She found the prospect of talking about her feelings and facing the biological facts of her friend's death more frightening than holding onto her guilt and giving up her life as an athlete and a scholar.

Confusion, Withdrawal, and Isolation

Younger grieving children may become confused over their feelings of unreality, as if in a "waking nightmare" (LeShan, 1978, p. 22), dreaming of the deceased person as though the person were still alive, as if someone had played a cruel trick. Some may take on a look of indifference (Grollman, 1978) as a defense against the conflict and actually may deny that a person is dead. In these cases of denial, experts say adults should allow children to keep their fantasies until they indicate they are ready to face reality (Carroll, 1985). They also may feel that they lack permission to discuss or question a parent's remark such as, "I wish I could just die too," yet they believe the desperate statement must be true (Schaefer & Lyons, 1988). Some children may opt to withdraw, believing that, if they had not loved the deceased person so much, they would not be hurting so much now. Therefore, they conclude that by avoiding love and intimacy, they will avoid future pain (LeShan, 1978). Thus, some children develop distancing strategies to limit their number of close relationships (DeSpelder & Strickland, 1987). Also, parents who are grieving themselves may be unavailable to participate in typical school or recreational activities. This self-absorption adds to their children's sense of isolation. Nongrieving peers also may contribute to children's withdrawal by teasing or shunning them, thinking that what killed a parent or sibling is contagious (Donnelly, 1988).

Confusion

Bewilderment and disbelief are especially strong in adolescents, whose typical response is often avoidance and escape. They often do not know what normal grieving is (i.e., an acceptable display of sorrow). Therefore, they are leery of showing their natural fear because others might see their display as different, inadequate, or abnormal—a horrible experience in their eyes (Rafael, 1983). Answering "I don't know" to questions about feelings may be a tactic for avoiding giving the appearance of being different from others (Donnelly, 1988).

Anniversary Reactions

All people in grief—children as well as adults—move in and out of the above negative emotional states. A wise helper knows that an apparently resolved issue may show up again at a later time. Besides occurring at an expected period after a death, these responses may reappear on anniversaries of special significance to a child—holidays, birthdays, or significant dates and occasions previously spent with the person now deceased (Fox, 1984; Osterweis & Townsend, 1988). Because children may not recognize the connection with their unexpected surge of feelings, helpers would be providing children a solid service if they talk about why this loss is happening at this particular time.

VISIBLE SIDE OF CHILDHOOD GRIEF

Besides a child's hidden inner turmoil, often readily observable behaviors show up in the classroom that can alert the teacher to a more complicated bereavement. A younger child may show anger and aggressiveness in resistance to "being good"; the deceased "was so good that God wanted him in heaven." Avoid reprimanding or correcting a child for being angry at a deceased person (Carroll, 1985). With children 8 to 12 years old, anger may be expressed openly in aggressive games or in victimizing younger siblings and friends. A child may turn on playmates with sudden anger and hostility (Grollman, 1990), perhaps caused by teasing from other children. Boys especially may become aggressive in their responses and play (Donnelly, 1988; Rafael, 1983). Also, note that a child may be caught in a self-fulfilling prophesy, as parents and educators often label as "difficult behavior" the general irritability accompanying children's inner turmoil following a death (Rafael, 1983). According to Rafael (1983), some young adolescents become bossy while grieving. They take on an adult facade of apparent control and power, perhaps as a defense against feeling helpless and afraid. Immediately after the death of one 14-year-old boy's invalid father, the son showed great fright and felt an uncontrollable longing for his father, even though he had been aggressive and violent toward the son. Later on, however, the boy became demanding and began giving orders to his mother and younger sister, insisting that he no longer missed his father and that, in fact, he was now in charge of the family. He immediately wanted to change his name to an aggressive and destructive TV character who never showed any feelings (Rafael, 1983). In the volatile aftermath of experiencing the death of a loved one, children and teenagers may exhibit a full range of emotions and will latch onto a specialty that offers a feeling of control and stability, even if they are temporarily deceiving themselves. Listening to them in the midst of their emotional vortex and giving them a chance to share some of their immediate thoughts and feelings will help them regain a genuine sense of control sooner.

Roller Coaster Emotions

Hyperactive actions, incessant talk, laughing instead of crying, and even exhibiting self-destructive behavior, all may occur in order to bring on punishment for an assumed guilt and badness (Rafael, 1983; Schaefer & Lyons, 1988). Such contradictory, distance-provoking behavior actually may be a request for closeness. One study (Rafael, 1983) described an eight-year-old boy who was reported by his teacher to have increasing problems with disruptive behavior in school. After his father's sudden death, his mother was overcome with grief, anger, and feelings of desertion to the point that she lost sight of her children's needs and their own feelings of abandonment. Finally, through counseling, the child was able to express the real source of his anger and frustration. Often a parent, such as this overwhelmed mother, is also helped indirectly by talking with the counselor concerning what appears to be "the child's problem."

Bodily Distress

Just as with adults, a child may experience any number of physical symptoms in reaction to his/her deeper pain. Symptoms may come in symbolic form; for example, a child who feels that he/she cannot talk about the loss may develop a sore throat or tightness in the throat (Carroll, 1985; Grollman, 1978). Symptoms can include a variety of breathing problems, skin eruptions, lethargy, exhaustion, insomnia or perpetual drowsiness, tightness in the chest, allergies, altered eating habits, enuresis, persistent abdominal pain, headaches, blurred vision, and girls' menstruation may stop for a few months (Carroll, 1985; Grollman, 1978; Hinton, 1972; Rafael, 1983; Schaefer & Lyons, 1988).

School Problems

Various studies show that overall, children struggling with loss and death show poorer school adjustment than nonbereaved children (Kamerman, 1988; Rafael, 1983). Problems include an increased disinterest in school, preoccupation with the distress at home, brooding about the deceased, a general lack of concentration along with difficulty in following directions and a greater tendency to lose things, a reluctance to participate in activities, and a dread of competing. Conversely, school children who have a catastrophic illness may push themselves to get things done and may become angry when people take too long in answering their questions or requests (Carroll, 1985; Donnelly, 1988; Hinton, 1972; Osterweis & Townsend, 1988; Rafael, 1983; Schaefer & Lyons, 1988).

Other school performance problems include a decline in grades, especially for girls; test anxiety; examination failure; and, for older adolescents, dropping out of school. Children may refuse to attend school at all, especially in the case of sibling death; they fear leaving home and having someone else from the family die while they are away (Donnelly, 1988; Osterweis & Townsend, 1988; Rafael, 1983).

Risk-Taking and Sexual Behaviors

In *The Anatomy of Bereavement,* Rafael (1983) discussed the daring behavior of some bereaved young people. Boys may take risks such as wild driving, delinquent acts, drinking or taking drugs, and testing authority, all as a release of tension and in order to provoke punishment. Adolescent girls may become promiscuous in an attempt to gain nurturing and reassurance as well as indulge in the other sorts of risk-taking. In one case study, Rafael reported a 14-year-old girl who felt that no one in her family cared for her now that her father had died. After his death, she overheard her mother say that the daughter would be fine because she was young and had never shown much affection anyway. The mother stated that her daughter was likely not affected at all by the father's death. The girl decided to "show them." She later reported,

> The boys thought I was great—I really turned it on for them—everything I had. I'd be all excited, and they thought I was pretty sexy. I'd feel good at first, especially when they would hold me afterward, but then it would wear off, and I'd feel bad and dirty. They used to tell me they loved me. I knew they didn't mean it, but it made me feel good, because at least for a while I'd feel someone cared, now that I didn't have Dad. (Rafael, 1983, pp. 163-164)

DEVELOPMENTAL STAGES AND RESPONSES TO GRIEF

Although teachers are already well-acquainted with the ordinary behavioral patterns of school-age children, they might find it beneficial to consider youngsters' specific conceptions about death. Also, teachers might benefit by viewing children's reactions to loss from a developmental perspective, precisely because grief does not touch the majority of children at any one time and certain patterns may be overlooked. In discussing the similarities and differences in the various age groups of bereaved children, three important factors must be kept in mind. First, in spite of age group, children develop at different speeds due to cultural influences, temperament, and general life experiences (Kastenbaum, 1981). Second, for all children, the meaning of death is reexamined as the their lives change and their understanding unfolds through a natural growth process (Grollman, 1990). Lastly, children may resolve their grief successfully at one age, only to face new challenges with the same loss at a subsequent developmental stage (Rafael, 1983). Such was the case with a preadolescent girl I counseled who adjusted adequately to the death of her father only to discover a new feeling of loss and deprivation several years later when she entered high school without her beloved father to guide her.

Conception of Death

Most experts agree that by eight years old, if not before, children come to see death as an irreversible natural process that can happen to anyone, including themselves (Rafael, 1983). However, children do not necessarily accept that death *must* happen to everyone, especially themselves (Grollman, 1990). Even in the 8- to 12-year age range, children still may fluctuate between seeing death as final and as reversible although, with a life-threatening childhood illness, children in all age groups are likely to have an understanding of death at an earlier age (Rafael, 1983). Buckman (1988, p. 157) told of one child with cancer who, when asked his age, replied, "I am 11 years, 4 months, and 3 days old, and I am dying inch by inch." By adolescence, children usually understand as well as adults do that death is universal, inevitable, and irreversible, and thus adults need not show so much caution when considering their words in talking about death (Rafael, 1983; Schaefer & Lyons, 1988). Recent findings by various researchers indicate that previous information about children's personification of death is no longer applicable, at least among American children. Kastenbaum (1981) stated,

> Perhaps the world of childhood has changed enough from the time of Nagy's research to replace personification with more objective and scientific-sounding responses. "Death is like the computer's down and you can't get it started again," one 7-year-old told his mother recently. (p. 252)

A classroom exercise of drawing a picture about death might be useful to both teacher and students in testing these findings.

Those who study children have noted certain specific differences among them according to age groups. Schaefer and Lyons (1988) pointed out that children aged 5 to 9 are likely to see death as contagious and need an adult to reassure them that dying is not infectious. Unique for 8-to 12-year-olds is their acute sense of fairness about life and death. They hold a tangible belief that a birth should occur for every death. They also exhibit a tendency to see death as a punishment for wrongdoing or unkindness. In this same age group, children value black and white standards and they often hold firm beliefs about propriety, such as the absolute requirement to conduct a meaningful burial ceremony and ritual for any animal that dies. Given these intense attitudes among students of elementary school age, teachers might help students who have lost a classmate to organize a small group ceremony or memorial service, followed by a short discussion.

Adolescents usually see death as a natural enemy, questioning the purpose of a life that can be stopped short without notice (Schaefer & Lyons, 1988). When teenagers suffer a catastrophic illness, they are most likely to feel resentment. Just as they are beginning to understand their own potential in life, they must come to grips with the end of their life. Out of anger, such terminally ill adolescents often fail to take prescribed medicine, or they ignore medical advice out of anger (Buckman, 1988). Teachers are in an excellent position to help teenagers understand their grief and emotions and to literally teach them how to act in a crisis. (Additional strategies for teachers will appear later in this chapter.)

"Magical thinking" regarding death affects all ages of boys and girls with slight variations. For young children, magical thinking consists of believing death can be controlled (Schaefer & Lyons, 1988), perhaps bargained with, or even killed (Carroll, 1985). As children develop a sense of conscience, an untimely death can lead to a strong sense of personal guilt; children often believe that their ill wishes and thoughts actually can kill another person (Schaefer & Lyons, 1988). In these cases, someone these children trust needs to inform them that they have no such power. Irrational connections are also common, such as believing grocery stores cause death because a grandparent suffered a fatal heart attack in one (Carroll, 1985). Although adolescents understand intellectually that one can neither stop nor cause a death by thoughts alone, they also may revert to this kind of thinking, just as adults do, as a defense against the anxiety of impending death or grief. On the other hand, adolescents generally feel unique and special, so much so that they believe that even highly risky activities will not provoke death for them (Rafael, 1983).

In all age groups, young people yearn for a person they have lost and they daydream of a life where the relationship is still intact. Younger children and adolescents alike, however, often are wary of openly expressing their yearning for fear of seeming helpless or childish. The culture does not support public expressions of grief and open displays of sadness and loss. When children repress this legitimate longing, they often show a greater tendency toward pathological mourning (Rafael, 1983).

Need for Approval

According to Schaefer and Lyons (1988), a sense of propriety appears among 8- to 12-year-olds, and both the bereaved child and the child approaching a bereaved classmate may question how to act and what to say in order not to look different or appear stupid. Contradictions in young people's behavior seem to abound. If embarrassed, or if they just don't know how to behave around a bereaved classmate, they may act silly or laugh or become abruptly quiet. They need the guidance of adults in what to say and how to act toward a bereaved peer.

A Flood of Emotional Messages

Observers of childhood grief have found that adolescents especially demonstrate contradictory reactions, such as an hysterical outburst followed by embarrassed laughter; or they may idealize the dead person, followed by condemnation (Schaefer & Lyons, 1988). They seem to fluctuate between invulnerability and a sense of impending disaster (Grollman, 1978), independence and dependence, and wanting comfort yet feeling a need to be strong (Donnelly, 1988). Adolescents have the added burden of being overly concerned with their own body image (Tull & Goldberg, 1984). They hate to be seen crying for fear of looking weak as well as ugly (Schaefer & Lyons, 1988). The preadolescent with a catastrophic illness may feel singled out, picked on, separated from other children, and may experience a sense of unfairness; the adolescent may add feelings of disgrace and shame as well. Adolescents experience the death of a parent as the greatest loss, especially in their earlier years when they have not yet completed their own sense of separation (Rafael, 1983). Rafael (1983) noted several patterns of response. Some children take the bereavement very quietly, as if withdrawn, with little major change in their behavior except for some falling off in schoolwork. They seem to be marking time until life becomes secure again.

A Teacher's Role in Bereavement

achers become especially important as a consistent relationship in a
'fe. Children often express their emotions in a particular way, and an
er can make the classroom seem a safe place compared to the latest

crisis at home. Also, a child may retreat into some symbolic or obsessive behavior as a way of linking up with the deceased. One 11-year-old boy would
lie in his room, his headphones on, listening for hours to a favorite hymn of his
father's, which repetitively included the phrase, "Oh, Father, I long to be with
you." Finally, a child may take on an adult behavior such as bossiness. Rafael
described a seven-year-old girl whose mother died and who began at once to
take on a motherly role in the family. "She fussed about, bathed and dressed
her younger brother, and even encouraged his regression to use his bottle again"
(Rafael, 1983, p. 102). Although she yearned for her mother, she rose to the
family's needs, repressing her own longing for care and maintaining an identification with her mother through her new role. Another seven-year-old child
was observed caring for her dying mother during the day but allowing her
father to care for and comfort her in the evenings. After her mother's death, the
father continued to encourage her to express her grief, and the pattern of post-
death compulsive caregiving did not emerge.

During the Gulf War crisis, a news telecast introduced a family in which
the mother went to the Middle East to fight in the war while the father remained home with the children (two sons and a daughter about 9 or 10). In the
interview, the father admitted relying on the daughter to take over her mother's
household responsibilities and the care of the three males of the house. The
daughter reported that she missed her mom and especially did not like having
to be the "woman of the house," although she acknowledged assuming a motherly role and responsibility. One can easily imagine that if the mother had died
in the war, the daughter would have continued as surrogate mother for a long
time to come. The implication for the child would have been that not only did
she lose a parent but also her childhood.

Denial

All ages have a tendency to react to illness and death with automatic
denial, wishing that the information were not true. Rafael (1983) pointed out
that younger children may carry on with laughter and play as if nothing has
happened, even becoming wild in behavior, and may be perceived as uncaring,
unloving, or unaffected. By ages 9 to 12 years, the denial is usually more temporary, and the child's distress soon pours out to a sensitive listener. One boy
of seven learned that his mother had "gone to Heaven and would not be returning." He immediately ran off to play in what appeared to be happiness and
excitement. "He became, however, more and more difficult to manage. He did
not cry. He had many wild and rowdy games throughout the house, crashing
his toy cars into the furniture and becoming very aggressive" (Rafael, 1983, p.
101). Eventually, in visits with a counselor, he was able to admit his helpless-

ness. After open discussion, he settled into a more natural sharing of memories and feelings with his family.

Biological Interest

According to Schaefer and Lyons, children aged 8 to 12 years are most interested in the biological aspects of death and the technical details of what happens to a person's body. The same children, however, may not yet grasp simple details, as shown in questions such as, "Is the lid closed when a casket is put into the ground?" Students in this age group most likely would enjoy participating in and be fascinated by a step-by-step demonstration of a funeral (Schaefer & Lyons, 1988, pp. 22-24, 109).

Factors to consider in assessing a young person's level of grief and emotional needs include the closeness of the child to the deceased, the way the death occurred, the way a messenger conveys the loss to the child, and the support and attitudes the surrounding adults display. Added to these factors, a child's own developmental level applies. In many cases, children in each age group have their own unique inner responses; consequently, they will respond differently, depending on developmental age, to what adults say (or do not say) and how they say things. Teachers and other adult helpers are in an excellent position to offer help to grieving children during the course of a day's activities. The following sections are suggestions for helping.

HELPING A GRIEVING CHILD

Equally important in dealing with grief is knowing what not to do. The suggestions here and in the next section are mainly for teachers, but any caring adult in a position to help should follow these guidelines. Many occasions, of course, call for teachers and other school staff members to refer children to professional or pastoral counseling. Teachers are already overloaded with responsibilities and no one is asking them to become full-time counselors as well. A brief checklist of the helping behaviors that I describe below may be useful for everyone.

Observe	Label Interpretations
Listen	Create a continuing dialogue
Accept	Encourage the child
Ask questions	Create security
Answer questions	Become informed
Explain	Refer to professional counseling

With careful observation, a teacher can compare a child's behavior to previous behavior and what has been normal patterns for that child. This will help a teacher in deciding what approach to use in conversations or activities and when to refer children for professional help. In noticing even subtle changes in a classroom, teachers can discover a valuable opportunity to interject comments or lessons about death and grief.

As a teacher, do not forget that you too are part of the children's class. In one story I heard, a second-grade teacher's father died unexpectedly, and, while she was on bereavement leave, a substitute teacher taught her class. The children were naturally curious and concerned about their teacher's loss. In assuring them that their teacher would return soon, the substitute explained that the teacher's father had died and that she most probably would be feeling badly about his death for some time to come. She encouraged the children to ask any questions now but not to bring up the subject when their teacher returned in order to prevent upsetting her or making her cry. Upon the teacher's return, she sensed some tension among the children but attributed it to the disruption they felt in her absence. During the first day, however, one of the children "accidentally" burst out with a remark about her dead father, and the teacher realized that the children were genuinely interested in her loss. Although talking about her painful grief was difficult, she recognized the importance of the children's being able to talk about their teacher's hardship. Having addressed the topic head-on, everyone learned from the exchange, and the children soon felt no further need to bring up the subject.

Listen and Accept

More than anything, children need and want someone they respect to acknowledge and accept their feelings (DeSpelder & Strickland, 1987). Rather than engaging in discussions of right and wrong, children should have an opportunity to ramble, talk crudely, and ask questions in an atmosphere of safety and acceptance (Kavanaugh, 1985). Listening to what children are really saying is essential, and not to what one thinks they should say (Schaefer & Lyons, 1988). We need to offer relaxed and patient attention, doing more listening than telling and without trying to explain or reassure at the start (Kastenbaum, 1981; Kavanaugh, 1985). The technique of "active listening" can be very useful. By paraphrasing a child's remarks without judgment, advice, or added comment, teachers let children know that they truly have heard their students and that what they have said is neither shocking nor bad (Adler & Towne, 1990).

Allow Children to Cry

Crying provides a release of tension as well as a nonverbal way of honoring the deceased while expressing one's deepest pain and yearning. In talking with a children about their loss, remember that you are not the cause of others' tears. The tears are usually right below the surface waiting for a safe time to flow. On the other hand, no one should urge children to display unfelt sorrow. Some children are not able to cry easily or will not feel comfortable doing so in a school setting (Grollman, 1978).

Ask Questions

An initial discussion with a bereaved child's family is always the wisest first step in clarifying that child's feelings and awareness. A family will be helpful in letting a teacher know how much they have shared with the child and what personal boundaries, if any, they wish the teacher to respect. Conversely, a teacher's evaluation of a child since the illness or death will be a valuable link in the family's own understanding of their child's experience. After talking with the family, ascertain from the child what he/she already knows of the illness or death and of death in general. For example, "What does the doctor say about your illness (or your grandfather's illness)? What do your parents say?" Children may have distorted ideas, and, in sharing these notions with you, will help you better understand their fears. How close is or was the child to the ill or deceased person? How will the loss upset the child's routine? This information will help determine how a child is adjusting and the best approach to take with that particular child.

Some typical questions with which to open up a conversation might include the following: Can you tell me a little about the death? What happened that day? Can you tell me about your grandmother's illness? How serious is it? Might she die from it? What have you been feeling since your grandfather became ill? How has this illness affected your life at home? At school? How have you (or your friends and family) managed since the death? Bertman (1984, p. 56) stated, "It is essential to help a child recall the happy and sad, or not so good, times with the deceased. Such a review of a relationship can ward off the unhealthy tendency to glorify or idealize the dead person." A conversation that facilitates this kind of review might include a question such as, "Tell me about your mother. What kinds of things did you do together?"

Answer Questions

Even if children already have engaged in conversation about the death—perhaps over and over again—a teacher can expect children to repeat certain types of questions. These questions may vary slightly, but they show the level of a child's thinking and feelings (Jackson, 1978). Some examples are as follows: What is death? What makes people die? What happens to people when they die. Where do they go? Did I cause this to happen? Will it happen to me? Who will take care of me now? When is he coming back? Will she ever move again? Is she sleeping? Why can't they fix him? Is he cold? How will he eat with dirt on his face? There also may be questions about the afterlife as well as a worry that the dead person will seek revenge, that others will die too, and that basic needs will not be met (Grollman, 1990; Osterweis & Townsend 1988; Schaefer & Lyons, 1988). Although the tone of some of the above questions may sound "young," I have noticed variations on such questions coming from even eighth- and ninth-graders. When teachers present an emotionally safe environment without judgment or expectations, children are willing to expose their hidden concerns.

Answers about death are most problematic for those aged five to nine years old, for even the words themselves can be confusing. Many words or their sounds have double meanings already, such as perish and parish, or the idea of expiring versus an expiration date. Schaefer and Lyons (1988, pp. 20-21) reported one story of a child who thought his dead father spoke to him from a shoebox, confusing the words "soul" and "sole." Euphemisms are equally confusing to children. Statements such as "death is like sleep" can cause a child to fear going to sleep. To say the child "lost" a parent implies that the parent can be found and returned. Expressions such as "has passed away," "has left us," "has gone," or "is departed," may be comforting to adults but leave children wondering about their true meaning and even if the act of "leaving" was deliberate on the part of the deceased (Schaefer & Lyons, 1988). Ultimately, young children are trying to understand death on a simple, practical level. DeSpelder and Strickland (1987) pointed out that, tempting as it may be to relay imaginative answers to kids such as fairies taking the child's pet off to play or angels carrying a body out of the grave after all the people have left, adults should tell the truth. Even if small children seem captivated by these make-believe comments, when they later realize the truth, they most likely will sense that they cannot trust such important adults in their lives as parents and teachers. Most children are satisfied to hear simple and direct answers to their questions. If children want to know more, they will ask at that point if they feel safe and trusting.

When answering children, honesty about one's own limitations is the best route to follow, especially when one does not have an answer to a question. Overall, children think concretely and often are not developmentally ready to understand abstract responses, such as "death is a beginning." Grollman (1990,

p. 46) suggested supplying an answer such as, "Lot's of people think about death in different ways, but no one has the final answer. Tell me what you think." Elisabeth Kubler-Ross (Kubler-Ross, in Carroll, 1985, p . 201) struck a balanced perspective in suggesting that "Why not me?" is just as valid a question for an illness as "Why me?" In all conversations, the important focus is on a child's response and feedback.

Children under the age of nine seldom speak openly about being afraid to die but keep their communication indirect and in the third person singular (Carroll, 1985; Rafael, 1983), perhaps asking a question such as, "What if a person . . . ?" Teachers and other helpers must be alert for such a form of questioning or comment and should not respond in an offhand manner but rather should ascertain as much as possible what the child specifically has in mind. When a child asks, for example, "Why are people always shooting each other?" the real question may be, "Am I going to be killed?" Or, in a classroom conversation about death, students may blurt out, "How old are you?" when they really mean, "Are you so old you are going to die, too?" (Schaefer & Lyons, 1988, p. 120). Read between the lines. With a difficult question such as, "When will I feel better?" adults may tend to assume the questioner's meaning and answer with more detail than is needed or with confusing information that does not address the true question. To be safe, ask specifically what children mean rather than assuming you know.

Explaining Death

According to Schaefer and Lyons (1988, p. 124), explanations should typically include phrases such as, the body "gets sick" (illness) or "wears out" (old age) or is "hurt" (accident) and "stops working." Make clear that the death is no one's fault and that the child will not automatically die. Carroll (1985) pointed out that technical explanations, impersonal logic, or emotionally distant explanations only will push children away, whereas sensitivity without sentimentality shows them that significant adults value their feelings at a time of an important loss. Carroll suggested, "Keep the tone on an even, sympathetic level, and avoid oversentimentalizing. Let the talk be thoughtful and weighty but not necessarily solemn. Serious does not mean gloomy. Serious can also mean reflective, earnest, even meditative" (1985, pp. 160-165). Schaefer and Lyons (1988, p. 125) suggested beginning a conversation about the news of a death with, "A terrible thing has happened and we are all very sad." Also, because communication generally consists of as much if not more attention to nonverbal cues as to the spoken word (Adler & Towne, 1990), adults must keep their body language consistent with the verbal message in order to avoid negating what they are saying.

Homicide and Suicide: Controversial Topics

In the case of homicide, an opening statement might include, "Sometimes people do very bad things" (Schaefer & Lyons, 1988, p. 124). According to Carroll (1985), dwelling on lurid details is not helpful. Instead, answer the questions the children have. They may appear fascinated, but, concurrently, they may be developing unspoken fears. Telling a young child the facts about a suicide is a point of controversy among experts. Some authors (Conley, 1984) have recommended against directly telling a younger child about suicide, but all writers agree that, whatever the age of the child, the news bearer also should say that suicide is never a solution to problems and that surviving children are not responsible for the person's death. (See chapter 9, "Depression and Suicide: Injecting Hope," by Park and Boyd.)

Answering Funereal Questions

When children ask about funerals—details on cremation, embalming, cosmetics, and the like—adults ought to answer factually, simply, and impartially, perhaps mentioning that some people make these choices and others do not, depending on the family's circumstances and personal comfort (Schaefer & Lyons, 1988). Besides the technical consideration of burials, Carroll (1985) suggested that an explanation of funerals should include several additional points: a discussion of the purpose (i.e., to see the person one last time and to say good-bye and a time to support one another); what takes place at a funeral; why people seem sad and cry; and how people should act at a funeral.

When teachers or other adults do answer questions, they should verify that children have understood the true intention of the answer. One effective way of assessing an answer's usefulness is to ask children what the answer meant in their own words.

Explaining Grief Simply

Teachers are in an excellent position to educate children about the causes and normal range and phases of grief. For grieving children, a mini-lesson on grief will help put their experience in context; for nonbereaved children such explanations will help them in developing compassion for their grieving classmate or friend. A class discussion also can be helpful, especially if such a meeting arises naturally within the usual lessons of the day. A nonintrusive and gentle approach is to suggest possible reactions that children may have (such as those listed earlier in this chapter) without directly confronting or questioning the class, thereby allowing children to see or examine their position without embarrassment. Eda LeShan's *Learning to Say Good-by: When a Parent Dies* (1978) is a classic that presents an excellent demonstration of this style of communication. Carroll (1985, pp. 160-164) added, "Telling stories in the third person is a nonthreatening corrective technique designed to slip smoothly around (children's) natural defense system." Almost despite themselves, children assimilate the messages without shame or pressure. When talking to a young child about a specific death, make the explanation a third-person story: "Grandmother became ill, went to the hospital, became more sick, and then died."

Since guilt is a natural part of grieving, making sure children have a realistic understanding of how the death happened is important. Children need to realize that the actual death was a biological occurrence and not an event they caused (Schaefer & Lyons, 1988). Guilt for anyone is often unreasonable—certainly for children guilt is typically inappropriate. Nevertheless, adults ought to allow children to tell their own story including any personal role they imagine for themselves in the death. After listening and after a child feels genuinely heard and understood, let the child know that wishing does not cause or stop death, and that the child had nothing to do with the death, for all people die sooner or later. Avoid connecting suffering and death with sin and wrongdoing (Grollman, 1990).

Label Interpretations

In discussing an afterlife, one needs to label beliefs as such rather than as universal truths. Thus, children are free to develop their own understanding about death (DeSpelder & Strickland, 1987). A family's religious and cultural beliefs should guide what children appropriately hear about death. Respecting a family and its values is the best way to convey respect for children in a family. Because experts generally agree that using religious explanations can be controversial (Osterweis & Townsend, 1988), teachers would do well to begin with a talk with the family about both their beliefs and their wishes about their child or children.

Create a Continuing Dialogue

Rather than waiting or planning for the one important talk that may never come (or may be prematurely interrupted), maintain a continuing dialogue as occasions arise. The death of animals, scenes in movies, newspaper articles, TV presentations—all provide a chance to keep the dialogue going. In a general classroom discussion of death (as the subject comes up naturally), start first with nonthreatening examples and proceed gradually in keeping with the children's ability to understand. An explanation might include the life cycle of plants or small animals (not pets). Kastenbaum (1981) has predicted that after such conversations, children with troubling responses may be subtle about expressing these disturbing feelings. Children are likely to make such overall responses gradually, and they may express their trauma in a variety of ways. Perhaps a conversation may seem complete with all the delicate issues resolved, but some children probably will be working things out in their minds in an ongoing process. Adult confidants need to remain accessible and supportive.

> Teachers and other school personnel occupy a unique position in relation to a bereaved child. They are with the child for many hours of the day—often a greater part of the child's waking day than is spent at home. Children may turn to their teachers for comfort, information, and help. Since teachers, unlike members of the child's family, are not themselves mourning the loss, they are able to objectively observe the child's behavioral responses to the death, to offer emotional support to the child, and to mobilize mutual support among the child's peers. Parents, too, may turn to teachers for help. After a death in the family, parents may check to find out how the child is doing socially and academically. They may also ask the teacher to help calm particular anxieties expressed by the child and to help modify grief-related behaviors. (Osterweis & Townsend, 1988, pp. 1-2)

Encourage

Many children need encouragement to express their grief openly. When someone is dying, or even after a death, teachers can help. Any bereaved or ill child can share personal experience as a class project. Children, for example, may talk about their version of what happened at the funeral or on the day of the death. Where were they when they received the news? Who told them? What exactly did the informant say? How did they feel? What did they feel they should do? What did they actually do at that time? One child's responses can help other children open up and provide an opportunity to interject their own experiences about death. Some youngsters may wish to bring a special memento or photograph of the deceased. Seeing a tangible example from a student's quality world placed respectfully in a classroom will lend both support and comfort to a young grievant.

Bertman (1984) stated that repetitions of words and rituals not only make the blunt event more real, but also, ultimately, can create the conditions in which children can find the necessary emotional and psychological distance from the shock. "Teachers cannot provide too many opportunities for students to retell or relive their stories, especially in the company of other caring and non critical friends" (Bertman, 1984, p. 56). Company itself brings relief compared to the unbearably painful experience of evoking the image of a dead loved one when alone. Carroll (1985) suggested that, as children adjust to life without the deceased, encouraging a hobby, sports, or outdoor activity might help counteract depression.

Create Security

Teachers can help children gain stronger feelings of security by simply allowing them to continue participating in a normal routine and typical classroom activities while accepting understandable departures from the routine (Kastenbaum, 1981). By remaining an active participant, children gain both a sense of direction from encouraging adults and a sense of personal power when they might otherwise feel helpless. In the case of adolescents, teachers do well to respect teenagers' great need for privacy (Conley, 1984). To create a successful connection with adolescent students, we all must respect their normal need for seclusion and privacy under these painful circumstances. We must respect a natural need for separation but balance this consideration with a concerned vigilance. Bereaving adolescents want to know that an adult is available and accepting without feeling pummeled with questions or being singled out (Donnelly, 1988). Consistency from adults is the key with children of all ages. Teachers who promise a grievant a specific time for a talk or other activity absolutely must follow through with this plan or verbally acknowledge any changes in schedule and make new arrangements (Bertman, 1984).

Become Informed: Transcultural Contacts

Educating oneself about a child's impending loss or devastation from a death is a top priority for teachers and counselors. Becoming informed about a catastrophic illness will help caring adults support children and, when necessary, encourage them to slow down, recognize their physical limitations, and temporarily find less strenuous activities for play (Tull & Goldberg, 1984). People working with seriously ill children do not need medical details, but do need to learn enough to recognize common symptoms and effects on personality (Bertman, 1984).

Another form of self-education teachers may elect is to ask children in a class to talk about their families' cultural and ethnic customs and values about death and dying. Children from different backgrounds learn about death in different ways. Two small studies have been conducted on these lines, the first concerning American-Chinese families (Kastenbaum, 1981), and the second a comparative study of Los Angeles Blacks, Anglos, Hispanics and Japanese (Kalish & Reynolds, 1981). In the first study, the Chinese parents were especially reluctant to discuss death with their children and maintained a death taboo. In the second study, American-Japanese families were the most evasive about death and most reluctant to disclose the truth about an impending death in the family. The implication of these findings for teachers of Asian-American school children is that school may be the first or only place a American-Japanese child is free to discuss death. In spite of the enormous amount of death and violence on television, Anglo children are perhaps least likely to come in actual contact with death and dying, according to the investigation. When a personal loss occurs, they may be the least familiar with the feelings that emerge. Again, teachers can help ease things. Finally, in the cross-cultural study, Hispanics were the most willing to kiss the body at a funeral. Seeing this custom as a family value can alert teachers to a grieving child's distress when parents may have urged touching or kissing the deceased family member before that child was emotionally ready to do so. In all such cases, the best source for discovering and applying cultural traditions is the family itself. An open discussion in the classroom of ethnic differences and similarities can be educational and helpful for both teacher and students, and this conversation does not have to focus on death and grief. Finding pen pals with school children in sister cities throughout the world would be an enjoyable way students may incorporate learning about cultural differences and similarities, including diverse customs and values related to death.

Refer to Professional Counseling

With adult guidance and support, most children will be able to understand and resolve their grief successfully without the need for professional therapy. Rosen (1986) suggested four behaviors that we might expect to see in normal bereavement as children successfully manage their grief: first, behaviors that help them accept the reality of the loss; second, behaviors that assist them in dropping nonadaptive responses that they no longer find helpful; third, behaviors that help children cope with conflicting feelings; and fourth, behaviors that help them reestablish a sense of continuity and safety in the world.

Behaviors to Help Accept Loss. Specific examples of coping behaviors include focusing on school activities, keeping an object that the deceased had owned, talking about the loss, looking at a picture of the deceased, crying, maintaining a normal routine, and accepting parents' religious explanations regarding the loss. Writing about the loss, even something as simple as writing the word "dead," also can be helpful. To understand how simple writing can be and still be effective, Patricia Hovey (Bertman, 1984, p. 51), an oncology social worker, described a seven-year-old boy's experience. After his mother died, the child said to his grandmother: "We're going to have to tell people Sally doesn't live here anymore. How do you spell died?" He held onto mail that had come addressed to his mother. Later, his grandmother found three signs taped to the front and back doors and to the mailbox: "Sally Died Today."

How Long Should Children Grieve? Determining whether or not children could benefit from professional counseling often depends on the intensity and length of time grief symptoms last (Grollman, 1990) and their own readiness to accept help (Donnelly, 1988). Most people initially deny or entertain guilt, to name but two grieving behaviors; however, continuing to deny the death after many months, or maintaining a sense of guilt beyond a reasonable period of time alerts helpers to the special needs of these children. The issue is not how a child grieves—for almost any initial behavior in the face of grief is a normal response to shock—but rather how long they continue these initial grieving behaviors.

Atypical Grieving

Children's grieving style is generally briefer than adults' expression of grief. Adults' grieving symptoms sometimes stay consistent well into a second year or more. Most experts agree that children are usually able initially to suffer their grief and loss and then readjust within several months to a level close to their previous normal lifestyle, with occasional feelings of sadness and temporary grieving behaviors. If, after several months, children continue their pattern of initial severe grieving symptoms, professional consultation and counseling are in order. Rafael suggested three disabling grieving patterns: suppressing grief, distorting grief, and chronically grieving. Suppressing grief may include depressing, avoiding social activities, overlooking one's personal hygiene or one's physical appearance, absorbing oneself in constant daydreaming, apparently abstaining from grief altogether, or refusing to talk about the deceased. Distorted grief includes hectic overactivity and an inability to relax as before the death, persistent self-blame, guilt and anxiety, overidentification with the deceased, and compulsive caretaking of others. The third type of complicated grief, chronic grief, includes extreme fatigue or ill health, indifference to once-enjoyed activities, expectations of reunion with the deceased, exaggerated dependency on a surviving parent, and extreme idealization or degrading of the deceased (Grollman, 1990; Rafael, 1983).

Danger Signs

Some problems need professional help immediately, of course. Examples are reliance on drugs and alcohol (chapter 8), suicidal tendencies (chapter 9), and aggressive, destructive acts, such as vandalism or stealing (chapter 12). In other cases, children may feel comfortable and willing to talk with a professional counselor soon after the loss, regardless of the type of symptoms they exhibit.

In general, a supportive and helpful encounter with grieving children is akin to a revolving wheel in which teachers continually move back and forth from three different stances: listening and watching; asking questions to draw children out and make sure they truly understand what is going on; and finally, explaining honestly and simply what they want or need to know.

In summary, implement the following do's and don'ts when you are around a bereaving or seriously ill child:

- Do not ignore or dismiss unusual behavior. Do note unusual behavior and investigate causes.
- Do not tell children not to cry or not to talk about it. Do let them cry as long as they need to do so. They will not need as long as you think.
- Do not say, "Be cheerful, think happy thoughts, and carry on." Do encourage children to talk if they so desire, and listen to them.
- Do not say, "Things could be worse." Do acknowledge that this loss is a big change for them and may be scary.
- Do not tell children to be little adults or be the parent's little helper. Do assure the children that they will continue to receive all the help they will need.
- Do not compare children to their dead sibling. Do let the children know they are individuals in their own right.
- Do not try to divert children's grief. Do provide time for their questions and discussion.
- Do not discount questions or give fanciful or philosophical answers; avoid euphemisms; do not dwell on disturbing details. Do answer questions simply, directly, and honestly.
- Do not scold or correct children for having negative feelings. Do accept their feelings as valid for them.
- Do not assume that you know what children are feeling or what their experiences are. Do ask them what they already know and how they feel about their experiences.
- Do not take all questions at face value. Do read between the lines.

- Do not assume children understand their own feelings. Do explain the general stages of grief and the natural range of feelings that grieving people have.
- Do not immediately discount children's feelings of guilt. Do explain, after careful listening, that they are not responsible.
- Do not wait for one crucial talk. Do maintain a continuing dialogue as opportunities arise.
- Do not ignore the importance of saying good-bye. Do find opportunities to create a full circle—with specific beginnings and clear endings.
- Do not break promises or be inconsistent. Do follow through on agreements and maintain routines.
- Do not single children out or embarrass them. Do respect privacy while being accessible and available.
- Do not ignore the effects of illness. Do become informed about symptoms and physical limitations in catastrophic illness.
- Do not ignore differences in ethnic and cultural backgrounds. Do learn about family customs.
- Do not underestimate children's troubled behavior or assume this phase will pass with time. Do refer to professional or pastoral counseling as appropriate. If in doubt, seek a consultation about youngsters with a counselor.

Practical Activities to Help a Grieving Child

The following are possible school activities that teachers can adapt to a classroom as a whole or to individual children. As always, note that various ideas work for some people and not for others. An intervention should fit children's personality and specific needs, for not all of the following may be comfortable or appropriate with particular children or teachers. Many other adult helpers in various settings can use some of these approaches as well.

Self-expression. The treasure in letting a child draw freely is that the child's inner world is made more visible. This can be a vital tool in understanding what the child is feeling and how to approach him/her, and many experts agree that, for the child, the act of drawing, even without words, is as therapeutic as if a heartfelt conversation had taken place. You might specifically suggest certain types of drawings or leave the content entirely up to the child, who will draw from his/her own inner perspective (Furth, 1984). When asked to draw a family picture, one hospice child I know of drew everyone except the dying father around a dinner table, reflecting the child's sense of impending loss. Encouraging a child to draw the characters in a bad dream or nightmare gives the child some power over the dream and the ability to manipulate the fearful parts into less threatening images. Similar drawings about a threatening illness allow the child to express fears by showing the disease as a powerful monster or a tiny bug that can be stepped on and stopped. Examples of children's visual ideas about disease can be found in Murray and Jampolsky's *Another Look at the Rainbow* (1982), a follow-up of the Center for Attitudinal Healing's first book, *There Is a Rainbow behind Every Dark Cloud* (1979). Both books show a wide variety of pictures children drew to express feelings about their own illness or the illness of a sibling. When asked to draw something about a deceased person, hospice children often depict the person in a heavenly setting or at peace in a garden or meadow, which helps the child to internalize a sense of comfort in the loss. Another form of drawing is found in the concept of a coloring book about grief and loss. *Saying Good-bye* (1989), by Jim Boulden, combines text and cartoon figures to talk about the various feelings children might experience.

Molding or pounding clay around a theme of death and dying can be a powerful way for the child to work with personal aggressive feelings about the loss (Bertman, 1984). Other suggestions include collages or making "feelings masks" with an outside (public) face and an inside (private, secret) face reflecting the child's deeper feelings concerning the death. For younger children, or for a more convenient project, faces can be made on paper plates with crayons, or glue and objects, such as beads, yarn, or dry macaroni. Scrapbooks can be made including photos, poems, newspaper clippings, magazine articles or pictures of a deceased person. In trying to understand the homicide of her brother, one young teenager with whom I had spoken made a scrapbook of newspaper articles about victims and offenders and still added and referred to it even several years later.

Class projects might include planting a memorial tree (Schaefer & Lyons, 1988), placing a bookshelf in the library in a classmate's memory (Grollman, 1990), or dedicating the yearbook or class picture to the child's memory. A class mural can be made about the person (or death in general) or a class storybook where each child contributes a page about the person or about what grief or death is like. The class can work together in projects of sympathy, such as making condolence cards (or "hope you are feeling better" cards) or growing and sending flowers. An optional field trip to a local cemetery is educational, and I have noticed that students often remark how beneficial they found glimpsing other bereaved people bringing flowers and visiting a grave. Going as a group to visit the parents of a deceased classmate, especially months after a fellow student's death, is often beneficial for the parents as well as for the students (Kubler-Ross, 1983). Children also may wish to visit a sick classmate in the hospital. Because an ailing child may not feel well enough to meet a large group, or a hospital may not allow such groups, a class may wish to pick one or several representatives who can arrange a special visit and then report to the others.

Therapeutic Play. Ernest Becker, in his Pulitzer Prize winning book, *The Denial of Death,* wrote the following:

> The serious work of all play: [Play] reflects the discovery and exercise of natural bodily functions; it masters an area of strangeness; it establishes power and control over the deterministic laws of the natural world; and it does all this with symbols and fancy. (1983, p. 31)

Psychologists who study children see that they often act out loss or illness in the same way they act out other family dynamics. This behavioral rehearsal allows them to see concretely what they are thinking and feeling and to create a sense of control (DeSpelder & Strickland, 1987). This view is consonant with choice theory. All humans, children included, are constantly trying to stay in control by matching sensory pictures from the environment with internal mental pictures. By the age of five, a child's imagination has developed far enough to imagine himself in someone else's situation and also to imagine something of the unknown (Donnelly, 1988). As children experiment with death anxieties, courage, and fear, they often play games where they create imaginary perils and monsters (Kastenbaum, 1981; Schaefer & Lyons, 1988).

Including games of visualization in their more structured play can help bereaving children. Parents can ask their children to "lock up" bad memories or nightmares in a big box and place the parcel on a high shelf in a closet. In this way, children's troubles are still present where children can reclaim these at will; however, these mementos are safely tucked away where the child does not have to be disturbed by them. The strategic therapy idea of having troubles within reach usually seems more comforting than losing them forever, for complete disappearance may mean losing part of one's own life. You can guide children in an imaginary trip into a garden or a space ship where they meet a wise being who gives them a special gift or tells them something important. This fantasy can be an opportunity for a child to "hear" from a deceased loved one or to receive some special inner symbol to help with the transition.

In practicing letting go or saying goodbye, a child might talk to a photo (Bertman, 1984; Schaefer & Lyons, 1988) or write the deceased a letter. Home Hospice of Sonoma County California's children's grief group, "Just for Kids," used to have children write a message on a slip of paper and put it inside a helium balloon, which they then released into the sky. Environmental concerns caused adult organizers to replace this practice with the unique idea of wrapping the messages around the legs of homing pigeons and then releasing these messengers to fly back to their nest in the next town. An angry or aggressive child might receive permission to hit a pillow or a ball, throw old pottery against a wall, or use a tennis racket to beat a rug or blanket over a clothes line. After overtly showing their frustration and anger, children may take a quiet walk or enjoy some rest time while concurrently discussing their feelings. A less direct form of working with children's aggression is suggesting that they become involved in activities, sports, clubs, or physically demanding hobbies such as gardening or building something tangible (Carroll, 1985).

Many board games are available concerning facing and overcoming danger, allowing children to solve their problems and identify their feelings. Catalogues of books, games, and art projects on self-awareness, motivation, and emotions are also available.

Bibliotherapy. All teachers throughout the ages know of storytelling and story reading exercises. Educational and psychological experts, however, have mixed opinions about reading fairy tales because many of these classics have frightening and even gruesome aspects. In working with the themes of death and dying, teachers and counselors need to let children create their own ideas. Sensitive adults can carefully select pictures of powerful looking archetypes, both "dark," representing death and the frightening aspects of life, and "light," representing goodness, peace, and protection. In my own work I have found that, depending on their developmental level, children, adolescents, and adults will make up any variety of stories, myths, or fairy tales. These fantasies depict the battle between the forces at hand, and allow them to express some of their own inner battles. Rosen (1986, p. 53) described another example of "thematic apperception"—children telling a story from pictures. Rosen described a projective test that Eugenia Waechter developed in her study of death anxiety in children with fatal illnesses. An assumption in asking an individual to create a projective story for evaluative purposes is that children are likely to be discussing their own needs, concerns, and worries as they describe a picture. Psychometrists select intentionally vague pictures to avoid influencing storytellers in too narrow a direction.

Children and adolescents today have access to many fiction and nonfiction books regarding this chapter's treatment of death and dying. Many of the reference books listed at the end of this chapter include bibliographies for children.

Film and Video. There are also films and videos available for various school ages through county school districts that approach the topic of death and dying both directly and indirectly. Earl Grollman provides a video series called "Talking About," which covers many aspects of loss and includes one cassette specifically for younger bereaved children. (Talking about Death with Children, 15 minutes and in color, is available from Batesville Management Services, P. O. Box 90, Batesville, IN 47006.) At the conclusion of his book, *Talking about Death: A Dialogue between Parent and Child,* Grollman (1990) presented an annotated list of age-related films.

To summarize, useful activities to help grieving children include the following:

- Drawing: free association, feelings, one's family, characters in a nightmare or dream, the illness, something about the deceased person, and coloring books;
- Creative projects: clay, collages, "feeling masks," scrapbooks;
- Memorial projects: Tree planting, library bookshelf, yearbook or class picture dedication, class mural, group story-writing;
- Sympathy projects: Making condolence or "thinking of you" cards, growing and sending flowers, cemetery field trip, visiting parents of deceased classmate, and sending a representative to visit a sick classmate;
- Free play: "Death games," imaginary danger, hitting a pillow, throwing pottery, and beating a rug;
- Structured play: visualization of boxing and shelving troubles or encountering a wise being, writing a note to deceased and letting it go, table games, and physical sports; and
- Bibliotherapy: Reading stories to children, children reading on their own, film, and video.

COMMUNITY SUPPORT FOR GRIEF

Many communities provide guidance, including support groups, for children facing a life-threatening illness in the family, or in themselves, and for children experiencing a bereavement. Also, if the teacher knows of other parents or children in similar circumstances, it would be highly appropriate to ask their permission to connect them in support. Isolation is a major debilitating factor in bereavement, so there can never be too much support available. As Rafael (1983, p. 102) stated, "If adequate family continuity, plus surrogate or other care, is available, much of the distress will have settled by the end of the first year, although the parent will be remembered with sadness and regret."

CONCLUSION

So often we speak to children in ways we think are best, but we guess wrong. We want to encourage them and subdue any fears they may have—in short, we do not want them to suffer. We tell a child not to cry, things could be worse, be cheerful, think of happy things, carry on, partly because we think our reminders will help and partly because we ourselves cannot bear to see the child in pain. These kinds of injunctions, however, tend to stifle the child's natural expressions of grief, which are usually brief, episodic, and emotionally cleansing.

Often, after a parent has died, a child is encouraged to "be the man of the family" or to "take mother's place"—burdens that many adults have trouble carrying. Sometimes parents try to alleviate the child's pain by "replacing" the loved one right away, such as in bringing in a new pet to replace a dead one, or even to divert the child's attention away from his/her grief over the deceased. In the classroom, additional diversionary tactics only reinforce the message to the child that he/she must not feel the loss but must move into the future as quickly as possible. If you realize that the child needs to tell, question, and express feelings, the most helpful approach is not to divert but to create a safe atmosphere for this expression.

Teachers may wish to dismiss a child's unsettling questions about death because they sound bizarre and disruptive in a classroom. Questions such as, "Do worms eat the person?" are difficult to answer even on an adult level; however, to discount them or to tell the child not to think such morbid thoughts only convinces the child that these reactions are wrong and should be kept hidden. A simple acknowledgment that the child's loss is a big one and may be scary may be enough for the child to feel safe in the world, knowing that his/her teacher understands.

With a balance of compassionate listening, careful observing, explaining, answering questions, and educating, a teacher is in an excellent position to aid any grieving child in his/her journey through loss and pain. With a supportive and informed atmosphere in the classroom, the child will be better equipped to experience feelings and make a smooth transition into the next phase of life.

BIBLIOGRAPHY

Fulton, R., Eric, M., Greg, O., & Scheiber, J. L. (1978). *Death and dying: Challenge and change.* Redding, MA: Addison-Wesley Publishing Company.

Kalish, R. A. (Ed.). (1984). *The final transition.* New York: Baywood Publishing.

Kalish, R. A., & Reynolds, D. K. (1984). An overview of death attitudes and expectations. In R. Kalish (Ed.), *The final transition* (pp. 25-49). New York: Baywood Publishing.

Kastenbaum, R. J. (1978). The kingdom where nobody dies. In R. Fulton et al. (Eds.), *Death and dying: Challenge and change* (pp. 202-207). Redding, MA: Addison-Wesley Publishing Company.

Liddle, H. A. (Ed.). (1989, March). *Journal of Family Psychology.* Newbury Park, CA: Sage Publications.

REFERENCES

Adler, R. B., & T. N. (1990). *Looking out/looking in: Interpersonal communication.* Fort Worth, TX: Holt.

Anthony, S. (1972). *The discovery of death in childhood and after.* New York: Basic Books.

Becker, E. (1973). *The denial of death.* New York: Macmillan.

Bertman, S. (1984). Helping children cope with death. In J. C. Hansen (Ed.), *Death and grief in the family: Family therapy collections* (pp. 48-58). Gaithersburg, MD: Aspen Systems Corporation.

Boulden, J. (1989). *Saying goodbye.* Desktop published, P. O. Box 9358, Santa Rosa, CA 95405.

Buckman, R. (1988). *I don't know what to say: How to help and support someone who is dying.* Ontario, Canada: Key Porter Books.

Carroll, D. (1985). *Living with dying.* New York: McGraw-Hill.

Center for Attitudinal Healing. (1979). *There is a rainbow behind every dark cloud.* Berkeley, CA: Celestial Arts.

Conley, B. (1984). Interdisciplinary care in adolescent bereavement. In J. C. Hansen (Ed.), *Death and grief in the family: Family therapy collections* (pp. 61-72). Gaithersburg, MD: Aspen Systems Corporation.

DeSpelder, L. A., & Strickland, A. L. (1987). *The last dance: Encountering death and dying* (2nd ed.). Mountain View, CA: Mayfield Publishing.

Donnelly, K. F. (1988). *Recovering from the loss of a sibling.* New York: Dodd.

Fox, S. S. (1984). Children's anniversary reactions to the death of a family member. In R. A. Kalish (Ed.), *The final transition* (pp. 87-101). New York: Baywood Publishing.

Furth, G. M. (1981). The use of drawings made at significant times in one's life. In E. Kubler-Ross (Ed.), *Living with death and dying* (pp. 65-94*).* New York: Macmillan.

Grollman, E. (1978). How does a child experience grief? In R. Fulton et al. (Eds.), *Death and dying: Challenge and change* (pp. 208-214*).* Redding, MA: Addison-Wesley Publishing.

Grollman, E. (1990). *Talking about death: A dialogue between parent and child* (3rd ed.). Boston, MA: Beacon.

Hansen, J. C. (Ed.). (1984). *Death and grief in the family: Family therapy collections.* Gaithersburg, MD: Aspen Systems Corporation.

Hinton, J. (1972). *Dying.* New York: Penguin Books.

Jackson, E. (1978). When to talk about death. In R. Fulton et al. (Eds.), *Death and dying: Challenge and change* (pp. 198-201). Redding, MA: Addison-Wesley Publishing Company.

Kalish, R. A., & Reynolds, D. K. (1981). *Death and ethnicity: A psychocultural study.* New York: Baywood Publishing.

Kamerman, J. B. (1988). *Death in the midst of life: Social and cultural influences on death, grief and mourning.* New York: Prentice-Hall.

Kastenbaum, R. J. (1981). *Death, society and human experience* (3rd ed.). Columbus, OH: Charles E. Merrill.

Kavanaugh, R. E. (1985). *Facing death.* New York: Penguin Books.

Kubler-Ross, E. (1983). *On children and death.* New York: Macmillan.

Lehman, D. R., Lang, E. L., Wortman, C. B., & Sorenson, S. B. (1989, March). Long-term effects of sudden bereavement: Marital and parent-child relationships and children's reactions. In H. A. Liddle (Ed.), *Journal of Family Psychology* (pp. 344-367). Newbury Park, CA: Sage Publications.

LeShan, E. (1978). *Learning to say good-by: When a parent dies.* New York: Avon Books.

Murray, G., & Jampolsky, G. G. (Eds.). (1982). *Another look at the rainbow: Straight from the siblings.* Berkeley, CA: Celestial Arts.

Osterweis, M., & Townsend, J. (1988). *Helping bereaved children: A booklet for school personnel.* Washington, DC: U.S. Department of Health and Human Services.

Rafael, B. (1983). *The anatomy of bereavement.* New York: Basic Books.

Rosen, H. (1986). *Unspoken grief: Coping with childhood sibling loss.* Lexington, MA: Heath.

Schaefer, D., & Lyons, C. (1988). *How do we tell the children?* New York: Newmarket Press.

Schumacher, J. D. (1984). Helping children cope with a sibling's death. In J. C. Hansen (Ed.), *Death and grief in the family: Family therapy collections* (pp. 82-88). Gaithersburg, MD: Aspen Systems Corporation.

Tull, R. M., & Goldberg, R. J. (1984). Life-threatening illness in youth. In J. C. Hansen (Ed.), *Death and grief in the family: Family therapy collections* (pp. 74-77). Gaithersburg, MD: Aspen Systems Corporation.

Chapter 17

PARENTAL INVOLVEMENT WITH CERTAIN SCHOOL PROBLEMS

Larry L. Palmatier

Editor's Note

Everyone connected with the school must focus on eliminating fear and coercion so that the system itself is not a place that damages anyone or dishes out pain in any form. The focus of all reform efforts is on the system, not on blaming the constituents. Glasser made this point eminently clear in a 1996 statement to his Institute faculty; he does not believe that any school district interested primarily in a disciplinary program can become a quality school district. Faulting learners contributes nothing to overhauling a system within which learners are behaving or misbehaving.

Focusing on discipline is misguided because everyone is aiming at the wrong target. As educators take aim at the system itself, they will be working to create the conditions that foster community, collaboration, and enthusiasm for learning. In short, they will be redefining the cultural norms that guide behavior within schools. After transforming the schools at the core, blaming and punishing will no longer characterize these learning places. The new quality norms will insure respect for positive and responsible relationships at all levels. Students coming to school with crunched egos and damaged hearts will find a safe harbor that buoys their minds and spirits and facilitates their enjoyment of learning. Helping kids make better decisions about getting along well is not a form of stimulus-response disciplining (Kohn, 1993).

HOW BATTERING AFFECTS KIDS

When I was a little boy—about a week ago—I saw my share of interpersonal strife at home. I heard even more conflict than I directly observed. My dad was 18 and my mother 16 when they got married in 1931. As a four- or five-year-old, third of the first five children in phase 1 of my family of origin, I vividly remember worrying that my mother might die during one of my dad's angry outbursts. The most dangerous encounter I can recall was my 28-year-old dad chasing her through an adjacent field of tall dry weeds and bruising her so badly that her arms and face were black and blue when she finally dared to come back home, shaken and traumatized.

Endless Cycle of Blaming One's Parents

Today, with a half-century perspective, I know that any boyhood experience I may now label a raw deal makes sense only in the exact framework of my life at that particular time. I also know that even though early danger and physical abuse affect children, those traumas need not ruin their lives or compel all young observers or victim-observers to repeat the violence as adults. Fortunately for me and my four siblings in that family grouping—my last two brothers came along 10 and 12 years later—my dad outgrew his knee-jerk tantrumming. He settled down over the next few months and soon stopped the physical threats and poundings completely. I remember this permanent reprieve coming within months of his chasing me with a leather belt when I was eight years old. He strapped me sharply several times after I fell to the ground in a desperate attempt to curl out of reach or, at least, to minimize the lashing. My two older brothers bore the brunt of my dad's wrath more than I did. Throughout these coming up years, my older sister enjoyed 100% immunity from his temper. How can I explain his dropping parenting through fisticuffs? Perhaps he came to his senses rationally, or maybe he looked around one day and noticed that he had four strong boys with a flair for his stubborn style.

Putting Security and Safety Needs in Perspective. Years later, I learned a family secret about my dad's dad. My paternal grandfather had abandoned his entire family without a word of warning. He slipped away from a little farm in Illinois, leaving my future father and nine siblings, and my Irish grandmother who persisted in the arduous task of raising 10 kids on very little money or other resources. I wondered how anyone could do such a thing? In due time, I learned more about my paternal grandfather. Abandoned at an early age, he and his twin brother eventually made their way to an "orphan train" that ran across the country back in the early part of the century. At each stop, prospective parents would meet the train and choose the youngsters they would adopt. In time, the two adolescent brothers met two twin sisters from County Tyrone in northern Ireland and married them. My future grandmother had left Ireland with her 15-year-old twin sister (and millions of others) to escape the deadly effects of the infamous famine that ravaged the emerald island. Most of her American brood were lucky to get through the sixth grade in school, and all of them grew tired of the main food staple—potato soup. In 1925, my dad was one of three boys in the family between the ages of 12 and 16 who left the farm and headed for the largest town that side of Chicago in search of factory jobs.

Alternatives to Blaming Parents. The tendency to blame parents is pervasive. Some blamers move to the graduate level course and blame their grandparents too. I admit that periodically I felt victimized as a young boy and scared of my dad's swearing and hot temper. After regularly visiting an elementary schoolmate at his house, I gained a totally different perspective when I caught glimpses of his aging grandfather who lived with his family. Grampa was a mean-spirited alcoholic who made my dad sound like a Sunday School teacher. Whenever the old man took a break from boozing, he would emerge from his cluttered room in a messy undershirt and sloppy trousers. He would swear at everybody and slug any of the boys he could reach. I saw him as totally unpredictable and I avoided him like the plague, lest he snarl and attack me as a mad dog might. My worries about home suddenly seemed quite minimal.

I concluded that, as bad as things were from time to time at my house, I did not have a tragic life. Thinking back, I have far more pleasant memories than dismal ones—a hundred to one. My dad spent most of his time doing good things for us rather than beating on us. He would do a soft-shoe tap dance on the kitchen linoleum and sing, in a 1940s rap-equivalent, "Chicken in the car and the car can't go, C-H-I-C-A-G-O, Chicago." His favorite treat was taking us on Sunday drives to one or another of his brothers' farms where my aunts' chicken dinners were tasty and generous. He would give us kids a turn sitting on his lap and steering the car down those rural gravel roads. On Saturday evenings, he drove the whole family to a small country town park for free outdoor movies, cartoons, and a strawberry ice cream cone at the soda fountain down the street. By focusing on these fun times, I learned early to leave the dull past behind and live without resentment. The memory of my dad laughing at all my jokes helped too. The question that comes out of this review of my own early childhood terror about the dark and the boogie man in the closet is, "What are today's young children to do in the face of intensive danger?" Chapter 7 presents specific ideas for handling suspected abuse in all its forms. My purpose here is to clarify teachers' responsibility for balancing the personal and the academic and for involving students' families in working out conflicts at school.

Should Teachers Help Students Solve Personal Problems?

My plan is to present some fairly common "raw deals" from young children's lives today, along with some not-so-common suggestions that counselors can use as interventions. Teachers also can use some of this information in spotting trouble in the bud and reporting the dangers to the proper authorities. I do not propose that teachers become professional therapists, but I believe their jobs will be easier and more satisfying when they gain more information about their students' lives outside of school. Standing in a classroom and looking out at 32 heads in need of a fill-up is a narrow interpretation of teaching. Learning about serious disturbances in students' lives does not automatically mean that teachers will be blown away by the information. They can be strong and model for children how they may choose to view some of these troubles. They also can make appropriate referrals through the school counselor if they learn of serious problems they cannot help manage.

Some say that teachers should not need to grasp the technicalities of counseling or that they have only a limited interest in becoming personally involved with their students. "Teachers should teach and healers should heal" is the standard line from critics. With Glasser, however, I think any sincere professional educator can learn to speak with students in ways that not only minimize antagonism, but also invite attention and commitment to personal and social responsibility. The success teachers are having in moving to quality school practices proves they are capable of adjusting to a new and enhanced classroom role. Teachers need to know their students personally because young learners do not automatically shed their outside stressors when they step onto the school grounds. If outside preoccupations intrude too much on students, they will find being in a classroom difficult and concentrating on subject matter especially burdensome.

Teachers Are Not Social Workers

What teachers do is meet with students in classrooms and communicate with them. Communication is all about human relationships. Should teachers who, by occupation, are in the business of communication draw an artificial boundary about certain topics? The answer is yes. Just as using a classroom as a political forum is wrong, eliciting very personal information about students' families and other relationships outside of school is going beyond their job description. At the same time, teachers are not ignorant about troubles. They manage their own lives and they are in the best position to spot warning signs in their students' classroom interactions. Without hunting for confidential stories, they can speak personally with students about day-to-day classroom behaviors and lend a listening ear one-to-one with children or adolescents who show signs of stressing. Teachers must respect the limitations of their role. They also deserve to know the context of their students' lives to the degree this information will help them teach better. They also have a right to information that a parent decides will be useful for them to know. The danger of a teacher seeing a student as a victim is a possibility, but this risk is minimal when any counseling a child receives follows the principles in this book.

Solve School Problems at School and Home Problems at Home

I will report on some students' conflicts and then suggest various ways of thinking about these dilemmas and of intervening to resolve the troubles. Teachers may or may not play a direct role in helping students sort out some of these conflicts, but at least they will be more fully aware of the family and larger social context of their young charges. Glasser's standard advice on judging the appropriateness of problems that teachers, school counselors, and principals should tackle is the following: Solve school problems at school and home problems at home. To this general rule—solve school problems at school—I add one simple idea. Make an intelligent referral when you become aware of a student's home problem or a combination home and school problem. An example of a home problem could be an alcoholic uncle living in a trailer on the family's property. Educators have little business delving into this condition unless they find that the uncle is abusing the children in some form. A combination home and school problem might be a father telling his son to fight at school or he will beat the boy at home. Once the school becomes aware of this double bind, someone with proper training should address the matter with the family because the family matter becomes the school's problem. Finally, when teachers have some background information about their students' distractions in the classroom, they can better understand their students' behavior without making excuses for them. Beyond understanding, they can see the behavior differently and plan some *practical problem-solving strategies* that will benefit their students immediately. Most teachers would agree that helping their students regain responsible control of their lives is a top priority for all educators. Like it or not, teachers do have the frontline responsibility for defining the context for enjoyable relationships and classroom management.

PROBLEM-SOLVING STEPS THAT WORK

Even though the focus in this chapter is on creating quality schooling, teachers need to see how the system itself affects children's behavior. Those who misbehave usually carry around a personal history of harshness or at least their share of tough experiences. Even someone generally regarded as a "troubled" child, however, often will relax physically during a first family counseling appointment. In light of this common phenomenon, we might conclude that children's problem behavior is not the real heart of the whole family's complaint. Their misbehavior is the most frequent complaint of other family members, however, and a counselor's first task is to work out a solution to the presenting complaint or inconvenience. The family therapy literature offers various words for signaling a family's distress. The late Virginia Satir referred to the most visible casualty in a family as the one who "carries a symptom" (1967, p. 1).

Most often, a child or adolescent "wears the symptom" for a family, leading outsiders to conclude that children conveniently volunteer for the role of scapegoat; or perhaps they believe that, if they become a serious nuisance, they can rescue certain individuals or even an entire family. Madanes (1984) has suggested viewing the symptom as a metaphor for a family's problem, and Minuchin and Fishman (1981, p. 18) speak of "parentified" children. Also, some people assume that a problem kid is the broken or defective part of a system and that everyone else will be fine after a counselor "fixes" the squeaky wheel.

Systems theory, however, takes a less judgmental position on the topic of pinning problems on a particular culprit. Blaming is unsuitable because any problem serves only to sound an alarm that the family's communication system has somehow gone awry. Other phrases that counselors commonly employ for the most apparent point of difficulty in a family are "index person," the "symptom bearer" (Minuchin & Fishman, 1981, p. 28), or the "identified patient," known simply as the IP (Boscolo, Cecchin, Hoffman, & Penn, 1987, pp. 108-109).

Children Try to Solve Problems with Problems

Generally, human beings do not set out to create problems. Most often, we set out to fix problems. Are children who work at cross purposes with adults smarter than we think? Perhaps they choose to act out in a conscious but reckless effort to become the medium through which a whole family finds help. Perhaps, troublemakers so often visibly relax at a first meeting because they have managed to get their parent or parents to go to a counseling appointment. Experienced counselors are supportive of a family but do not highlight a child's role in this scenario. Even though the job of an IP is an important one to the whole family system, giving too much public acknowledgment by featuring a child's problem at a session might give an IP too much power and encourage a youngster to bully the whole system further. When outsiders comment on symptom bearers during a session and surprisingly credit them for making the family counseling happen, most IPs tune in and listen intently. Even though a counselor downplays an IP's role, solving the presenting symptom is a top priority if the family is to make any progress. Using an acting out child as a ruse for sneaking up on the system's flaws would not be fair or effective.

HOW MUCH INFORMATION DO TEACHERS NEED?

As noted earlier, knowing the social context of children's behavior can be useful to school professionals. No teacher can reform the world, but knowing a little about students' home life helps teachers understand students so they can make some reasonable adjustments at school. Ironically, a teacher can know too much about students. Learning every detail of students' personal challenges can bog down even the most willing teacher and make objectivity impossible. Instead of holding out possibilities for students, a teacher who has become too much an insider may find it too easy to make excuses for those who are having a difficult time.

A Little Girl Tries to Teach Her Mother

A 27-year-old mother of two children—a 10-year-old boy and an 8-year-old girl—met with a school counselor ostensibly about her daughter's tendency to throw wild temper tantrums, but only at home. I sat in the second session as a consultant. As serious as the daughter's emotional displays were, however, Bernice was more interested initially in using the counseling time to discuss her own personal stressors. The university and a local public school district teamed up to run a school-based family counseling program. As a routine practice, parents help us to (a) separate out the topics they see as most pressing, (b) negotiate a problem, and (c) set some priorities. More information on this cooperative program appears in chapter 18.

A Mother's Pattern Continues. Bernice's story was that she recently had left an abusive relationship of five years—her third in a series of such connections with male partners. Because she lacked money, she had moved back to her mother's house and all of her sickening earlier life experiences came back to haunt her. Predictably, her mother had not changed one iota. She and her late alcoholic husband had been very abusive of Bernice as a young girl. The mother never cooked a meal or took her children anywhere. From all appearances, the mother knew nothing about shopping, budgeting, or managing a bank account. Most serious of all, she would slip out of the room at the slightest display of emotion and go hide in her bedroom. She then would turn off the lights, get into bed, and pull the blankets up over her head just as children who cover their eyes and think no one can see them. The more the grouchy and self-focused mother followed her lifetime pattern, the more frustrated the soft-spoken and affectionate Bernice felt.

Besides this background information on her abusive parents and the series of her abusive adult relationships, Bernice added two points. She reported an endless fear of an ever-present dark cloud looming above her head. She thought that one day this permanent shroud would swoop down, envelope her, cover her mouth as a cellophane wrapping, and suffocate her. This fantasy probably would stop most people dead in their tracks. Secondly, in response to a question about what she did for fun, Bernice was embarrassed to admit that she had few interests and participated in no sports. Parentified children have little time to bounce a ball out in the yard.

Helping Mother Take Effective Control. By seeking constant attention, eight-year-old Carmen actually was trying to help her mother. Before moving to the daughter's problems, however, the counselor and I presented Bernice with concrete suggestions for handling her three most serious worries. Her home-work was to do three tasks: (a) make a list of all fun activities she was putting off and resist the urge to do any of these things for at least one more week; (b) decide exactly where the looming shroud floated and consciously move the little devil to a convenient spot on her right-hand side, approximately 20 feet in the air; and (c) write the letter to herself that her mother *should* write her but never will.

Bernice Carries through on Her Plans. The second meeting was remark-able in its brevity and in the new hope that Bernice had discovered. She first listed many fun activities that she wanted to do—many involving her chil-dren. Secondly, she took charge of the looming death threat and felt the cloud move far out of sight behind her. Third, she wrote herself the letter she would have enjoyed receiving from her mother. Collectively, these steps gave Bernice a whole new lease on life and cleared the path for her to concentrate on her daughter's needs. She began the second session with a comment: "I thought I had gone bonkers. My whole week was better. The yellows were yellower, the greens greener, and the blues bluer." Only after reaching this point did she reveal that her daughter, Carmen, gave her trouble through her tantrumming style at home.

How Did the Daughter's Tantrumming Help? Finally, during the third meeting, Bernice confided that her daughter showed little control of her emo-tions at home and often played out a full-blown temper tantrum. I asked for more details and soon tentatively arrived at two conclusions: (a) the young girl felt that she had missed out on some of her girlhood because of her mother's continuous moves and her choices of mean partners; and (b) Carmen felt that, because her mother was much too soft in dealing with men, she herself would come to her mother's rescue.

I decided to tell Carmen that she used her tantrums to demonstrate how her mother could behave more forthrightly and, thus, stop allowing others to take advantage of her. Operating on these two premises, I suggested that Bernice let Carmen sit down beside her on the sofa every evening for a week and read her stories from a book written for much younger girls because Carmen had missed out on some of those earlier years. Secondly, I recommended a more conventional practice in counseling families with tantrumming children. Periodically, the mother was to stage the girl's outbursts so that she, not her daughter, was setting the schedule for Carmen's brash displays. Every evening for a week, mother was to prearrange a time for Carmen to throw a tantrum and to extend the charade at least five minutes beyond the usual duration.

Results of Tantrumming Advice. I knew that the small plan we had worked out—helping the family reduce the number and intensity of Carmen's tantrums—would be useful to the degree that mother and daughter were willing to play the game. I sensed that if Bernice could show her daughter that she was becoming stronger, the daughter would have far less to worry about and would find dropping the tantrums an easier task. The easiest way to prove her new found strength to her daughter was for Bernice (a) to avoid future relationships with abusive boyfriends, (b) to be more direct and communicative with her own mother, and (c) to ask forthrightly for what she wanted.

A GOOD GIRL STARTS SHOPLIFTING

Tina was only 11 years old when a store sleuth caught her shoplifting. The juvenile authority referred her for mandatory counseling (an oxymoron, of course). Prior to this incident, she had been a docile, charming, and successful student, so, naturally, when she involved the legal authorities, her teachers and family showed surprise and concern. Concurrently, she began dressing in the dark-colored jackets of a local professional football team with a reputation for smashing their opponents. She let her former neatness slide and seemed to be heading straight into the gutter with reckless abandon. What was going on in Tina's life? How could those who knew her best account for her abrupt turnabout?

Adjusting to Big Changes at Home

As the story unfolded at the first meeting, Tina was having difficulty adjusting to her mother's recent decisions to stop shooting up on heroin and to seek help with her addiction after seven years of abuse. The girl's mother began her downhill plunge when Tina was only four years old. In her desperation, she turned over child care duties to her mother. Tina seemed more emotionally attached, at this point, to her maternal grandmother than to her own mother.

The main problem that emerged at the first court-ordered counseling meeting was that Tina was sassing back whenever she spoke with her mother. She bluntly told her mother, Diane, to shut up. I decided that any parent who had struggled with an addictive substance for as long as she had is usually tentative about almost everything. She was not sure she could sustain her abstinence and was sending Tina ambiguous signals. Therefore, with the mother's agreement, I suggested that the daughter triple the number of times that she told her mother to shut up on any given evening at home. We ended the session on this note.

When mother and daughter returned the following week, I asked Diane if Tina had continued her sassy comments and how both of them had done on their homework. I learned that Tina had, indeed, been mouthy and obnoxious in Diane's eyes. When Diane answered my next question, I felt more confidence that she would be able to stick with her resolve to stay clean and sober. My question: "What did you do when Tina told you to shut up 18 times in one evening?" Diane responded, "I told her to knock that shit off." The mother had decided that she was back home and that she was the parent. Any ambiguity that the daughter clung to would dissipate as her mother took charge of the household. Diane had discovered that her daughter would be unsure of the rules at home if she herself did not feel she had a right to resume her place in the family. An excellent resource on the topic of recovering parents is Nelson, Lott, and Intner (1995).

Permission to Succeed. After several more counseling meetings—one with Tina and her friends alone and mother observing the girls over closed circuit TV—we staged one final session in front of a class of graduate counseling students. The purpose of that appointment was to obtain public statements of support for Diane in her struggle to regain her bearings and to live without drugs. Present were Diane, her mother, and Tina. First, we asked Diane's mother if she would give her adult daughter permission to succeed. She quickly said a definite yes. Sensing that Tina would not give her consent to her mother's success, I decided to ask her grandmother what she thought Tina would say if we asked her for the same permission. Grandma said she did not think that Tina would approve publicly of her mother's decision to turn her life around and give up drugs. Meantime, Tina assumed a neonatal position on the couch and looked frightened. We suggested that she did not have to say anything right now because, being an 11-year-old, her job was to manage her own life and not to take responsibility for a 33-year-old woman.

Outcome. In the next few weeks, the counselor who had been working with Tina at the school reported that the girl had allowed herself to relax and once again was dressing and acting her age. At that point, we referred the family to a community-based counseling program for continued assistance as mother and daughter completed the transitional phase in this battle for freedom and a satisfying relationship. We obtained Diane's permission to keep the teacher informed of those parts of the counseling that affected Tina's classroom behavior.

PROBLEMS OF DIVORCE
AND SOLUTIONS FOR CHILDREN

Some common themes and tactics for children of divorce are in order here because of the vastness of the problem and the impact on schools (Ables & Brandsma, 1977; Guerin, Fay, Burden, & Kautto, 1987; Hansen & L'Abate, 1982). For every problem and attempted solution, an alternative (and better) behavior or solution exists, but the paths out of trouble are easier for both the counselor and the student to see when the counselor first reframes a student's futile tries as meaningful and not fully effective. Here are some examples of common problems associated with divorce.

Problem 1: Children typically feel responsible for causing the divorce of their parents.

Solution: Draw boundaries and give children something explicit to do and say. "My counselor told me to say this to you: Right now I would like to go to my room (or out to the patio or the backyard) because when you argue so strongly, I feel scared and helpless."

Problem 2: Divorcing couples often use children as "courier pigeons" to carry their hostile messages about each other.

Solution: If parents insist on communicating their harsh messages to each other via the children, have them do so in writing and have the children hand carry the notes and letters in sealed envelopes so that they do not know the contents. Avoid putting the children in an untenable position and do not read the messages in front of the courier.

Problem 3: Children often try to rescue one or both of their parents by taking on a distressing symptom as the family goes through the process of divorce.

Solution: Swearing, withdrawing, acting out, running away, starting fires all can serve many purposes, including attempting to keep the parents together and thwarting the divorce.

Problem 4: Parents just as often may try to rescue children from the experience of divorce.

Solution: Parents can try putting on a happy smile and projecting an aura of being socially unafraid of the future, but children can read the lines between verbal and nonverbal messages. Have parents openly acknowledge the divorce and the painful losses everyone will face so that children do not take on the authorship of the divorce decision or feel that the divorce is designed to "get rid of the kids."

Problem 5: After children feel the direct shock of divorce, they may replicate the conflict in their family by arranging a comparable breakup with a close friend in a dramatic effort to understand divorce more realistically.

Solution: Trying on divorce for size may lead children to antagonize their best friends to the point of getting them to give up on the friendship. Thus divorce comes to the classroom.

Symptom as Metaphor

Cloé Madanes (1984) described the notion of symptom as metaphor for the larger complaint in the family. How does the child's problem represent the family's current challenge? A girl recognized her mother's helplessness and incompetence to take proper medical care of herself. Therefore, the girl took dangerous risks that brought her into frequent contacts with medical services that she hoped would extend somehow to her mother. The girl's symptomatic behavior was a metaphor for her mother's own helplessness and neglect of herself. Other examples of metaphor follow that may help explain particular symptoms, along with suggestions for resolving the accompanying complaint. These stories depict the perceptual bias that youngsters may hold and suggest ideas that counselors or teachers may use in assisting children to wriggle out of their interpersonal binds.

Story	Symptom, Metaphor, & Solution
1. Symptomatic Behavior: A nine-year-old girl periodically throws tantrums at home.	**Ineffective Behavior:** The girl worries that her docile mother will go on letting men abuse her. **Metaphor:** The girl chooses tantrumming as a tool for teaching her mother to speak up and take care of herself. **Solution:** Invite mother to spend more time reading little girl stories to her daughter and also structuring and scheduling the tantrums.
2. Symptomatic Behavior: A "big tough boy," age six and a half, cries a lot after his mother splits up with her boyfriend of six years.	**Ineffective Behavior:** Little Tommy independently expresses the pain of separation from the only dad he ever knew. He holds his tongue at school, except to cry endlessly. He talks now and then but only about his misery. His peers make fun of him and keep their distance from him because of his singular focus. **Metaphor:** He helps his mother face the losses she ignores. **Solution:** Invite the boy to keep his sadness a secret from his teasing classmates, and, because he still carries fond memories of his earlier times, have him pretend to be a baby at home. This way, he feels better instantly, and his family must allow him to cry when he feels sad.
3. Symptomatic Behavior: An 11-year-old girl is mistrustful when her mother, absent for seven years, decides to discontinue drug use and resume her parental duties.	**Ineffective Behavior:** The girl tries shoplifting, and this thievery compels mom to find professional counseling for them. **Metaphor:** The daughter signals her mother that she wants to hold onto something that she is unsure she has a right to have. **Solution:** Have both generations—the IP's own mother and her daughter—state their positions on the client's decision to cease drug use and support the mother as she takes charge at home.

4. Symptomatic Behavior: A 10-year-old boy alternates visiting his divorced parents. The parents pull him in opposite directions by sending messages to each other through him.

Ineffective Behavior: The mother thinks that her son brings home some "vile stuff" about her after visiting his father and stepmother for a weekend. The mother admits pummeling the boy for information on the visit and then experiencing the reports from her former husband as "salt in the wounds."

Metaphor: Both parents unwittingly put their son into a role of middle man who communicates their conflict and vile feelings.

Solution: While visiting his dad, the boy is to fill a small vial with anything that represents the parents' conflict—dirt, salt, a piece of a banana peel. Upon his return home, mother is to refrain from pumping him for information. He and his mother are to go somewhere together and nonverbally empty out the vial's contents. The only messages he is to deliver to his parents are those they agree to write down and place in a sealed envelope.

5. Symptomatic Behavior: Two kindergarten boys are having a rough time and begin to swear loudly in the classroom.

Ineffective Behavior: The kindergarten boys swear to express the family's trauma and confusion. In one family, the parents are going through an acrimonious divorce. The second boy is living with his paternal grandmother who reluctantly tolerates drug use by her two adult sons (including the boy's uninvolved father) and looks the other way when the boy's father and uncle openly watch X-rated movies at home.

Metaphor: Both boys are announcing the vulgarity and desperation at home.

Solution: Encourage the grandmother to give her two adult sons their walking papers and structure an agreement that the boy will go to the other grandmother if his father and uncle stay. In the other case, have the parents do their squabbling about divorce away from their five-year-old.

6. Symptomatic Behavior: Single-parent families and kids may have troubles.

Ineffective Behavior: Single parent families have special needs.

Metaphor: The lone parent must stand all the watches and this never-ending duty explains their discouragement and sheer exhaustion.

Solution: Support groups for single parents may be helpful.

7. Symptomatic Behavior: Quality time between parents and children is not always easy.

Ineffective Behavior: Kids require time that their parents often do not have or take.

Metaphor: When children feel neglected in their family, they sometimes try to steal some time from others and create extra turmoil at the very time their parents may be especially vulnerable.

Solution: Avoid junk food, allow enough sleep and rest; and spend at least some quality time together.

THE BOY WHO THOUGHT HE WOULD DIE

The following story of a 10-year-old boy unfolded at a day treatment program for severely emotionally disturbed youngsters. I played a consulting role to a special education counselor at the school in southeastern England. Nigel steadfastly refused to touch anything at the school because he was afraid that if his hands came in contact with anything, he would die. He was living with his British mother in England while his Iranian father was off on a business trip to his home country. Adding to his bad luck, the Iranian authorities had arrested Nigel's dad and thrown him into jail. His mother was not sure about the father's status with the legal system, his safety, or his release date. Prior to his overseas trip, her husband had confirmed her worse fear by demanding a divorce. For her part, the mother did not hide her anxiety about entering the future as a single parent.

An Insensitive Teacher Employs Coercion

The preliminary case information helps paint an accurate context for this boy's difficulties. The school had tried many different angles in hopes of coming up with a cure for Nigel. Two of the specific methods the staff had tried were behavioral techniques and psychodynamic group work. These efforts to pin down the social contingencies and to find new ways to manipulate the self-perpetuating reinforcers met with little success. Analyzing his youthful psyche was equally ineffective. Sadly, one of the teachers decided to take the bull by the horns and ignore the boy's pleas for understanding. On a field trip to a swimming pool, the teacher heard about Nigel's fear of touching things and decided to handle this petty fear in an expeditious manner. The teacher grabbed the boy and promptly tossed him into the pool. This impulsive and insensitive act added to the crisis, of course, and the mother decided then and there to make a trip to a child psychiatrist's office for medication for her son.

Touch and Die Metaphor

I suggested that the counselor ask the mother just how terrified she was feeling these days and, also, for her private thoughts on the level of danger that the husband currently faced. She confirmed that she was at her wits end over money worries and the threat to the boy's father. She viewed everything that was going on as life and death issues.

Solution for the Withholding Boy. I advised the counselor to obtain the mother's permission to set up a meeting with the boy and to offer him this idea: "As you know, your parents are facing some very serious problems. Do you agree that their problems are difficult—even life and death concerns?" The boy agreed the parents had their work cut out for them and that the danger to dad was extremely serious. The counselor continued, "We believe that your unwillingness to touch anything is an important statement on your part. From now on, we are going to read your message as 'hands off my parents' problems. Hands off death!' We want you to know that we understand how difficult this time is for you. Please feel free to keep your hands away from touching anything and we will know that you know you cannot take on your parent's problems."

Results of This Suggestion. The very next day on a school-sponsored field trip to a sand dune fronting the Atlantic ocean, the boy touched everything around him for the first time since coming to the school. The counselor reported that he ran through the brambles and rolled in the sand. In a short time, he returned to his regular school, knowing that he did not need to have a serious problem to visit the counselor whom he liked very much. In a three-week, six-month, and two-year follow-up, I learned from the counselor that this boy did not need further treatment for his original decision to refrain from touching anything. He narrowly escaped taking heavy drugs that his mother would have endorsed had she consulted a psychiatrist for the boy's strange behavior.

THE MOTHER WHO HID IN HER CLOSET

Carina sped away from school for the 40th time—and this was only the second quarter of the school year! As usual, her two sons, each with a different father, had slept in and missed their school bus, so she had to drive them in her beat-up, 17-year-old Pontiac. The principal decided to refer the family to our counseling program at the school.

I held the first session in front of a university counseling class. The mother, Carina, was willing to try anything to get help with her sons—Joseph, age nine, and Reggie, age eight. Her main complaints were the boys' missing the school bus every day, their incorrigible behavior that included attacking her, and their foul language. Because we met in the context of doing family counseling with a school-related problem, I asked Carina to describe her main concern. She explained that she often would go to her bedroom closet, lie down on the floor in a fetal position, and shout and scream that she wanted to die.

Changing a Problem from Noun to Verb

Counselor: *Then what happens?*
Mom: *The boys come into my room fighting and hollering and pound on me.*
Counselor: *How does this problem relate to your frustration with their getting to school on time?*
Mom: *I don't know where to start with them and with the mess at home.*
Counselor: *Would you be willing to let me talk with them alone about the bus?*
Mom: *Yes, I sure would.* (Mother excitedly takes a cup of coffee and a doughnut and leaves the room).
Counselor: *Boys, tell me about the way things are at your house when you are getting ready for school in the morning.*
Reggie: *We usually don't get up on time.*
Counselor: *Is that a problem?*
Joseph: *Yeah, 'cuz then my mother has to drive us to school and she doesn't like to do that.*
Counselor: *So you usually miss the bus.*

Boys: *Yeah.*
Counselor: *Would you like to do something about catching the bus?*
Joseph: *Okay.*
Reggie: (Shrugs his shoulders)
Counselor: *How about this plan: Reggie, you don't have to listen. You're too young. Joseph, how many times do you think you could catch the bus next week and get to school on time?*
Joseph: (Pause) *Five.*
Counselor: I think that would be too much. I would think you are just trying to get me off your back. How many days would be more believable?
Joseph: *Four?*
Counselor: *Still too many. How about three? Do you think you could catch the bus on time on three of the five days next week?*
Joseph: *Yeah. I could do that very easily.*
Counselor: *Good. Now, Reggie, remember: you don't have to do any of this because you're just a little brother.*
Reggie: *I can do it too.*
Counselor: *Is this plan all right with you, Joseph, if your teacher or her aide telephones me on those days when you arrive on time?*
Joseph: *Sure.*

As one might imagine, Joseph got on the bus every day during the following week and arrived at school on time. Reggie did not want to be pegged "the little brother," of course, so he, too, took the bus every day. The counselor did go to the school and check in with the boys during recess to make sure they knew he cared about them and was following through. He also presented the boys with little surprises—a soccer ball for Joseph and colored pencils for Reggie who had volunteered that he liked to draw. Every day over the next week, the teacher's aide telephoned the counselor with the report that "Joseph took the bus today." Five weeks later, after perfect attendance for both boys, Joseph won the "Student of the Month" award. (The gifts were not intended as reinforcers. These prizes were tokens of friendship and the counselor meant to show the boys that he genuinely cared about them.)

Solving the Presenting Symptom First. Meanwhile, back to the meeting with the mother. She reentered the classroom after the bus plan was complete and talked more about her worry about the boys' fighting with each other and with her.

Mom: *What do I do when they chase me and hit me?*
Counselor: *This may sound strange to you, Carina, but I do not see what your boys are doing as assaulting you in order to hurt you. I*

think they are worried about you because you constantly tell them how you are feeling overwhelmed. They come to your rescue. I may be wrong, but I think they hunt you down, pester you, and hit you in the closet to make sure that you stay alive.

Mom: *I never thought of it that way.*

Counselor: *Are you willing to think of some more things a bit differently?*

Mom: *Mm. Depends.*

Counselor: *I was thinking of an idea that may or may not do much for you. If you are willing to try some minor suggestions, I will tell you what I have in mind that might help you. I guarantee if this suggestion does not work, it won't bring any harm to anyone.*

Mom: *All right, I guess. Things can't get too much worse.*

Counselor: *My idea is simple. When do you have a little peace and quiet for yourself?*

Mom: *In the early morning before the boys wake up.*

Counselor: *You told me you would try something new. I suggest that you use that early morning quiet time for yourself. Take a note pad and play some quiet music that you like and write out your plans for the day. Make sure that you do all of this in your closet. Your boys will get up and will probably notice where you are. I will be interested to know how this plan works out for you.*

Mom: *I'll try.*

Counselor: *I accept the try, Carina. I take that word to mean, "I am rehearsing the plan in my head before I actually implement it in real life."*

Mom: *Lately, I have been telling myself that "help is on the way."*

Counselor: *Please do me one small favor, Carina. Would you change your sentence from "Help is on the way" to "I am getting help." I would say that we have done enough for one day. What do you think?*

Soon after that first meeting, the boys stopped swearing, chasing down their mother, and beating up on her. They told me later they were not as worried about her because she was getting counseling. Besides, they had concluded they could keep their mother alive without pounding on her.

MULTIPLE PROBLEM FAMILY: NEGOTIATING THE NEXT PROBLEM

Over the next few weeks, the mother presented one new item each week, exposing her perception that hers was a multiple problem family. Beyond the sibling rivalry, Carina reported a messy house, little money, an eviction notice to move from their rented house, and trouble communicating with her parents. When it rains, it pours! Each week, the mother divulged more information as she gained confidence that we were not going to report her to the authorities for welfare fraud. Some further difficulties were physical abuse from Carina's current boyfriend, separation from the boys' maternal grandparents because of the brothers' caustic manner with each other, spousal abuse, suicidal threat, no beds for the boys, and car trouble. Naturally, we had a mandate to report neglect and abuse if we had reasonable suspicion to believe anyone were harming the boys.

Summary of Outcome

We accomplished all the goals we co-created after 12 meetings over approximately 8 months. She ended up calling me at home at the end of the school year to inform me that she was planning to take the boys on a camping trip along with her new boyfriend who liked youngsters and was not abusive. This change represented a far cry from Carina's plans at the end of our first meeting. She left that initial session with two things she agreed to do. First, she changed her statement, "Help is on the way" to "I am getting the help we need." Second, she agreed to continue to enter her closet every morning, but, instead of fretting and depicting desperation, she would take a notebook with her and plan her day from inside the closet while listening to the sounds of pleasant and calming music. She did both of these plans and each had a strong effect on the boys as they saw her taking the bull by the horns instead of letting the bulls of the world gore her at will.

Locating the Problems: School, Home, and School and Home

I worked with the family on school problems before moving to the other pressures and helping the mother solve each of these one at a time. The priorities for a counselor are rather standard. In this case, help the boys first because their symptomatic behavior is the presenting problem. Their hassles successfully brought their mother some professional help. After stabilizing the most obvious complaints, move on to more complex topics if the parent agrees. By dividing the problems into (a) school, (b) home, and (c) home and school troubles, the family received more than emotional support or a patient ear. After 12 meetings over the next 8 months with the mother and two sons, the mother alone, her current abusive partner alone, and the mother's parents alone, the family had made many improvements together. The woman had given her mean partner "the boot," following the counselor's mandatory reporting of child abuse to Child Protective Services. In the end, Carina met a new man who was not abusive and who did not angrily pick the boys up by their ears.

THE FATHER WHO BETRAYED HIS TWO SONS

A 14-year-old boy was in Juvenile Hall for becoming violent and damaging property. Authorities arrested his 16-year-old brother at the same time for similar behavior, but the older fellow was assigned to a different correctional setting. The counselor who consulted me on this case was an art therapist who learned the story from the younger brother. In short, the two brothers had been in an automobile accident and had received a significant insurance settlement. This money was resting in a bank as future college money. Their father knew of the plan and decided to take matters into his own hands. He not only absconded with the funds but also abandoned the family in the same step. The young men were shocked at their dad's deception and betrayal and took their frustration to the streets. This decision landed them in the juvenile justice system.

Art Therapy and the Conditions of Change

The art therapist worked with the 14-year-old boy to give him the chance to express any of his fury over the violation of love between father and sons. The young man went through the motions of putting paint brush to paper and sorting out the humiliating abuse he had experienced. His heart was not in his artistic projects, however, and he was thinking of ways to escalate his poor social record at the agency by intensifying his refusal to participate.

Motivation Is a Key. Before any adolescent in a detention center will take a personal risk, he/she must see the merit in moving in any new direction. I judged that the counselor first needed a powerful cognitive reframe before she could reasonably expect either of these two brothers to show any vulnerability. We both knew that no one can motivate another person. All the counselor could do was present some information to the boy and let him motivate himself. I laid out a proposal to the counseling trainee and she applied the plan with zest and courtesy.

Reclaiming Their Birthright. First, the counselor told the young man that for him not to be deeply hurt and to feel a serious sense of frustration at what happened would mean that he was not really attached to his father and his family. We read his antisocial activities in the face of the shocking news of his dad's departure with his money as a measure of his prior trust and commitment. The counselor noted that his continuing to feel furious and helpless made some sense in light of his viewpoint, but he also could take a surprising step if he were so inclined. The boy was willing to listen to a suggestion on the off chance that a novel idea might help him regain his sense of purpose.

The counselor noted that he and his brother both felt an overwhelming sense of betrayal. They then took this feeling of injustice and acted out their frustration by damaging public property. This sequence led them to the jail for youth. Why not rethink the scenario and consider ways they might regain the upper hand. Their father's behavior could not cause them automatically to ruin their entire lives. What if they were to share the betrayal and connect with others who could likely understand their bad luck?

Sharing the Betrayal. Instead of keeping his misery to himself, perhaps the boy could write out his story and share his betrayal with others. We settled on 90 fifth- and sixth-graders from a school in a low-income part of town because many of these students may have experienced a similar feeling of abandonment by a parent. Armed with a common frustration and sense of powerlessness, the younger students would receive Bill's story and, in groups of three, would write their own endings to his story. He would receive his story back with 30 new endings to consider. We arranged the project in such a way that he would judge the elementary students' efforts and award all the participants a small prize of one dollar per student from a petty cash fund we had established in the school. In this way, he would find himself of being in a position of being magnanimous in relation to his story and not petty as his father had been. He too will win a prize for his story. Then he will read a new ending to his life's story every day for a month, accepting ideas that he liked, changing these suggestions to fit his own goals, and rejecting other proposals as he saw fit.

One can see easily that connecting one's story to others in a similar bind can help a person feel a new sense of community and hope. Realizing that many others have encountered abusive treatment by those who should love and guide them can make a youngster feel less alone. Hearing all the creative ideas from the students on the same side of the tracks could prove a powerful boost to one who felt so desperate and alone. Bill decided to risk the contact.

A Dollar and Sense Perspective. In order to discover exactly how much schooling Bill would need in order to retrieve some of his lost money and move on with life, the counselor began by asking Bill to write down the exact amount of money that his father had stripped away from him. The next question was to determine how long it would take him to earn the money back. The answer to this question, of course, depended on the kind of job he would have. This led

Bill to specifying a job that would permit him to pay back the money in a reasonable period of time. This information affected the amount of education he would need to carry out his financial plan. All of this served to help Bill gain a sense of control over his own occupational fortunes and to take charge of his life from this moment forward. Bill was more willing to discuss these questions after he showed a willingness to share his betrayal. (For more information on taking the bull by the horns and writing one's way out of terrible straits, readers may choose to consult the narrative therapy literature (Hoyt, 1994; White & Epston, 1990).

POSTSCRIPT ON CREATIVE SOLUTIONS

We could continue looking at more case material showing harsh interference in students' lives. Ironically, students, families, and other clients do not always have to carry out the new plans for resolving a problem. I have found that merely creating an imaginary escape route from a current messy condition or scene is often enough to bring welcomed relief to many. This observation that people sometimes find relief simply by being aware of optional solutions does mean that those in a bind do not take new action in the face of pain and frustration. Picturing a way out of a dilemma is itself a form of solution. Planning a new tomorrow is taking action in the form of envisioning new outcomes and imagining ways to overcome any obstacles. The fact that this planning stage alone may bring a person relief from suffering is good to know. Finally, the keys to counseling with parental involvement are the same as individual counseling:

- connecting solidly with students in trouble;
- capturing the essence of their intensive quality world feeling about an intact, a threatened, or a lost value;
- concentrating on what they really want that they do not have by focusing on the perceptual error or frustration signal that is driving their behavioral system;
- collaborating together on formulating a new plan to correct the threat, unfairness, or damage; and
- cementing the friendship by sticking with a student and family through thick and thin.

BIBLIOGRAPHY

Adler, A. (1969). *The science of living.* New York: Doubleday Anchor Books.

Anderson, T. (Ed.). (1991). *The reflecting team: Dialogue and dialogues about the dialogues.* New York: Norton.

Ardrey, R. (1970). *The social contract: A personal enquiry into the evolutionary sources of order and disorder.* New York: Atheneum.

Bach, G. (1976). *The intimate enemy: How to fight fair in love and marriage.* New York: Avon.

Bandura, A. (1977). Self-efficacy: Toward a unifying theory of behavioral change. *Psychological Review, 84,* 191-215.

Becvar, D. S., & Becvar, R. J. (1996). *Family therapy: A systemic integration* (3rd ed.). Boston MA: Allyn & Bacon.

Berg, I. (1992). *Family based services: Solution-focused approach.* New York: Norton.

Bornstein, P., & Bornstein, M. (1986). *Marital therapy: A behavioral-communications approach.* New York: Pergamon Press.

Bradshaw, J. (1988). *Bradshaw on: The family.* Deerfield Beach, FL: Health Communications.

Corsini, R. (1989). *Current psychotherapies* (4th ed.). Itasca, IL: F. E. Peacock.

de Shazer, S. (1994). *Words were originally magic.* New York: Norton.

Dyer, W. (1990). *You'll see it when you believe it.* New York: Avon.

Ellis, A. (1988). *How to stubbornly refuse to make yourself miserable about anything—Yes anything!* Secaucus, NJ: Lyle Stuart.

Ellis, A., & Dryden, W. (1987). *The practice of rational-emotive therapy.* New York: Springer.

Fisch, R., Weakland, J., & Segal, L. (1982). *Tactics of change.* San Francisco, CA: Jossey-Bass.

Frankl, V. (1963). *Man's search for meaning.* New York: Washington Square Press.

Gattuso, J. (1996). *A course in love.* San Francisco: Harper San Francisco.

Glasser, N. (Ed.). (1989). *Control theory in the practice of reality therapy.* New York: Harper & Row.

Glasser, W. (1971). *The identity society.* New York: Harper & Row.

Glasser, W. (1984). *Control theory.* New York: Harper & Row.

Glasser, W. (1995). *Staying together.* New York: HarperCollins.

Goldenberg, I., & Goldenberg, H. (1980). *Family therapy: An overview.* Belmont, CA: Brooks Cole.

Gray, J. (1995). *Men are from Mars; Women are from Venus.* New York: Harper Collins.

Gray, J. (1996). *Mars and Venus in the bedroom.* New York: HarperCollins.

Hansen, B. (1996). *General systems theory beginning with wholes.* Bristol, PA: Taylor & Francis.

REFERENCES

Ables, B., & Brandsma, J. (1977). *Therapy for couples.* San Francisco, CA: Jossey-Bass.

Boscolo, L., Cecchin, G., Hoffman, L., & Penn, P. (1987). *Milan systemic family therapy.* New York: Basic.

Guerin, P., Fay, L., Burden, S., & Kautto, J. (1987). *The evaluation and treatment of marital conflict.* New York: Basic Books.

Hansen, J., & L'Abate, L. (1982). *Approaches to family therapy.* New York: Macmillan.

Hoyt, M. (1994). *Constructive therapies.* New York: Guilford.

Kohn, A. (1993). *Punished by rewards.* Boston, MA: Houghton Mifflin.

Madanes, C. (1984). *Behind the one-way mirror.* San Francisco, CA: Jossey-Bass.

Minuchin, S., & Fishman, H. C. (1981). *Family therapy techniques.* Cambridge, MA: Harvard University Press.

Nelson, J., Lott, L., & Intner, R. (1995). *Clean & sober parenting.* Rocklin, CA: Prima.

Satir, V. (1967). *Conjoint family therapy.* Palo Alto, CA: Science and Behavior Books.

White, M., & Epston, D. (1990). *Narrative means to therapeutic ends.* New York: Norton.

Chapter 18

CONFLICT RESOLUTION STRATEGIES: USING REALITY THERAPY AND CHOICE THEORY TO ASSIST CHILDREN IN MAKING BETTER CHOICES

Edward W. Chance
Patti L. Chance

Editor's Note

How can anyone concentrate on learning and getting along with others in a school filled with friction, boisterous arguing, and intimidating challenges and fighting? First and foremost, a school must be a safe *place where all students experience respect, are calm, and can let their guard down. With those criteria, I probably just eliminated a very large percentage of schools in the country from the list of qualifiers. Even in some otherwise safe communities, many students may feel nervous about their physical safety. Teachers, too, may have concern that they cannot totally relax at their work site, lest someone act out in a dangerous way.*

The reality is that all of society's problems spill over into the schools and the world is more difficult for all the reasons we have presented in the prior 17 chapters. However, all boasting aside, schools can solve problems that fighting poses in schools if the authorities will make eliminating physical threat a top priority goal. The formula for success in reducing and eliminating all violence and threats of violence is available. Most schools can turn a school around within a year or two if everyone is working together in a concerted effort. Here is my own proposal:

1. *Limit school enrollments to 200 to 300 students per school (or organize the school into several schools-within-a-school). Let each school create a special esprit.*

2. *Hire professional staff people from the district superintendent to the teachers, to the custodians, bus drivers, and yard duty assistants who are 100% committed to making school a safe, personal, and high quality place. Train everyone in effective communication and creative curriculum. Keep schooling personal and positive.*

3. *Establish a collaborative procedure for adopting rules of conduct and emphasize positive statements—for example, "Here, everyone receives respect." Include one simple zinger: "If you fight, you go home." Then follow through on this rule.*

4. *Train a cadre of student leaders in conflict resolution skills, following a plan such as the one Ed and Patti Chance present here. Most problems occur outside of class time. Structure the school schedule to accommodate the fact that most problems occur outside of class time. Move quickly on any threats.*

5. *Implement classroom discussions. These meetings can serve the three main purposes Dempster presents and, beyond these structured conversations, teachers can arrange special sessions to handle special problems.*

6. *Build into each classroom procedures for resolving conflicts among the students.*

7. *Organize school-wide forums for tackling problems outside the class room, especially cross-cultural rivalries or gang disturbances.*

8. *Retain full and direct control over school discipline. Avoid turning responsibility for school order over to a police officer or even a squad of police.*

9. *Involve structured teams of teachers and parents to address more sensitive areas. (See chapters 12, 14, & 15.)*

10. *Develop a more elaborate plan if needed, involving parents, community sports figures, reformed gang members, and other people and resources as needed.*

VALUE OF CONFLICT DEPENDS ON ITS SOCIAL FUNCTION

Whenever two or more human beings interact socially, sooner or later, *some conflict is inevitable.* Saying that conflict occurs naturally in the course of human interactions does not imply that friction is inherently bad or good. In fact, human beings and organizations are healthiest when they accept, encourage, and openly resolve the inescapable conflicts. Conflict, like stress, is *amoral* and means little until people assign meaning to a specific instance of disunity. In practice, people usually turn conflict into a benefit or a liability, seldom succeeding in holding real disagreement in neutral gear.

Benefiting from Conflict

Conflict can be useful, for example, when it serves a constructive purpose. People who tackle an interpersonal conflict head-on can strengthen their ties and become even closer. In an intimate pairing, conflict can serve as an opportunity two people may exploit to move past the cliché stage with each other. This progress can lead to deeper intimacy and, commonly, more honesty. A serious conflict in an organization can be the prelude to creative new products and renewed teamwork as by-products of the human efforts to resolve the threat. When conflict becomes destructive and hurtful, however, almost everyone agrees that its meaning changes from neutral or positive to negative.

Losing in the Face of Conflict

Destructive conflict has little potential to improve organizations or people. Such negative discord reflects itself in human interactions that imply pettiness, jealousy, feelings of unfairness, and a frustrating lack of control over one's life and environment. People involved in a destructive conflict exhibit such symptomatic behaviors and behavioral patterns as threatening, angering, withdrawing, verbally attacking, becoming physically ill, tensing up, and even resorting to violence. The actual basis for the sources of noxious disharmony may be indiscernible and often stay hidden.

Why People Express Conflicts. Constructive conflict, on the other hand, should be welcomed because this natural friction produces a creative tension that allows those confronting the conflict to grow intellectually and psychologically. The roots of constructive conflict are also much easier to recognize and accept. Some of the common reasons for interpersonal conflict may be differences in values and belief systems, disagreements over personal or organizational goals, and the means to actualize these purposes, an absence of information or disinformation, and, finally, disagreements over how to meet basic needs.

Although the behaviors that people choose to exhibit in a constructive conflict may reflect a type of defensive posturing or a test of their emotional limits, seldom do well-managed constructive conflict situations degenerate into destructive ones. In situations that people perceive to be out of control, however, people usually cannot stand by and idly watch the discord become ferocious and flip flop from neutral or constructive to destructive.

Both destructive and constructive conflicts occur in schools. Many of the destructive conflicts begin as simple misunderstandings that the protagonists could have resolved more appropriately if they were to view the challenges as constructive conflicts and manage them accordingly. Because people have strong basic needs for power, recognition, and belonging, they often change a manageable challenge into a destructive one. People have as many reasons to explain these irrational choices as they have conflicts.

A Choice Theory Definition of Conflict

Chapter 2 explains choice theory as a continual search for sensory pictures from the outside world that will match our mental pictures of what we want. When we are unsuccessful in finding a "controlled picture," that is, we cannot find a sensory picture to match a current want—we feel an annoying conflict. The pinch we feel as *an urge to behave* comes from the conflict of not having what we want. Conflict occurs *within an individual* when one's mental picture of wants is asynchronous with one's sensory pictures of objects and relationships in the world. To summarize, conflict is part of the feedback mechanism in our perceptual system that motivates us to pursue our basic needs.

An Interpersonal View of Choice Theory. In terms of choice theory, conflict occurs *between students* as they both act in a way to meet their needs. Students in conflict most often are choosing behaviors with which they are familiar. They have learned that yelling, grabbing, threatening, pushing, crying, or being stubborn are behaviors that have worked for them in the past. Even if these unproductive behaviors have not worked or are not working now, students have not learned any more effective behaviors to get what they want.

In reality, what many label *conflict* among students more accurately may be (a) clashes between students as they concurrently seek legitimate but conflicting goals or needs and (b) choosing ineffective behaviors in an attempt to *resolve* conflict. As stated previously, conflict is inevitable as humans interact with one another. The reason is that people are always on a "hunger search" to meet needs, and, periodically, these pursuits of needs will lead to competition and disputes. We seldom describe an interaction between students that results in compromise, sharing, or problem solving as a *conflict situation.* Yet, such bartering is a direct result from the dissension. The difference between compromise as conflict and the conflict that results in yelling, pushing, or shoving is that students are *choosing more effective behaviors* and are *resolving* the conflict in the negotiation sample. Students who resolve their conflicts learn to meet their needs at no one else's expense.

We can teach students more effective ways to resolve conflicts by injecting mediation strategies into the middle of a skirmish. By teaching students mediation techniques, we not only help them learn more effective behaviors, but also remove barriers to their own empowerment. Empowering themselves leads them to more self-control and responsibility.

In the example above of situations that we normally identify as conflict, students may yell, push, grab, or bully. These behaviors are always overt, usually disruptive, and too often dangerous. Consequently, teachers move swiftly to put an abrupt stop to these forbidden actions and to provide a solution to every problem.

Let us look at two third-grade boys pushing each other on the playground. After physically blocking the boys' pushing, the teacher learns that they were fighting over who would get to be captain of the game. The teacher intervenes and solves the problem by deciding that both boys are out of the game and must sit out during recess. What is so bad about imposing a logical consequence on the squabbling fellows? Hasn't the teacher resolved the problem once and for all? Perhaps, but the conflict stays alive—in their minds. The next day, the teacher wonders why these same two boys are "at it" again. The decree from on high solved the teacher's problem, but the two third-graders have not learned any more effective behaviors for resolving *their* problem.

HELPING STUDENTS SOLVE THEIR OWN PROBLEMS

In all fairness, from a time management viewpoint, the teacher acted efficiently at the time. After all, the teacher was supervising many children on the playground and could not take the time at that moment to help the boys resolve the problem themselves. How many disruptions can students avoid in the future, however, if a teacher or a counselor would show them more effective ways to solve problems or would give them more responsibility to solve their own problems?

Many conflicts which result in classroom disruption, referral to the principal, verbal assaults, or physical confrontations begin as simple misunderstandings or among students lacking skills and/or practice in resolving their own problems. By providing programs that allow students to resolve many of their own problems and that teach students the necessary skills to do so, schools can reduce the number of incidents that disrupt the educational climate and which take time away from the educational purposes of school.

Schools throughout the country are adopting mediation programs or incorporating conflict resolution strategies into their curricula. School mediation programs and curricula are adaptations of conflict resolution strategies used in business and labor negotiations, community and neighborhood programs, and precourt mediation. Mediation strategies include communication techniques such as active listening and paraphrasing. Mediators are taught *not* to take sides and *not* to offer solutions. The mediator's role is to help the disputants arrive at their own, mutually agreeable solution.

Mediation strategies are remarkably similar to the counseling techniques that Glasser (1965) first proposed in developing reality therapy. Furthermore, the concepts in Glasser's (1984) rendering of choice theory clearly explain the learning process and motivation for changing behaviors involved in mediation. The following explanation of mediation will correlate the steps and strategies of mediation to reality therapy and choice theory.

Reality Therapy as a Mediation Strategy

In the first step of mediation—*establish the ground rules*—the mediator explains the roles of the mediator and the disputants. After the introductions, the disputants must agree that they want to solve the problem. This decision to work out a remedy is a critical step in mediation because the adversaries themselves take on the responsibility for problem solving rather than leaving this duty to the mediator. Mediators must avoid taking sides in any dispute. Also, the disputants make a commitment to work out their differences by agreeing to the ground rules of mediation. In terms of reality therapy, the mediator is establishing a friendly climate and laying out the rules of engagement. The mediation process uses four simple rules:

1. respect yourself and tell the truth,
2. listen and do not interrupt,
3. be courteous and do not call anyone names, and
4. stay open and really work to solve the problem. (See Table 18.1.)

In the second stage of mediation—*stating the problem*—the mediator asks each disputant to tell his/her side of the story without interruption. The

TABLE 18.1
Conflict Resolution Process

I   SOCIAL INTRODUCTIONS AND GROUND RULES
A   "Hello, I am a playground mediator. I see that you have a conflict. Would
you like to work the problem out? All right, let me explain how mediation
works and how I may be able to help you both." (If students say no, explain
that their unresolved conflict could lead to more trouble and adult intervention.) The three parties move away from others on the playground.
B   Introduce yourself and have disputants introduce themselves.
C   Explain that you will not take sides.
D   Explain the rules and ask if both sides agree to abide by the rules.
  a   Respect yourself and tell the truth.
  b   Listen and do not interrupt.
  c   Be courteous and do not call each other names.
  d   Stay open and really work to solve the problem.

II   STATING THE PROBLEMS
A   Ask both students to tell their side, uninterrupted. Mediator never interrupts,
and firmly reminds the disputants if they interrupt each other.
B   Mediator *paraphrases* what Person 1 said—repeats the idea to Person 1's
satisfaction.
C   Ask the second person to tell his/her side, uninterrupted.
D   Mediator *paraphrases* what Person 2 said—repeats the idea in the
mediator's own words to the speaker's satisfaction.
E   Give each antagonist a turn to add any new points or comments.
F   Summarize their comments.

III PROBLEM SOLVING
(The following strategies should be used in helping the parties come to a *mutual*
agreement.)
A   Point out any *common ground.* Say, "I hear you both agreeing that. . . ."
B   Ask if either person can suggest a solution.
C   Ask Person 1 to tell Person 2's side of the story: What is Person 2 angry
about?
D   Ask if the other believes this restatement was an accurate account.
E   Ask Person 2 to explain why Person 1 is angry.
F   Ask Person 2 if Person 1 was accurate.
G   Focus on the *future*: "We've talked about what has already happened. What
do you want now? Where do we go from here?"
H   Ask both sides: "What can you do to make that happen?"
I   Ask Person 1: "What do you want Person 2 to do? What are you willing to
do?" Then, ask Person 2 the same questions.
J   Remember the *golden rule of mediation:* Do unto one as you do unto the
other.

IV   CONCLUSION
A   Write the final solution on the agreement form. (Remember, a good solution
will be *simple, short,* and *success oriented.* The final agreement, however,
belongs to the disputants and not to the mediator.)
B   Have all parties sign the agreement—adversaries and arbitrator.
C   Thank all the parties for coming.
D   If the disputants do not reach an accord, thank them for meeting together and
participating. Explain to them their options and/or future consequences.

mediator then gives each party a chance to add any statements, and, finally, summarizes the disputants' comments.

In reality therapy terms, the mediator is asking, "What are you doing?" The mediator is allowing both disputants to share their perception of what happened. Through this procedure, the mediator will gain information about the disputants' pictures of what they wanted to happen—what needs each was trying to meet.

In the third stage in mediation—*problem solving*—the mediator begins by pointing out any common ground: "I hear you both agreeing that. . . ." The referee then asks each disputant to suggest a solution. For each suggested solution, the mediator is careful to apply the *golden rule of mediation:* "Do unto one as you do unto the other." Giving each party equal time is very important. The mediator might say, for example, "Mary has suggested this solution. Mary, would this solution help you get what you want?" The mediator then would ask the other disputant the same thing about one of her suggestions: "Susan, would this solution that you have offered help you get what you want?"

At the third stage—problem solving—the mediator is helping both parties work out a concrete plan while clarifying and making reference to each person's pictures of how they want to meet their separate needs. This process requires that disputants choose alternative behaviors that will be more effective in helping them get what they want. In the long run, both disputants may have to make some alteration of their need-satisfying pictures in their quality world (Glasser, 1990). (See Table 18.2.)

The fourth and final stage in mediation is to *make a commitment to the solution.* Mediation uses a written contract between the disputants to seal their commitment. This agreement places responsibility for the plan's success on the disputants, not on the mediator. Occasionally, disputants will not reach an agreeable solution. When they are unable to come to closure on their strife, the mediator simply thanks the disputants for participating and explains further consequences which might result should they continue to fight and argue.

Mediation in a School Setting

While adults can and should use the mediation process described above to help students work out conflicts, the strategy is even more powerful in the hands of students who have received training as peer mediators. Students can learn this negotiating tool easily and be available to mediate minor disputes *before* they evolve into major disruptions. By training student mediators, teachers and

TABLE 18.2

Comparison of Mediation to Reality Threapy/Choice Therapy

Suggested Mediation/Steps for Students	Reality Therapy	Choice Theory
A Introduce yourself. Ascertain whether or not the students wish to solve their problem.	What do you really want? What are you doing now? Is it helping? Is it against the rules?	Get an idea of the exact pictures that both students have in their heads. What needs are they failing to meet?
B If yes, proceed. (Some schools designate a quiet area for problem solving.)		
C Get mutual agreement on four rules: a Respect yourself and tell the truth. b Listen and do not interrupt. c Be courteous and do not call each other names. d Stay open and really work to solve the problem.	Make a plan to get what you want. Get a commitment from each antagonist.	Ask them to agree to work on meeting all their needs. Identify the pathways by which they can succeed.
D As mediator, select the order of speaking.		
E Ask first person what happened and how he/she feels now.	What are you doing to get what you want? What are you *choosing* to do to meet your goals and needs?	What needs are you controlling for (trying to meet)? What do you want? What is your picture?
F Use active listening and paraphrasing. Repeat what was said.		
G Ask second person what happened and how he/she feels.	What are you doing now? What exactly are you *choosing* to do to get what you want?	What needs are you controlling for (seeking)? What do you want? What is your picture?
H Use active listening and paraphrasing. Repeat what was said.		

(*Table continues on next page*)

TABLE 18.2
Comparison of Mediation to Reality Threapy/Choice Therapy (*Continued*)

Suggested Mediation/Steps for Students	Reality Therapy	Choice Theory
I Ask the first person for alternative solutions.	Is your choice of behavior helping you get what you want? Make a plan to do better.	Think of some alternative pictures. Suggest some more effective behaviors.
J Ask the second person for alternative solutions.	Is your choice of behavior helping you get what you want? Make a plan to do better.	Think of some alternative pictures. Suggest some more effective behaviors.
K Help both students to arrive at mutually acceptable solution.	Make a plan to do better.	Choose some more effective behavior. Adjust your pictures to more acceptable and realistic ones. Check if these will help you meet your needs.
L Have both shake hands. Congratulate both for solving problem.	Get a commitment on carrying through with the new plan.	Control for success. Obtain a needs satisfying picture.
M Follow up with the two combatants as needed.	Make friends. Don't accept excuses. Don't interfere with logical or natural consequences. Don't give up easily.	Control for success. Go for a needs satisfying picture.

counselors can remove the barriers to students empowering themselves as they apply the new skills to solve their own problems. A peer mediation program is one way schools can contribute to the creation of an environment that helps meet students' needs for power and competency, recognition and status, and belonging.

Models for establishing peer mediation programs are in place in many schools throughout the country. Additionally, comprehensive curricular packages are available to help a staff member teach conflict resolution strategies. See the description of specific resources in the next section. Such curricula could be used in training peer mediators or incorporated into guidance or classroom programs for all students.

Programs in Practice

Mediation programs have been implemented in various locations and in a variety of settings, including elementary, middle, and secondary schools. In San Francisco, the Community Board Center for Policy and Training introduced school-based conflict manager programs in the early 1980s. Elementary student mediators wear brightly colored T-shirts identifying themselves as conflict managers, and they settle disputes on the playground. High school arbitrators settle disputes in a special room for mediation sessions (Roderick, 1987/88). In Las Vegas, Nevada, elementary students are serving as playground mediators with additional duties as cafeteria monitors. The principal at Ferron Elementary School in Las Vegas reported: "Our students are learning that issues can be resolved more effectively by talking them out than by fighting. . . . Students become active participants in enhancing a school environment that is friendly, safe, and happy through the Mediator Program" (Cahoon, 1987/88, p. 94).

Project SMART (School Mediators' Alternative Resolution Team) operates in four high schools and one junior high in New York City. In this program, trained student mediators resolve disputes and record the resolutions in the form of a written contract. Their follow-up reviews indicate that combatants fulfill more than 90% of the agreements mediators hammered out with them (Koch, 1986). Racine, Wisconsin operates a similar program in their middle schools (Gilmore Middle School, 1988).

One of this chapter's authors serves as an administrator in an elementary school with a mediation program that uses playground mediators to resolve conflicts before they escalate to the level where an adult must intervene. The success of the program is reflected by the fact that many students seek out mediators when a problem arises. The mediators' communication and problem-solving skills relate directly to an improved school climate of mutual respect and student responsibility.

Conflict Resolution Curriculum for Schools

Several good sources for teaching students conflict resolution skills exist in the form of packaged curricula and lesson plans. Primary among these pragmatic materials are the programs the San Francisco Community Board publishes. Their materials include an integrated curriculum for secondary schools and one for elementary schools. These programs include activities to teach about understanding conflict, improving communication skills, and making classroom applications of the training (Community Board Center for Policy and Training, 1987).

The Grace Contrino Abrams Peace Education Foundation has published two resource books: *Creative Conflict Solving for Kids* (Schmidt & Friedman, 1985) and *Fighting Fair* (Schmidt & Friedman, 1986). Based on Martin Luther King Jr.'s philosophy of nonviolence, the activities in these books involve studies in role playing, problem solving, and decision making.

Several curricula have their roots in Law Related Education projects. Examples of these include the Youth Negotiation Project developed by Harvard Law School and the dispute resolution curriculum developed by Vivian Einstein-Gordon for Chicago high school students.

These packaged curricula are designed to teach students mediation concepts and negotiation skills. Teachers could use these materials either as units in classroom programs or as training programs for student mediators.

CONCLUSION

In the course of normal living, conflict is inevitable from time to time between individuals and among people in all organizations. Destructive conflict, especially in schools, can destroy children's learning as well as teachers' ability to instruct. Conflict that is resolved in a constructive manner by utilizing mediation strategies based on the tenets of reality therapy and choice theory helps students experience greater control and learn how to meet their needs.

The opportunities for students to gain a sense of empowerment through the constructs of reality therapy and choice theory mediation provides a life-long impact. As children become adults, they will have developed a broader base of strategies by which they can meet their basic needs. Thus, they will be more productive as adults and waste less time in choosing inappropriate or futile behaviors. They will know how to compromise, listen, conceptualize ideas, interpret, plan, and understand their needs. As students gain this information and practice mediational skills, they are creating a more desirable future for themselves, where they choose violence less and make resolution the operational norm.

Conflict is inevitable. Resolving conflict through mediational strategies utilizing reality therapy practices and choice theory concepts provides a positive approach focusing on meeting basic needs and choosing effective behaviors.

REFERENCES

Cahoon, P. (1987/88). Mediator magic. *Educational Leadership, 45*(4), 92-94.

Community Board Center for Policy and Training. (1987). *Conflict resolution: A secondary school curriculum.* San Francisco, CA: Author.

Gilmore Middle School. (1988). *Conflict resolution.* (Unpublished document). Racine, WI: Racine Unified School District.

Glasser, W. (1965). *Reality therapy: A new approach to psychiatry.* New York: Harper & Row.

Glasser, W. (1984). *Control theory: A new explanation of how we control our lives.* New York: Harper & Row.

Glasser, W. (1990). *The quality school: Managing students without coercion.* New York: Harper & Row.

Koch, M. S. (1986, April 2). Schools can replace gladiators with mediators. *Education Week,* p. 28.

Roderick, T. (1987/88). Johnny can learn to negotiate. *Educational Leadership, 45*(4), 86-90.

Schmidt, F., & Friedman, A. (1985). *Creative conflict solving for kids.* Miami Beach, FL: Grace Contrino Abrams Peace Education Foundation.

Schmidt, F., & Friedman, A. (1986). *Fighting fair.* Miami Beach, FL: Grace Contrino Abrams Peace Education Foundation.

PSYCHOLOGY: SCIENCE OR CHARADE— FREUD'S POWER GRAB

Larry L. Palmatier

Contrary to popular opinion, psychology is all about human relationships. Many people carry around a lifetime delusion about psychology—that the subject refers only to a head trip. The word commonly refers to the science of human behavior, and the connotation is investigating mental disorders. Many skeptically ask how anyone could study scientifically a subject as broad as human behavior. Many say that human beings are so unpredictable that no scientific control is possible. Interestingly, the psychological theories that most closely fit popular cultural notions contain some of the most scientifically manageable concepts. Behavioral therapy may be the most empirical component within the general field because of an exclusive interest in observable phenomena. The shortcoming of pure behavioral thinking is an airtight disavowal of cognitive mapping. I call this kind of fuzziness "shooting-yourself-in-the-foot therapy," which insists on counseling someone with no reference to mental pictures about goals, hopes, dreams, and private logic. This approach to a topic that is, after all, *mostly* in a person's head is like swimming with one arm tied up around your head.

FREUD HOODWINKING
A CENTURY OF PURISTS

Most agree that the least empirical (i.e., verifiable) mental construct in all psychology is the original formulation that some hangers-on still consider to be scientific. The elaborate fictional web I am featuring here is psychoanalytic theory with its deep dark abyss known as the unconscious. We now call this black hole *unawareness* because no one can be aware of everything all of the time. Absolutely no one on the planet can deny that this intrapsychic convolution is *comprehensive*. Not as many folks will agree, however, that Freud's theory is *comprehensible*. Freud's elaboration makes decent literature as his story soon becomes as complex as a Kafka novel, brimming with mental figures of speech: psyche, id, libido, ego, superego, defense mechanisms, resistance, and—most sacred of all—transference. The culmination of this intricate pathogenic madness is one of the most perverse notions of all—repression! God forbid people ever again should have to hate themselves as a rite of passage back to sanity.

ALTERNATIVES TO FREUD

Many brilliant psychological theorists, creative strategists, and lesser known practitioners—Adler, Jung, Rogers, Skinner, Frankl, Szasz, Ellis, Laing, Erickson, Glasser, Beck, A. Lazarus, R. Lazarus, Mahoney, Haley, Minuchin, Madanes, Watzlawick, Weakland, Satir, Berg, de Shazer, O'Hanlon, Lankton & Lankton, Furman, Ahola, Fisch, Montalvo, Zluski, Beck, White, Epston, Vrend, Dyer, and many other thinkers—all have rejected Freud's and his contemporary imitators' focus on absurdity as cruelty to humans. They see all these pathological terms as nebulous cognitive hoaxes that have terrorized humanity for almost a century.

THE ICEMAN DREDGE

The "Willie Mammoth" mentality of dragging the frozen form from the depths of the icy sea is now only a fictional charade therapists maintain for entertainment purposes only. Sadly, the charade is cruel, and the managed care forces are having some success in stopping these practices. In the U.S., insurance companies are mandating to therapists to delete all forms of *endless therapy* from their repertoires. Fortunately, so many alternatives to psychodynamic therapy exist that pathologizing represents only about 10% of the possible psychological avenues today. Unfortunately, the reverse percentages are closer to the truth of actual practice. Probably 90% of therapists are still of a psychodynamic persuasion.

RATIONAL KEY TO HEALTH

Sanity literally refers to good health. In psychology, the word sanity mostly means being *rational*. Ideally, sane is coming to mean the state of being *well-balanced*—rational, emotionally responsive, behaviorally competent and flexible, physically fit, sensually attuned, interpersonally comfortable, and open to the fullness of life. All therapies—Freudian and counter-Freudian—address one or more of these seven dimensions of human behavior and living: thinking, feeling, acting, physiologically processing, sensing, socializing, and willing to wonder. The more emphasis on twisted feelings and hidden thoughts and devious meanings, the more Freud-like the therapy. The more focus on practical behavior, clear goals, logical thinking, healthy habits, and positive respect for self and others, the less Freud-like the therapy.

OPERATIONALIZING GOALS

The most empirical theories today are the simplest formulations. Nothing is as straightforward as Skinner's (1976) question: "Did you get out of bed this morning?" (His next question was the confusing one: "What environmental contingencies made you get up today?") First, Skinner kept everything simple and normal, then he proceeded to remove all self-efficacy from the client by crediting outside stimuli with controlling power. True, individuals could learn to organize the environmental factors that push their lives around, but, in the end, free choice is only a Skinnerian illusion. A substantive critique of Skinner's philosophy comes from Kohn (1993) who cited study after study showing the serious limitations of trying to condition and train a self-regulating and self-helping human being. In spite of these quirks within the observable traditions, however, psychology now can be a science more than ever before. The main reason for this exciting possibility is ironic: we can account for therapeutic effects now because so many theorists have depsychologized the playing field and the rules of interpersonal engagement. The less convoluted explanations for human behavior make for more concrete research and even predictability of human behavior.

THE WILLIAM GLASSER DECLARATION

Like so many other pragmatists, William Glasser, M.D., a psychiatrist, has discarded all medical notions of mental health and also fundamentally rejected the concept of mental illness (he and all those listed above). By focusing on the only endeavor all humans do from birth to death—namely, behavior—Glasser has pruned the psychology tree down to (a) succeeding (having what you want) and (b) failing (not having what you want). He has defined behavior as people's best attempt at a given moment to meet their needs and get what they want. He has eschewed hedonism by including social responsibility when suggesting that people have what they want *at no one else's expense.* Glasser has stated that, when all is said and done, only one psychological problem exists: people do not have something that they want. For many, this agonizing deficit is not being able to get someone else to do what they want them to do. Finally, Glasser has rejected all discipline programs that attempt to coerce students into conforming while ignoring the role the system itself may play in any given conflict within a school.

Glasser on Choice Theory

Glasser's most significant recent contribution appears to be deciphering Powers' (1973) control theory and developing these ideas so that clients can find relief within their lifetime. As a feedback model, control theory is a key cybernetic system that accounts for 100% of human behavior. In contrast, Skinner's work with rats follows the percentages in statistical research. Thus, lab research suggests probabilities. This method can account for only 96%, with a low probability that a given event happened merely by chance (or 75%, 92%, or any other meaningless number). As a closed loop, negative-feedback system, choice theory explains 100% of human behavior. Human beings take action only in the face of an unmet need. For information on choice theory, see chapter 3.

Cause of Behavior

Once people grasp how their inner control system operates and once they understand that all people always are trying to match the world up to their mental pictures, the intrapsychic fable becomes even more ludicrous. We now can predict reliably that people carrying large perceptual errors—not seeing in the world what their mental picture tells them to find out there—will take drastic action to eliminate the pain from the discrepancy between the mental picture of their current want and their sensory picture of what they actually have. Some will push and shove and try to change the world. Others will examine what they can do to change their behavior to end up a winner. The most common choice in the midst of serious conflicts seems to be resorting to medication to soothe the perceptual error in their heads.

MEASURING THERAPEUTIC EFFECTIVENESS

Outcome studies now provide the best data to support the science of human behavior. Psychology is more credible when researchers can show the following changes, accomplished briefly, and find that the improvements last for months or years in follow-up studies. First, the old psychology, with weekly therapy sessions, typically lasting for one to three years:

Complaint	Outcome
Transference issues	Three years to partial independence
Repressed rage	Pounds pillows (forever) when furious
Splitting	Identifies mother as culprit
Superego nudges Id, especially at parties	Patient adjusts to living alone

What about the new psychology? Notice how the language shifts to more practical, tangible, observable terminology. Five of these cases required one meeting; none lasted longer than five sessions.

Complaint	Outcome
Couple is splitting up over new baby proposal	Couple has a baby and stays together
Boy fears he will die if he touches anything	Boy starts touching everything normally
A woman, abused as a child, picks abusive males	Woman changes her pattern
Young girl goes berserk at school; mother is furious	Girl settles down; mother is calm
Boy desperate over move from abusive step-dad	Boy adjusts to shock; enjoys other kids
Man spends a lifetime of torment over tragedy	Man finds peace of mind about tragedy
Mother attends school for a year with child	Mother stops attending in two days
Adult daughter always fights with her mother	Daughter sees mother as a consultant
Woman cannot find a long-term relationship	Woman meets man and marries
Daughter often tantrums at home	Daughter drops tantrumming

Nothing is more empirical (i.e., verifiable) in outcome studies than finding out if the complainant no longer has the presenting problem—that is, is no longer doing the behavior that led to the complaint. For an elaboration of this epilogue, see Palmatier (1996). (Permission was granted by the *Journal of Reality Therapy* to use the material included here.) Nothing is less empirical than Freudian outcomes. The reasons for this problem of no documentable results in traditional psychology is that psychodynamic therapy is nebulous, long-term, and aims to elicit insight and not behavior change.

CONCLUSION: MOVING BEYOND CRISES

Schools have a commission to guard a sacred trust—their country's children and youth. But no institution can merely *house* people. For good or ill, some change in those people is inevitable. Why not intend positive outcomes? Therapy is for anomalies. The normal course of events in school is not therapizing youngsters but creating the conditions in which they can develop favorably and learn basic and creative topics and skills. Whatever schools do will have an effect, one way or another. Results can be useful, so-so, or damaging. This book is all about removing the barriers that limit schools in their primary mission of teaching students who want to learn. My wish is for teachers to take heart, to work together, to obtain the materials and moral support that they need and deserve, and to enjoy the challenge and privilege of relating to younger human beings who embody the future.

REFERENCES

Kohn, A. (1993). *Punished by rewards.* Boston: Houghton-Mifflin.

Palmatier, L. (1996). Freud defrauded while Glasser defreuded: From pathologizing to talking solutions. *Journal of Reality Therapy, 16*(1), 75-94.

Powers, W. (1973). *Behavior: The control of perception.* Chicago: Aldine.

Skinner, B. F. (1976). *About behaviorism.* New York: Vintage.

INDEX

ABOUT THE CONTRIBUTORS

Mary B. Ballou holds a Ph.D. in Counseling Psychology from Kent State University, an ABPP Diplomate in Counseling Psychology and Fellow status in APA. She is an Associate Professor of Counseling Psychology at Northeastern University in Boston and also has an active professional practice in counseling and consulting. She has authored numerous articles, chapters, and books, several development feminist therapy. Currently she is committee coordinator in the Feminist Therapy Institute.

Kimberly Barrett, Ed.D., is a lecturer and clinical supervisor in the Department of Psychology at the University of Washington, where she is also a faculty member for the Addictive Behaviors Research Center. Dr. Barrett specializes in work with children, adolescents, and families.

Albert O. Boyd, Ed.D., is a professor in the Health Sciences Department, Santa Rosa Junior College, and is a psychiatric mental health counselor, Santa Rosa, California.

Barbara I. Bratter, MSW, is a graduate of Columbia College and George Brown School of Social Work at Washington University. She completed a postgraduate internship at the Child's Guidance Clinic at Yale University where she served as a consultant to three schools helping create a group psychotherapy program. She has taught, served as part of the clinical staff, and now does administration at The John Dewey Academy, Great Barrington, MA.

Carole Jaffe Bratter, MA, is a Phi Beta Kappa graduate of H. Sophie Newcomb College (Tulane University) and Teachers College, Columbia University. Prior to working at The John Dewey Academy, Carole worked cooperatively with her husband helping gifted, drug-dependent, alienated adolescents become more responsible and productive. She is co-founder of The John Dewey Academy, Great Barrington, MA, and serves as its vice president.

Eleven years ago, *Thomas Bratter* founded with his wife The John Dewey Academy (Great Barrington, MA) to prove to mental health clinicians and educators that when placed in an uncompromising environment that demands excellence and integrity, gifted, self-destructive, and drug-dependent adolescents can transcend their irresponsible pasts. Providing intensive, individualized instruction and treatment, this residential school has admittedly ambitious twin goals: (a) to help students (re)gain their self-respect and (b) to convince colleges of quality to admit graduates who seal permanently their pasts and in so doing maximize their future educational, professional, and social options.

Linda K. Brewer, MSW, L.C.S.W., BCD, is project coordinator for the Title IV-E Child Welfare Training program in the School of Social Work at San Francisco State University. She maintains a private practice in San Francisco and is a doctoral student at the University of San Francisco in the Counseling Psychology program.

Edward W. Chance, Ph.D., is Professor of Educational Administration and Higher Education, University of Nevada Las Vegas.

Patti L. Chance, M.Ed., is a teacher and counselor with Clark County Schools, Las Vegas, Nevada.

Steven Eckert, LCSW, is the Director of North Peninsula Family Alternatives (NPFA), a counseling agency serving youth and families in South San Francisco. He has been involved with NPFA's provision of the Juvenile Sexual Responsibility Program since its inception in 1987. He is the past Clinical Director of the San Quentin Pilot Sex Offender Program, 1990-1994.

Jan Francis, MA, MFCC, has been in the field of bereavement and care of the dying since 1972, and her work has included many years with Home Hospice of Sonoma County. Since 1985, Francis has been teaching psychology classes, including "Death and Dying," at Santa Rosa Junior College, California. She holds a California license in Marriage, Family, and Child Counseling.

William Glasser, M.D., is the developer of Choice Theory, the author of numerous books on counseling and education, and a lecturer.

Larry Litwack has an Ed.D. from Boston University, an ABPP Diplomate in Counseling Psychology, and is a Fellow of Division 17 of the American Psychological Association. he is Professor of Counseling Psychology at Northeastern University and is consulting psychologist for the LABBB Collaborative, a Quality School in Lexington, Massachusetts.

Lynn Loar, LCSW, Ph.D., is the education coordinator of the San Francisco Child Abuse Council. She designs and implements training programs for providers who work with inner-city children and families at risk of abuse, neglect, and community violence. She was Director of the Sex Offender Treatment Program at San Quentin State Prison (1990-1994).

Mary T. Parish, Ed.D., is an assistant professor at Saint Mary's College in Moraga, California, and a lecturer in the Graduate Counseling Program at Chapman College, Concord, California. She is the counseling training coordinator for the graduate counseling program at Saint Mary's College. She is a member of the State of California, Office of AIDS HIV Trainers Group and is the Secretary of the Board of Directors, AIDS Alliance, serving Alameda and Contra Costa Counties. She served for eight years as the coordinator of HIV Testing Services and Support Groups for Contra Costa Country Health Services.

James C. Park, Ph.D., is an adjunct professor at Santa Rosa Junior college, Sonoma State University, and the University of San Francisco. Dr. Park is also Director of Youth and Family Services within the Department of Public Safety at Rohnert Park, California.

Terence E. Patterson, Ed.D., is a licensed psychologist and teaches ethics and family systems at the University of San Francisco, Department of Counseling Psychology.

Bruce Peltier, Ph.D., is a clinical psychologist in private practice and Associate Professor at the University of the Pacific Dental School in San Francisco. He lectures at the University of San Francisco in the Counseling Psychology Department.

Morgan Peterson, Ed.D., has a doctorate in counseling psychology; is past director of crisis counseling for police officers, San Francisco Police Department; is a consultant on gang behavior, Carlsbad, California; and teaches criminal justice, Palomar College, San Marcos, California.

Sarah Rafton is a counselor at Seattle Children's Home in Washington, working with emotionally disturbed and behavior disordered children and adolescents. She holds a B.A. and an M.S.W. from the University of Washington.

Sherry Tennyson, Ed.D., has worked with youth, particularly at-risk, for 18 years. She has facilitated workshops/groups concerning youth issues, has taught in an alternative school setting, and is currently program director at a family resource center in San Francisco.

ABOUT THE AUTHOR–EDITOR

Larry Palmatier, Ph.D., holds California licenses in psychology and marriage, family, and child counseling, and a school counseling credential. He is a professor of counseling psychology and chair of the department at the University of San Francisco. During the first 13 years of his career, he was a junior high school teacher of Spanish and English, director of a county schools program for innovative teachers, and a teacher educator at UC Berkeley and the University of Utah in Salt Lake City.

Larry is married and has a daughter, three sons, and three granddaughters. In addition to his university teaching and a private psychotherapy practice, he consults with teachers and administrators on creating quality schools. As a faculty member with the William Glasser Institute, Larry conducts training in choice theory and reality therapy. He currently is completing two companion books on choice theory counseling and transforming school systems with quality management.